MW00533340

The United States and th

Lester D. Langley, General Editor

This series is dedicated to a broader understanding of the political, economic, and especially cultural forces and issues that have shaped the Western hemispheric experience—its governments and its peoples. Individual volumes assess relations between the United States and its neighbors to the south and north: Mexico, Central America, Cuba, the Dominican Republic, Haiti, Panama, Colombia, Venezuela, Peru, Ecuador, Bolivia, Brazil, Paraguay, Argentina, Chile, and Canada.

The United States and the Americas

Paraguay and the United States

Frank O. Mora and Jerry W. Cooney

Paraguay and the United States: Distant Allies

The University of Georgia Press
Athens and London

© 2007 by the University of Georgia Press
Athens, Georgia 30602
All rights reserved

Set in 10/14 Palatino by Newgen
Printed and bound by Integrated Book Technology, Inc.
The paper in this book meets the guidelines for permanence and durability of the Committee on Production Guidelines for Book Longevity of the Council on Library Resources.

Printed in the United States of America

11 10 09 08 07 C 5 4 3 2 1
11 10 09 08 07 P 5 4 3 2 1

Library of Congress Cataloging-in-Publication Data

Mora, Frank O.
Paraguay and the United States : distant allies /
Frank O. Mora and Jerry W. Cooney.
p. cm. — (The United States and the Americas)
Includes bibliographical references and index.
ISBN-13: 978-0-8203-2467-8 (hardcover : alk paper)
ISBN-10: 0-8203-2467-1 (hardcover : alk. paper)
ISBN-13: 978-0-8203-2932-1 (pbk. : alk. paper)
ISBN-10: 0-8203-2932-0 (pbk. : alk. paper)
1. United States—Foreign relations—Paraguay.
2. Paraguay—Foreign relations—United States.
3. Americans—Paraguay—History.
4. Paraguay—History—19th century.
5. Paraguay—History—20th century.
I. Cooney, Jerry W. (Jerry Wilson), 1940– II. Title.
E183.8.P3M67 2007
327.730892—dc22 2007005843

British Library Cataloging-in-Publication Data available

Nivardo Mora,
One can only aspire to be half the man,
husband, and father

My nephew,
Jeffery Kieth Hergert,
1955–2005

Contents

Preface xi

Acknowledgments xiii

Introduction 1

1. A Troubled Beginning 5
2. A Distant Relationship 38
3. War and the Search for Peace 66
4. Civil War and Hemispheric Security, 1939–1954 92
5. Our Man in Asunción: Anticommunism, 1954–1961 125
6. Alliance for Progress and the Ricord Affair, 1962–1976 160
7. Human Rights and "Democracy by Pressure," 1977–1989 193
8. Safeguarding Democracy in Paraguay, 1989–2000 231
9. Epilogue 260

Notes 267

Bibliographical Essay 301

Index 319

Preface

In a conversation with Franklin Delano Roosevelt in 1941, author John Gunther surprised the president by stating that he had visited Paraguay as well as the other Latin American countries he investigated.[1] That surprise was understandable. Although Paraguay had gained its independence in 1813, had maintained relations with the United States since the 1850s, and was an original member of the Pan American Union, few Americans knew anything about this republic situated in the heart of South America. More often than not, they would have confused it with another South American republic, Uruguay.

Even today Paraguay rarely enters the consciousness of North Americans. If they know anything about it, they picture a jumble of dictators, fanciful notions of refugee Nazis dreaming of the Fourth Reich, or, at most, peasants sipping yerba mate—a tea native to this region.[2] Paraguay has likewise received little attention from most North American specialists in Latin America. This lack of attention is understandable. Until the mid-twentieth century, this republic did not play a significant role in any assessment of United States national interest. North Americans had few investments in, or commerce with, that isolated area, and unlike the circum-Caribbean, there was no compelling geopolitical reason to pay it much attention. And until the 1940s, a visit to Paraguay usually required a journey by ship to Buenos Aires and then a thousand miles upriver by steamer to Asunción. Few North American tourists, commercial travelers, or government functionaries visited this republic. Much changed with the advent of the air age, World War II, and then the North American hegemony over the Western Hemisphere. Yet even today Paraguay ranks low in U.S. economic, political, or strategic interests.

Although Paraguay has never loomed large in North American consciousness, the converse is definitely not true. Over the past seventy years, the international policies of the United States have had a vital impact upon Asunción, and the North American cultural and economic impact has also been crucial. In addition, on several occasions from the 1850s to 1940s, various odd conflicts arose between the two nations, mostly of an episodic nature, but significant for an understanding of the role of the United States in the larger region of the Río de la Plata.

Relations between the two countries have taken on greater importance since the U.S. attempts to mediate in the Chaco War between Paraguay and Bolivia (1932–35). Hemispheric Solidarity in World War II, the Cold War in Latin America, the "balance of power" in the Río de la Plata, and the question of U.S. support for, or aid to, Latin American dictators—all became matters of interest in the last half century of Paraguayan-U.S. relations. In the latter instance, the long dictatorship of Alfredo Stroessner (1954–89) spanned much of this era and the course of Paraguayan-U.S. relations during his regime is illustrative of the ebb and flow of realpolitik on the part of both nations. Not only did Washington have definite diplomatic goals, but so did Asunción. The relative disparity of power and wealth between the two nations did not necessarily hinder Paraguay's pursuit of international advantage in its relations with the United States. After the fall of the dictator Stroessner in 1989, Paraguay encountered difficulties in its transition to democracy. The U.S. policy in this era was to support firmly that process. Washington was still concerned, however, about human rights matters, trafficking in drugs, money laundering, and intellectual piracy.

The organization of this study is essentially chronological—from the beginning of diplomatic contact between the two nations in the 1840s to the first years of this century. Until the 1930s, however, Paraguay and the United States were relatively distant countries. The United States had very few interests in Paraguay, and Paraguay was not greatly concerned with the far northern power. That lack of engagement changed for the two just prior to World War II. For that reason, treatment of international relations between the two republics is heavily weighted in favor of the last seventy years.

Acknowledgments

Our many years of reading, observing, and reflecting on Paraguay have left an extensive accumulation of people and institutions in Paraguay and the United States to thank. Here we can acknowledge only a few.

From the conception of the book Lester Langley, general editor of the United States and Latin America Series, consistently offered support and much patience during the project's long gestation. We greatly appreciate the opportunity to express our views on Paraguayan-U.S. relations. Once the manuscript was completed, Lester provided important editorial and substantive comments that improved the quality of the work. Others, including the reviewers, provided helpful ideas and encouragement at times when it seemed this project would not see publication. We also wish to thank Efraím Cardozo and Edwin Lieuwen, who many years ago encouraged Jerry Cooney to work on this topic. The stimulating conversations with Thomas L. Whigham, particularly in regard to the personality of Charles Ames Washburn, aided greatly.

In the United States, this project received indispensable encouragement and financial support from gracious and outstanding individuals at three institutions. At Rhodes College, the Seidman and Buckman families provided invaluable funds for the many research trips to Paraguay taken by Frank Mora. The administration at Rhodes and colleagues in the Department of International Studies, specifically Brenda Somes and Andrew Michta, always provided much encouragement and motivation.

During Frank's sabbatical year (2002–3), Andy Gomez and Jaime Suchlicki provided the monetary and office support at the Institute for Cuban and Cuban-American Studies, University of Miami, where much of the final stages of the research and several chapters were completed. This book would not have been completed without their kind offer. Frank's friends and mentors at the Department of International Studies welcomed and encouraged him to complete the manuscript.

Also during this time, a trip to Kansas offered Frank more than an opportunity to visit the archives of the Paraguay-Kansas Partnership in Wichita; it allowed him to meet Professor Charles L. Stansifer and his wife, who were so kind in opening their home and archives to him. While in Lawrence, Frank met and interviewed many wonderful folks who had been an integral part of the partnership.

The outstanding leadership and faculty at the National War College provided a wonderful collegial and intellectual environment that greatly facilitated the completion of the manuscript. Their continued support is greatly appreciated.

In Paraguay there are many remarkable and supportive people whom we admire and call family. The influence and contributions of friends and scholars such as José Luis Simón, Ricardo Scavone, Fernando Masi, Diego Abente, Domingo Rivarola, Marcial Riquelme, Roberto Cespedes, Domingo Rivarola, Roberto Quevedo, and Milda Rivarola can be seen throughout this manuscript. We are forever indebted for all they taught us about their wonderful country.

On a personal note, as with other projects, Ivette G. Mora, Frank Mora's spouse, closest friend, and mother of their two wonderful children, Daniella and Frankie, made the whole project possible. She means more to him than she can imagine. Finally, Nivardo Mora, Frank's father and role model, taught him much about character and integrity. To him Frank dedicates this book.

Paraguay and the United States

Introduction

The nation of Paraguay has its origins in the great Spanish Conquest of the 1500s that swept over much of the Americas. Those conquerors and explorers of the Upper Plata failed to discover great civilizations and precious metals. By necessity, they created an agricultural and pastoral society utilizing the labor of the local Guaraní Indians. For several centuries this portion of the Spanish Empire remained a backwater, beset on the west and north by hostile Indians and on the north and east by the often hostile Portuguese Empire.

The only viable access to the outside world was the all-important Paraguay-Paraná River system that led to the South Atlantic. Gradually, the Spanish-Guaraní descendants of the conquistadores developed a crude export economy of yerba mate—a tea esteemed by many in South America. Yet never did Paraguay develop the wealthy, glittering society of the more favored parts of Spain's American empire. Only in the last fifty years of colonial rule, under the impetus of imperial economic and administrative reforms, did Paraguay tentatively share in the growth of the platine regional economy.

The isolation of this region in the colonial period, its unique Hispano-Guaraní culture, and the self-reliant ethos forced upon the people by a long defense of the province all fostered a sense of particularism that emerged in the turmoil of Spanish American independence in the early 1800s.[1] Paraguay achieved independence in 1811 as a consequence of the Buenos Aires rebellion against Spanish authority in 1810. Briefly, the province remained loyal to Spain and defeated an invading army from Buenos Aires. Encouraged by that success, the provincial militia then rebelled against royal authority and after several years of political confusion, Dr. José Gaspar de Francia assumed dictatorial power. This austere, middle-aged lawyer ruled the new republic sternly, honestly, and efficiently until his death in 1840.[2]

Dr. Francia fanatically defended the sovereignty of his country against the machinations of Buenos Aires or any other party that dared question Paraguayan independence. At the same time he pursued a policy of nonintervention in the affairs of surrounding states, avoiding the postindependence regional rivalries that might have compromised Paraguayan sovereignty. Fortunately for Francia, those very rivalries diverted attention from Paraguay. In 1818 the dictator closed Paraguay to all political contact with the outside when the United Provinces of the Río de la Plata (the predecessor of Argentina) refused to concede that independence and continued to interfere with Paraguay's access to the Atlantic. From 1818 to 1840 few foreigners entered Paraguay; few Paraguayans left; and only a trickle of carefully controlled trade at designated locales entered or left the republic. The dictator guaranteed internal peace and interfered little with the traditional life of his countrymen. That calm was enforced with a heavy hand, however. Nonetheless, during his generation of rule and isolation, Dr. Francia not only created the Republic of Paraguay but also fostered a strong nationalism.

In this era of El Supremo (as Dr. Francia became termed), Paraguay knew few diplomatic contacts, even with its most important neighbors, the new Brazilian Empire and the United Provinces of the Río de la Plata. Francia distrusted Brazilian motives in the Río de la Plata as much as he did those of Buenos Aires.[3] As for contact with European nations or the United States, neither Paraguay nor those faraway powers had any reason to engage in meaningful diplomatic intercourse.

In early 1822 after the United States acquired Florida from Spain and no longer had to mollify that power, Washington recognized five Latin American governments, the United Provinces of the Río de la Plata being one.[4] U.S. policy toward the Río de la Plata was governed by three factors: the sympathy for Spanish American independence, an increasing import of hides and other extractive products of this region, and the development of the Monroe Doctrine.

By the time of the 1810 revolt of Buenos Aires, Yankee sea captains had already forged close ties with local merchants and exporters. The War of 1812 only temporarily interrupted commerce with the United States, and exports northward—mainly hides, tallow, and salted beef for transshipment to the Caribbean—grew so steadily over the next thirty years that by the 1840s North American ports were second only to British ports as the ultimate destination of porteño exports. The origin of these platine exports was overwhelmingly that of the province of Buenos Aires with few exports from the interior.

Paraguay, in contrast, produced little that Yankee businessmen desired. Yerba had no market in the United States. Tobacco might eventually have found a market in North America, but transportation costs prevented any meaningful commerce with overseas consumers (and the United Provinces also imposed duties on Paraguayan exports). The Paraguayan economy, before and after independence, was regional in nature and had little relevance to the United States. No economic motive existed for the State Department to challenge the United Provinces' claim to Paraguay, or to push for any liberty of commerce on the Paraná River. Such actions could only threaten a flourishing oceanic commerce with Buenos Aires.

In 1817, bowing to congressional pressure for the recognition of Spanish American independence, Washington dispatched two agents to the Río de la Plata to investigate economic and political conditions there. Significantly, in their lengthy reports Paraguay was mentioned only briefly and then in context of its isolation. In contrast, the reports analyzed in great detail the political condition and economic possibilities of Buenos Aires.[5] While not stated, it was obvious that any internal dispute as to the sovereignty of Paraguay was of little interest to the United States.

Much the same disinterest was revealed in North American concern over the possibility of European intervention in this region of Spanish America. In 1823 when the Monroe Doctrine was announced, Paraguay was then the only Spanish American state with no seacoast, as well as being difficult to access by means of the Paraná River. Any European threat to the Upper Plata would necessarily have been part of a more serious assault upon the United Provinces. Indeed, as far as the Monroe Doctrine has been concerned, Paraguay rarely has played a significant role in North American eyes—even during the strident anticommunism of Alfredo Stroessner at the height of the cold war.

For nearly a generation this region was of little or no concern to the United States. Dr. Francia's isolation was considered a curiosity but warranted no action. And that lack of official interest was echoed among individual North Americans. By the early 1840s Yankee merchants, adventurers, and diplomats had penetrated many parts of Latin America; to the authors' knowledge, none by this time had visited Paraguay. Nonetheless, neither the policy of isolation nor the lack of North American interest survived that decade. Internal changes in Paraguay, as well as altered international conditions, brought forth the first contacts of the United States with Asunción.

1 A Troubled Beginning

Dr. Francia's death in September 1840 left Paraguay in confusion as the dictator had made no provision for a successor and an ineffectual junta of army officers assumed temporary power. By the following March a national assembly authorized the establishment of a consulate composed of Colonel Mariano Roque Alonzo and don Carlos Antonio López, a lawyer turned landowner. Alonzo was rapidly pushed aside as López assumed administrative control of the nation and then was elected president in 1844—a position he held until his death in 1862.[1]

Don Carlos faced much the same set of international problems as Francia: the need for recognition of Paraguay's sovereignty, disputes over frontiers, and lack of freedom of navigation for Paraguayan ships on the Paraná River. Gradually, with many controls in place, he opened Paraguay to visitors and merchants from abroad. Within two years of taking power don Carlos entered into communication with those European diplomats resident in the Lower Plata, U.S. representatives in the port cities, the Empire of Brazil, and especially with Juan Manuel de Rosas, governor of Buenos Aires and de facto leader of the Argentine Confederation.

In early 1843 the minister plenipotentiary of Paraguay to the Argentine Confederation, Andrés Gil, was in Buenos Aires fruitlessly attempting to gain recognition and freedom of the rivers from Rosas.[2] Rosas proved to be the greatest obstacle to international recognition and freedom of the rivers. Paraguayans dispatched to Buenos Aires found that caudillo polite in conversations but unwilling to accept that Paraguay was not a part of the Argentine Confederation. Nor would he relax Buenos Aires's control over river traffic to the estuary. The closer relationship that Paraguay had forged with the city of Corrientes undoubtedly strengthened his resolve in this matter, for Corrientes had long opposed Rosas's political power in the littoral.

Paraguay did score some minor successes on the diplomatic front in the early 1840s. Bolivia recognized Paraguay in 1843, followed by Chile in 1844 and Uruguay in 1845. At the time, Brazil was embroiled in a civil war in its southernmost reaches with complications of covert platine involvement. Rio de Janeiro would take no action relative to Paraguay until that was solved. European powers and the United States decided that any recognition of Paraguay would be premature given the Argentine Confederation's claim to Paraguay, as well as the hostility of Great Britain and France to Buenos Aires brought about by Rosas's meddling in the Uruguayan civil war.

Nonetheless, political conditions in the Río de la Plata in the 1840s were changing, yielding a gradual erosion of Rosas's power. By mid-decade French and British hostility to the porteño dictator resulted in a blockade of Buenos Aires. French merchantmen, escorted part of the way by a French war steamer, sailed to Asunción. The Empire of Brazil finally crushed the rebellion in the southernmost reaches of its realm, and that power had no love for Rosas because Buenos Aires had given support to anti-imperial forces. However, Rosas still controlled the Confederation, and not until he was removed from power could López attain Paraguay's objectives.[3]

Although the United States failed to respond to the initial feelers from the López government, U.S. diplomats in the Lower Plata had some knowledge of conditions in Paraguay thanks to informal conversations with representatives of that republic. One result was the first U.S. business contact with Paraguay as the U.S. consul in Buenos Aires suggested that Henry Gilbert, a countryman and merchant in Buenos Aires, might undertake the first minting of coins for the Paraguayan government. Unfortunately, a squabble ensued between Gilbert and the Paraguayan government over the means of payment for Gilbert's services; the squabble would continue until the mid-1850s when Gilbert was finally forced to accept Asunción's terms.[4] Another encounter on the part of U.S. businessmen occurred in late 1845 when three U.S. merchantmen joined the French-escorted convoy that penetrated Rosas's blockade of the Paraná and sailed to Asunción to market their goods.[5]

Edward A. Hopkins and the Approach to Paraguay

The activities of the French and British fleets in the Río de la Plata raised concerns in the United States about a danger to the Monroe Doctrine—an understandable but unfounded fear. In June 1845 Secretary of State James Buchanan authorized Edward A. Hopkins as a special agent to Asunción to inform López of the deep interest that the U.S. government felt in the "success and prosperity" of Paraguay and to investigate the Argentine Confederation's claim to Paraguay and the assertion of exclusive rights of navigation on the region's rivers. If it was the Confederation's goal to exclude world commerce from Paraguay, Asunción could count on Washington's good offices to help open the rivers.

Before Hopkins could commit the president of the United States on the matter of recognition, the special agent had to satisfy himself that "Paraguay is in fact an independent nation and capable of maintaining her independence." In addition, Buchanan ordered Hopkins to report on the people of Paraguay, their support for the present government, the racial makeup of the nation, state finances, marketable goods, the U.S.-made items that might be sold in the republic, and the military capabilities of the republic.[6]

This young agent—only twenty-two years of age at his appointment—was a true son of the era of Manifest Destiny and, as such, exhibited some of the worst characteristics of that flamboyant and exuberant age. His self-confidence, self-interest, and brashness were obvious, yet somehow attractive to many of the officials he met in Washington and later in Paraguay.[7] Hopkins immediately sailed south to Paraguay, stopping at Rio de Janeiro to confer with Henry Wise, U.S. minister to the Empire of Brazil, about Rosas's involvement in Uruguay's civil war, which had precipitated an Anglo-French naval blockade of Buenos Aires. Wise was also troubled about a Corrientes rebellion against Rosas and Paraguay's ongoing difficulties with Rosas. The foreign minister of Brazil suggested that the United States and Brazil employ every means necessary to end the struggle in Uruguay. Their joint action would then reduce or eliminate the European action in the

Río de la Plata, a presence that was quite worrisome to both Brazil and the United States. Washington had given Wise no guidance relative to the Brazilian proposal, but on Hopkins's arrival he perceived the special agent as a useful associate in his project of peace for the platine region.

Flushed with enthusiasm, Hopkins then traveled overland to Asunción, arriving there about November 8. Within a month, he had several interviews with President López and wrote his report on Paraguay's government, people, land, and products—an account filled with admiration and wonder about the country and boasting of his own accomplishments. Shortly after Hopkins had arrived in Asunción, President López agreed to an alliance with Corrientes that obligated Paraguay to dispatch twelve thousand soldiers across the Alto Paraná to aid that province in its struggle with the Rosas-dominated Argentine Confederation. Hopkins tried to dissuade him from that action, but López asserted that Paraguay had no choice. The U.S. agent reported López's promise to reduce the force to four thousand and to take no action unless attacked (a most doubtful assertion on Hopkins's part). Several times López assured Hopkins that a successful U.S. mediation would be viewed with much gratitude.

Yet, as the president repeated, any permanent accord depended upon Rosas's recognition of Paraguay's full independence. As for the offer of mediation, Paraguay would need a treaty, guaranteed by the United States, that secured the republic's limits and free navigation of the Paraná. If those conditions could be met, the Corrientes alliance would then have no purpose. However, until those conditions were met, Paraguay would have to look to its own interests and take actions it deemed necessary. The U.S. agent also held conversations with the Brazilian minister to Paraguay and found him equally opposed to European intervention in the Plata. That representative feared that Paraguay's adventure in Corrientes would sow the seeds of even greater conflict in the Plata. His government's policy, instead, was to persuade Rosas to grant recognition to Paraguay and freedom of the rivers. Hopkins deplored the possibility of increased European penetration in the Plata and assured the Brazilian that this ran counter to U.S. policy (or at least to the policies of U.S. minister Wise in Rio de Janeiro) as well.

In any case, throughout this despatch runs a continual suspicion of the motives of the French and British.[8]

What Hopkins omitted in his despatch was a personal motive in advancing peace in the Upper Plata. He had asked President López for a steamship monopoly on Paraguay's rivers and informed the astonished president that a group of U.S. capitalists stood ready to invest three hundred thousand dollars in the republic. For any entrepreneurial plan to succeed, however, peace in the Plata, recognition of Paraguay's sovereignty, and free navigation of the Paraná were critical. With this, Hopkins revealed the moneymaking zeal that he never abandoned in all his relations with Paraguay. In the pursuit of profit, he saw the opportunity to do well by doing good. In any case, the Paraguayan government did not grant the steamship concession, but it would not be the last time that this American mixed diplomacy with the pursuit of personal gain.

Hopkins had informed Wise in Rio de Janeiro of the conversations with López, and Wise was pleased with Hopkins's "success." By February of 1846 Hopkins was again in the Brazilian capital. Even though Wise had still not received an authorization or encouragement from the State Department for his plans to bring peace to the Plata, the two decided that Hopkins must sail to Buenos Aires and coax Rosas to some agreement. Hopkins lacked accreditation to the Argentine Confederation, and Rosas's foreign minister was all too aware of Hopkins's pro-Paraguay prejudices. López, of course, could not accept Rosas's conditions, and a state of semi-hostility between the two continued for the next six years. On hearing of Rosas's stance, Hopkins proposed that the Confederation declare war upon France and Britain, confiscate British and French property, recognize the sovereignty of Paraguay, and conclude a treaty with Brazil. Accompanying these proposals were various personal insults aimed at Rosas. As soon as the State Department heard of this intemperate outburst, it offered the most profound apologies to the Buenos Aires government, and Rosas was gracious enough to accept them.

Washington had already decided to recall Hopkins because he had exceeded his instructions. The government had dispatched Hopkins to Paraguay solely to ascertain if the United States should recognize that republic. Hopkins had been authorized to convey to López the best wishes of the United States, but no more. Hopkins's actions violated "two time honored principles which have long regulated the policy of the United States toward foreign nations." First, he meddled in a controversy between two nations. Second, his actions would encourage the "intervention of foreign European Powers in the affairs of independent American nations." Buchanan stated that the Paraguay-Corrientes league against Rosas would drive those two into the arms of Great Britain and France. And that pact would make it impossible for the United States to "interpose their good offices with the Argentine Government." The December 1845 war between Paraguay and Corrientes on one side and the Argentine Confederation on the other made it impossible at present for the United States to welcome Paraguay into the family of nations, but the U.S. president hoped that this action might soon occur. The secretary of state softened the blow by assuring Hopkins that undoubtedly all "proceeded from the best motives and that you were actuated by an eager desire to serve your country."[9] Before departing the Río de la Plata for the United States Hopkins informed López that he would continue the struggle for U.S. recognition—a promise that he kept. However, any recognition of Paraguay by the United States was now in limbo, given the continuing problems in the Río de la Plata. Essentially, Buchanan in 1846 accepted the Argentine contention that recognition of Paraguay would only benefit the British and French and that the United States did not care to do.

When Hopkins returned to the United States he reported to the secretary of state that Paraguay was indeed a viable nation. Buchanan, however, maintained his stance that the Paraguay-Corrientes alliance, as well as Rosas's policy, made recognition of Paraguay impossible. For the next several years the restless young American acted as a publicist for economic prospects in the Upper Plata, publishing extensively in various magazines and sending memorials to the State Department. Returning to the Río de la Plata, he traveled extensively, dropping into Asunción on visits and there advocating economic schemes for Paraguay's advancement (and his own). Steamships on the Paraguay, agricultural schools, manufacturing companies—all flowed from his prolific pen.

While Hopkins was promoting Paraguayan economic opportunities and lobbying the Millard Fillmore administration for a diplomatic appointment to Asunción, great political changes occurred in the Plata. The long regime of Juan Manuel de Rosas of Buenos Aires drew to a close as his former lieutenant, Justo José de Urquiza, turned against him. In December 1850 Brazil and Paraguay signed an alliance clearly aimed at the porteño dictator, and by May of the next year Urquiza had constructed an alliance of Uruguay, Brazil, and much of the littoral provinces to depose Rosas. Paraguay held back from that alliance. Even so, in February of 1852 the Urquiza alliance ousted Rosas. With his fall any rationale for European intervention in the Plata disappeared, a happy outcome for the U.S. government, which recognized Paraguay in 1852. Three months later, on the heels of victory, the new government of the Argentine Confederation formally acknowledged Paraguay's independence and the right of free navigation on the Paraná and other interior rivers.[10]

Business or Diplomacy?

With the fall of Rosas the Fillmore administration moved to conclude treaties of commerce and navigation with the republics of this region. In March 1853 representatives from the United States, Britain, France, and Sardinia joined in concluding treaties of friendship, commerce, and navigation with don Carlos, as well as formally recognizing Paraguay. The U.S. treaty provided for a most-favored-nation status for U.S. shipping and commerce, as well as the normal provisions for the protection of merchants, port usage, duties on goods, exemption from Paraguayan military service for Americans residing in the republic, and consular exchange. One interesting provision guaranteed to U.S. merchant vessels the right of free passage of the Paraguay to Asunción, and the same right on the right side of the Paraná to Encarnación. Don Carlos was suspicious of the Brazilian pressure for the completely free navigation of the Paraguay River into the Brazilian Mato Grosso. On security grounds, he had no wish to grant the precedent for full navigation of the Paraguay River. In any case, however, he immediately ratified the treaty.

In the meantime, Edward A. Hopkins had been named U.S. consul in Paraguay. After his appointment, Hopkins and a group of Rhode Island businessmen incorporated the United States and Paraguay Navigation Company. The enterprise was capitalized with one hundred thousand dollars to build and sail ships on the rivers of South America, as well as to conduct other business. As general agent of that company in Paraguay, Hopkins received a salary and other benefits.[11] Although plagued by shipwrecks, the company succeeded in sending Paraguay several types of modern machinery—steam engines, agricultural machinery, cigar-manufacturing equipment, and a sawmill, as well as the men to operate this equipment.

Hopkins assumed his post as consul in Asunción in November 1853. There he received the blessing of don Carlos for various entrepreneurial projects—even though López evidently learned of the projects only on Hopkins's arrival in Paraguay. President López provided the U.S. entrepreneur with government housing for the U.S. technicians, the right to import all machinery free of duties, and the right to purchase land and slaves and to hire convict labor at low wages. When Hopkins encountered cash problems in the operation of his cigar and brick factories, the Paraguayan government even loaned him 11,500 pesos.

The dreams of Hopkins fitted well into don Carlos's plans for the modernization of the Paraguayan economy. Unfortunately, Hopkins's personality was a major obstacle to good relations with the president and other Paraguayans. His own U.S. employees thought him "swaggering," "bullying," and "tyrannical." In his business proposals to the Paraguayan government, Hopkins was arrogant, overreaching, and determined to have full control over all his proposed projects. He made no secret of his mission to "civilize" Paraguay and openly criticized the 1853 treaty, arguing that it did little to protect foreign business in Paraguay. Don Carlos had no tolerance for such behavior, and following a dispute between Hopkins's brother and a government soldier, the president took measures obviously designed to rid the country of this irritating American and his company. The first assaults were directed at Hopkins in his capacity of entrepreneur. First, he was asked to sell his rights in the United States and Paraguayan Navigation Company to the government. He refused. Then on 16 August, López declared invalid the sale to the company of a small plot of land adjoining the company's headquarters at San Antonio and insisted that the title be returned to the original owner. Pointedly, on 23 August troops occupied that headquarters. Hopkins protested, arguing that the U.S. government would offer him, as it would any citizen, "powerful and constant protection." He appealed for support from the U.S. commander of the U.S.S. *Water Witch,* currently in platine waters. He also sent to Secretary of State William L. Marcy a long, rambling, and disjointed plea in which he defended all his actions. In it he severely criticized López, found fault with the Treaty of 1853, attacked Brazilian foreign policy, and condemned the lack of respect he felt the commander of the *Water Witch* had accorded him. He concluded that letter with his resignation as consul.[12]

On 24 August additional decrees concerning the carrying of arms by foreigners, assembly of noncitizens, rights to navigation, rights of land possession, and commercial patents all fell upon Hopkins. These measures were purely discriminatory, yet the Paraguayan government was within its rights inasmuch as the Treaty of 1853 had not yet been ratified by the United States. The most telling measure was the demand that all foreign establishments then in operation obtain a license to continue. This was obviously aimed at Hopkins, as no others then existed. Hopkins applied for such a license but was refused on the grounds that he had signed the application as general agent for the company—a title now expressly forbidden. The cigar factory in Asunción was sequestered, and the government forbade the further operations of Hopkins's company in Paraguay. Hopkins reacted forcefully, informing the Paraguayan government that he would file claims against it. Finally on 1 September, under a pretext of his mistreatment of Paraguayan laborers, the government revoked his *exequatur.*[13]

The *Water Witch* Controversy

As in the case of Hopkins's exuberance over the commercial possibilities offered by Paraguay, the voyage of the *Water Witch* to the Río de la Plata also had its origins in Manifest Destiny. From the 1830s through the 1850s, the U.S. Navy became a spearhead for overseas commercial expansion. Promoting foreign trade and access to ports were important naval duties and often effected in conjunction with exploration and navigational investigation.[14] The State Department and Department of the Navy had digested Hopkins's reports on Paraguay by the 1850s, and his public addresses and articles had also awakened some interest in this region of South America. The interior of the Río de la Plata, it was believed in Washington, might very well be a fertile region for the sale of U.S. products.

The secretary of the navy selected Lieutenant Thomas Jefferson Page as commander of the platine expedition and instructed the young officer that "the primary objects of the expedition are the promotion of commerce and navigation."[15] On the voyage south, Page acquired from Brazil and the Argentine Confederation special permission for the *Water Witch* to navigate the rivers of these two countries draining the Río de la Plata. On entering Paraguayan waters he received permission from President López to proceed to Asunción. There he was warmly welcomed, and López even permitted the U.S. commander to construct a small auxiliary vessel in the Bay of Asunción for shallow water exploration.

Paraguay was then engaged in diplomatic difficulties with Brazil relative to boundary questions along the Mato Grosso frontier. Any voyage of the *Water Witch* north to Brazilian territory would set a precedent for Brazilian navigation on the Paraguay—a liberty don Carlos was loathe to permit. Nonetheless, perhaps because he desired the United States to ratify the recent Treaty of 1853, President López gave permission to Page to sail north to Bahía Blanca in Paraguayan territory, but no farther. Page ignored López's wishes. The *Water Witch* proceeded as far as Corumbá in Brazil. Perhaps Page felt justified since he did have Brazilian permission to enter imperial waters. In any case, President López was infuriated.

As the *Water Witch* sailed south, relations between Paraguay and the United States worsened in August of 1854 when Hopkins's personal relations with the president exploded. Page had no desire to become involved in Hopkins's difficulties. He rejected Hopkins's criticism of the Treaty of 1853 as it was a highly dubious action for a consul. Still, he sailed to Asunción to expedite the consul's departure. At first Page requested that don Carlos provide transportation for Hopkins's party downriver. The government replied that Hopkins was free to leave after he supplied an inventory of his and the company's property.

When the former consul attempted to pass customs, officials informed him that land titles and papers of the company must be handed over to the Paraguayan officials. Page now became angry and defended Hopkins's right to the papers. Then the U.S. commander waved a red flag at López by informing the president that Brazil had granted to the United States further rights of exploration in the Mato Grosso. Page asked for government permission to pass through Paraguayan territory to the north, a very unwise request given López's growing sensitivity about Brazilian pressure to open the Paraguay River.

The situation escalated; Page became much more hostile to López when the Paraguayan government refused to accept the U.S. commander's communications regarding the land titles and voyage to Brazil since they were written in English. Finally, because of the government's delay in authorizing the party's departure, Page lost control. He demanded leave to go and pointedly turned the ship's cannon on the presidential palace. On 30 September, after Hopkins's party was allowed to board the *Water Witch,* Page departed Asunción. Within a week of Hopkins's departure, the Paraguayan government closed national waters to foreign ships of war—obviously in response to Page's actions. That decree was quickly followed by Page's receipt from Washington of the revised Treaty of 1853. A subordinate officer delivered the treaty to Asunción by way of private steamer, but again Page refused to have the explanations for the changes in the treaty and accompanying communications translated into Spanish. Again the Paraguayan government refused to accept those communications and the treaty itself.

For the next four months the *Water Witch* explored only Argentine waters. However, in late January 1855 Page ordered a junior officer, Lieutenant William N. Jeffers, to assume command of the U.S. ship and proceed up the Alto Paraná to collect navigational information. Following the Paraná channel on the Argentine side, the *Water Witch* ran aground on a sandbank. On freeing the vessel, Jeffers attempted to ascend the river again, using the northern channel in the portion of the river claimed by Paraguay. A canoe from the Paraguayan fort of Itapirú delivered to the U.S. ship a copy of the closure of rivers decree, but as it was in Spanish, the U.S. commander, following the example of his superior, refused it—even though as in the past a translator was present. The *Water Witch* approached the fort closely, ignoring the message, and then ignored an unshotted cannon warning. Finally the Paraguayans fired a warning shot in front of the ship. Their aim was poor, and the U.S. vessel was hit. After a brief exchange of cannon fire, the *Water Witch* was gravely damaged; with helmsman Samuel Chaney dead, the ship turned away to Corrientes. The Paraguayan government, on hearing of this incident, dispatched a note to Secretary of State Marcy defending Paraguay's actions and assumed that the United States would punish the commander of the ship for jeopardizing U.S.-Paraguayan relations.

When the damaged warship arrived in Corrientes where the U.S. expedition then had its headquarters, Lieutenant Page was furious. He immediately departed to Buenos Aires to request permission to equip another warship to destroy the fort of Itapirú. The U.S. commodore wisely refused, citing the need for approval from Washington for such action. The secretary of the navy approved Page's action, possibly because Page used a bit of creative geography to maintain that the main channel of the Alto Paraná flowed near Itapirú, thus placing Jeffers in international waters. At the same time, the Navy Department also commended the restraint of the U.S. commodore. Page may have taken some satisfaction when shortly after the *Water Witch* incident Brazil sent a strong naval expedition up the Paraná to Paraguay's frontier and, by that show of force, compelled López to grant passage of Brazilian vessels through Paraguayan territory to the Mato Grosso.

In Washington, the administration of Franklin Pierce was not happy with these problems with Paraguay; Pierce termed López's actions "violent and arbitrary." Bedeviled as he was by internal sectional politics, the U.S. president still preferred a diplomatic approach. Furthermore, Secretary of State Marcy was extremely dubious of Hopkins's conduct. He questioned the claims against Paraguay by the United States and Paraguay Navigation Company (amounting to a fantastic $935,000) and had little use for the conduct of Thomas Jefferson Page. Only upon the urging of Samuel G. Arnold, a prominent Rhode Island politician and also an officer of and shareholder in the company, and Senator Philip Allen of Rhode Island did Marcy agree to raise the issue of claims. His major concern, however, was to attain ratification of the Treaty of 1853. To that end, Marcy dispatched Richard Fitzpatrick as special commissioner to Asunción.

Fitzpatrick handled the negotiations somewhat clumsily. In any case, he insisted upon treaty ratification before discussing other outstanding differences. The Paraguayan position was precisely opposite—no ratification until the Hopkins and *Water Witch* problems were resolved. The Paraguayan foreign minister assured Fitzpatrick that President López wished to negotiate a new treaty if the U.S. government sent a representative with appropriate instructions and powers. At this point, the next move had to come from Washington.

One can understand López's impatience. Within less than a decade he had experienced the failure of Hopkins's mediation attempt, the consul's disgraceful conduct in 1853, and the ensuing *Water Witch* imbroglio. All made him wary of U.S. diplomacy. Nonetheless, he erred. Had Paraguay ratified the 1853 treaty, a significant stumbling block to the establishment of normal relations would have been removed and the atmosphere cleared for further discussion. Nor did the Paraguayan president bother to ascertain what the consequences might be for Paraguay.

A Naval Fleet to Paraguay

President James Buchanan had taken office in Washington. As it had during the Pierce administration, the Navigation Company continued its complaints against Paraguay. In July 1857 company officials suggested that a naval blockade of Paraguay might be imposed to compel Paraguay to settle its claims. Buchanan did believe that the United States needed to take some action given all the problems with Paraguay. In June 1858 Congress charged the president to use both military and diplomatic means to bring these matters to a successful conclusion. Throughout this squabble Paraguay suffered the consequences of inadequate diplomatic representation abroad. Don Carlos was personally suspicious and secretive and was not willing to allow any independence of action to the few diplomats that Paraguay then had. The consequences of the republic's long isolation during the Francia era meant a scarcity of men able to conduct foreign affairs—even if López had allowed them to do so. Only in 1856, at the urging of Louis Bamberger, the U.S. consul in Asunción, did López appoint a consul—a U.S. citizen—in New York. And he was handicapped by the lack of any instructions from Asunción. López simply had too narrow a vision of international relations. On the other hand, the Brazilian foreign office urged Paraguay to find a peaceful solution to the conflict, but by 1857 López appeared resigned to war.

President Buchanan ordered Commodore William B. Shubrick to prepare the largest naval expedition ever to leave the United States up to that time. Eleven steam-driven warships, seven sailing war vessels, and supply and hospital ships were readied, as well as sufficient marines and sailors to constitute a respectable landing force.[16] The diplomatic aspect of the mission was not neglected as Buchanan appointed as minister plenipotentiary Judge James Butler Bowlin, a prominent and well-respected Saint Louis politician with experience in diplomacy. Bowlin had gained a reputation as a forceful, no-nonsense diplomat in his previous post in Colombia, and no one doubted that he would press Paraguay hard. His instructions included a demand for an immediate indemnity from the government of Paraguay for the family of the dead helmsman of the *Water Witch*. Furthermore, Paraguay must explain and apologize for its treatment of Page and Fitzpatrick. Either the Treaty of 1853 or a new treaty must be signed, ratified, and exchanged. Finally, Bowlin was instructed to press for an indemnity of $935,000 to satisfy the claims of the Navigation

Company, although he was authorized to accept $500,000. If Paraguay refused to pay that latter sum, then the indemnity was to be turned over to arbitration. However, in that arbitration convention Paraguay must admit "its liability to the company"—thus loading the dice against López's government. Should Bowlin fail to achieve an agreement with López on these issues, then the emissary was to turn matters over to the commodore of the expedition. At that point, Shubrick's contingency order was to blockade the Paraguay River to prevent commerce and to attack and destroy the Paraguayan fortress of Humaitá and any others that might bar the fleet's passage to Asunción. Arriving at the capital he then would demand its surrender and take possession of the city, by force if necessary.

Justo José de Urquiza, the president of the Argentine Confederation, followed quite closely the U.S. preparations and strongly urged his Paraguayan counterpart to accept Argentine mediation of this dispute. As usual, López feared ulterior motives, but at least Urquiza's offer presented the two parties with a way out. Meanwhile, as the U.S. fleet departed for the Río de la Plata in October 1858, López ordered the strengthening of Humaitá, a fortress on a strategic bend in the Paraguay River barring any easy passage to Asunción. Cannon and infantry were rushed to this fortress together with Paraguay's small fleet. In the face of the U.S. naval threat, López believed he had certain advantages. The U.S. fleet carried too few troops for large land actions; Paraguay had a largely self-sufficient economy that could weather an economic blockade; and the Paraguayan president knew that the internal problems of the United States might soon lead to a civil war in that country. Even so, any naval hostility could damage Paraguay and weaken it to the point that either Argentina and Brazil, or both, might take advantage of his nation's misfortune. In the end, at Urquiza's urging, López gave way on the *Water Witch* issue.[17] He would negotiate with the United States a new treaty of friendship, commerce, and navigation but stand firm on the claims of Hopkins's company. As events proved, Bowlin had no real problem with that position. While Urquiza deserves credit for swaying López to a peaceful resolution of the conflict, his intervention was hardly altruistic. The Argentine president thought it an excellent opportunity for his own government to assert its boundary views upon Paraguay, thus preserving peace in the Plata on his own terms.

The U.S. fleet steamed north to Corrientes, where it halted while Bowlin and Schubrick continued up the Paraguay in one of the warships. Since the Paraguayan border officials were informed of the peaceful nature of this voyage, the warship had no difficulty in passing Humaitá. Neither Paraguay nor the United States could gain by naval action on the Paraguay River. Humaitá, it was obvious, would have been a hard nut to crack, and many of the U.S. ships were well fitted for oceanic action, but not riverine sailing. On the other hand, Paraguay certainly would not have benefited from any altercation. Its export economy would have been wrecked, and if the U.S. fleet had managed to force the river, Asunción was vulnerable. In addition, López was still concerned about Brazil's policy toward Paraguay. Paraguay needed no new enemies.

Moreover, Bowlin grew still more dubious about the validity of Hopkins's claims, particularly after discussions with Bamburger, the U.S. consul to Asunción. If those claims were suspect, this certainly weakened any justification of the United States to use force to redress differences with Paraguay. For that matter, by 1858 Hopkins wished that Bowlin had the power to settle for less than five hundred thousand dollars.

In the course of discussions with the president, Bowlin took some liberties with his instructions, easing the way to agreement on all parts of the U.S. demands, other than Hopkins's claims. López offered $250,000 as settlement—a more than generous amount. However, Bowlin informed the president that his instructions called for a flat settlement of $500,000 or arbitration. Through Urquiza, Bowlin quietly let López know that Paraguay would receive impartial and fair treatment. In this matter, as in others, Urquiza played a useful and appreciated role and later received the grateful thanks of Bowlin for expediting the negotiations.

On 4 February 1859, a new treaty of commerce and navigation was signed. The following year, with no difficulty, both parties ratified it. It differed little from the unperfected treaty of 1853.[18] Paraguay deplored the Page and Fitzpatrick incidents, and the family of the dead helmsman of the *Water Witch* received a generous compensation. All undoubtedly were relieved that a mutual and peaceful accommodation was achieved. President Buchanan was pleased with Bowlin, and in his annual message of December 1859 he stated that all the difficulties with Paraguay had been satisfactorily settled.

Rejection of the Hopkins Claims

On the same day that the treaty was signed in Asunción, Bowlin and the Paraguayan foreign minister signed a convention for arbitration of the Hopkins claims. By that agreement, a commissioner appointed by the president of the United States, in conjunction with a Paraguayan counterpart, had to "investigate, adjust, and determine the amount of claims" submitted by the United States and Paraguay Navigation Company.[19] After hearing testimony and investigation of documentary evidence, the commission issued its decision on 13 August 1860: "that the said claimants, the United States and Paraguay Navigation Company, have not proved or established any right to damages upon their said claim against the government of the republic of Paraguay; and that, upon the proofs aforesaid, the said government is not responsible to the said company in any damages or pecuniary compensation whatever, in all the premises."[20]

One can disagree with few of the commission's findings. Perhaps the only claim worthy of some consideration was the damage suffered by López's ruin of the company's business in Paraguay during August 1854 when he deliberately embarked upon the expulsion of Hopkins and the United States and Paraguay Navigation Company. In that instance, no more than twenty thousand to thirty thousand dollars would have been justified, and even so, the company left debts behind. Company officials proved inordinately avaricious, however, and their demands, as well as the conduct of Hopkins, obviously outraged Cave Johnson, the U.S. representative on the commission, in both a legal and ethical sense. López was at one time willing to pay $250,000 just to rid Paraguay of this irritant. The company wanted more; it got nothing.

Cave Johnson received general public and congressional approval for his forthright decision. The Paraguayan government was also pleased with the commissioners' decision, but not so President Buchanan. The naval expedition had cost perhaps as much as three million dollars. Buchanan submitted the settlement to the Senate for consideration in February 1861 but stated that the commissioners had been limited by the convention to ascertain the damages to the company—not their validity. Buchanan's attorney general (as later did Abraham Lincoln's) had informed the president that by awarding no damages the commission had exceeded its powers, thus making the settlement null and void. The Senate took no action on Buchanan's message. The commission's view was that damages might have run from zero dollars to the entire amount claimed by the company; the commission awarded the lower number.

Had President Buchanan accepted the decision, much effort might have been saved over the next decade. Although future administrations attempted to reopen this matter with Paraguay, all failed. After the commission's award, Paraguayan governments simply and correctly stated that they accepted the decision as a valid one.[21]

So ended the initial phase of relations between the United States and Paraguay. Never in the 1840s and 1850s was there any real conflict of interest between the two nations. Yet by the late 1850s a real danger of war had developed. What then occasioned the misunderstandings and incidents that engendered the friction between both republics? Certainly, personalities played a role in this friction—the major problem being the erratic and self-serving behavior of Edward A. Hopkins. Then too, the actions of Lieutenant Page certainly added to the growing estrangement between Washington and Asunción. But those two Americans do not bear the entire blame. As secretary of state, Buchanan should never have given special agent status to Hopkins in 1845, given the latter's inexperience and obvious problems with authority. Later in 1851–52 the Fillmore administration erred in Hopkins's appointment as consul when full evidence of his unfitness was at hand. In a minor sense, the suspicious personality of Carlos Antonio López, as well as his limited vision of international relations, contributed to the tension between the two nations. Yet it is obvious that he was more sinned against than sinner.

When the crisis between the two countries reached its peak, the diplomatic skill and pacific intentions of James Bowlin can only be applauded. Bowlin realized that he bore the honor of the United States in his negotiations with Paraguay, and he succeeded in defusing a perilous situation. In this, he was ably seconded by Commodore Shubrick. When the Arbitration Commission met, Commissioner Cave Johnson dispensed justice concordant with the honor and good name of the United States. The wisdom, forthright character, and integrity of these three served the United States well.

The Paraguayan War

Under pressure from Rhode Island investors, the administration of Abraham Lincoln continued Buchanan's policy of noncertification of the Hopkins claims arbitration and appointed Charles Ames Washburn commissioner to Paraguay to reopen negotiations. Washburn, selected mainly because of the influence of his prominent Republican brother, Elihu, had no success in Asunción. The government of Carlos Antonio López now considered the matter closed. Washburn decided to remain in Asunción, reporting to Washington on Paraguay and the Río de la Plata, and in 1862 was promoted to the post of minister to Paraguay—even though U.S. interests in that faraway republic did not warrant that level of representation.[22] Washburn did have relatively good relations with Carlos Antonio López, but not with the latter's son and successor, Francisco Solano López.

The U.S. minister had little idea that the great war of the Triple Alliance versus Paraguay (1864–70) was about to erupt. The immediate cause of the war was the Brazilian Empire's military intervention in a Uruguayan civil war, which President Francisco Solano López considered a danger to Paraguay's interests in the Río de la Plata. Even before the intervention, Brazilian pressure against Paraguay in the 1850s for free passage of the Paraguay to the Mato Grosso, as well as boundary problems with the empire, had prompted Carlos Antonio López to expand his nation's armed forces. After Rio de Janeiro ignored Solano López's protests, Paraguay seized a Brazilian steamer in Paraguayan waters and immediately launched a successful invasion of the Mato Grosso. Then President López ordered a disastrous attack on Brazilian territory along the Uruguay River. In the course of that campaign Paraguay violated Argentine territory. In early 1865, Brazil, Argentina, and Uruguay concluded a wartime treaty against Paraguay. By 1866 Paraguay was desperately defending its southern frontier of the Alto Paraná River.[23]

So unconcerned was Washburn that after the beginning of the war, but before Argentina joined it, he took leave to the United States for personal reasons. He returned in late 1865 with a young bride and spent the next year fuming in Corrientes, Argentina, since the Brazilian admiral of the fleet blockading the Paraguay River did not allow him free passage to Asunción. Nor did the admiral of the U.S. squadron in South Atlantic waters render him any aid in returning to his legation. Finally, after many complaints to Washington, a U.S. naval vessel arrived and carried the minister to the Paraguayan capital.[24] Francisco Solano López judged the minister's arrival as a sign of Washington's favor for his cause, and Washburn enjoyed relatively good relations with the Paraguayan president for a brief period.

The War of the Triple Alliance, or Paraguayan War, erupted when the United States was still fighting its Civil War. By late 1866, however, U.S. policy toward the Paraguayan War was essentially in place, although never explicitly stated. Under no circumstances would the United States become embroiled in that war because no U.S. interests were involved, and the United States, with its Civil War less than two years in the past, was war weary. Although there was some concern that the war might open the path to European intervention and thus an assault upon the Monroe Doctrine, the confinement of that conflict to the Upper Plata by late 1866 rendered that danger minimal. Furthermore, France, withdrawing from its Mexican fiasco and preoccupied with the growing threat of Prussia, and Great Britain, seeing no profit from any platine intervention, were then the only two European nations with the power to intervene, and they had no interest in such an action. Another vague concern of Washington officials was that any possibility of trade in the Upper Plata was doomed as long as the war continued. On the other hand, the State Department little understood the depth of Brazilian hatred for Solano López and Rio's determination to be rid of its dangerous neighbor. Nor did Washington realize how President Bartolomé Mitré might use the war as a useful vehicle to consolidate Argentina. Essentially then, the United States adopted a passive policy toward the war, hindered by the State Department's inability, or unwillingness, to consider the war in the Río de la Plata from the viewpoint of the belligerents.

President López, at the onset of the war, displayed no foreign policy directed at powers outside of the Río de la Plata. Even when the war turned against Paraguay in 1865, there was no attempt on the part of Asunción to engage the United States. There was little commerce between the two nations, and if López had any consideration for extra-hemispheric powers, it was to Great Britain and France that he looked. Only for the brief period of Washington's mediation attempt in late 1866 and early 1867 did López feel that the United States might be useful to Paraguay. However, the failure of that venture, as well as the obvious reluctance of the United States to challenge the allies over the blockade of the Paraguay River, persuaded him that nothing could be expected from the far north. To be sure, the presence of Minister Washburn in Asunción from late 1866 onward did give some legitimacy to López's government, but that was of little value to the war effort. Finally, when all was lost by 1869, there was a desperate approach to the United States by a Paris-based Paraguayan diplomat, but as will be seen, it had no chance.

The very cautious policy of the United States did not preclude the possibility of Washington's mediation in the conflict. In late 1866 Secretary of State Seward believed that the time was opportune for such an offer. He stated that the United States had no intention in interfering in the war, but in the interests of peace, and should the belligerents all desire mediation, Washington would offer its good offices. The House of Representatives quickly endorsed Seward's overture and sent a resolution via the U.S. ministers to the warring nations. In the course of discussion in Washington, however, Seward's original proposal had subtly changed and became an offer of mediation. This the allies received coldly. By early 1867, with the Brazilians contributing the preponderance of manpower and resources in the struggle against Paraguay, the Río government now believed that Solano López could be crushed by force of arms, and that an outright military victory was desirable. Argentina and Uruguay shared Brazil's view to varying degrees. Although the allies had no wish to alienate the United States, the offer of mediation was not welcome.

The allies rejected not only mediation but also any outside interference while they prosecuted the war against Paraguay. Nonetheless, only a few months after that rejection Alexander Asboth, the U.S. minister to Argentina, pushed U.S. mediation upon the Argentine Foreign Ministry to the point of a diplomatic dispute. Finally, Secretary of State Seward decided to soothe the Argentines, and Asboth made amends. Later, in 1868, in an attempt to test again the waters, the U.S. minister in Rio de Janeiro, J. Watson Webb, also made an overture to reopen the mediation question, though this time in a more discreet manner. He had no more success than Asboth.[25] The Brazilians politely declined, citing the same reasons as before. By that time the Paraguayans had retreated from the fortress of Humaitá, and the allies saw a full military victory on the horizon.

"A Tyrant So Absolute and Cruel"

Other than the futile mediation attempts, Washburn found little to do in Asunción in late 1866 and 1867. A diary kept by his wife and him reveals the tedium of their existence. They had little contact with the upper-class families of the capital, either through the asunceños' choice or their own; and only a few diplomats and other foreigners remained to relieve their isolation. Communications with the United States were slow, not only because of distance but because the allies placed obstacles to private and official mail leaving Paraguay. Boredom, frustration, and isolation from the outside world were Washburn's lot, and his discontent was shown in letters to his brothers, despatches to the State Department, and official letters to U.S. diplomats accredited to the allies. Furthermore, Washburn now considered López "a tyrant so absolute and cruel."[26] Secretary of State Seward found his complaints tiresome and often did not even bother to reply. Only J. Watson Webb, the U.S. minister to Brazil, managed to continue a civil relation with Washburn, though even he privately deplored the ill temper and far-fetched accusations that the minister in Asunción so casually displayed.

The neutralization of the Paraguay fortress of Humaitá that guarded the entrance to the Paraguay River by the surrounding allied army in early 1868 indirectly worsened relations between Washburn and President López. The Brazilian fleet now had free run of the Paraguay River and bombarded Asunción itself. That threat induced López to transfer his capital to Luque, a small interior town a short distance from Asunción. He also ordered the complete civilian evacuation of the capital. As early as October 1867, the U.S. minister had anticipated the abandonment of the capital. When asked by anxious foreigners and Paraguayans what he would do if the government fled, he responded:

> I tell them that I shall stay at my post until I am ordered to leave it by my government. If the enemy come and bombard the town they can bombard my house, but I shall keep my flag flying and shall not leave it; and if they or anybody else shall blow up the town they can blow me up with it, for I shall not leave my post except I am carried away a prisoner and by force. This determination seems to have given great confidence to people who think many evils may be averted by my remaining here. . . .
>
> Should the evacuation of the town be ordered—and I believe it will be if the war last much longer—it is uncertain whether the foreigners will or will not be permitted to remain. If they are not, I apprehend many will ask admission to my premises and request protection, which it would be hard to refuse and might be embarrassing to grant. As against the enemy, however, I have not hesitated to say that this legation will give whatever protection it can to whomsoever, save notorious criminals, may resort to it in time of danger.[27]

For the duration of his service in Paraguay, Washburn never wavered from his determination to remain in Asunción and provide protection to those who asked. The State Department commended his determination to remain at "your post of duty" and also approved his intention to grant asylum in the legation, "as far as it can be done without compromising your neutral character or that of your country."[28]

In the confusion of the civilian evacuation of Asunción, foreigners and Paraguayans deposited money and other valuables at the U.S. Legation. Since he took no inventory, Washburn refused to assume responsibility for the money and jewelry left there.[29] Even so, this humanitarian action led to a long diplomatic controversy between Paraguay and the United States over the ownership of the items deposited and would drag on until the 1920s.

Another consequence of the fall of Humaitá was the increased governmental oppression and persecution of foreigners and Paraguayans. Some foreigners, under suspicion of conspiracy, turned desperately to Washburn for protection. He did what he could to shield the few Americans and other foreigners in Paraguay, but that aid placed Washburn under suspicion. Through 1868 the tension grew so great that Washburn feared for his life and the safety of his family. By that point the only diplomatic function that Washburn could perform was somehow to protect himself and those around him.[30] He realized that even though he and his family might be saved by his diplomatic status, others in the legation faced great danger. He informed Porter Bliss, an American to whom he had given shelter in the legation, that should the Paraguayans arrest him, "you have my full authority to say anything about me which may either mitigate your sufferings or prolong your lives; not a word of it can ever be believed by anyone outside of Paraguay, nor by any one in Paraguay unless it be López himself."[31]

Minister Washburn's burdens were somewhat relieved by the near absence of compatriots in wartime Paraguay. Even so, there was the curious case of James Manlove, an adventurer from Maryland, who claimed to have been a Confederate major under Nathan Bedford Forrest. Manlove had earlier met Washburn in Brazil in 1865. Later that year, in Buenos Aires, the two met again, and Manlove broached a scheme to obtain letters of marque from Paraguay and then, with nominal Paraguayan ownership of vessels and nominal Paraguayan captains, prey upon Brazilian shipping in the Atlantic. The U.S. minister opposed this, realizing the embarrassment it might bring his country if it came to pass. He then refused to ask the allies for permission for Manlove to pass through their lines into Paraguay. The adventurer was not to be denied. He traveled upriver, ingratiated himself with the allies, and surreptitiously slipped through their lines into Paraguay in early 1866. There, President López was suspicious of this American, probably believing him a spy, given his passage through enemy lines. The Paraguayan government rejected the privateering proposal, and Manlove was now trapped in Paraguay. Washburn did dole out funds for his upkeep, as did the Paraguayan government, but the American's position was precarious. He could not gain a measure of protection by being added to the legation's staff, given the proposal he had made. In mid-1868, after the fall of Humaitá and during President López's persecution of "traitors," Manlove, by López's orders, was executed by a firing squad.[32]

Conspirator or Not?

Regardless of the dubious nature of evidence presented by the López government after the retreat from Humaitá in 1868, it is yet an article of faith, even in today's Paraguay, that there was indeed a conspiracy to overthrow Solano López. In any discussion of plots, the name of Charles Ames Washburn always appears. Defenders of the Paraguayan president have always claimed that the U.S. minister organized the movement to topple López. No evidence of plots or connection with plotters has appeared within Washburn's private and official correspondence. A statement in a later House investigation of his conduct in Paraguay remains the best word on the conspiracy claim: "the inherent falsity and absurdity of the charge carries with it its own, and its strongest, refutation."[33]

One has to have sympathy for the tremendously difficult position in which Washburn found himself. Nonetheless, in the personal sense he certainly had deficiencies. He lacked prudence, was extremely arrogant, and carried violent prejudices to the extreme. Not only did he display open contempt for the Paraguayan president, but he was proud of his openness. From the onset of his mission he hated Francisco Solano López: "It may not have been diplomatic, and certainly was not courtier-like, but I took a sort of malicious pleasure, when everybody else in the room was standing, to sit in a conspicuous place, indifferent whether the President were standing, or not."[34]

Another War for a General

Washburn's departure left the United States with no representative in Paraguay. Normally, this would have meant little—most other powers lacked representation as well. However, there yet remained the matter of Porter Bliss and George F. Masterman, both members of the legation to whom López refused permission to depart with the Washburn party. After Secretary of State Seward accepted Washburn's resignation in June 1868, a search immediately began for a successor, and within a month Seward selected Major General Martin T. McMahon as minister to Paraguay.[35]

In late August 1868 the new minister sailed for the Río de la Plata accompanied by his three younger sisters. His instructions from the State Department were rather sketchy. The United States supported the full sovereign rights of all nations but wished no

> alliances or engagements by which they might become parties in the conflicts of other nations. They have asserted and faithfully maintained neutrality in the unhappy war which has so long existed in the valley of the La Plata. Nevertheless the United States regard wars between the several states of this continent with sincere regret, and they have, therefore, constantly tendered their good offices to the belligerents for the purpose of procuring an end of hostilities and a restoration of peace among the nations of South America. This is the spirit of the instructions which have been given to your predecessor and they will be found sufficient for your guidance.[36]

At stops in Brazil he became aware of the confused nature of Washburn's departure and the travail of foreigners in Paraguay. General J. Watson Webb, the U.S. minister to Brazil, recommended to McMahon: "You have no duties to discharge in connection with Paraguay. López by an act of war against the United States, has cancelled alike your duties and your instructions, and nothing remains for you to do but to consult the honor and dignity of your country by remaining here, or in the La Plata, until you hear from Washington."[37] In Buenos Aires, McMahon met with Washburn, who emphatically recommended that he have no communication with the López government until Washington had been apprised of Washburn's recent problems.[38] Washburn evidently believed, however, that McMahon might take up residence in Paraguay as he recounted the matter of valuables left in the legation. He anxiously requested his successor to inquire after the well-being of Paraguayan and European friends of the Washburn family.[39] McMahon then arranged for the care of his sisters in Buenos Aires and joined Rear Admiral Charles H. Davis aboard the USS *Wasp.*

In the seven months of McMahon's residence in Paraguay, very little of a diplomatic nature transpired between him and the Paraguayan government. He found himself isolated from Washington inasmuch as despatches to and from him had to pass through allied lines, and the Brazilian high command deliberately delayed such communications in their effort to delegitimize the López regime in the eyes of the world. Even so, the short stay of the new minister is interesting in its contrast to the Washburn period. McMahon rapidly formed a close personal relationship with President López. The young American was a romantic and saw the war as Paraguay's heroic struggle against a powerful alliance bent on the destruction of the republic. He perforce sympathized with the effort of López to defend his nation and was willing to overlook qualities in the Paraguayan leader that others found detestable. Then too, his military background may well have inclined him to a "freemasonry of generals." Or the young man may have been flattered by the extent of confidence a president and leader of a nation at war gave him. In any case, McMahon never abandoned his sympathy for the

Paraguayan cause and defense of López, even when that subjected him to severe criticism by foreigners and his own compatriots.[40]

A rather unthinking action by McMahon was greatly criticized by foreigners. On 23 December 1868, just before McMahon left for Piribebuí, a new Paraguayan capital, President López, with the full knowledge and permission of McMahon, named the latter as executor of his will. In that testament the president left his entire estate to his mistress and mother of his children—Eliza Lynch.[41] Whatever one thinks of the López family, McMahon's assumption of responsibility for the personal financial affairs of the Paraguayan leader was unwise. Within a week of its execution, victorious Brazilian troops captured the will and other papers revealing the sudden friendship between the Paraguayan and American. The allied command rapidly made it public. A drumbeat of criticism ensued, an attack upon McMahon in the Argentine and Brazilian press that increased in intensity for the remainder of his stay in Paraguay. The allies accused McMahon of being in the pay of López—a charge he indignantly denied. Others, with more justice, spoke of a gullible naïveté since López obviously had deceived the American as to the nature of the Paraguayan government and its aims. An extreme accusation in the Argentine press even had the American accepting López's order to command the Paraguayan Army.[42]

At Piribebuí McMahon suggested to López a means to end the hostilities. The U.S. minister would arrange an armistice, López would voluntarily go into exile, and the allies would abandon Paraguayan territory. This was a rather naive proposal. After all, by 1869 the allies had finally tasted victory and were determined to prosecute the war to its conclusion. Moreover, by this juncture the courtesies of communication between belligerents had been generally discarded. Even McMahon, a neutral diplomat, often could not persuade the Brazilian army to accept his communications for transmission to Washington. As with other mediation attempts, McMahon's was futile.

Finally, in early May 1869, two U.S. naval officers passed through allied lines with despatches for the U.S. minister—one being his recall to the United States. Earlier in the year, the Andrew Johnson administration debated closing the Paraguayan mission since the United States had no commerce with that republic and hardly a handful of citizens there. Secretary of State Seward opposed the abandonment, and no action was taken.[43] The new Ulysses S. Grant administration, however, decided to clean up what many saw as an embarrassing imbroglio. Evidently, the steady drumbeat of criticism of the American's closeness to López had considerably complicated Washington's relations with Rio and Buenos Aires alike.

A Black Eye for the Navy

McMahon passed through Asunción on his departure from Paraguay. In that city, now under Brazilian occupation, he angrily noted that victorious Brazilian troops had looted the U.S. Legation and thrown records into the street. Downriver in Buenos Aires, he found the Argentines chilly as they considered him López's stooge. Since yellow fever was raging in Brazilian ports, he returned to the United States by way of Europe. He arrived at much the same time that Congress opened an investigation into the conduct of Washburn and the actions of the U.S. Navy in the Río de la Plata—all in relation to the confused imbroglio that was characteristic of U.S. relations with Paraguay in the late 1860s.[44]

The investigation by the House Committee on Foreign Affairs began in Washington on 30 March 1869. Throughout the year, that body acquired documentary evidence from the State and Navy Departments, as well as taking testimony from many witnesses. Inasmuch as some officers and men of the South Atlantic Squadron were on duty, a subcommittee composed of three Republicans and one Democrat took testimony throughout the year, both in New York and Washington. Finally, the full committee in December 1869 issued a thirty-page report, summarized from extensive testimony and documentation and penned by the subcommittee, as well as all the testimony and documentary evidence taken during the investigation.

The ostensible ground for this investigation was the U.S. Navy's treatment of Bliss and Masterman following their rescue from Paraguay during the McMahon mission. The two claimed that not only had officers of the *Wasp* accepted López's contention that the two had engaged in a conspiracy, but that their previous confessions confirmed their guilt. The two claimed that the navy, on the voyage downriver in 1868, had unjustly treated them as criminals, and such treatment did not stop when the *Wasp* reached the estuary.

The House report supported Washburn's contention that Bliss and Masterman acted as members of the legation staff and expressed its outrage about the arrest of the two as well as their subsequent treatment at the hands of Paraguayan interrogators (they, the committee claimed, were no better than state torturers). In the eyes of the committee, the entire Bliss/Masterman affair demonstrated little more than López's tyranny and revealed that the "blessings of civilization are almost unknown in Paraguay." As for the charges against Bliss and Masterman, the report dismissed them as totally incredible and sustained only by testimony obtained "under a species of torture which hardly had its counterpart in the bloodiest annals of the Inquisition." The report endorsed the State Department's position that Washburn had acted correctly in his protection of the two. The matter of naval-diplomatic relations during Washburn's service concerned Rear Admiral Godon's refusal to carry Washburn to Asunción and the treatment Bliss and Masterman received by naval officers after their release from Paraguay and on their trip downriver.

In its report to the House the Committee on Foreign Affairs presented several resolutions. The first was that Rear Admiral Sylvanus Godon "failed to discharge his duty" when he neglected to aid Minister Washburn to travel to Asunción in 1865–66. Bliss and Masterman were part of the personal suite of Minister Washburn and as such were entitled to his protection. The arrest and detention of Bliss and Masterman were a violation of international law and an insult to the United States. The president of the United States was correct in withdrawing Minister McMahon from Paraguay and terminating all further diplomatic discourse with the López government. Both Bliss and Masterman were not treated with due courtesy by the navy after their rescue from Paraguay. And finally, the committee stated that it was the duty of naval officers to provide all reasonable assistance to the diplomatic representatives of the United States, and that any refusal or discourtesy of those officers toward diplomatic personnel should entail an inquiry and possible punishment by the Navy Department.

Were the conclusions of the majority valid? Certainly when judging Washburn's defense of Bliss and Masterman, as well as the treatment of the two by Paraguayan authorities, they were. Admiral Godon's actions, the testimony of subordinates and other U.S. diplomats besides Washburn, and Washburn's own words and papers justified the committee's censure of Godon. Admiral Davis, by contrast, was treated a bit too harshly by the committee. Certainly, he appeared dilatory in readying a ship to rescue Bliss and Masterman, but the arrival of the new minister, General McMahon, complicated matters. Then too, when Davis brought McMahon to Paraguay in 1869, both he and McMahon wished to avoid any unnecessary conflict with Paraguay, while at the same time effecting the rescue of Bliss and Masterman. In such a case, it is probably not best to second-guess the responsible commander on the scene—regardless of the appearance of subservience to López. The really telling complaint against Davis concerned the treatment of Bliss and Masterman after they were rescued. The navy accepted at face value the statements the two made before their release. That blind acceptance revealed a great naïveté as to conditions in Paraguay. The navy then paid no attention to their subsequent explanations, and Davis, as commander of the squadron, must bear much of the responsibility for their treatment as criminals.

There are some curious aspects about this House report and the resolutions—both majority and minority. Although the original resolution calling for an investigation failed to mention the Paraguayan policies of the Lincoln, Johnson, or Grant administrations, even today it seems surprising how little the investigation and report dealt with the "Washington end" of U.S. relations with Paraguay. Instead, all evidence and testimony were concentrated on the events in the Río de la Plata, and regardless of the thrust of evidence and testimony, the main figure in the investigation was always Charles Ames Washburn. After taking testimony and evaluating other evidence, the majority simply accepted his version of the Bliss-Masterman affair, as well as his version of the conflict with the naval authorities. While the word "exoneration" did not appear in the report, a careful reading reveals that the majority felt that no blame or criticism should be assigned to the U.S. minister.[45]

The Last Gasps

During most of the war Paraguay did little to influence U.S. opinion or, for that matter, the U.S. government. At the war's outbreak, Paraguay had no diplomatic representation in Washington, only a U.S. citizen, Richard Mallownay, who acted as its consul in New York City. Mallownay's only recompense was proceeds from consular fees, and he never saw it as his duty to "lobby" for the republic. What money Francisco Solano López allocated for the presentation of his cause he directed at France and Great Britain. The lack of an effort in the United States gave free rein to the allied diplomats in Washington to create a pro-allied opinion or at least counter any growth of sympathy for Paraguay. They also were on hand to take care of any diplomatic problems relating to the war. In this, Domingo Sarmiento, the able author, politician, and publicist, took the lead as Argentina's minister to the United States. He not only had greater access to the press but was well connected with U.S. intellectual circles. The Empire of Brazil was well represented in Washington but handicapped by some diplomatic difficulties with the United States remaining from the U.S. Civil War when that empire was too supportive of the French-backed Mexican Empire of Maximilian.

By 1869 the lack of any effort to champion Paraguay's cause in the United States concerned Gregorio Benites, the Paraguayan chargé d'affaires in Paris. Benites was one of the able young Paraguayans whom Carlos Antonio López sent abroad to gain an education. He recognized that with Paraguay's cause in great doubt, neither France nor Great Britain would do anything to aid his homeland. On the other hand, the cultivation of the United States might pay dividends, even at this late date.[46] In 1869 he visited the United States to try to summon sympathy for his nation in the press and Congress, advancing the supposed threat to the Monroe Doctrine that an allied victory might bring—or alternatively, the danger to U.S. interests that a Brazilian hegemony in the Río de la Plata might pose. It was no use. Secretary of State Hamilton Fish in the new Grant administration received Benites rather coolly during an interview and replied negatively to his plea for U.S. mediation in the war. Fish knew from past experience that the allies wanted no outside mediation, particularly with full victory in sight. And there was no way that the United States could force mediation upon them. Benites also had an interview with President Grant. That discussion was friendlier in manner than the meeting with Fish, but Grant fully supported his secretary of state. The Paraguayan diplomat departed sadly, though he left convinced that the United States harbored no anti-Paraguayan feelings.

The final attempt to gain U.S. aid to Paraguay came with the visit of a son of President López to North America in 1870. The Paraguayan leader had destined Emiliano Victor López for a public career, and on his visit the young Paraguayan gained the attention of the *New York Herald,* one of the few prominent newspapers to assume an open and crusading pro-Paraguayan stance. Emiliano became a press celebrity with a fleeting fame as the *New York Herald* promoted a short tour for him in the Northeast. As in the case of Benites, the young López had an interview with Hamilton Fish and tried to persuade him to send another minister to his father's government. Fish essentially replied that the new pro-allied provisional government in Asunción seemed to have affairs well in hand. No new U.S. representation to Francisco Solano López's government was forthcoming, and the marshal's forces, now reduced to a starving, straggling band in the wilderness of northeastern Paraguay, soon met its fate at the hands of the Brazilian Army.

2 A Distant Relationship

General McMahon departed Paraguay shortly before the allied victory in August 1869 at Piribebuí that effectively ended organized resistance by Marshal López. In the same month the allies established a new provisional government that faced a prostrate Paraguay, economically ruined and with more than half its population dead.[1] Even so, Washington's policy after the War of the Triple Alliance was to favor the continued independent existence of Paraguay, and officials monitored closely the negotiations between the victors and Asunción, as well as the negotiations among the victors. If Paraguay disappeared, it might well have brought new tensions between Argentina and Brazil.[2]

Despite that concern, Washington maintained no diplomatic presence in Asunción. After the recall of General McMahon, no U.S. minister resided in Paraguay or was accredited solely to that nation as ministers to Paraguay also held accreditation to Uruguay. Neither the State Department nor the U.S. Congress believed that there was need for a minister in Asunción, noting the few Americans present in that republic and the negligible commerce with Paraguay. Ministers, or chargés d'affaires, occasionally visited the republic as part of their duty, but such visits were usually courtesy calls.

In the early 1880s Paraguay approached William Williams, the U.S. chargé d'affaires in Montevideo, about the desirability of a U.S. consul in Asunción, but Williams stated that there was little need for such an agent. Asunción persisted in its request, and in 1888, Frank D. Hill accepted the post of U.S. consul in Asunción, ending the long absence of U.S. representation. He was an able man, and the Paraguayan government was pleased. The decade of the 1890s brought further pressure from Asunción for the United States to appoint a minister solely to Paraguay. Economically, postwar Paraguay offered little to U.S. capitalists. What foreign investment Paraguay received from the 1870s to the 1910s came mainly from Argentine or European sources—in the latter instance, mainly British.

Hopkins Returns with New Ideas

In the immediate postwar era, only one U.S. businessman perceived any gain from Paraguay. That entrepreneur, Edward A. Hopkins, returned to the republic after pursuing various projects in Argentina in the late 1850s and 1860s. In mid-1869 the provisional government granted him a permit to establish a sawmill in Villa Occidental, a small settlement in the Chaco just across the Paraguay River from Asunción. He commenced operations, but on 28 September the government, in an attempt to raise revenue, imposed license fees on businesses.[3] Hopkins refused to pay that fee, stating that he was now on Argentine territory, even though he had earlier sought permission from Paraguay for the enterprise. After a month of this dispute, the commander of Argentine forces in Paraguay ordered his troops to occupy Villa Occidental and informed Asunción that the Chaco was "exclusively Argentine, and that the Paraguayan authorities have nothing to do with it."[4] Paraguayan officials charged that Hopkins had induced the commander to that action to avoid the business fee.[5]

The Argentine occupation of Villa Occidental prompted Hopkins to undertake a more ambitious project—the construction of a railroad from the Paraguay River to southeastern Bolivia to provide an outlet for Bolivian goods. Of course, he planned the eastern terminal at Villa Occidental, and through the early 1870s Hopkins maintained the right of Argentina to that region of the Chaco. The Argentine government was sufficiently impressed with Hopkins's proposal to form a commission to investigate its feasibility. However, before any meaningful work was accomplished, the region through which the railroad would run was awarded to Paraguay in an arbitration decision of 1878.

A Town Named Hayes

In the Paraguayan Chaco, near the capital of Asunción, lies a medium-sized town by the curious name of Villa Hayes (formerly Villa Occidental)—named after Rutherford B. Hayes, seventeenth president of the United States. More than any other U.S. president, Hayes is honored in Paraguay for his arbitration of a boundary dispute with Argentina. Paraguay, occupied by the victorious Brazilian and Argentine armies, was in mortal danger of being divided completely between the two victors. Only mutual suspicion between Rio de Janeiro and Buenos Aires saved Paraguay. The victors pressed earlier territorial claims in the boundary treaties accompanying the peace agreements, and Paraguay lost large sections of territory.

In the Machaín-Irigoyen Treaty of Limits of 3 February 1876, Argentina confirmed its possession of the disputed Misiones as well as various disputed islands in the Alto Paraná and received in the treaty the entire Chaco region south of the Pilcomayo River. As a counterweight to the greater occupation presence of the Brazilians in Paraguay, Argentina particularly desired the region around Villa Occidental, north of the Pilcomayo. By the terms of the Treaty of the Triple Alliance of 1865, Buenos Aires claimed the Chaco Boreal littoral north from the Pilcomayo River to the Río Verde and all the Boreal north of the Pilcomayo, citing its effective occupation from the late 1700s. The Brazilian Foreign Ministry adamantly opposed any extension of Argentine territory past the Pilcomayo. Rio de Janeiro encouraged Paraguay to stand fast on its claim to the Chaco Boreal, and Argentina gave way. The Paraguayans succeeded in placing their right to the southern Chaco Boreal in arbitration before the president of the United States.[6]

After some seven months of reviewing the issue, the U.S. State Department recommended that President Hayes render a judgment favorable to Paraguay. On 12 November 1878, the president awarded to "the said Republic of Paraguay the territory on the western bank of the river of that name, between the Río Verde and the main branch of the Pilcomayo, including Villa Occidental."[7] The two most important pieces of evidence that swayed North American judgment were an *expediente* of 1782 that revealed Paraguay's forts, villas, Indian reductions, and other Chaco establishments, and accounts of the Reducción de Melodía, founded in the late colonial period close to the present-day city of Villa Hayes. An odd aspect of the State Department's deliberations on this matter was a prior Paraguayan settlement in the Chaco on the site of the future Villa Occidental that was not included in the Paraguayan evidence. In the 1850s Carlos Antonio López had established in the Chaco the colony of Nueva Bordeos with French settlers. The colony survived only a few years, but the State Department noted that the Argentine government had never protested its establishment, nor had it ever denied Paraguay's right to establish it.

An unexpected result of the U.S. decision to accept the task of arbitration was the protest of the nation of Bolivia that the North American action ignored its rights. Bolivia, through claims of colonial jurisdiction over this region, argued that Argentina and Paraguay had no right to request any third-party arbitration that ignored the rights of Bolivia. The Bolivian government further stated that during the war it had been assured by the allies that the Andean nation's rights to the Chaco would be respected. La Paz maintained that between 1871 and 1876 Paraguay had also stated to Bolivia that the latter's rights would be reserved in any settlement of the Chaco frontiers.[8] Because Bolivia had not been a signatory to the Paraguay-Argentine treaty, Secretary of State William M. Evarts remained unpersuaded. And for the moment, Washington took no further notice of Bolivia's position, although this question never went away.

Hopkins Redux, Claims, and a Missing "Jewel Box"

The Hayes Award was the most important diplomatic action between Paraguay and the United States in the generation after the War of the Triple Alliance. However, two controversies left over from the prewar era and the war itself bedeviled U.S. representatives for several decades: the renewal of the Hopkins claims and the disposition of the valuables, the Paraguayan "jewel box," that had been deposited in the U.S. Legation in 1868 upon the evacuation of Asunción. Trivial as these matters may seem now, these two problems involved an inordinate amount of time and frustration.[9]

Minister Washburn had refused to accept any responsibility for those valuables in 1868, either on his part or for his government. No inventory was taken and no receipts issued.[10] When he left Asunción, the valuables, belonging to both Paraguayans and foreigners, remained in the legation until it was looted by Brazilian soldiers in 1869. The Brazilian high command made an effort to recover the valuables—both money and jewels—and transferred them to Rio de Janeiro, but they also made no effort to take an inventory. In 1871, this time with only a descriptive inventory, the valuables were passed to the hands of James R. Partridge, the U.S. minister to Brazil, then to a bank in Rio, and later to Partridge's personal possessions when he returned to the United States. Only in 1884 when the State Department acknowledged requests from Paraguayans for the return of their possessions did the Partridge family deliver the valuables to the U.S. government. There is no question that in this odyssey items and money disappeared. Even then, various claims could not be acted upon inasmuch as the State Department demanded a rigorous proof of ownership with which none could comply.

In the meantime Edward A. Hopkins demanded that the State Department reopen the claims case, supposedly resolved in 1860. Under political pressure, Secretary of State Hamilton Fish reluctantly agreed, although he had grave doubts about the wisdom of that action. In 1872 Minister John L. Stevens discussed the claims with José Falcón, the Paraguayan minister of foreign relations, to no avail. Falcón expressed surprise and contended that the 1860 decision had settled the matter. Stevens then reported to Washington that it was futile to pursue the claims, and that Paraguay, impoverished after the war, could in no way pay such claims anyway.

But Hopkins persisted, and in 1885 he found a partisan in the U.S. chargé d'affaires to Paraguay and Uruguay, Judge John F. Bacon. On a trip to Asunción the next year he found the Paraguayan foreign minister, José Segundo Decoud, quite unreceptive. Decoud was an astute diplomat and politician who used delay, obfuscation, internal politics, and even the "jewel box" issue to fend off Bacon. In mid-1887 Bacon returned to Paraguay, and it then appeared that a monetary settlement might be reached. A partisan press campaign capitalized on Hopkins's past misdeeds, alleged a raid upon the treasury, and agitated for the return of the "jewel box."[11] The Chamber of Deputies rejected any agreement. Bacon perceived the fine hand of Decoud, who was no longer minister of foreign relations, in the whole affair, but he also believed that the "jewel box" issue killed the agreement. Bacon was still persistent, but eventually even he realized that no agreement could be reached. Finally, the Hopkins claims were dead.

The return of the "jewel box" became an important political issue in Paraguay. In 1895 José Segundo Decoud, again foreign minister, demanded its return and restitution of whatever had been lost from it since 1871. The State Department still insisted upon adequate proof of ownership, but the circumstances of its deposit in the legation in 1868 precluded such proof. The whole matter dragged on for another thirty years until 1924, when an aged Paraguayan widow asked for the return of heirlooms she assumed to be among the valuables of 1868. The State Department proposed that the remaining valuables be handed to the Paraguayan government with the understanding that the United States admitted no liability. Asunción agreed. In a display of pomp and ceremony what now remained was returned to Asunción. The Paraguayans, in general, were pleased with this resolution even though the contents proved to be of little value.

Pan-Americanism and an Errant Gunboat

The difficulties surrounding the Hopkins claims and the "jewel box" affair were important issues for the Paraguayan government, but they had little impact on other more "normal" relations between the two nations. In the 1880s, Secretary of State James G. Blaine called for an organization of American states to regularize economic relations in the Western Hemisphere and to prevent a repetition of such internecine wars as that of the Triple Alliance and the War of the Pacific (1879–83) between Chile on one side and Bolivia and Peru on the other. The first call for such a conference in 1881 had collapsed because of internal Republican Party politics, but at the end of the decade Blaine, now secretary of state again in the Benjamin Harrison administration, tried again. He repeated his call for a conference, and in 1889 at the first Congress of American States the Pan-American Union was created.

Paraguay's delegate to the first Pan-American Congress was the seasoned José Segundo Decoud, who had played a role in the Chaco arbitration, served several times as foreign minister, and dominated Paraguayan foreign policy in the last quarter of the nineteenth century. The 1889 Congress was Paraguay's first venture in an international assembly, and Decoud enthusiastically supported the idea of a Pan-American Union—if not all the treaties proposed by the United States at this conference. As foreign minister and diplomat, he represented a country with boundary problems with more powerful neighbors as well as unpayable debts to the victors of the recent war. Even now, Brazil still exerted much influence in Asunción, and not necessarily to Paraguay's advantage. The rapidly growing Argentine Republic controlled Paraguay's river access to the outside world. Any international assemblage in which Paraguay at least had a voice could only help that poor, weak nation. At the Washington conference Decoud made an eloquent plea for arbitration. That desire, as well as support for the Pan-American Union, remained a cornerstone of Paraguayan foreign policy for the next thirty-five years.[12]

Unlike its South American neighbors, Paraguay was less critical of the more assertive U.S. role in Latin America in the 1890s as exemplified by Asunción's nonreaction to the U.S.-Chilean confrontation (1891–92) and the Venezuelan boundary crisis of 1895. At the outbreak of the Spanish-American War in 1898, Paraguay declared and maintained strict neutrality. Relations were relatively good with the United States, and the sinking of the *Maine* created some Paraguayan sympathy for the United States.[13] Although there was a Spanish-born community in Asunción, no great economic or emotional tie drew Paraguayans close to the "mother country." The Spanish-American War was for Paraguayans simply another foreign war.

But one incident during this war created trouble for both Paraguay and the United States. In late May 1898 the Spanish gunboat *Temerario* entered Asunción Bay, claiming it had engine problems.[14] At this time, international law regarding obligations of neutrals relative to belligerent ships in their waters was somewhat vague. Nonetheless, most nations had adopted the principle that such a ship might enter and remain only for repairs, fueling, or taking on provisions—all within a definite time limit. In this case, however, the Spanish Legation requested asylum for the vessel and agreed to the Paraguayan government's condition that by international law the warship be interned in Paraguay until the end of the war. Paraguay asked that the vessel be disarmed, also according to international law for interned ships. The captain of the gunboat refused to disarm his craft, and Paraguay then ordered its departure in twenty-four hours. Then the captain requested a stay before departure to repair engine damages. On inspection, authorities then gave the *Temerario* thirty days to make the necessary repairs, which may have compromised Paraguayan neutrality, which was complicated by Asunción's desire not to alienate either the United States or Spain and also by Paraguay's inability to enforce its neutrality.[15]

The Paraguayan Chamber of Deputies decided to send a report of the ship's problems to the United States. Some deputies maintained, however, that they owed no explanation to Washington inasmuch as Paraguay alone was responsible for exercising its neutral obligations. As in so many troublesome diplomatic difficulties of this era, the chamber turned to José Segundo Decoud, who was then serving in that body. Decoud persuaded the deputies that there was no harm in replying to the questions of Consul John N. Ruffin, who was then rather irregularly assuming the powers of a chargé d'affaires. But as Decoud astutely suggested, the chamber should offer no explanations to those questions unless they came by way of the U.S. minister, William R. Finch, in Montevideo. Only Finch had the authority to deal with Paraguay on such matters, and this procedure precluded any interjection by Ruffin—as well as giving Paraguay more time to consider answers.

In the end, after all this discussion, the Paraguayan government decided that in accordance with international law, the *Temerario* should be disarmed. The Spanish Legation asked for a delay to confer with Madrid, but the Paraguayans refused. In early June the *Temerario* slipped out of Asunción Bay. Finch now was justifiably angry and concerned since he had no way of ascertaining the gunboat's whereabouts. The ship cruised on the Paraguay-Paraná river system until it returned abruptly to Asunción in late August. Its captain then requested an indefinite stay in Paraguayan waters. Decoud referred the matter to Finch and stated that should the United States object to the captain's request, Paraguay would honor the objection. By this time the war had ended. Finch had no objection and probably breathed a sigh of relief that the matter was finally settled.[16]

It might be tempting to view the *Temerario* incident within the theme of the new emergence of the United States into Latin America at the end of the nineteenth century. However, Finch's insistence upon Paraguay's duties as a neutral was nothing more than what any nation would demand in any war. Rather, if one seeks to place Paraguay into the new thrust of the United States, it is better to look at the arrival of U.S. investment in that land and Paraguay's participation in the Pan-American Union.

Trade and a Troubled Consul

In the 1890s, however, trade between Paraguay and the United States was of little importance to either nation. High U.S. tariffs on platine exports as well as a lack of regular U.S. steam liners to the Río de la Plata had already driven the international commerce of the region into European hands. Although the State Department exhorted representatives in the Plata to press for greater U.S. business, the poor response reflected those disadvantages. In the case of Paraguay, the United States also contended, and rightfully so, that Paraguay's high tariffs on U.S. products violated the most-favored-nation clause of the 1859 treaty. In response to that charge, José Segundo Decoud, now minister of the economy, broached the possibility of reciprocity in commercial relations, hinting at the need for a strong partner to ensure its economic progress. Reciprocity did not occur. However, the discussion was indicative of a newly awakened commercial interest of the United States in this region, as well as Paraguay's search for additional security through the aegis of a distant great power.

Paraguay's foreign relations during this era suffered from the violent transition from the generation-long Colorado Party rule to that of the Liberals. In that struggle, commerce on the rivers suffered when the Liberals acquired in Argentina an armed riverboat that mounted a blockade of the Paraguay River. The beleaguered Colorado government, lacking a navy, could do nothing. In desperation the Paraguayan government turned to U.S. consul John N. Ruffin, who had enjoyed good personal and professional relations with powerful Colorados. The besieged Colorados informed Ruffin that they favored some type of U.S. intervention, such as a gunboat to clear the river. Consul Ruffin asked Washington about that request and also if he might call upon the Brazilian government for naval intervention. Paraguay also wanted undetermined goods—probably arms—from the United States and was anxious that such goods not be intercepted. Washington refused on the understandable grounds that it could not guarantee free passage of the Paraguay River without very undesirable international complications.

The Colorado Party plea for U.S. help was an act of political desperation. In November 1904 General Benigno Ferreira, the revolutionary chieftain, assumed power, dissolved Congress, purged the Paraguayan Army officer corps, and appointed a provisional president. The Liberal triumph, however, did not bring political peace. For the next ten years, infighting among the victorious factions (complicated by Argentine and Brazilian meddling) kept the republic in turmoil. A consequence of the shift in power was an assault, personal and political, upon the person of the U.S. consul John N. Ruffin. Ruffin, it appears, had neglected to repay a loan to him by a prominent Paraguayan, who brought a civil suit to recover the money since Ruffin had departed Paraguay in 1905 and it was not known if he would return. Other residents of Asunción also accused Ruffin of neglecting his duties and swindling Paraguayans in various business activities.

The Paraguayan Foreign Ministry then involved itself with a charge that Ruffin had been supplied with $7,500 in Argentine pesos by the former Colorado government for the purchase of a small steamboat. The new Liberal government had not received the boat and now demanded that Ruffin either return the money or deliver the craft. The U.S. consul had not responded to Paraguay's demands, and the U.S. government received an official protest from the Paraguayan foreign minister. The State Department replied that it would place no obstacle to the collection of just debts. Finally, in a confused denouement, Ruffin was charged by the new government (echoed by Minister Finch in Montevideo) with having irregularly approached a British arms seller in Buenos Aires on behalf of the new Paraguayan regime. Asunción declared in early 1905 that Ruffin was persona non grata and desired that he not be returned to Asunción.

Revolution, Power Politics, and Uncle Sam's Stepchild

Paraguay's political turmoil of the early twentieth century played out against the backdrop of recurring problems—persistent Argentine and Brazilian meddling in national politics—and the uncertainties created by the role of the United States. Liberals such as Cecilio Báez, Manuel Gondra, Eligio Ayala, and others did not pay much attention to the new policies of the United States. In the first years of the first decade of the twentieth century, they had a more immediate concern about the problems of intervention by their two great neighbors. Paraguay owed both Brazil and Argentina reparations from the War of the Triple Alliance. There was no way that those debts could ever be paid—and everyone knew it. Paraguayans, on the other hand, considered that the continuing debt not only constrained their freedom of foreign policy but also was a hindrance to the attraction of foreign capital.[17] Given Paraguay's overriding concerns about their relations with their two great neighbors, Asunción's views, therefore, of the new interpretation of the Monroe Doctrine were more theoretical in nature and somewhat mixed. In any case, no Paraguayan commentator seriously believed in the danger of U.S. intervention in southern South America.

Often ignored in consideration of Theodore Roosevelt's policy is the U.S. drive to conclude arbitration and extradition treaties with Latin American nations. In a practical sense, the "big stick" could not be employed throughout the entire hemisphere, and Roosevelt, for all his rhetoric, knew that negotiation of differences through diplomacy was always preferable to the last resort of force. Minister Edward O'Brien approached the Paraguayan government about such treaties, noting that the last such agreement had been concluded between the two nations in the 1850s. Paraguay proved agreeable, and a Treaty of Arbitration was ratified in 1909. Later in 1914, the two nations concluded another treaty for the Advancement of Peace. This helped to implement and further define the arbitration process. These two treaties, however, were really not that useful since normal diplomacy covered most intercourse between Asunción and Washington. The treaties did, however, reveal that both parties desired good relations.

The lack of a U.S. minister accredited solely to Paraguay had irritated the Paraguayan Foreign Ministry since the 1890s. U.S. ministers to Paraguay, resident in Montevideo, also found the arrangement awkward given the nine hundred miles that separated the Uruguayan capital from Asunción. After the beginning of the twentieth century, the United States focused more attention on Latin America as a result of the Spanish-American War, the "new imperialism," and the rise of the Pan-American Union. And by the second decade of the century there was greater U.S. investment in Paraguay, as well as a modest growth in trade between the two republics.

There were also regional political concerns that favored a U.S. mission in Paraguay. It was in the U.S. interest to retain Paraguay as an independent buffer state between Brazil and Argentina, given the political tensions of the day between Rio de Janeiro and Buenos Aires. By the 1900s the United States and Brazil had achieved an understanding that served the interests of both nations.[18] The Baron Rio-Branco, the very able foreign minister of Brazil in this era, had no objections to a U.S. interventionist policy. Indeed, he considered many of the problems faced by his nation in the Río de la Plata to be similar to those confronting Washington in the Caribbean. The 1904 revolution that ejected the Paraguayan Colorados had damaged Brazilian influence in the Upper Plata. The growing strength of Argentina and the control of the Paraná River route to Asunción by Buenos Aires made it nearly impossible for Brazil to resort to gunboat diplomacy against Paraguay. Irritated by the political instability in Paraguay after the 1904 revolution, the baron suggested to Washington that the United States dispatch several naval vessels to Paraguay to restore order.[19] The United States had no intention of taking such a drastic step. Paraguay now fell more and more under the influence of Buenos Aires. In light of that development, Brazil desired the appointment of a U.S. minister to Asunción as that might moderate the growing Argentine influence.

At the time, many observers believed that a U.S. minister resident in Asunción might exert influence in favor of moderation in Paraguay. And finally, the appointment of a minister would remove the humiliation that Paraguay felt, as it was the only nation in Latin America lacking a U.S. resident legation. Eligio Ayala, an able foreign minister, complained that in regard to this absence, his nation was "Uncle Sam's stepchild."[20]

A strong argument in favor of a U.S. mission solely to Paraguay occurred in July 1908 when Minister Edward O'Brien visited Asunción to negotiate treaties of arbitration and extradition. As chance had it, a rebellion against the Benigno Ferreira government erupted during his stay there. O'Brien joined with other foreign representatives in Asunción to arrange a cease-fire and a safe conduct for the deposed president and other members of his government. O'Brien informed the new government that his actions implied no recognition of the new government selected. In any case, it did reveal that a resident minister had prestige and influence that a minister some nine hundred miles away in Montevideo did not.

In 1913 Paraguay finally emerged from the chaos of the last decade. Brazil essentially ceded to Argentina a dominant position in Paraguay, and the ensuing political stability strengthened the hands of those in Washington who favored a separate mission to Asunción. In that year the State Department overcame the financial objection to the expense of a legation in Asunción. After forty-five years of absence, a U.S. minister, Daniel F. Mooney, accredited solely to Asunción, took his post in May 1914.

While U.S. diplomats in the Río de la Plata observed the political turmoil that raged in Paraguay from 1904 to 1913, and the State Department debated the wisdom of a U.S. minister accredited solely to Paraguay, almost unnoticed was the onset of significant U.S. investment in that republic. In the latter part of the nineteenth century, European and North American capital invaded Latin America. Paraguay, mainly due to its isolation, had not interested U.S. investors, but that was about to change with the arrival of Percival Farquhar.

As a young man, Farquhar cut his teeth upon U.S. investments in Guatemala and Cuba. In the 1890s and early 1900s, through U.S. holding companies and with French capital he created the "Farquhar Syndicate" of the Brazilian Railway Company, vast Brazilian cattle lands, and packing companies.[21] In 1909 Farquhar embarked upon his most ambitious project, a trans-Andean railway to connect the Pacific coast of Chile with the Atlantic ports of southern Brazil. Essentially that rail route would pass through the Yguazú region, central Paraguay, the Argentine Chaco, and then over the Andes to Antofogasta in Chile. Many doubted the economic feasibility of that dream, as much of this territory presented daunting terrain, required necessary immigrants and development to return revenues to the railroad, and demanded a great capital investment. Farquhar paid no attention to the difficulties.

The first impact upon Paraguay of the Farquhar Syndicate occurred in 1910 when the Brazilian Railway Company purchased a controlling interest in the Paraguay Central Railway Company.[22] Manuel Rodríguez, a principal shareholder and president of the Paraguayan company, realized that he did not have the resources to withstand the syndicate's projected railway. When the Argentine government failed to support him in face of the syndicate's plans, Rodríguez decided to join Farquhar, rather than oppose him. He profited greatly from the sale of his shares to the syndicate and then became indispensable to Farquhar as the latter's "point man" in Paraguay. Through Rodríguez, the syndicate acquired strategic investments in the republic, as well as amazingly advantageous railroad concessions as he dispensed largesse to Paraguayan politicians.

Within six years of the 1904 revolution the successful Liberals had split into two contending groups—Cívicos and Radicales. The ambitions of the leaders of these two factions were driven less by ideology than by personal interests—and their desire to profit by control of the revenues of the state. In 1910, a Cívico government was at odds with the Villa Morra Tramway Company, a traction company that served Asunción and was detested by the public for bad service and high fares. It recently had been acquired by the Paraguay Central Railway Company—the latter now part of the Farquhar empire. That squabble persuaded Farquhar to throw his weight behind the Radicales.

In early 1912, following a bloody rebellion against the Cívicos, the Radicales took power. In return for its aid, the Farquhar Syndicate had a clear path to complete its economic penetration of Paraguay. It obtained various railroad concessions (mostly to forestall any competition in its goal of a south Brazil–Asunción connection). Then for revenue-producing cargo, the syndicate bought supportive industries, particularly in 1912 the Industrial Paraguaya company that profitably exploited yerbales and hardwoods. Through the purchase of shares the syndicate acquired control of this enterprise in 1912. The Paraguay Central Railway was extended to Encarnación on the Alto Paraná River, where it connected with the Argentine railroad network by a railroad ferry. The capital's electrical generation company fell into the syndicate's hands, and, finally, the syndicate acquired vast cattle and quebracho lands in the Paraguayan Chaco (quebracho being a native tree rich in tannin for the curing of hides).

All this was accomplished through a bewildering and complex process of holding companies, issue of watered stock to finance takeovers, and much political corruption. It was "frenzied finance" at its worst since it depended upon sufficient revenues from Farquhar's Brazilian railway interests and a steady influx of foreign capital, mainly from French banks. At the height of the expansion in Paraguay in 1912, however, economic conditions in Brazil changed for the worst. By early

1914 the French banks that had previously supplied capital for the syndicate's expansion worried about the health of the enterprise and refused further credit. The advent of World War I entailed further curtailment of European investment. The temporary wartime economic dislocation that hit Brazil (and also Paraguay) in the latter half of 1914 was the final blow to the syndicate. In December of that year it no longer could meet financial obligations and was forced into receivership.

In the forced reorganization of Paraguayan assets the Paraguay Central Railway fell to British investors, as did the Industrial Paraguaya. British investors also acquired the electrical generation monopoly of the capital. Farquhar and U.S. investors in the former syndicate did salvage much of their investment in the Chaco cattle lands when, in 1917, the New York–based International Products Corporation was formed out of the wreckage. That company's aim was to raise and process cattle, as well as to exploit the quebracho resources of the Chaco lands.[23]

The failure of a railway route to southern Brazil signified that through command of the river outlet to world commerce, Argentina would maintain a dominant, and often baleful, impact upon Paraguay's economy. The republic did profit from the expanded North American cattle industry in the Chaco, and income from U.S. and other companies in that region by the 1920s amounted to nearly two-thirds of Paraguay's foreign exchange earnings.

The Coming of the Cattlemen

Of all the Farquhar investments in Paraguay, the cattle industry contributed the greatest U.S. presence, but it was a presence that arrived after the pioneering efforts of other foreign investors. In the 1880s the ruling Colorado government embarked upon a policy of easy purchase of public lands to replenish the treasury and spur land development to provide the economic stimulus for future tax revenues. Argentine, British, and Paraguayan capitalists purchased large tracts of valuable cattle, timber, and yerba land at bargain prices.[24]

One Montana cattleman realized that turn-of-the-century Paraguay offered him a great opportunity. Granville Stuart (U.S. minister to Uruguay and Paraguay during the second Grover Cleveland administration) paid several visits to Paraguay in the mid-1890s. On surveying the state of the cattle industry and the availability of cheap land, he tried to persuade a former business associate to raise capital for a ranching venture in the republic. The banking industry in the United States, however, had not yet shaken off the impact of the 1893 depression, and credit was simply not available. The election of William McKinley in 1896 sent this Democrat appointee back to Montana with his dream of cattle ranching in Paraguay abandoned.[25] Better than a decade had to pass before economic conditions in the United States and new views of investment abroad brought U.S. capital.

In late 1910 Percival Farquhar met with George Lewis (Tex) Rickard, a well-known cattle raiser, professional gambler, miner, and boxing promoter to discuss the possibility of cattle production in South America. Farquhar proposed that Rickard investigate the purchase of rangeland along the proposed railway line to Chile and then act as a salaried manager of the large enterprise the syndicate contemplated. The U.S. rancher, never one to discount himself, replied, "Salary be damned. This is a 50-50 deal, with your money and my savvy about cattle."[26] The U.S. cattleman arrived in the Río de la Plata in early 1911. Rather than scout out land in Argentina along the proposed rail route, Rickard followed the advice of a U.S. diplomat and traveled to Asunción, where he was impressed by the opportunity of inexpensive cattle land in the Gran Chaco. He then sailed for France, where Farquhar was raising capital and conferring with syndicate members. They agreed upon Paraguay and somehow—perhaps by cable—Rickard hired some twenty U.S. cowboys. He and his hired hands arrived in Buenos Aires in mid-1912, sailed upriver to the Argentine Chaco, and then traveled by horseback overland through the Paraguayan Chaco to Asunción. His earlier impression was confirmed; this was good cattle land.

In August 1912 the syndicate chartered the New York and Paraguay Company in Delaware with a capitalization of $1.5 million. That firm's charge was the acquisition of Paraguayan land and the raising and processing of livestock. At first it acquired about four million acres across the Paraguay River in the region of Concepción, stocking the property with forty thousand head and importing blooded bulls from the United States. The Farquhar Syndicate then purchased six million additional acres in the Chaco and quickly owned or controlled about ten million acres—perhaps a fifth of the Paraguayan Chaco. Puerto Piñasco, the major Chaco headquarters of the company, eventually boasted electricity, schools, a hospital, jail, homes for workers, river cattle boats, a railroad, and a processing mill to tap the quebracho resources of this region. Its meatpacking plant was located near Asunción.

In 1913 the New York and Paraguay Company reorganized under a Maine incorporation as the Paraguay Land and Cattle Company, still controlled by the Farquhar Syndicate. Rickard continued as manager, part owner of the vast property, and director of the new company. Reports reached the syndicate of Rickard's energy: "Tex fearlessly riding through the Gran Chaco quebracho forests and grasslands of the Paraguay Land & Cattle Company, infested by hostile Indians who refrained from attacking the bold Texan."[27] Those accounts may have been a bit far-fetched as Rickard spent as much of his time in Buenos Aires and Asunción as in the bush, but no one can deny his energy in establishing the company's presence.

With the knowledge and permission of the company, Rickard engaged in some independent ventures in Paraguay. He promoted a packing plant to process and ship downriver chilled beef for eventual European consumption. Distance, problems of shipping, and ferocious opposition from Argentine chilled beef interests defeated that plan. Initially more successful was his investment in a packing plant at San Salvador, north of Concepción. From that establishment the British government in the first days of World War I purchased a large quantity of canned beef. The British accepted and utilized the product but then refused payment to the plant on the grounds that a majority of its stockholders were German nationals. The San Salvador operation collapsed. Then, in 1916, other U.S. investors acquired the plant's assets and ran it successfully until 1920 when it, like so many Paraguayan ventures, failed as a consequence of post–World War I economic dislocation. At much the same time, with the collapse and liquidation of the Farquhar Syndicate in 1914, Rickard played a large role in salvaging its cattle and quebracho interests for the U.S.-based International Products Corporation (IPC). Out of the wreckage of the Farquhar syndicate and its subsidiary, the New York and Paraguay Company, Rickard acquired some 468,000 acres in the Chaco interior, that land comprising the extent of his Paraguay Land and Cattle Company.

Rickard proved an excellent choice to establish the syndicate's interests in the Chaco, and he retained ownership of his large cattle ranch there until his death. By 1915, however, he was tiring of the Paraguayan cattle venture and desired to return to his first love—boxing promotion. He spent no more time in South America, leaving his ranch in the hands of managers. On his death in 1929, his estate owed Paraguay back taxes on his property. His widow sold that land to another U.S. cattleman to pay the taxes and also received a comfortable profit.

In the wake of the syndicate's investments came a new group of Americans to Paraguay—managers, clerks, technicians, and cowboys. As might be expected, the most colorful figures were the southwestern cowboys who started to arrive in 1912. They were a wild, incorrigible bunch of hell-raisers, many on the run from the law in the United States. Some stayed with the U.S.-owned ranches, but most found it more enjoyable (and perhaps profitable) to turn to riverboat gambling and even rustling.

Among them was George West Musgrave, known in Paraguay as Bob Stewart. Musgrave had been a leader of the southwest U.S. "Black Jack" gang that in the first decade of the twentieth century robbed banks and trains. To escape the increasing attention of the law, Musgrave sailed for Paraguay and then worked as a manager for Rickard for a brief period. But rustling offered more opportunities. He established a small spread in the Chaco with registered brands that easily could be impressed over those of Rickard and other ranchers. By the late 1910s and through the 1920s, he stole cattle out of the Chaco and east of the Paraguay River and drove the livestock to the Brazilian Mato Grosso. If conditions proved favorable, he also smuggled contraband cattle from Brazil to

Paraguay. Musgrave easily corrupted the Paraguayan border guards, and other than a few gun fights with outraged ranchers, he had few problems with his nefarious pursuits.

When not engaged in livestock theft, Musgrave turned to gambling. Many considered him a cheating card sharp, but his skill with a six-shooter and his obvious personal courage lent him much immunity. For all his faults, many Americans and Paraguayans genuinely liked Musgrave. He was a generous, loyal friend (if you had no cattle to be stolen) and an engaging fellow. He made no pretense about being other than he was—a real U.S. desperado. By corruption, his reputation as a gunman, native intelligence, bonhomie, and an instinctive knowledge of when it might be time to visit Argentina or Brazil, he evaded justice for the forty-odd years he was in the Río de la Plata. The last survivor of the wild American West, he died peacefully in his sleep in Asunción in 1947.[28]

Not all U.S. cowboys in Paraguay were gamblers, hell-raisers, or rustlers. One, who knew Musgrave well, was Robert Eaton. His tale, however, is one of the 1930s through the 1960s as he progressed from cowboy to respected Chaco cattle rancher and a pillar of the U.S. community in Paraguay.

A Growing Trade

The U.S. cowboy presence in Paraguay proved less consequential than that of other U.S. entrepreneurs. The Farquhar Syndicate and Tex Rickard led the way for other U.S. meat packers in Paraguay, notably Swift and Morris. All took advantage of the great demand for canned beef brought about by World War I. When the war ended and demand suddenly dropped, most U.S. meat packers survived as they had capital to weather the hard times. They, in company with important French, Argentine, and British interests, dominated the Paraguayan economy during this era, profiting greatly from a deliberately weak Paraguayan peso and selling their products to markets with strong money.[29]

U.S. manufacturers found Paraguay to be a small but steadily growing market for their goods in the 1910s and 1920s. With Europe at war from 1914 to 1918 and unable to supply Latin America with finished goods, Paraguay, in common with other Latin American nations, turned to the United States. Major imports from the United States included machine goods, farm implements, firearms, chemicals, textiles, and even some processed food items. By the 1920s, U.S.-made automobiles and trucks began to find a market as well. Most of this commerce was transshipped through Argentine intermediaries since few U.S. sales representatives made the long journey upriver to Asunción and few U.S. companies expressed any desire in establishing direct commercial ties with Paraguayan customers. Buenos Aires offered better communications, shipping, and banking. Observers deplored the lack of U.S. business houses in Asunción and the absence of direct marketing to Paraguay.

The balance of trade was greatly in favor of the United States. By the late 1920s nearly 20 percent of Paraguay's imports originated in the United States, while that country absorbed only 1 percent of Paraguay's exports.[30] The IPC earned most of its income from quebracho exports. Swift and Morris operated meatpacking plants. Another U.S. firm in the export of quebracho was the New York and Paraguay Company. While incorporated in Buenos Aires, the sole streetcar company in Paraguay, the Asunción Compañía de Luz y Tracción, had significant U.S. capital. While the pattern of investments was greatly similar to prewar years, the amount of U.S. investments had increased from an estimated $3 million in 1914 to $15 million in 1928.[31]

As for Paraguay, hides and quebracho made up the great bulk of exports to the United States. That export, however, was not enough to counterbalance imports.[32] After World War I, economic power had shifted from the City of London to Wall Street, and North American investments and finance were increasingly felt in South America. Paraguay, however, had little concern about a U.S. economic predominance. By accident, rather than design, foreign investment in Paraguay in the 1920s was well distributed among various investor nations—the United States, Britain, France, Belgium, and Argentina—and no single nation became the target of nationalist resentment.

A Very Distant War

The U.S. investment in the Paraguayan cattle industry occurred just prior to World War I, as did the appointment of a U.S. minister resident in Asunción. Other than wartime prosperity brought about by demand for beef products and quebracho, Paraguay was little affected by the conflict.[33] The resultant prosperity redounded to the benefit of the Radical government, and with increased state revenues, Paraguay enjoyed a period of internal peace. Strict neutrality was the only sensible course of action. Neutrality, however, did not preclude an often-voiced sympathy for the Allies. Many in the small group of governing Liberals evidenced affection for French culture. Many also had business connections with British and French companies that were quite prominent in the Paraguayan economy. Manuel E. Gondra, foreign minister at the time the United States entered the war, best described Paraguay's wartime policy: a "strict neutrality in face of the European conflict, and continental solidarity when the United States first, and then Brazil, entered the war."[34]

For the first two years of the conflict Paraguay had seen no particular reason to justify its neutrality, as such action was simply the right of any sovereign power. Nonetheless, in a note from Gondra to U.S. minister Daniel F. Mooney in February 1917 when the United States broke relations with Germany over the latter's unrestricted submarine campaign, Gondra carefully made clear his government's sympathy for President Woodrow Wilson's earlier peace initiatives. Paraguay also felt that such submarine warfare posed a threat to the "legitimate interests of neutral powers on the free sea." Gondra was concerned that a war by the United States upon any of the European belligerents might gravely affect the "international life of the republics of this hemisphere whose political, moral, and economic solidarity has been continually solidifying over the last thirty years." Finally, the foreign minister stated that if the Pan-American Congress that had been postponed on the war's eruption in 1914 were reconvened, Paraguay would be pleased. That conference could then deliberate upon the economic and legal rights of the neutrals of the Americas during the conflict.[35] In all, Gondra made clear that Paraguay would maintain its neutrality but revealed his concern about the future of inter-American relations should the United States enter the conflict. Whatever the United States might do, Paraguay was determined not to irritate that power and continued to support the Pan-American system. Two months later the United States declared war upon Germany.

For the remainder of the war, Paraguay maintained its neutrality but always reassured the United States of its commitment to solidarity among American nations. Asunción did favor an international conference of American states to deliberate upon a uniform conduct of those states in view of U.S. participation in the war. That idea found no reception in Washington inasmuch as President Wilson was conducting his war and had no desire to have his hands tied by any Pan-American conference or policy. At the same time, relations remained quite good between the two republics as the United States well understood Paraguay's policy of neutrality and had no problems with it. The appointment of Manuel Gondra as Paraguayan minister to the United States in late 1917 revealed the strong desire of Paraguay that nothing disturb good relations with Washington. Certainly, it did not harm the relations between Asunción and Washington that at the outbreak of the war, the U.S. minister to Paraguay was Daniel F. Mooney, a skilled diplomat and quite popular in the republic.

An interesting aspect of the impact of the U.S. declaration of war was the outpouring of pro-Allied sentiment by important members of the Paraguayan elite. In print and at public meetings in 1917 such luminaries as Antolín Irala, Cecilio Báez, and José P. Guggiari—among others—lauded the goals of the Allies and the ideals of President Wilson.[36] Certainly these prominent Liberals and Colorados were generally more sympathetic to the Allied cause, but now they also realized that U.S. entrance into the war signified a significant change in world power, and one that would have consequences in the Americas and Paraguay.

In the early years of the century, a few travelers from the United States visited the Republic of Paraguay, and some even spent considerable time there. The most prominent visitor was former president

Theodore Roosevelt on his 1914 expedition to the Brazilian wilderness. He passed through Paraguay and left a short but interesting account of his river voyage north from Asunción. On board ship Tex Rickard, an old acquaintance from Roosevelt's ranching days, regaled him with tales of cattle raising in the Chaco. Although Roosevelt's stay in Paraguay was brief, and his observations somewhat superficial, he evidenced in his account of the expedition an empathy with the Paraguayans.[37] A few other U.S. travelers followed and left accounts of their visits.[38] Other than some serious works by North American missionaries, most accounts repeated the standard clichés of the "Jesuit Republic," the debilitation of the tropics, and other trivialities that unfortunately are still employed.

Not all Americans sped through the republic. By the 1890s various Protestant churches in the United States took a missionary interest in Paraguay. Among the first was the Methodist Episcopal Church of the United States, already long established in Brazil and Argentina. At the onset it confined itself to establishing a school in Asunción and ministering to the spiritual needs of the small U.S. community there. It later expanded its activities to the countryside. By all accounts it was quite tactful in its activities and avoided any rancor with the dominant Catholic Church.[39]

Others followed, and by the late 1920s a half-dozen different missionary groups from the United States operated in Paraguay—among which were the Methodists, Seventh-Day Adventists, Baptists, and Disciples of Christ. Although most foreign missionary societies established schools, that education was linked closely to their proselytization goals. However, there were exceptions. In 1920, with the financial support of the United Christian Missionary Society, the Disciples of Christ established the Colegio Internacional in Asunción with an avowed purpose of advancing the moral education of students, regardless of their faith. The educational standards of this institution were high, and a successful effort was made to attract Paraguayan teachers of proven competence to its classrooms. Rapidly, it began to serve students from Paraguay and northern Argentina, and many of the political and business elite of Asunción enrolled their children in it.[40]

The efforts and influence of U.S. educators in Paraguay, as well as the possible realization on the part of the ruling Liberal elite that U.S. power in the hemisphere was growing, prompted the Paraguayan government by the first decade of the 1900s to subsidize the education of ten Paraguayan youths a year in U.S. universities. Paraguay also began to look to the United States for inspiration in the structural reform of the republic's primary school system, and a U.S. book publisher was profitably supplying school texts to the republic.

Most missionary societies focused first on the capital, but by the 1910s they extended their efforts to towns in the countryside. The reaction to their presence was mixed. The Catholic clergy, with reason, viewed these activities with suspicion, if not outright hostility. For the most part, however, the newcomers found a cautious (if at times somewhat confused) welcome on the part of the Paraguayan populace. These missionaries, of all the Americans who visited or lived in the republic, probably had the most understanding and knowledge of rural Paraguay.[41] From their efforts, and the work of Protestant missionaries of other nationalities, sprang the small local Protestant community that grew steadily in numbers throughout the century.

The Rockefeller Commission

Americans also contributed to improving Paraguayan public health. By the 1920s the Paraguayan government understood that the health of its population was deplorable. Tuberculosis, diarrhea, poor diets, and a host of other ailments afflicted Paraguayans, and few doctors—especially in rural areas—were available. Hookworm proved the most debilitating disease, however, afflicting some 80 percent of the population and contributing to 20 percent of all deaths. An earlier antihookworm campaign in Asunción and the capital's immediate environs had revealed the magnitude of the problem, but nothing had been done to combat this disease in the countryside. In 1923, the Rockefeller Foundation, fresh from its success against hookworm in the United States and other tropical areas of the Americas, signed a five-year agreement with the Paraguayan government. A Paraguayan Sanitary Commission was established the next year with a U.S. doctor as technical expert. The first year the foundation funded 50 percent of the costs of the commission; the Paraguayan government the other 50 percent. Each succeeding year the Paraguayans assumed 10 percent more until by 1928 the financial burden of the campaign became solely their responsibility.

The director of the Rockefeller Foundation effort in Paraguay, Dr. Fred L. Soper, had much experience in the United States and tropical regions in combating hookworm. In this effort to establish the first, if rudimentary, public health program in Paraguay, he discovered several serious challenges. The incidence of infection was so high so that all Paraguayans needed to be medicated against the parasite.[42] The lack of privies, both in towns and the countryside, meant that infected feces could reinfect Paraguayans, the great majority of whom had no shoes.

The commission fought this battle on several fronts. Nothing could be done about the lack of footwear. But medicine against hookworms was available and could be distributed freely. Fanning throughout the campo, or countryside, doctors and public health experts established centers of health instruction and clinics. They presented slide shows in churches and schools detailing the effect of hookworm and strongly urged villagers and peasants to construct and use privies as a method of reducing reinfection. They initially had considerable success in the countryside and small towns. A difficulty encountered, however, was to persuade the populace to use this simple sanitary device continually.

Government cooperation in this effort was vital—particularly as funding for rural sanitation would be completely in Paraguayan hands by 1928. Furthermore, the anti-hookworm campaign required an ongoing effort, or any progress made in the 1924–28 period would be erased by reinfection. Unfortunately, in the last year of the agreement the Paraguayan government reduced its contracted funding, rather than assuming the responsibility it had earlier promised. With war clouds looming over conflicting Paraguayan and Bolivian claims to the Chaco, monies were diverted to the purchase of arms. Sadly, the Rockefeller

Foundation withdrew from the republic, as it did not feel it could accept any financial responsibility beyond its original commitment. It did return in the late 1930s when the Paraguayan government again addressed the issue of public health.[43]

A Hope for Collective Security

After World War I many of the Paraguayan elite were enthusiastic about Wilsonian idealism and international cooperation in the pursuit of peace. Paraguay was a weak, poor nation bounded by powerful Argentina and Brazil and also by Bolivia, which increasingly was contesting Asunción's claim to the Chaco. It was only natural that Paraguay wished to put its trust in diplomacy, international agreements, and arbitration to protect its interests. Manuel Gondra, a leading Paraguayan statesman of the era and the republic's foremost foreign policy architect, hailed the promise of the postwar era in Paraguay's support of international cooperation and the Pan-American Union.[44]

A few years later, at the Fifth Meeting of Foreign Ministers of the American republics, Gondra's doctrine for the peaceful solution of disputes among American republics was adopted. Essentially, the Gondra Doctrine, embedded in a treaty ratified by all American republics, spelled out in detail the arbitration procedure when normal diplomatic solution of international differences failed.[45] And in the same decade Paraguay willingly participated in the various functions of the Pan-American Union.[46]

By now, however, the United States had become disillusioned with Wilsonian idealism in the conduct of foreign relations and had turned its back on the League of Nations. Even so, it well understood the rationale for Paraguay's postwar foreign policy. In the peaceful, prosperous years of the 1920s few incidents marred the good relations between the two nations. Of course, some Paraguayans had misgivings about the continued U.S. occupation of various Caribbean states. While supportive of the Pan-American Union, the Paraguayan Foreign Ministry also worried about the dominant role of the United States in that organization. And yet, the Caribbean was distant from Paraguay, and any unease about intervention there and the operation of the Pan-American Union warranted no gratuitous irritation of the northern giant. Even at the 1928 Havana Meeting of American Foreign Ministers that witnessed a spontaneous and extremely critical Latin American assault upon the U.S. intervention in Nicaragua, Paraguay kept to a muted course and condemned U.S. policy only in weak terms.[47] By that time, Asunción had a major foreign policy problem in the offing, and irritating the United States was not in Paraguay's immediate interest.

3 War and the Search for Peace

During the administration of Herbert Hoover (1929–33) and the first administration of Franklin Delano Roosevelt (1933–37), the U.S. Latin American policy underwent significant transition. Both Hoover and especially Roosevelt spoke of a new relationship with the other American republics—what FDR called the "Good Neighbor." Depression-era diplomacy had as one of its objectives the increase in trade between the United States and Latin America. Paraguay had not seen North American military intervention since the 1850s, and since that era no U.S. interest in the Upper Plata warranted such action. Although both countries would have welcomed an increase in trade during the Depression, Paraguay's potential as a market for goods paled in consideration with larger Latin American markets. But it was a conflict, the Chaco War that raged between Bolivia and Paraguay from 1932 to 1935, in which the United States encountered a seemingly intractable foreign policy problem with Paraguay. Attainment of peace required much attention from the State Department, much patience on the part of diplomats, and an inordinate amount of frustration.[1]

The Chaco—arid, hot, and dusty in the wintertime, swampy and mosquito ridden in the summer—extends from the Paraguay River in a generally northwestern direction toward the foothills of the Bolivian Andes. On the southwest it is bounded by the Río Pilcomayo and to the northwest by the Río Negro. In the colonial era, the hostile terrain and warlike nomadic Indians had discouraged the Spanish from any settlement or even extensive exploration of the region. By law, the Chaco was subject to the Audiencia of Charcas in Upper Peru (now Bolivia), but none of the surrounding Spanish settlements exerted any power over it.

That lack of concern continued into the national era. As the heir to the Audiencia of Charcas, Bolivia claimed the region but did little to explore it—let alone exploit it. The Paraguayans had some knowledge of the fringes along the Paraguay River, but they too were ignorant of the interior. In the colonial era, some minor missionary work had been carried out in the Chaco littoral under the direction of the bishop of Asunción. From that little exploration, the missionary work, and tenuous contact with the Indians of the Chaco near the Paraguay River, the new republic of Paraguay claimed ownership over this region. Later, during the era of Carlos Antonio López, the Paraguayans established a few minor military posts on the Chaco side of the Paraguay River. Even so, Paraguay's sway over the Chaco was confined as much to the eastern fringes as was Bolivia's to the western periphery.

This casual attitude toward the ownership of the Chaco changed by the last decades of the nineteenth century. In the War of the Pacific (1879–83) Bolivia lost its Pacific coastline to Chile, becoming a landlocked nation. Many nationalists now contended that the economic future of their country depended upon the possession of the Chaco, and with it a viable oceanic outlet by the Paraguay-Paraná river system.[2]

For Paraguay, from the 1880s the Chaco became more important economically. Favorable land laws enabled foreigners (mainly Argentines) to obtain great tracts of land in the Chaco. Cattle raising on a great scale ensued, as well as the extraction of quebracho. Tax revenues on Chaco products were critical for the Paraguayan state. By the 1920s as much as two-thirds of Paraguay's foreign exchange earnings came from this region. Not surprisingly, Paraguayans believed that their nation must retain the Chaco in order for Paraguay to survive economically.[3]

Another nation had large, though indirect, interests in the Chaco. By the 1920s Argentine economic and political influence was so great in Asunción that Paraguay could well have been termed a client state of Buenos Aires. Argentine territory commanded all the important access routes to Paraguay. The greatest foreign investments in Paraguay—land, cattle, quebracho, and yerba extraction—were Argentine. Not only might Argentine interests in the Chaco be in legal jeopardy if Bolivia ever succeeded in its extreme claims, but should Paraguay be shorn of this region and political and economic chaos ensue, then there was a definite possibility of renewed Argentine-Brazilian contention in the Upper Plata. Gradually Argentina secretly encouraged Asunción to resist Bolivian pressure.

From the 1880s through the 1920s Paraguay and Bolivia conducted futile negotiations over the ownership of the Chaco. Often, internal political turmoil delayed, or even prevented, negotiations.[4] For Paraguay, however, the most significant negotiation in the period was the Pinilla-Soler Protocol of 1907 that assigned two zones to the Chaco, one ceded to Paraguay and the other subject to arbitration by the Argentine president. Both Paraguay and Bolivia were enjoined from making changes in the status of the Chaco and were forbidden to extend forward their respective possessions until each government accepted the arbitration. This protocol was quite favorable to Paraguay, and Asunción ratified it immediately. Bolivia did not and in 1910 rejected the entire proposal. Nonetheless, the status quo line of the 1907 protocol became an article of faith in future Paraguayan negotiation. Continually after 1907 Asunción raised the status quo line as a necessary condition for any successful resolution of the Chaco dispute. To La Paz, however, it made no difference. By the 1920s in the Pilcomayo region, the central Chaco, and around the Río Negro, Andean establishments had far passed the status quo line.

By the 1920s contention over the Chaco was no longer a matter of negotiations between chancelleries. Nationalistic fervor swept up the small educated class in both nations. School texts proclaimed "The Chaco is Paraguayan," or, conversely, "The Chaco is Bolivian." Nationalists seized upon the Chaco question, utilizing maps, postage depictions, historical justifications, and popular ballads.[5]

The governments of both nations bear much of the responsibility for the whipping up of this excessive nationalism; and the ruling politicians found it was a double-sided sword. Any future attempt to find a compromise would bring an accusation of "weakness" or "sellout." For two politically fragile countries, "weakness" on the issue was a potential threat to both regimes. By the middle of the decade the situation had worsened. Bolivia now claimed the entirety of the Chaco—all the way to the Paraguay River. At the same time, a revamped Bolivian army accelerated the construction of a line of fortines (small military camps) that stretched from Bolivia's small enclave on the Paraguay River north of Bahia Negra south-southwest to the Pilcomayo. That military line, the Bolivians calculated, would bar the Paraguayans from any further penetration to the interior and effectively block Paraguayan expansion that was effected through cattle raising, quebracho extraction, and the new Chaco agricultural colony of the Mennonites. The Paraguayan government took quiet precautionary actions by purchasing arms from abroad and increasing its reconnaissance of the Chaco and quietly made plans for an expansion of the Paraguayan army should mobilization be required.[6]

From the perspective of three-quarters of a century, it is surprising that third parties in the 1920s, including the Argentines, failed to perceive the danger of war. U.S. representatives in both capitals noted the diplomatic maneuverings of both Paraguay and Bolivia, the rising nationalism over the Chaco question that increasingly straightjacketed any peaceful solution, and Bolivia's arms purchases. Washington could do little beyond advocating a diplomatic settlement. The United States could exert no significant diplomatic, economic, or military pressure on the two governments. Furthermore, Washington was then under increasing pressure from Latin American nations to abandon the interventions that had flowed from the Roosevelt Corollary to the Monroe Doctrine.

Prelude to War

In 1927, after lengthy discussion, Bolivia accepted Argentina's offer of good offices for further Chaco negotiation between Paraguay and Bolivia. Paraguay was hesitant. Nationalist fever in Asunción heightened when a Paraguayan army officer wandered into a Bolivian outpost on the Pilcomayo and was captured. When he attempted to escape, a guard killed him. Bolivian authorities defended the action on the grounds that the officer had violated Bolivian sovereignty. Paraguay angrily rejected that claim of sovereignty, and tensions between the two republics rapidly accelerated.

Both nations agreed to Argentine mediation of the affair, but it came to naught as each government hardened its positions, and Asunción strengthened its Chaco forces. Paraguayan units probed north toward the Río Negro, and on 5 December Guaraní forces attacked and captured a Bolivian fortín, Vanguardia. This was no inadvertent clash but a deliberate assault—perpetuated by a Paraguayan commander on the scene without the knowledge or permission of Asunción. Bolivia alerted its own forces in the Chaco and broke diplomatic relations with Paraguay. Then, in the western Chaco, Bolivian forces retaliated by overrunning the Paraguayan outposts of Boquerón and Mariscal López.

Only the general lack of war preparedness on both sides prevented an immediate outbreak of hostilities. By coincidence the International Conference of American States on Conciliation and Arbitration was meeting in Washington, D.C., and it stepped forward with its good offices. Both parties, apprehensive over the December incidents, agreed to establish the Commission of Investigation and Conciliation to investigate the Chaco dispute. The commission convened in Washington and consisted of delegates from Paraguay, Bolivia, Cuba, Mexico, Colombia, Uruguay, and the United States. In January 1929 the two nations signed a protocol for the settlement of problems arising from the clashes of the previous month; in August the commission declared that Paraguay bore the responsibility for the Vanguardia/Boquerón incidents, and circulated a draft treaty for the settlement of the Chaco dispute. The treaty called for juridical arbitration, but the Villa Hayes zone was reserved for Paraguay and the region around Bahia Negra for Bolivia.

Both parties rejected the draft treaty, regardless of earlier rhetoric about acceptance of arbitration. Nonetheless, on 12 September the commission, repeating its findings of Paraguayan responsibility and ignoring the reluctance of Paraguay and Bolivia, called for a preliminary arbitration of the Chaco dispute. That too was rejected.

By this time Secretary of State Henry Stimson had become directly involved in the Chaco negotiation. Given the commission's report of Paraguayan culpability in the December 1928 attacks, Stimson concluded that if Paraguay rejected the recommendations for conciliation, the commission would announce Paraguay's culpability in the affair. Asunción, under duress and uncomfortable because of the finding of responsibility, reluctantly accepted. In pursuit of peace the first commission was replaced by the Washington-based Commission of Neutrals in early October.

For Stimson there was another problem. In August 1929, the Argentine president, Hipólito Irigoyen, termed the conciliation efforts then held in Washington, D.C., "outside interference." Stimson attempted to placate Irigoyen by offering acceptance of Buenos Aires as a venue for negotiation. Argentina then responded that it did not desire to make any new proposals relative to the Chaco. In any case, the U.S. government recognized that the position of Argentina in any further resolution of the Chaco dispute had to be addressed.

Paraguay accepted the conciliation report of the Commission of Investigation and Conciliation. Bolivia did not. La Paz saw no need inasmuch as that commission had indirectly named Paraguay as the aggressor. Nonetheless, the protocol of 12 September 1929 was technically in force. Uruguay accepted the frustrating charge of trying to implement it, but opposition in both Asunción and La Paz, requests for modification, and quibbling over terms delayed the agreement for the return of the fortines until April 1930.

La Paz's demand that the Paraguay River constitute Bolivia's eastern boundary hardened with the settlement of the Tacna-Arica dispute that removed Bolivia's last hope for a Pacific outlet. For all of 1930 and the first half of 1931, there was no more movement on the diplomatic front. Several minor military encounters occurred in the Chaco, and the war of words between La Paz and Asunción grew hotter. Charge and countercharge about military buildups resulted in Bolivia breaking relations with Paraguay.

That rupture offered the Argentine government an opening to supersede Washington as a site of negotiations, and Buenos Aires offered its good offices to settle the dispute. Asunción agreed; La Paz did not. The upshot of Argentine action was La Paz's offer for a non-aggression pact between Paraguay and Bolivia and Bolivia's return to Washington and the Commission of Neutrals. In September 1931 this commission announced that discussion of such a pact would soon begin.

In the following month skirmishes in the Chaco accelerated. The neutrals still did not know if Bolivia would send a negotiator. Prodded by the U.S. State Department, nineteen American countries asked Bolivia to send a delegate. Surprised by this action, the Bolivian government agreed and returned to the peace table. Amid rumors of greater arms shipments and independent attempts of conciliation by various Latin American governments, the neutrals hammered out a draft non-aggression pact. Bolivia informed U.S. assistant secretary of state Francis White, the chair of the Commission of Neutrals, that it accepted the pact, subject to a few minor revisions. Paraguay presented some serious objections demanding, on the surface, security guarantees and compulsory arbitration. White now assumed, correctly, that Asunción did not desire such a pact, which would have left Bolivia in control of the regions of the Chaco it had recently gained, and Asunción officials now believed that they could not risk an unfavorable arbitration.

In any case it was too late. In June 1932 Fortín Carlos Antonio López in the central Chaco fell to a sudden assault by the Bolivian army. After intensive discussion in Asunción, Paraguay announced it was withdrawing from the Washington negotiations. A mood of frustration was evident in Asunción. Since the September 1929 protocol, diplomacy had not favored Paraguay. Its attacks upon Vanguardia and Boquerón had been condemned, and it had tacitly admitted Bolivia's legal possession of Vanguardia. By late 1931, Paraguayan statesmen were convinced that diplomacy had weakened the nation's position in the Chaco. The attack upon Fortín Carlos Antonio López in June 1932 offered a way out from negotiations that Paraguayans perceived as working against their interests.

An Apprehensive Minister

During the period of greater tension between Paraguay and Bolivia before the outbreak of the Chaco War, the U.S. minister to Paraguay was Post Wheeler, the first career diplomat posted to Asunción.[7] From his arrival in Paraguay in late 1929 to a temporary departure to the United States for health reasons in late 1931, Wheeler observed the deterioration of relations between Paraguay and Bolivia. He understood the danger of a representative identifying too closely with his host country but concluded that Bolivia was indeed the aggressor in the Chaco and that the Commission of Neutrals would take no meaningful step to resolve the crisis as long as its chair, Francis White, continued to insist that Paraguay conciliate Bolivia.[8] The Paraguayans now completely discredited the Commission of Neutrals and especially White, whom they believed overly partial to Bolivia. Wheeler himself came to share that opinion of White.

As war increasingly loomed in mid-1932, Wheeler strongly recommended to his superiors the idea of a mutual withdrawal of forces and U.S. arbitration of the entire question. Paraguay was quite open to such an action, but only if the arbitration was accompanied with guarantees by the United States. The Hoover administration, grappling with the dire economic and political consequences of the Great Depression, would not assume that responsibility. According to Wheeler, White told him that the time for arbitration might be later, perhaps "'when Paraguay comes to her senses and knows she can't whip Bolivia.'"

White then advanced an armistice based on the actual position of both armies in June. According to Wheeler, President Eusebio Ayala accepted the proposal, but Bolivia demanded conditions that Paraguay could not accept. Asunción newspapers carried a story out of Washington and attributed to White that there would be no resolution of the Chaco dispute until a "decisive victory." That ambiguous statement was interpreted by Paraguayans to mean a Bolivian victory. Wheeler noted: "The reaction was violent. There was bitter resentment against the Neutrals and an abortive demonstration against the United States."

In mid-1932, with the Bolivian seizure of Paraguayan positions in the central Chaco, full war erupted between the two republics. Paraguay then abandoned negotiation with the Commission of Neutrals. Wheeler was so disgusted with U.S. policy that he later stated that he personally informed the Paraguayan government that it was his opinion that Paraguay should declare war. He also claimed that he communicated that action to the State Department, well knowing that it might effect his termination. It did not. White simply acknowledged that despatch and let the matter die.

The United States had failed to settle the Chaco question. Never during this period did it fully realize that Paraguay was becoming more desperate in the face of the Bolivian threat and that Paraguayan leaders were steeling themselves for war rather than meekly accepting the increasing Bolivian pressure. Realistically, however, the United States had few useful tools to work with in this dispute. As Leslie Rout so aptly pointed out in his study of Chaco War diplomacy, the only tools that Washington possessed were "moral force and reason." In a dispute considered vital to both parties, those were weak instruments in the hands of any outside power trying to find a peaceful solution. Neither Paraguay nor Bolivia was vulnerable to any type of economic pressure from the United States. Financial inducements (a positive word for bribery on a national scale) would have been futile in face of the intense nationalism evident in both nations. As for military force, the United States never considered that option as no question of national interest could have justified it. Rout does suggest that the United States might have disengaged itself from all negotiations, allowing another group to take stronger steps than the United States could envision. Perhaps both parties might have accepted a forced peace if it had been accompanied by a direct threat of military intervention. But not even Argentina would have assumed the risk.[9]

When war erupted in the Chaco, Washington expressed its concern but could do little during the conflict. The State Department had relied upon the Commission of Neutrals, directed by Assistant Secretary of State Francis White, to resolve the Chaco dispute. The failure of that body left it few options. Further, Argentina was determined to exclude outsiders from any role in Chaco diplomacy. Thus, for a period of three years, the United States had little influence on wartime diplomacy.

Nonetheless, the commission thrashed futilely until its death in mid-1933, proposing truces, troop withdrawals, and other means to restore peace. The weakness of that body was evident in July 1932 when Argentina, Brazil, Peru, and Chile (ABPC) decided to pursue an independent path of war diplomacy, but during the war Argentina played a critical role in advancing Paraguay's aims. In late June 1933 the Commission of Neutrals issued its last communiqué before disbandment. In it White made clear his bitterness against Argentina as an obstacle to the commission's peace efforts. Buenos Aires, however, paid no attention. White and the State Department had to recognize that any likely peace in the Chaco had to recognize Argentine interests. The United States had only minor interests in the Chaco, but it did have significant interests in Argentina that must not be jeopardized.

Argentina opposed the Commission of Neutrals, but its hostility did not translate into any effective action by the ABPC powers to end the war. The new grouping had the power to deny any outside intervention in the Chaco conflict but found it difficult to act in a positive manner. The spirit of denial was quite evident by December 1932 when some nineteen neutral American nations supported the final peace proposal of the Commission of Neutrals. The ABPC ignored that plea, and its non-action essentially signaled to the world that the Commission of Neutrals was dead, but the ABPC proved no more effective than the commission.

After some initial setbacks in late 1932 and early 1933, Paraguay began a series of offensives that within two years brought its armies to the foothills of the Andes. Although poorer than its enemy, and with a smaller population, Paraguay possessed a greater social cohesion among its soldiers. Its military leadership was quite effective. General José Félix Estigarribia possessed great strategic abilities as he led the Paraguayan army from one success to another in Chaco campaigns. President Eusebio Ayala proved a most competent wartime president as he mobilized political and economic support for the war effort. For the Paraguayans, possession of the Chaco meant national survival. For Bolivian conscripts, wrenched from their highland homes and having little understanding of the war, the Chaco signified a green hell of confusion, defeat, and all too often death by machine gun bullets or sheer thirst. Eventually peace came, but not before at least a hundred thousand Bolivian and Paraguayan combatants perished.

Now the cause of peace was passed to the League of Nations. Initially most Latin American nations were dubious about the league intervening in what was essentially an American affair, but both Paraguay and Bolivia were members of the league and supposedly bound by its charter. As ever, Argentina's position was critical. Foreign Minister Carlos Saavedra Lamas had initially appeared to welcome the league's intervention but rapidly turned hostile to it since Buenos Aires was determined to defend Argentina's primacy in foreign affairs of the Río de la Plata against all comers.

In 1933 the League of Nations reluctantly took cognizance of the war, particularly as one member, Paraguay, had by this time declared war upon a fellow member of the league. At first the league called upon the ABPC powers to act for it and later dispatched a commission of inquiry to the Río de la Plata. The commission arrived in Montevideo when the seventh Pan-American Conference of foreign ministers of the American republics was convened. At that conference, U.S. secretary of state Cordell Hull endorsed the league's efforts to find peace in the Chaco. Again the United States and Latin American nations urged a conciliatory solution to the Chaco War, and for a brief period an uneasy truce between the two combatants was concluded.[10]

For the most part, this U.S. effort to bolster the League of Nations had no success in bringing about a peace. Hull, as well as the league, discovered that Argentine determination to exclude other parties from this conflict was an insurmountable obstacle. In addition, the commission's attempt to bring Paraguay and Bolivia to negotiations was hindered by Paraguay's determination to pursue a course of arms after an impressive victory in late 1933.

In May 1934 the league's commission of inquiry issued its report, concluding that neither combatant really wished arbitration. The league refused to assign to any party blame for the failure of its efforts but recommended to its members an embargo of arms shipments to Bolivia and Paraguay. By December 1933 some thirty-nine member states and two nonmembers—Brazil and the United States—had taken various legal steps to forbid arms sales to the belligerents. Other arms-producing nations did not limit sales, and the league's embargo was a failure. Bolivia had placed various arms orders in the United States and prior to Washington's embargo had received some shipments. With the embargo's proclamation most of the pending sales were nullified. Some orders, however, were at the point of shipment when the U.S. embargo went into effect and were allowed. Asunción protested the latter exception, but the State Department paid little attention. After all, it was well aware that Paraguay, relying upon European suppliers, was taking full advantage of loopholes in the league embargo. Although the U.S. embargo was not perfect, it was enforced with more rigor than exercised by most other nations.[11]

The League of Nations advanced a peace formula in 1935. Argentina opposed it, and eventually Paraguay, flushed with recent victories, rejected it. At that point, the league proclaimed Paraguay as the aggressor and lifted the arms embargo on Bolivia. Paraguay then resigned from the league and suffered no loss of foreign military supplies. The league was powerless in the face of Argentine opposition, and concern over the rise of Hitler in Germany prompted Britain and France to conciliate Buenos Aires. Essentially Paris and London gave Argentina and Chile full freedom to use their influence upon the belligerents as they saw fit. The league, as Francis White had predicted, had had no more success than the ill-fated Commission of Neutrals.

"Standard Oil's War"

No perception of the Chaco conflict has had a longer life than the tale that international oil companies, pursuing their own economic interests, played a covert role in the war. A yet popular account relates that Standard Oil of New Jersey was influencing Bolivia, and that British petroleum interests were behind Paraguay. More common, particularly in Paraguay, is the assumption that the major player in this scenario was solely Standard Oil.[12] The basis for this story is that Standard Oil possessed oil-producing concessions in the eastern foothills of the Bolivian Andes and desired to expand its extraction of oil by tapping rich oil deposits in the Chaco.

Where were those Chaco oil deposits? None have been discovered in the past fifty years of exploration of the territory gained by Paraguay in the war. And the claim that the explorations were a success but the wells secretly capped to await higher prices is scarcely credible.

Bolivia's concessions to Standard Oil granted in the 1920s and early 1930s did not fall into Paraguay's earlier territorial claims; only as Paraguay's armies advanced to the foothills of the Andes did those oil fields become a matter of importance for Asunción. Was the Bolivian drive to the Paraguay River secretly part of Standard Oil's desire for a pipeline to the Upper Paraguay for tanker export? Not only did that river have inadequate depth for tankers of the era for much of the year, but slackened demand during these years of the Great Depression, as well as the minor production of the Bolivian fields, precluded the capital investment for such a pipeline. Barging oil downriver would have demanded Argentine ports for transshipment, and the cooperation of the Argentine government in such a project was quite dubious given its opposition to the introduction of Bolivian oil. Finally, if Standard Oil indeed was a secret supplier of arms and money to Bolivia, either before or during the war, it was a rather strange association inasmuch as relations between La Paz and Standard were greatly strained almost from the beginning of drilling in the 1920s.

The first proponents of the "Guerra del Standard" thesis appear to have surfaced in 1932–33 and were Argentine nationalists, largely associated with *Editorial Claridad* in Buenos Aires. Not only was the accusation against Standard Oil a stick with which to beat the Bolivians as Argentine sympathy for Paraguay grew during the war, but the company, having left Argentina in the mid-1920s after disputes with the Argentine government, was now considered to be a regional oil competitor after development of its oil fields in Bolivia. Blackening the name of the North American company aided Paraguay, might weaken a regional competitor of YPF—the Argentine state-owned oil company—and might reinforce Argentine nationalism. An intriguing aspect of the development of the myth is how it also was seized upon by the Latin American left in its campaign against foreign exploitation of national resources.[13]

As for Paraguay, this interpretation of the origins of the war was a useful political explanation. For those who wished to minimize their country's responsibilities for the war, the hidden hand of an outside power offered a handy absolution. If Paraguay did not gain its inflated demands at the conclusion of the war, a ready scapegoat was at hand. Finally, the Paraguayan victory in the Chaco War—a victory not only against Bolivia but also Standard Oil—was a matter of nationalistic pride.

Standard Oil was faced with a public relations problem. If it protested too strongly that it was not supporting Bolivia in that dispute, it faced the wrath of nationalists and the Bolivian government as a "traitor in our midst." However, any public support for the Bolivian cause was obviously just as dangerous. The company opted for neutrality, and the lot of neutrals is not a happy one. In 1937, after a decade of conflict over production, taxes, and export problems, the Bolivian government nationalized the holdings of Standard Oil in Bolivia—a poor reward if indeed the company had supported the Bolivian war effort. For those who hold to the myth, this action was taken by Bolivia because not enough support was given. Standard found itself in a no-win situation.

Enter the "Kingfish"

The accusations that Standard Oil was a hidden actor in the Chaco War gained considerable currency when Senator Huey Long (known as the "Kingfish") entered the fray.[14] From May 1934 to January of the next year, in a series of four speeches on the floor of the U.S. Senate, Long criticized the "forces of imperialistic finance," most notably Standard Oil and the Rockefeller interests, as being responsible for the war between Bolivia and Paraguay. Paraguay, he asserted repeatedly, was the rightful owner of the Chaco as confirmed by the earlier Hayes Award, and only Standard Oil's desire for the oil of that region had prodded Bolivia to war. The oil company had corrupted Bolivian leaders and financed that nation's mobilization for war.

The Paraguayan press was ecstatic over Long's charges. Now their interpretation was "confirmed" by an important North American statesman.[15] With Long's accusations, President Eusebio Ayala of Paraguay, who earlier had been dubious about the Standard Oil involvement, now, at least diplomatically, accepted it as true. Senator Long became a hero in Paraguayan eyes, and a Bolivian Chaco fort, recently captured by Paraguay, was renamed after him. In Washington, the Bolivian legation protested to Long that he was mistaken as to the role of Standard Oil. Long ignored that protest and rejected Bolivian arguments. He further criticized Bolivia for that nation's appeal to the League of Nations.

Senator Long's campaign against Standard Oil and Bolivia spread rapidly through Latin America, and diplomats reported to Washington on the publicity it had engendered. The Bolivian minister issued a well-reasoned defense of Bolivia in an attempt to refute Long's charges and distributed it to all members of Congress.[16] That response was also distributed by the State Department to all its representatives throughout Latin America—not because the State Department had any interest in defending Standard Oil, but because, as it stated, too many Latin Americans made no distinction between U.S. enterprises and the U.S. government. The State Department did not want U.S. neutrality in the Chaco War to be compromised, but Bolivia's defense and the State Department's action had little impact compared to the flamboyancy of Long's assertions.

Long attacked Standard Oil and Bolivia's claims and also launched assaults on the foreign policies of Presidents Herbert Hoover and Franklin D. Roosevelt, the U.S. State Department, United Fruit, the League of Nations, the World Court, and other available targets. He delivered the final and most telling speech on the Chaco in late January 1935. The Roosevelt administration had become concerned about the impact of Long on the conduct of Latin American affairs, and the State Department briefed various senators to answer his charges. Senator Long, however, had the initiative in the debate, shifting the emphasis and topic as he willed. Furthermore, it appears that he had been well primed by Paraguayan sympathizers with documents, maps, and other evidence, all prepared and selected to further the Paraguayan cause. Those senators who engaged him in debate were not as well prepared by the State Department. Even when they pressed Long on dubious assertions relative to the Chaco, they were at a disadvantage. In typical Long fashion, he cleverly shifted the debate to an assault on the World

Court, then to criticism of the League of Nations, then to the activities of Standard Oil in the United States, then to the "nefarious" activities of the Chase Manhattan Bank.

The Chaco War gave Huey Long the opportunity to throw dirt upon Standard Oil, an old enemy from Louisiana politics. Long had successfully ridden the wave of anti-Standard sentiment in Louisiana. He saw no reason why that crusade might not be translated into national political advantage for him as well.

In the course of his Senate campaign against Standard Oil and its purported actions in the Chaco War, Huey Long displayed the oratorical and political skills that made him such a formidable public figure in the early 1930s. Indeed, his participation in the Chaco controversy may well have been "only demagoguery," as Pablo Max Ynsfrán, then counselor to the Paraguayan Legation in 1934, stated some thirty years later. It was also a very impressive and influential demagoguery. In his argument, as Michael L. Gillette states, Long "displayed a remarkable faculty for giving pertinence to the irrelevant, for emphasizing the few facts he did have, and for stretching his contentions to bridge the inherent gaps. In short, he took a virtually untenable position and maximized its credibility, a talent characteristic of Long's unique brilliance."[17]

The Search for Peace

By late 1934 the advance of the Paraguayan army in the southwest and central Chaco threatened Bolivia's eastern Andean foothills and, not incidentally, the oil fields of Camiri. In recompense for the sacrifices endured, Asunción eyed Bolivia's oil region as a prize of war. The Andeans, however, were now fighting on more favorable terrain and defending their homeland. Their army had been reorganized, and more capable officers came to the fore. In addition, Bolivian supply lines were now shortened while those of Paraguay were stretched too far. Although Paraguay had been victorious in the past two years, its resources of men, material, and finances had been stretched to the limit.

Successful Bolivian resistance in early 1935 signified the beginning of a different war, one in which Paraguay could not gain spectacular victories as it had in 1933 and 1934.

For two years various parties had advanced peace proposals only to see them rejected. In early 1935, however, Chile and Argentina laid a joint peace proposal before La Paz and Asunción. Although neither belligerent formally accepted the proposal, mutual war weariness and military stalemate prompted them to leave the door open to negotiations. In April, Argentina and Chile invited Brazil, the United States, and Peru to join in negotiation. That invitation was more optimistic than the situation really warranted, but from the joint proposal eventually came the Chaco Peace Conference and, after several years of intense and often frustrating negotiations, the Chaco Peace Treaty.[18]

The United States agreed conditionally to the peace conference invitation, followed by Brazil. In May the five-nation mediation group—Argentina, Chile, Brazil, the United States, and Peru—met in Buenos Aires. Uruguay was then invited to join and accepted. The foreign ministers of Paraguay and Bolivia received invitations to the Argentine capital for the purpose of negotiation and quickly accepted. With representatives of the belligerents present, the mediating powers in late May advanced various peace proposals.

After initial rejection of various proposals, breakthrough came in early June when Bolivia accepted the Paraguayan demand for guarantees during a cease fire, but only if Paraguay accepted a de jure arbitration of ownership of the Chaco. The mediating powers then hammered out a plan for international inspection of the demobilization of both armies in the Chaco to a minimal level and the establishment of a military frontier between the two. Bolivia and Paraguay pledged to acquire no new arms during the period of negotiations. War responsibility would be fixed, and a postwar conference would be held on trade, transit, and navigation in the Upper Plata. Eventually, La Paz and Asunción would sign a pact of non-aggression. On a critical aspect—the question of a time limit for negotiations before the preparation of arbitration—Bolivia was outmaneuvered as Argentina simply stated it would not abandon the negotiations in any instance until the territorial question or the arbitration process was settled. On 12 June 1935 the formal signing of the protocol ending Chaco hostilities took place, and hostilities terminated two days later.[19]

These negotiations were rushed, and the U.S. State Department had some serious doubts about many provisions. It felt that the stated objectives of the protocol were too ambitious and that the wording of the document was vague in many instances and could only give rise to squabbling over the intended meaning. In these views Washington was correct. However, the protocol was a compromise document designed to bring the belligerents to the peace table and had to offer something to everyone—even to some of the mediating powers who pursued their own interests in the search for peace. In this, even with the ambiguities that abounded, the protocol served its purpose.

The first U.S. delegate to the Chaco Peace Conference was the ambassador to Brazil, Hugh Gibson, a skilled diplomat who was better suited to the European scene. He found the Buenos Aires negotiations messy and pessimistically believed that peace was impossible to attain. He was anxious to return to his post in Rio and was replaced as ambassador to the conference by Spruille Braden in November 1935.[20] Braden had wide experience in Latin American business as well as diplomacy in that region. Both Secretary of State Cordell Hull and Under Secretary of State Sumner Welles respected Braden's ability and gave him wide power to achieve one important end—a lasting peace between Paraguay and Bolivia.

Braden played an important role in the ensuing peace negotiations and found, as had been expected, that the attitude of Argentina was critical to any success. Braden was extremely pragmatic in his search for a Chaco peace—so much so that he was quite willing to discard any remnants of Wilsonian idealism such as open diplomacy or the recent Stimson doctrine of nonrecognition of territorial conquest. He accepted open violation of international law in regard to prisoner repatriation, as acceptance was necessary to keep the peace talks progressing. He promoted a sham arbitration at the end of the conference in order to reduce the political danger to La Paz and Asunción when territorial matters were resolved. Braden accepted the world as it was.

Washington was now convinced that Argentina must be placated and its interests in the Upper Plata must be considered. For that reason, Buenos Aires was the logical seat of the conference, and the Argentine foreign minister, Carlos Saavedra Lamas, assumed a dominant role. U.S. views of Saavedra Lamas were not complimentary, and Braden found the Argentine minister to be egotistical, untrustworthy, and duplicitous. While much of that animosity may have sprung from continuous personality conflicts, other Latin American representatives (as well as some Argentines) shared similar views. Even so, the vagaries of Saavedra Lamas had to be endured, and in an attempt to placate him Washington even supported his desire for the Nobel Peace Prize. He gained that honor in 1936, but the United States gained little in return.

Argentina desired to protect its extensive investments in the Chaco, and Paraguay's victorious march to the Andes ensured the Argentine goal if any territorial decision by the Peace Conference validated that conquest. Also important to Buenos Aires, though hidden, was a desire to attain control over the export of Bolivian oil. It was acceptable if Paraguay conquered the oil-producing region, since Argentine domination of Paraguay's economy would redound to Buenos Aires' advantage. Should Bolivia retain that region, Buenos Aires still might gain indirect control over oil exports due to its geographical advantages. Resentment in La Paz over Argentine support for Paraguay in the Chaco War did not prevent Saavedra Lamas from pursuing his goal during the negotiations. After all, resentment or not, Argentina's dominant economic and geopolitical position in this region was simply a fact of life that Bolivia had to recognize.

Asunción was grateful for Argentine support during the war but also recognized warily that Saavedra Lamas pursued national interests. Brazil could do little to diminish Argentine influence in Asunción but could block complete Argentine domination of eastern Bolivia. Chile also desired a Chaco peace but one that did not greatly increase Argentine power or turn Bolivia back to its traditional insistence on an outlet to the Pacific. With all these subcurrents of national interest among the mediating powers, as well as politically driven intransigence by Paraguay and Bolivia, it is no wonder that few observers gave the Chaco Peace Conference much chance of success.

Spruille Braden realized that the main task of the Chaco Peace Conference was the solution of territorial claims to the Chaco. However, there were several preliminary problems to be solved before that central issue could be addressed. It was relatively easy to ignore the questions of war responsibility and a postwar economic conference, but the demobilization of armies, the rearming of the belligerents during the truce, the repatriation of prisoners of war, and the security of the military frontier attained at the time of the cease fire of 12 June 1935 required much attention. The mediating powers did not deal with these preliminary issues sequentially but considered many at the same time. It is, however, convenient to analyze them separately.

Demobilization of the belligerents' armies in the Chaco proceeded with surprising ease. Both nations were economically exhausted. As Paraguay felt the economic burden more than did Bolivia, it reduced its armies more rapidly. By September 1935 both armies reported that only about five thousand troops remained under arms. In the protocol of June 1935 both Bolivia and Paraguay had agreed that neither would rearm while the cease-fire was in effect. Almost immediately both parties ignored that promise. Delegates to the Chaco Peace Conference were aware of those transgressions but decided to ignore them since under the June protocol there was no way to impede shipments. Under the protocol, limitrophe nations were not responsible for barring the passage of arms destined for Paraguay or Bolivia. In all justice, the fiasco about rearmament resembled the failure of the League of Nations arms embargo of a few years earlier.

Spruille Braden, in February 1936, called for some means of monitoring arms shipments. The other delegates ignored his request. Though in 1937 the conference did vote to investigate the matter, Paraguay's intransigence forced the mediating powers to back down. Braden persisted, but by late 1937, recognizing that no other delegates wished to face this issue, he was forced to abandon his quest. In retrospect, it was just as well. Neither Bolivia nor Paraguay would stop rearming, and nothing the conference might do would persuade them otherwise.

In the early stages of the Chaco Peace Conference, Hugh Gibson and then Spruille Braden encountered serious problems as successive chairmen of the committee on the repatriation of prisoners of war. At the conclusion of hostilities in June 1935, Paraguay had taken approximately eighteen thousand Bolivian prisoners of war, while Bolivia reported about twenty-six hundred Paraguayan prisoners. The main obstacle to the repatriation of prisoners of war was Paraguay's demand for 3.5 million Argentine pesos for the maintenance of prisoners while in captivity. According to international law, maintenance of prisoners was the responsibility of the captor nation, but Asunción demanded that the opposing nations pay each other for the cost of prisoner maintenance. At the same time, Paraguay attempted to link prisoner repatriation to the legal recognition of the June 1935 military frontier between the two forces in the Chaco.

The peace conference was in danger of collapse over these issues, but Saavedra Lamas saved the day by pressuring Asunción to reduce its demands. At the same time, the Argentine foreign minister knew that Paraguay had to be given the opportunity to back down gracefully. He insisted that Spruille Braden travel to Asunción to break the deadlock. Braden, for all his differences with the Argentine minister, gave Saavedra Lamas full credit for finding a way out of a bad situation.

In Asunción President Eusebio Ayala and Braden agreed that the conference would establish the amount to be paid by Bolivia for prisoner maintenance. In no way was the military frontier earlier set by the Neutral Military Commission established by the Chaco Peace Conference a recognized territorial division. The Paraguayan government approved this new agreement since the provisions for security of the military frontier established by the 12 June 1935 Protocol were no longer valid. Asunción furthermore would not block the presence of the Neutral Military Commission to guarantee security measures in the Chaco. Finally, Paraguay abandoned any demand for the investigation of war responsibility.

Another conference protocol of 21 January 1937 affirmed the Braden-Ayala agreements. By the terms of that protocol, Bolivia received four hundred thousand Argentine pesos for prisoner maintenance, and Paraguay received 2.8 million pesos for its expenses. To many in Bolivia it appeared more like a ransom of Bolivia prisoners than a true repatriation. Even though La Paz accepted the protocol, it was political dynamite for the Bolivian government to pay the 2.4 million peso difference. According to an amusing account by Braden, the large mining companies in Bolivia privately contributed the money for repatriation because the war wrought havoc on their operations.[21] With money in hand, repatriation commenced in April 1936 and was over by July of that year. The exchange of prisoners was accompanied by recriminations and protests, and the entire matter reeked of cynicism, but pragmatically it did remove an obstacle to the further search for peace.

An unexpected outcome of the Braden-Ayala agreements was the overthrow of the Liberal regime of President Ayala. Nationalist army officers were outraged at what they perceived as abandonment of Paraguayan rights, and the new regime in Asunción threatened nullification of that accord. At this juncture, the Chaco Peace Conference revealed its power as the mediating powers quietly threatened the new Paraguayan government with nonrecognition should it renege on the agreement. Reluctantly, Asunción stated that it would observe all past Paraguayan commitments to the Chaco peace process. Even so, the confusion attending the military coup in Asunción delayed the peace process, and the same problem would also arise in Bolivia. Long and tedious negotiations were still in the offing.

A Difficult Peace

The optimism that greeted the peace protocol in mid-1935 was dissipated by 1937 as delegates to the Chaco Peace Conference encountered several great problems. Paraguay and Bolivia witnessed more internal political turmoil as governments in both nations were overthrown. That, of course, signified not only the change of delegates to the peace conference but also a reformulation of Chaco foreign policy for both parties.

At the same time, certain mediating powers took advantage of the peace process to pursue their own interests in the Río de la Plata. According to Spruille Braden (and his account is substantiated by other delegates and the diplomatic record), the greatest offender was

Argentina. Carlos Saavedra Lamas, the Argentine foreign minister and chair of the peace conference, was determined to gain advantages for Argentina during the quest for a Chaco peace. Even though many knew that Argentina had greatly supported Paraguay during the hostilities, Saavedra Lamas gained (not without difficulties) a railroad agreement with Bolivia by which Argentina would control the export of oil from Bolivia's Santa Cruz region. This Argentine quest for platine advantage prompted Brazil to conclude its own railroad agreement with Bolivia. All this was complicated by Argentina's fear that Brazil and Chile would re-create the former "diagonal" policy by which the latter two nations could counter Argentine pretensions.

The vague language establishing a cease-fire line in the June protocol also caused interminable problems for the delegates, mainly over the control of a portion of a road that led from Argentina to the Bolivian oil region of Camiri. During the war Paraguay had seized a portion of this access route and insisted on control over this road after the cease-fire. Finally, after much wrangling, the matter was resolved. The many disputes over the cease-fire line were referred to as a "security" problem inasmuch as both Paraguay and Bolivia desired the most favorable positions should the peace process fail and war again resume. At the same time, both parties realized that if peace did result, a de facto possession of territory enhanced their bargaining position.

Spruille Braden later recounted that by mid-1937 he had persuaded the Chaco Peace Conference to dispatch delegates to La Paz and Asunción to persuade both capitals to move forward on the peace process. By this time, both Bolivia and Paraguay had engaged in significant rearming, even though that action was contrary to the June protocol. Members of the Bolivian military, which by now controlled that nation through a junta, had regained their confidence, and Braden, who had been dispatched to La Paz, found them ready to resume hostilities. The U.S. delegate taxed the junta and the Bolivian president, Germán Busch, with their breach of the protocol and, according to his account, presented them with an outrageous and successful bluff.

Without authorization from Washington, Braden claimed that Bolivian intransigence in the search for peace would be considered an unfriendly act not only by the United States but also by the other mediating powers. The junta reconsidered its position, and Braden obtained a personal interview with President Busch. After intense discussion, the Bolivian leader agreed to boundaries that Bolivia could accept and agreed that his nation would support the dispatch of the foreign ministers of both Bolivia and Paraguay to the peace conference when negotiations reached a favorable state. Busch also agreed to the arbitration of a zone of territory roughly behind the cease fire positions held by the Paraguayan army.[22]

By March 1938 Braden was confident enough to predict to the State Department a peace treaty within four months. He was encouraged, not only by his informal agreement with President Busch, but by the departure of Saavedra Lamas from the Argentine Foreign Ministry and consequently from the Chaco Peace Conference. The new foreign minister, José María Cantilo, was much easier to work with and realized that peace was extremely desirable. Once the tentative agreement was accepted by Bolivia, the new Paraguayan government of Félix Paíva reluctantly agreed to send its foreign minister to Buenos Aires as well. With both the Paraguayan and Bolivian foreign ministers in Buenos Aires by May 1938, prospects for a treaty were enhanced. The mediating powers advanced proposals similar to the informal Busch-Braden agreement, and the outcome was predictable. Bolivia accepted them, and Paraguay rejected them. Braden turned to the Argentine press to mobilize public opinion and convinced most of the delegates to ignore Paraguay's intransigence. He even went over the head of the Argentine foreign minister to appeal successfully to the Argentine president to advance the peace process. This pressure probably did have some impact, and Paraguay found it was increasingly isolated at the peace conference. Gerónimo Zuibizaretta, the Paraguayan foreign minister and staunch defender of his nation's interests, finally had to compromise and produced a memorandum that was workable within the mediating powers' proposals. Braden was understandably elated, but ruffled feathers had to be smoothed, and Zuibizaretta quickly began to reconsider his own memorandum.

At that point, José Félix Estigarribia, victorious commander of the Paraguayan forces during the hostilities, made a dramatic appearance and intervened to save the prospective peace. Estigarribia had been appointed minister to the United States by Asunción in early 1938. In Washington he blossomed as an excellent diplomat who cultivated a relationship with Secretary of State Cordell Hull and Under Secretary Sumner Welles. Those two concluded that Estigarribia, who defended Paraguay's gains in the war, also desired a workable peace. In the midst of a possible last-minute breakdown in the Buenos Aires negotiations, Estigarribia arrived in the Argentine capital on 2 July. After rapidly reviewing the conference proposals, Estigarribia, with no authorization from Asunción, assumed the leadership of the Paraguayan delegation. As Efraím Cardozo, a young Paraguayan delegate, later stated, only a Paraguayan of Estigarribia's prestige and "great moral authority" could have successfully taken such a drastic step, and Asunción quickly confirmed his action.[23]

The logjam was now broken, and the peace treaty was signed on 22 July 1938.[24] Finally a Chaco peace was obtained. All the American nations involved in the long search for peace were properly grateful to Estigarribia, and soon the United States made that gratitude evident.

In the peace treaty the contentious problem of disputed territory, roughly behind the Paraguayan line after the cease-fire, had to be settled by arbitration. That proviso was deliberately inserted into the peace treaty so that both La Paz and Asunción might save face and not encounter great nationalistic opposition to the treaty. Since the arbiters were the same mediating powers of the conference, much of the territorial division had actually been decided prior to the treaty. Thus, the arbitration proceeded with few difficulties.

The search for a Chaco peace accord tested the patience of all participants, no less the United States. Spruille Braden was given great leeway by the State Department, and all involved, both friends and enemies (and he had many of both), recognized his significant role. The overall objective of the United States was to find a lasting peace, and in this Braden succeeded.

However, beyond the peace in the Chaco, some discerning statesmen were vaguely aware that Paraguay and the United States had entered into a new relationship. For nearly a hundred years of contact between the two nations, relations had been episodic in context. The Chaco War and resultant peace accord transformed U.S.-Paraguayan relations, even though it may not have been apparent at the time. Now Paraguay became a factor—small to be sure, but yet a factor—in the formulation of U.S. hemispheric policy in the face of international challenges. All this was soon apparent in the context of the Hemispheric Solidarity of the late 1930s, the coming of World War II, and postwar U.S. policy.

For Paraguay, the consequence of U.S. involvement in the Chaco peace treaty was somewhat ambiguous. Some Paraguayans, such as Estigarribia, recognized that Paraguay's conquests by 1935 were about all that could be expected and that peace was desirable if these conquests could be assured. Others felt betrayed that the peace accord had not gained more for Paraguay. Even today there are Paraguayans who feel that Braden and the mediating powers deprived Paraguay of control of the oil-rich Andean foothills. In any case, while U.S. participation in the long peace conference revealed its concern for the affairs of the Río de la Plata, no Paraguayan anticipated in 1938 the impact of the United States upon their nation in the ensuing decades.

4 Civil War and Hemispheric Security, 1939–1954

As previously noted, the Chaco War elicited considerable attention from the United States as being antagonistic to the political and economic interests of the Good Neighbor Policy. Furthermore, the drive for hemispheric solidarity was threatened by the rancor engendered by this war. As a result, Washington (and other hemispheric powers) brought diplomatic pressure to bear on Bolivia and Paraguay, especially during the Chaco Peace Conference, allowing the focus to return to promoting trade and hemispheric cooperation. However, the Good Neighbor Policy, with its emphasis on expanding political and economic partnerships and alliances to secure a peaceful, cooperative, and prosperous hemisphere, was only one factor explaining Washington's growing interest in southern South America. Another was the aggressive tone of the foreign policies of Nazi Germany and Fascist Italy, and their efforts to extend their influence in Argentina, Bolivia, Brazil, Chile, Paraguay, and Uruguay became an issue of concern to policymakers in Washington.

In the mid-1930s Germany realized the economic value of South America as a market for its industrial goods and source of raw materials needed to fuel its economic expansion (and ultimately to support strategic goals in Europe).[1] Latin America "was the richest raw material producing area in the world free from the control of any Great Power."[2] Germany made significant financial and infrastructure contributions; however, Berlin's main economic drive centered on commercial expansionism.

Economic penetration, however, was not the only means of infiltration that worried the United States. Over a million and a half German colonists and descendants lived in Latin America by the mid-1930s, most of them in southeastern South America. Not following the Italian pattern of acculturation, Germans resisted assimilation and affirmed their identity through schools, newspapers, broadcasts, and expatriate organizations. These potential "fifth column" Germans had immigrated before World War I and established agricultural communities in the northern region of the Río de la Plata basin. The success of the colonists' agricultural and financial projects and reputation for hard work gained them much respect among locals. Despite their influence, many Germans opted not to integrate into their surroundings, preferring to maintain their distinct ethnic identity by continuing to speak German and establishing educational, religious, and cultural organizations to serve the immigrant community. They also maintained close ties to Germany.

German immigrants, along with diplomats and professional spies, engaged in a number of overt and covert activities for the Third Reich. The most important concern of many in Washington was that Germany and Italy were attempting to cultivate pro-Fascist military leaders, who could, under the influence of German military missions and advisers, usurp political power and turn against Washington and its continental solidarity policies. It was evident to Washington that the region's armed forces—a traditional bastion of political power and nationalist sentiment—harbored an ideological sympathy and admiration for Germany, its Wehrmacht and Luftwaffe, and its success in having taken over much of Europe.

Paraguay Comes into Strategic Focus

It was not until the Chaco War that the United States began to pay much attention to political developments in Paraguay and regional matters in southeastern South America. The Febrerista Revolution and the regime's totalitarian inclinations raised some minor concern in Washington, but German expansionist strategy in southeastern Paraguay struck a far more threatening tone. At the end of 1938, fewer than three dozen Americans were in Paraguay, and only three U.S. companies did business there—Asunción Port Concession Corporation, IPC, and

Algodones, S.A. (with investments amounting to less than $2.5 million). Total trade with Paraguay ($1.5 million in 1938) amounted to less than 1 percent of U.S. trade with Latin America. As Michael Grow notes, perhaps not a single nation in Latin America was more remote from U.S. influence and interest than Paraguay.[3]

Germany had a far greater presence than the United States in Paraguay, which made Paraguayans not only more familiar with but also sympathetic to and appreciative of German culture, politics, and society. According to one estimate, there were twenty-six thousand Germans in Paraguay out of a population of one million. The immigrant community provided the main vehicle through which Paraguayans learned about Germany. Immigrants from the fatherland had first arrived in the late nineteenth century and again after the First World War, settling in agricultural colonies between Villarrica and Encarnación. By the mid-1930s, they had established farms and ranches, along with scores of small businesses devoted to mechanical repair and construction. Some five thousand lived in Asunción, many engaged in such business activities as banking and commerce that put them in close contact with Paraguayans. Germans acting as commercial agents for foreign companies carried much economic weight in Asunción. In consequence, they enjoyed considerable influence in the capital's business community, developing close professional and personal ties (through marriage) with influential families in Asunción. Their economic success, industriousness, technical skills, and penchant for discipline and order won Germans the admiration and friendship of Paraguayan intellectuals, business and political leaders, and military officers.

As in much of South America, German immigrant families maintained much of their identity. They not only retained their German citizenship but practically transplanted religious, cultural, and educational institutions to the region. Even before the Nazis came to power in Germany, Hitler's agents began establishing themselves in Paraguay by using the extensive network of German educational, religious, and charitable institutions "to diffuse and inculcate Nazi ideas among young Germans" and subsequently sympathetic Paraguayans. This was particularly the case with the large number of German schools in

Asunción and Villarrica. An intelligence report by the U.S. military, authored by Lieutenant Colonel Thomas F. Van Natta, military attaché in Asunción, noted: "Nazis took control of the governing board of German schools removing teachers and principals not sympathetic to National Socialism." Schools and other colonist institutions became centers of recruitment and propaganda for the Nazis, not only helping socialize and convert Germans but also facilitating the penetration of German ideological and economic presence in Paraguay. In 1931 the first Latin American Nazi Party was established in Paraguay—the first Nazi Party created outside of Germany and Austria.

By the mid-1930s portraits of Hitler and Nazi swastikas along with Italian symbols were openly displayed in a number of German and Paraguayan establishments. Nazi agents used film, newsreels, newspapers, and pamphlets to gain adherents among Paraguayan elite and to develop allies among intellectuals and nationalist authoritarian officers whom they invited to weekly social events at German locales in Asunción. By the late 1930s, a significant number of Paraguayan government officials and military supported the Third Reich. For example, cabinet members of Colonel Rafael Franco's Febrerista government, such as Gómez and Luis Freire Esteves, ministers of interior and finance, respectively, actively admired Europe's corporatist-totalitarian states.[4] Some leaders of the Liga Nacional Independiente, the ideological and organizational nucleus of Franco's government, also sympathized with National Socialism.

Most significant, military and police officers were noticeably supportive and enthralled by Fascist and militarist regimes in Europe and Asia. Colonel Mutshuito Villasboa, Paraguay's national police chief and founder of the pro-German faction of militant, authoritarian nationalist officers known as the Frente de Guerra (created in 1938), named his son Adolfo Hirohito, in honor of the two Axis leaders. The head of the national police academy, Captain Rolando Uberti, an ardent supporter and admirer of Italian fascism, directed cadets to display Nazi swastikas and Italian Fascist insignias on their uniforms.[5] Uberti and Marcos Fuster, head of General Higinio Morínigo's secret police, were close to Nazi agents in Paraguay and founded a Fascist underground group known as the Ring of Sacrifice.[6] High-ranking military officers, such as the noted hero of the Chaco War and the commander of the First Calvary division (also known as the Campo Grande military base) who led the February 1936 uprising, Colonel Federico Smith, believed, as did many Paraguayans by 1939, that Hitler's government was the best thing that could have happened in Germany. Colonel Smith and other distinguished Chaco War veterans associated with Frente de Guerra argued that Paraguay should counter U.S. interests and reject Liberal ideology in favor of close links with the German economy and the establishment of a pro-Fascist regime in Paraguay. For many Paraguayan officers, fascism's emphasis on nationalism, state power, and national unity was viewed as the country's best and only alternative to the corruption, instability, and fragmentation of Liberal rule.

It was not until the threat from Germany's strategic incursion into Paraguay and the start of the Second World War that Paraguay raised much concern in Washington. For Paraguay, the conflict in Europe severed economic links between Germany and Paraguay, forcing Asunción to abandon its strategy of playing the United States and Germany against each other. With exports to Europe largely cut off and the end of imports of finished goods, such as machinery, Asunción's options were limited though its needs remained high. Washington relied on an effective mix of diplomatic and material inducements with a propaganda campaign that spread the gospel of U.S. culture and democracy to draw Paraguay into an expanding U.S. sphere and away from that of Nazi Germany. Several U.S. government agencies became heavily involved in helping the United States strengthen cooperative ties with Paraguay. The key entities included the Export-Import Bank, created in 1934 to stimulate U.S. exports by providing low-interest credits to foreign governments interested in purchasing U.S. goods, the War Department (military missions and Lend-Lease), and the Division of Cultural Relations of the State Department and its successor, the Office of the Coordinator of Inter-American Affairs (OCIAA). The OCIAA was of particular importance; it focused on "promoting mutual progress and understanding in the Americas . . . through a multifaceted program of ideological, cultural and financial persuasion . . . meeting Nazi propaganda with American propaganda." A fourth organization, the Institute of Inter-American Affairs, also was important in Paraguay as it provided financial and technical assistance for the development of health, educational, and agricultural sectors.

Not long after the Liberal post-Febrerista government of President Félix Paíva named Chaco War hero General José Félix Estigarribia Paraguay's minister to the United States in May 1938, bilateral ties were enhanced. The United States was enthusiastic about the return of a Liberal government in 1937 and considered General Estigarribia, known for his strong pro-U.S. sympathies (though ideologically more in tune with Italian and Spanish fascism), as the political leader capable of countering Nazi influence in Paraguay. The United States was impressed by the general's leadership qualities when he assumed control of the Paraguayan delegation to the Chaco Peace Conference in Buenos Aires (July 1938), completing negotiations and the signing and ratification of the treaty before the end of the month. President Roosevelt and Under Secretary of State Sumner Welles, a U.S. diplomat with a long career in Latin America, were impressed by his character and leadership skills; they considered him "an intelligent and constructive-minded man . . . sincerely desirous of cultivating closer political and economic relations with the United States."[7] Suddenly, Estigarribia became Washington's man, and the general, a keen political strategist, was not about to lose an opportunity to promote his country and himself. General Estigarribia realized his excellent personal relations with U.S. government officials, along with sympathies for the Liberal government in the State Department, increased the likelihood that the Roosevelt administration would respond positively to an aid request from the Paraguayan government. Paraguay's economy stood to benefit and so did the general's political career.

In December 1938, Estigarribia presented the Export-Import Bank with a request for credits totaling $7.8 million, $3.3 million of which was to be allocated for the construction of a three-hundred-mile highway from Asunción to the Brazilian border. Estigarribia informed Warren Lee Pierson, president of the Export-Import Bank, that the road would have multiple benefits: "passing through Paraguay's most fertile agricultural region, it would lower farm to market freight rates and stimulate production of cotton and other export crops, tripling the volume of Paraguay's exports and reinvigorating the economy. Furthermore, by linking up with the Brazilian highway system, the proposed road would give Paraguay an alternate transportation outlet to the Atlantic, thus breaking Argentine stranglehold on Paraguay's foreign commerce."[8]

Estigarribia hoped the credit would not only stabilize the unstable political and economic situation in the country but also shore up the Liberal government and his own chance of becoming the party's next presidential candidate. While negotiations ensued in Washington with the assistance of his able counselor Pablo Max Ynsfrán, Estigarribia warned Liberal leaders that credits would fail to arrive unless he was guaranteed to be nominated as the Liberal Party's presidential candidate. On 19 March, General Estigarribia accepted the nomination and returned to Washington to finalize the negotiations.

There was much opposition from some quarters in the State Department and the Export-Import Bank to Paraguay's aid request, suggesting the proposal was "at best of dubious advisability." The State Department's international economic affairs adviser and some on Pierson's staff advised against approving the loan because of technical challenges, lack of qualified officials in Paraguay, and the negative impact on global cotton prices if Paraguayan production increased by 400 percent as expected. However, U.S. political and security imperatives in Paraguay and the need to support the pro-U.S. general who was likely to become the country's next president led Welles and the White House to urge the Export-Import Bank to approve the request without delay. In May Estigarribia was elected in absentia, and on June 13 President-elect José Félix Estigarribia and Secretary of State Cordell Hull signed an agreement that provided Paraguay with a $3 million credit for the highway and a $500,000 loan to strengthen the reserves of Paraguay's Bank of the Republic. The United States also provided technical advisers from the U.S. Tariff Commission and the Public Health Service to assist Paraguay's plan for modernizing its financial system and public health sector.[9]

This landmark agreement proved to be a turning point in U.S.-Paraguayan relations. Washington acquired the leverage that it never before possessed and that it used to thwart, if not eliminate, Nazi influence in the country, while ensuring that it would obtain future political and security concessions from Paraguay's governments when circumstances required. Similarly, for Paraguay the agreement marked the beginning of a new and important relationship that promised to have significant political and economic impact on the country. Never before, and not again until the mid-1950s, were U.S.-Paraguayan relations so close as during the Estigarribia administration. The June economic agreement also solidified the relationship between the Roosevelt administration and President Estigarribia. According to Sumner Welles, Estigarriba "said that I [Welles] could be sure that throughout his term of office as President of the Republic the first and foremost principle in his foreign policy would be the development and strengthening of the commercial and political relations between our two countries."[10]

The United States also hoped that Estigarribia's immense prestige within Paraguayan society and the Paraguayan military could stem the growing influence of fascism. Estigarribia assured Welles that he would not tolerate any further Nazi political, propagandist, or economic inroads into Paraguay. For example, the president blocked a German proposal to construct a petroleum pipeline from Bolivia to a Paraguayan port on the Paraguay River. He also rejected an offer from the German government to build a 220-mile highway from Asunción to the Brazilian border through Villarrica, establishing industrial colonies and factories along the road.

Paraguayan foreign policy clearly shifted in favor of supporting U.S. hemispheric security goals. Estigarribia instructed Paraguayan delegations to the First and Second Meetings of Consultation in Panama (1939) and Havana (1940) "to cooperate in the closest manner possible" with U.S. representatives, and during a visit to Washington the Paraguayan foreign minister told Sumner Welles that Paraguay desired "to cooperate to the fullest extent with the United States on all matters, whether they related to political or economic questions or to the question of military defense of the Western Hemisphere." This was a clear departure from Paraguay's position in December 1938, when at the Eighth International Conference of American States in Lima it challenged the urgency of U.S. alarm over Nazi German and Italian threats to the Americas and, under some pressure from Argentina, voted against a U.S. proposal to establish a formal mutual defense pact.[11]

Estigarribia's friendship with the United States was also motivated by his desire to counter Argentine influence and economic power, an objective that coincided with U.S. desires to limit Argentine influence throughout South America. With the war in Europe in full swing and Paraguay's export markets in Europe nearly inaccessible, Paraguay really had no choice but to seek a closer relationship with its new northern partner. U.S. leverage and Estigarribia's need for financial and technical assistance to help stabilize the economy and strengthen his domestic political position against pro-Argentine, Fascist elements assured Washington a strong ally. The relationship, though deeply lopsided, became mutually beneficial and exploitative. Much like he had done in 1939 to obtain the Liberal Party's presidential nomination by using the U.S. ploy, President Estigarribia was equally effective in playing the German alternative with the United States in an attempt to extract additional economic aid and cooperation from Washington. For example, he often warned the U.S. Legation in Paraguay of continued Nazi threats to his regime, particularly from German fifth columnists who were attempting to take advantage of Paraguay's financial situation to undermine his regime. In return for air-base rights for the U.S. military and a commitment to stamp out German influence in Paraguay, the Estigarribia government made a request for $17 million in August 1940. By mid-1940, Estigarribia had convinced the United States of the link between his government's stability and hemispheric security. As the U.S. Legation informed the State Department, "the matter of hemispheric defense and financial stability of the Paraguayan government [may] be considered as more or less related."[12]

As far as Washington was concerned, Estigarribia was its man in Paraguay in its struggle against fascism in the Western Hemisphere. Paraguay could be counted on to defend and support U.S. security priorities in the region. It mattered little that Estigarribia was a dictator.

After an attempted coup at the Campo Grande military base, the home of the First Army Corps strategically located on the outskirts of Asunción, on 14 February 1940 by officers sympathetic to the pro-Argentine, Febrerista opposition, Estigarribia declared a state of emergency and proclaimed himself dictator. In July a new constitution, Paraguay's fourth and one that lasted until 1967, was ratified (scrapping the 1870 Constitution that espoused the ideas of limited government, separation of powers, and the inviolability of private property); it created a corporatist state, modeled after that of Fascist Italy. Congress was stripped of most of its powers, while the president acquired broad powers to restrict political activities and intervene in the economy. During this time, the United States refrained from criticizing Estigarribia's authoritarian measures. For the United States, ideological inclinations and democratic credentials were secondary.

Frente de Guerra and the Morínigo Dictatorship

One consequence of the changes was a more active role for the Paraguayan military in national politics. Between 1936 and 1940, political-ideological divisions within the armed forces and Estigarribia's consolidation of power had kept pro-German officers from usurping control of the institution and state.[13] However, Estigarribia's accidental airplane death in September 1940 and the weakness of Paraguay's political parties gave nationalist officers the window of opportunity needed to consolidate their control. Immediately after Estigarribia's death, pro-Fascist officers demanded that one of their own, General Higinio Morínigo, the defense minister, be named president. Gradually, Morínigo consolidated his position and that of nationalist officers within the armed forces and government. Colonel Vicente Machuca, a popular officer of the nationalist faction, replaced the interior minister, Colonel Ramón Paredes, while Morínigo's most loyal supporters, Majors Victoriano Benítez Vera, Pablo Stagni, and Bernardo Aranda—members of the Frente de Guerra secret group—were promoted and placed in command of key military posts: commander of

Campo Grande, commander of the air force, and army chief of staff, respectively. Real power now lay with the military, specifically with pro-Fascist officers committed to slowing, if not reversing, the level of cooperation between the United States and Paraguay that Estigarribia cultivated.

To consolidate his Nationalist Revolution Morínigo turned to a small group of conservative Catholic intellectuals known as the Tiempistas (after their newspaper, *El Tiempo*) who favored establishing a paternalistic "social Catholic" dictatorship in Paraguay similar to the Salazar and Franco regimes in Portugal and Spain, respectively. Tiempistas held several key cabinet posts, including the Ministries of Foreign Affairs, Justice, Education, Agriculture, and Public Health. The foreign minister, Luis María Argaña, was the most prominent Tiempista in the cabinet; he helped shape General Morínigo's foreign policy and relations with the United States until 1944. The Frente de Guerra–Tiempista coalition was unapologetically authoritarian, advocating a "permanent military dictatorship, directed by honest patriotic military officers" and a small group of earnest, efficient, and dedicated technocrats.[14] Two U.S. ambassadors during this time confirmed the honesty and commitment to good governance of the Morínigo government but grew alarmed at its strong Fascist sympathies and unwillingness to fulfill Estigarribia's promise to curb German activities in Paraguay.

Before 1941 the Paraguayan officer corps, admirers of the Wehrmacht, expressed unabashedly their support for the German cause. Along with the Tiempistas, most officers believed that Europe's Fascist governments offered the best alternative to solving many of Paraguay's social and economic pathologies created by incompetent and corrupt liberal democratic governments. In addition to Germany's effective propaganda, the presence of a Vichy military mission—the only foreign military mission in Paraguay at the time—reinforced the view that the German military was superior and that the true threats to the Western Hemisphere were not the Axis powers but Western imperialists. Paraguayan elite opinion, now bombarded with pro-government news and propaganda, became increasingly pro-Axis. With no independent sources of news and information (many newspapers were confiscated), pro-Nazi newspapers and radio stations intensified their propaganda efforts with very good results. In August 1941, the U.S. Legation informed the State Department:

> Paraguay has offered a free field to German pamphlet and news propaganda . . . and the Germans are laboring in it tirelessly, intelligently and successfully to the point where they are taking over the public mind. . . . The atmosphere here is far less favorable to the democracies than was the case a year ago, and the government officials, army officers, and younger businessmen are coming to feel that Germany's victory is inevitable and will have beneficial results for South America and for Paraguay. It would look as if the influence of the United States had now reached a new low.[15]

Roosevelt Purchases Paraguayan Alignment

Within a year, everything that Washington had worked to achieve in Paraguay since the signing of the June 1939 economic agreement seemed to be slipping away. A new government meant that, in some ways, the United States had to refashion the relationship by disbursing greater largesse to Estigarribia's successor. Nazi sympathizers in South America looked with admiration at Hitler's military successes against the Allies in Europe, emboldening many, including the Frente de Guerra military group and some Tiempistas in Paraguay, to insist that their governments either remain neutral or become aligned with the German cause. As the German army rolled through much of Western Europe, and the U.S. War Department warned of potential German aggression in the Western Hemisphere, the Roosevelt administration tried to counter German influence by purchasing South American support regardless of the ideological proclivities of regimes in the region.

The Roosevelt administration, therefore, chose to cultivate Morínigo by broadening and increasing foreign aid programs to Paraguay. General Morínigo was not about to allow an opportunity for economic and military assistance, vital elements of regime survival, slip away. Despite opposition from his own military, he was prepared to provide Washington with military bases in exchange for economic aid. Between 1941 and 1943 Washington opened the economic spigot and turned on a charm offensive in an effort to obtain the hard and soft power leverage it could use not only to keep Paraguay within the U.S. orbit but also to structure Paraguay's domestic politics during and after the war "into a pattern more favorable to United States interests." In September 1941 the two governments signed an agreement in which the United States provided eleven million dollars in lend-lease military equipment to Paraguay. The terms of the agreement could not have been more favorable to Paraguay. According to a State Department liaison officer, "it would be unfortunate if other governments of the American Republics were to learn of the terms given to Paraguay . . . these are by far the most generous of our lend-lease offers to other American Republics."[16]

Throughout 1941, Paraguay expressed interest in obtaining additional credits from the Export-Import Bank; the United States drew out negotiations, hinting that Paraguay's request and other assistance would be provided if Paraguay reciprocated. In July the United States set aside $900,000 for additional financial cooperation with Paraguay, $400,000 for agricultural projects, and $500,000 for river and port works. These were relatively small amounts compared to those given to other nations but extremely important to Paraguay.[17]

A pivotal moment came at the Third Meeting of Consultation of Foreign Ministers (Rio de Janeiro—15–28 January 1942). After Pearl Harbor, an intense foreign policy debate ensued within the Morínigo government between the Tiempistas led by Foreign Minister Argaña, who insisted that Paraguay had no other practical option than to cooperate with the United States, versus nationalist officers, who believed that Paraguay's interests would prosper with an Axis victory.[18] Argaña argued that the United States had the capacity to reward and punish. With the Axis powers preoccupied with controlling Europe and the Allies dominating the high seas, Paraguay had no choice but to secure the means for coping with the inimical geopolitical circumstances by seeking a stronger relationship with the United States. Morínigo sided with Argaña and his civilian allies. Like the conclusions of many other Latin American leaders, Morínigo's decision centered on questions of political and economic advantage more than on abstract notions of hemispheric solidarity. Many years later, he said, "although Paraguay had great sympathy for the German regime, particularly the Army, I decided to align Paraguay with the United States because of the potential benefits or advantages. . . . I reached the conclusion that it was in Paraguay's interest that it be on the side of the Allies."[19]

Several symbolic but key measures were taken by Washington to cultivate the Morínigo regime. The most significant was when Sumner Welles suggested that President Roosevelt contact Morínigo with an offer to provide the general's son, who suffered from paralysis, with medical treatment at the Warm Springs, Georgia, hydrotherapeutic center where Roosevelt had received treatment. The U.S. government paid for the boy and his mother to travel to the United States for three months of therapy.[20] In an interview-autobiography, General Morínigo expressed his deep gratitude for the president's gesture, "one that I will never forget."[21] The second symbolic step was taken in February 1942 when diplomatic legations were upgraded to embassies, signaling the growing importance of bilateral relations. Finally, in early 1941 a source of friction in U.S.-Paraguayan relations was removed when Wesley Frost replaced Findley Howard as U.S. minister. Minister Howard had served in Paraguay since 1935. During his tenure he established close personal relations with Liberal Party stalwarts, particularly Estigarribia, and was openly disdainful of nationalist, Fascist, and Febrerista elements within the Morínigo government.[22] Soon after Estigarribia's death the new government expressed its strong antagonism toward Howard, the "Ministro Cowboy" who was known as a heavy drinker and who was inclined to receive guests at the legation in his bathrobe or, in a few cases, in much less. The minister's scandalous behavior and allegations that he was conspiring to overthrow the Nationalist Revolution (Morínigo claimed that Howard offered Paraguay's war minister the presidency if Morínigo was removed) made Howard an embarrassment for Washington. His dismissal in January 1941 was an important symbolic gesture indicating Washington's commitment to normalizing relations.

At the Rio Conference, Argaña supported U.S. resolutions, including its request that the Western Hemisphere sever relations with Axis countries, which Paraguay did on 25 February. However, developments in Europe and Asia continued to favor the Axis powers. And in Paraguay, Nazi influence and sympathies grew among key political, business, and intellectual groups. In the Paraguayan military many officers wondered if the regime's decision to support the United States at the Rio Conference was judicious. If the United States reneged on its general commitment made at the Rio Conference to provide military and economic assistance, it might jeopardize hemispheric solidarity and surely would have been a propaganda disaster. Not reacting quickly to support Paraguay's requests would undermine Foreign Minister Argaña's position vis-à-vis influential officials who had no interest in breaking with the Axis nations.

Much was at stake when in April Paraguay submitted a $7 million request for highway construction, sanitary works, and industrial development. The request was received with some skepticism by State Department and Export-Import Bank officials. This delay weakened the position of Foreign Minister Argaña, as the powerful Frente de Guerra officer group, still angered by Morínigo's decision to support Argaña's pro-U.S. position, sought to remove the foreign minister and reverse Paraguay's foreign policy in favor of the Axis powers. Tensions within Morínigo's government worsened as did bilateral relations when the State Department dispatched an emissary to Asunción to pressure the regime to, as Morínigo claimed, "openly persecute and remove all Germans from Paraguay . . . and confiscate all of their properties and possessions. An act I was not prepared to make." The U.S. ambassador in Paraguay quickly grasped the implications of U.S. vacillation and diplomatic pressures. Ambassador Frost warned that unless a "generous measure" of economic help was forthcoming, "we shall in short order have our first defection from the eighteen nations which pledged support at Rio."[23]

Within a month of receiving the Paraguayan request, the United States had approved a massive assistance package involving a series of cooperative and agricultural programs. The Export-Import Bank approved a grant of $3 million for "public works, agricultural, sanitary, and industrial development projects."[24] As Ambassador Frost noted, approval of this program "saved the situation" by preventing the pro-Axis military group from dominating the government. Through the Institute of Inter-American Affairs the United States funded the establishment of regional hospitals and pharmacies and the construction of the Ministry of Public Health and other public health centers involving U.S. technical advisers assigned to the Paraguayan government. The institute, through the Servicio Técnico Interamericano de Cooperación Agricola (STICA)—an agricultural and livestock cooperation program created in December 1942 to enhance Paraguay's capacity to increase its food supply—provided technical assistance, resources, and training to Paraguay's farmers.

As part of U.S. wartime hemispheric strategy, economic assistance dovetailed with the expansion of military and security links between the United States and Paraguay. The April 1941 lend-lease program started the process but brought mixed results from the nationalist, pro-German military. By the end of 1943 several key developments helped solidify U.S.-Paraguayan relations and weaken the pro-Axis faction. First, the late 1942 invasion of North Africa revealed Axis vulnerabilities, particularly the inability to control the sea lanes. Second, in April 1943, after some pressure from Washington, Morínigo closed Vichy France's military mission in Asunción. Third, in June General Morínigo's official visit to the United States to meet President Roosevelt at the White House was an unequivocal sign of mutual courting and establishment of a new partnership. This was followed by the August inauguration of Morínigo for a five-year term that at least gave the impression of a legitimate government in Asunción. Finally, the tide began to turn against the Axis powers in late 1943, weakening the ideological and political influence of nationalist military officers and allowing Morínigo and Foreign Minister Argaña to broaden bilateral ties to include the military and security. In October 1943 an agreement was signed establishing a Military Aviation Mission in Asunción followed by a similar agreement signed in December 1943 that brought a U.S. Army Mission to Paraguay.

Getting to Know One Another: Culture and Academic Exchange

Prior to this era, little if any interest in Paraguay existed among U.S. artists, scholars, and journalists. However, one important event that contributed to the development of Paraguayan studies in the United States was the 1939 purchase of the Manuel Gondra Collection by the University of Texas, Austin. Gondra (1871–1927) was one of the most respected scholars, writers, and statesmen of his generation, having served as president of Paraguay on three different occasions. The Gondra heirs sold the entire collection of 7,283 printed books, 2,633 pamphlets, 270 maps, and over 20,000 pages of manuscript sources. This collection became an invaluable source for scholars interested in studying Paraguayan history and helped create a generation of academics dedicated to the study of Paraguay.

The Roosevelt administration was helpful in initiating contacts between the two peoples. A significant and influential educational and cultural campaign led by Nelson Rockefeller and the State Department agency he directed, the Office of the Coordinator of Inter-American Affairs (OCIAA), played an important foundational role in helping expand exchange and understanding between the United States and Latin America. The strategic objective of the OCIAA was to promote security and solidarity in the hemisphere through programs of cultural interchange. One of the first and most important programs established by the United States under the rubric of cultural cooperation and propaganda was the Paraguayan-American Cultural Center (CCPA) founded in February 1942. The goal of the binational center was to "broaden ties of friendship and foment cultural relations between the United States and Paraguay and to promote the practice of values such as personal freedom and democracy in Paraguay." The CCPA became the U.S. Embassy's key instrument for disseminating U.S. values and culture throughout Paraguay.

The OCIAA propaganda in Paraguay was most visible in the form of informational motion pictures and filmstrips that were distributed and shown throughout the country, including some of the most remote towns or hamlets. Projectionists would tour the backcountry with a sound truck and gasoline generator, bringing motion pictures about U.S. culture, life, military, and politics into communities where movies had never been seen before. One U.S. cultural officer wrote of his experience on one of these tours:

> So untouched previously was the area visited that even the horses and oxen shied away from the truck as it passed along the road. . . . News of the trip had been announced in messages to the authorities of the towns visited and by radio, inserting the latter announcement in our local programs. As a result, there were great crowds everywhere. . . . From miles around people would come on foot, horseback and in ox-carts. All shows were open air ones, held either in the public square or the ample grounds alongside the church. Attendance averaged more than 1,500 and in San Juan Bautista and Piraya [sic] the crowd exceeded 2,500. There were constant expressions of admiration for the pictures.[25]

The United States also provided numerous scholarships, in different disciplines, for Paraguayans to study in the United States and awarded grants to a few Paraguayan scholars, such as social scientist Guillermo Enciso Velloso (later ambassador to the United States), to visit the United States to lecture at universities and engage in research when the opportunity presented itself. A distinguished specialist in pathology and rector of the National University of Paraguay, Dr. Juan Boggino, also visited the United States as a grantee. As a result of his observations in the United States, he encouraged more exchanges and publicly repudiated the anti-U.S. thesis of José Enrique Rodo expressed in his book *Ariel*. Journalists such as Oscar Schaerer, editor of *La Tribuna*, the most widely read newspaper in Asunción, were also invited to the United States to learn more about the country and the newspaper industry. In contrast to other countries, no awards were granted to U.S. professors and students to visit Paraguay.[26]

The other important mechanism of the U.S. cultural-propaganda campaign in Paraguay was the publication and distribution of *En Guardia* magazine. The magazine was distributed among cultural and education centers and influential political and intellectual figures in Asunción. It featured articles on the U.S. military and industrial power, South American liberators and intellectuals, and U.S. and Latin American culture. Finally, the U.S. educational system and work habit values were introduced to Paraguay by way of an educational agreement signed in March 1945 that provided financial and technical assistance for vocational programs in Paraguay.

During the war years Americans in relatively large numbers came into contact with Paraguay. Agricultural and forestry experts, public health specialists, engineers, military officers, diplomats, and experts and commissions of all varieties sprang forth from the cornucopia of U.S. aid. The upgrade of the U.S. Legation increased the staff of the embassy in Asunción so much "that the United States ambassador was warning the State Department of the danger of negative 'psychological repercussions' on the part of the Paraguayans if the number of official United States representatives expanded any further." The U.S. community swelled from fewer than 30 in 1939 to about 350 by 1944. The presence of Paraguayans in the United States increased thanks to the OCIAA programs, but their numbers remained relatively small compared to other South American countries.

Economic Ties: Accumulating Influence

Through the OCIAA, the United States also provided invaluable technical assistance to Paraguay in the areas of monetary and banking reform.[27] At the request of the Paraguayan government and with the assistance of the OCIAA, the Board of Governors of the Federal Reserve System made available to Paraguay the services of three members of its staff, in order to help in the preparation of basic monetary, central banking, and general banking legislation. Thanks in large part to U.S. technical advisers, these reforms represented the first effort by Paraguay to organize its monetary and financial life in a systematic and rational manner. By 1943 the deepening and broadening of U.S. ties and influence in Paraguay had not only overshadowed those of Germany and other European powers but were clearly beginning to replace those of Paraguay's traditional dominant partner—Argentina.

Though Paraguay was one of five countries not to sign a reciprocal trade agreement with the United States until 1945, bilateral trade increased from $1.5 million in 1938 to $5.5 million in 1945. The biggest increase was in Paraguayan imports of U.S. manufactured goods, specifically metals, vehicles, machinery, and chemicals. In a matter of five years, the United States went from being a marginal trading partner to Paraguay's second most important after Argentina.[28]

Paralleling the growth in trade and public economic assistance was a sharp influx of private U.S. investment capital into Paraguay.[29] In 1939 U.S. investments amounted to 17 percent of total foreign investments in Paraguay, the most important being the Asunción Port Concession Corporation and IPC. In the early 1940s, however, the number of U.S. companies increased in Paraguay as a result of Washington's expanded commercial ties with Latin America. The petroleum and tannin industries were overwhelmingly controlled by U.S. interests, while the United States also maintained a large share (61 percent) of the meatpacking industry. By 1945 the U.S. share of foreign investments in Paraguay was close to 30 percent. By the end of the war, the United States had become Paraguay's most important economic partner, surpassing the role of Argentina in several key trade and investment areas.

During his official visit to the United States, Morínigo had expressed interest in obtaining economic and technical assistance to explore Paraguay's petroleum reserve potential. The Roosevelt administration did not look favorably on public assistance for this project but encouraged Paraguay to seek assistance from private companies, including the Union Oil Company of California. In early 1944, after Paraguay granted it exclusive rights to explore for oil, a conflict ensued when Standard Oil of New Jersey expressed strong reservations at Union Oil's attempt to monopolize petroleum exploration in Paraguay. The U.S. Embassy intervened directly to settle the dispute. In the meantime, both companies sought to gain the government's favor by promising employment and financial benefits to members of the Morínigo regime if the government intervened. The Paraguayan government stayed out of the conflict as the dispute over petroleum exploration and exploitation in Paraguay remained a matter for the Americans to resolve.

In the area of telecommunications, the U.S. government urged the International Telephone and Telegraph Corporation (ITT) to establish a dominant presence throughout Latin America. The Export-Import Bank provided credits "to enlarge and modernize Latin American facilities." In Paraguay, telephone and radio-telecommunications systems were in the hands of a German-owned company. However, in 1944, as Morínigo made plans to expropriate the German company (to the delight of the U.S. Embassy) the U.S. government feared the Paraguayan government might decide to nationalize the telecommunication system. As a result, Ambassador Willard L. Beaulac wasted no time convincing the Paraguayan government of the technological and financial benefits of obtaining ITT's cooperation in developing a "modern domestic and international telecommunications system in Paraguay." A year later, ITT received the concession and near dominance of Paraguay's telecommunications system.

Working with Pan-American Airways, the United States embarked on a program to construct airports throughout Latin America. Officials in Washington were keenly interested in gaining special concessions for U.S. commercial airlines and exclusive rights, in case of emergency or war, for military aircraft. In Paraguay, Pan-American proceeded to obtain a long-term monopoly over all commercial operations at an airport it agreed to modernize near the Campo Grande military base. As with the petroleum dispute, the U.S. government intervened, forcing Pan-American and Paraguay to sign another agreement that allowed other U.S. airlines, such as Trans-World Airlines, to gain concessions and operate out of the airport that Pan-American was to modernize at no cost to the Paraguayan government. Another snag surfaced when Frente de Guerra officers, particularly Colonels Victoriano Benítez Vera and Pablo Stagni, strongly rejected granting a U.S. company the rights to build and operate such a strategic facility in Paraguay. They tried to convince Morínigo that accepting the contract meant not only subordinating Paraguay to U.S. interests but, more importantly for these pro-German officers, the establishment of a U.S. hub in Paraguay. Morínigo ignored his officers' warnings, hoping that the lure of U.S. economic and military aid would moderate their stance. When Pan-American engineers arrived in August 1942 to inspect the airfield and begin the planning phase of the project, they were surprised and frightened when a group of cavalry officers from Campo Grande (led by Colonel Benítez Vera) fired shots at the engineers, forcing them to flee the area and country and to suspend the project for several weeks. The State Department immediately protested, demanding that Morínigo control his military and recommit his government to completing the airport. An embarrassed Morínigo privately chastised his colonels and assured the U.S. Embassy that "no other interruptions would delay completion of the airport." The new international airport opened for business in September 1944.[30]

Prelude to Civil War: Denazification and Democratization

On 8 June 1943 General Morínigo arrived in the United States on an official state visit. He met President Roosevelt at the White House the next day, marking the first encounter between the heads of state of two countries that were not only so distant from one another geographically but also, until the late 1930s, generally of no great concern or interest to one another's respective governments and people. The Roosevelt-Morínigo handshake at the White House on 9 June confirmed how far relations had come in less than five years, but it also indicated a growing partnership based upon "mutual opportunism and reciprocal exploitation" that contributed to the expansion of relations and, consequently, accretion of U.S. leverage and influence over the next decade.[31] For Washington, the official invitation to have the Paraguayan president visit the United States constituted yet another effective symbolic step in a larger plan to continue wooing Paraguay into the U.S. orbit. For the Morínigo regime, the visit presented an opportunity to enhance the president's legitimacy at home and perhaps gain additional commitments of U.S. economic assistance.

Roosevelt and Morínigo had several private meetings where they discussed a range of issues, including the war in Europe, hemispheric affairs, and bilateral relations. Much time was devoted to the final issue. Roosevelt asked Morínigo why so many Paraguayans not only sympathized with Germany but, in fact, had publicly expressed their admiration for the Axis powers. Morínigo replied that Paraguay's historic ties with European intellectuals and military missions provided part of the explanation, but he insisted that support for the Axis was not political but military and was limited to the respect that some Paraguayan officers had for the Wehrmacht. There was no Nazi influence per se within the Paraguayan military, Morínigo affirmed.[32]

During much of the war, General Morínigo proved skillful in resisting U.S. pressures to restrict Axis activities in Paraguay while simultaneously assuring President Roosevelt that his government solidly favored the Allied cause.[33] Until 1944, the Paraguayan leader failed to close down the German network that used Paraguay as a base of operations and refused U.S. requests that Paraguay deport German Nazi sympathizers to the United States.[34] Indeed, he continued to award contracts to local Axis-owned businesses, openly tolerating the pro-Axis officers in his midst.

Moreover, in March 1944, Foreign Minister Argaña and his Tiempista colleagues in the cabinet resigned under pressure from Frente de Guerra officers. The precipitating issue was Argaña's compliance with the U.S. request that Paraguay not recognize the "profascist" regime of Major Gualberto Villaroel in Bolivia and the extreme nationalist military government in Argentina led by General Edelmiro Farrell and Colonel Juan D. Perón. Colonels Benítez Vera and Stagni strongly objected. In the end, the nationalist military officers got what they had been wanting for some time—the resignation of Tiempista cabinet members.

The Frente's victory was short lived, however, after the Allied landings in Normandy in June 1944. Continued U.S. pressures on Morínigo to stamp out Nazism in Paraguay led to the first serious effort in July–August 1944 to impose restrictions on German political and propagandistic activities and businesses in the country. Morínigo and an increasing number of non-Frente officers worried about ending up on the losing side of the war in Europe. They had no wish to alienate the United States—the emerging global military and economic power that had provided Paraguay with so much in the last few years. Finally, in August 1944, not long after D-day, Willard L. Beaulac, the new U.S. ambassador, arrived in Asunción with specific instructions to use U.S. leverage (i.e., withdraw or deny political support and material assistance) to pressure the Morínigo regime to eliminate all vestiges of Nazism in Paraguay and begin "to restore political liberties, hold new elections, and democratize Paraguay."

Ambassador Beaulac, an astute and aggressive diplomat, became one of the most influential and effective diplomats the United States ever had in Paraguay. His friendship and access to President Morínigo and instructions to do whatever was necessary to democratize Paraguay turned Beaulac into a powerful and influential domestic political participant. Not long after his arrival, the ambassador established a personal relationship with Morínigo (they met quite often) and praised the Morínigo government for the considerable progress achieved in developing Paraguay's infrastructure and economy.[35]

Beaulac was not particularly in favor of coercing the regime too hard on liberalization, not only because of his friendship with the Paraguayan dictator and Foreign Minister Horacio Chiriani (who might lose his job if perceived as kowtowing to U.S. demands), but also, as Beaulac's predecessor Wesley Frost often warned, because the absence of any democratic tradition made the prospect for democracy in Paraguay "exceedingly improbable."[36] Even so, Ambassador Beaulac pushed forward with Washington's policy. During a public ceremony that Morínigo attended at the end of 1944, Beaulac gave a speech that summarized the extensive inroads the Nazis had made in Paraguay. The ambassador worried about government reactions, but to his great surprise, Morínigo soon after began to deport leading Nazis in the country, "confining others in isolated towns, took over and denazified German schools, closed down black-listed firms, and took other helpful steps against Axis interests."[37] In February 1945, unwilling to risk losing U.S. development aid and a seat for Paraguay at the founding of the United Nations, Morínigo declared war on the Axis nations.

After 1945, economic and military aid increasingly became the lever with which the United States pressured Paraguayan politics into a pattern more favorable to U.S. interests. In Paraguay, continued U.S. aid was perceived by the elite as satisfactory compensation for an increased degree of subordination to U.S. leadership in international affairs and interference in domestic matters. It was simply viewed as the price for development aid. Once the denazification process was nearly complete, Beaulac reluctantly undertook a campaign to "encourage democracy . . . and liberal institutions in Paraguay."[38] The ambassador insisted in late 1944 that Morínigo concede a voice to the opposition by permitting it to hold public meetings. By March 1945 Morínigo was being pulled in two opposite directions. Beaulac made no secret that the future availability of U.S. foreign aid for development projects would depend on "the degree of evolution toward a Liberal, democratic government in Paraguay"; on the other hand, authoritarian nationalist officers such as Colonels Benítez Vera and Stagni insisted that the Paraguayan dictator resist U.S. pressure.[39] In their view, liberalization would bring instability and Communist takeover.

As Beaulac and Benítez Vera warred verbally, Morínigo desperately sought to find a middle ground. He tolerated public meetings and political dissent while refusing to hold elections. In the end, the Paraguayan leader's efforts to appease both sides only polarized national politics. In December 1945 the U.S. ambassador met with Morínigo to warn the president that "further United States aid would be related to the progressive democratization of Paraguay [and that] failure to correct the present situation would oblige our Government to withdraw the voluntary cooperation now being given to Paraguay and to refrain from giving additional cooperation."[40] Against the wishes of his officer corps and civilian supporters, the Paraguayan president gave in to U.S. warnings and threats, informing the armed forces in January 1946 that "foreign pressure had become too strong to resist," prompting him to announce his three-point democratization program.[41] In response, Washington signed a reciprocal free trade agreement with Asunción (after Morínigo had resisted doing so for nearly six years) and extended funding for its cooperative agricultural assistance program (STICA), suggesting that additional monies would be forthcoming if the Paraguayan government fulfilled its commitment to restoring freedom of the press and elections for the legislative assembly by the end of 1946.

Between January and June 1946, the United States kept up the pressure. As far as Beaulac was concerned, Morínigo would not stand in the way of liberalization. The threat came from Frente de Guerra officers who were vehemently opposed to the process and capable of subverting it by staging a coup. Although Ambassador Beaulac doubted that Paraguay could have fair and open elections for the legislature, he continued to insist that Morínigo plan for the election and negotiate with the Liberal, Febrerista, and Colorado parties. On the issue of negotiation, the Paraguayan president dragged his feet. Finally, in June 1946, with the support of key officers and the minister of interior, General Amancio Pampliega, a moderate liked by officers of different political persuasions, President Morínigo ousted Frente de Guerra officers from their strategic commands, giving him and Ambassador Beaulac the freedom to pursue aggressively the program of democratization.[42]

Not since the early 1930s had Paraguayans experienced such political and civil freedoms.[43] The press gained unprecedented freedom. Exiles from all political stripes returned, held public meetings, and organized mostly anti-Morínigo marches and rallies. As Paul Lewis described, under the coalition government made up of the military, Febreristas, and Colorados (a creation of the U.S. Embassy, according to Morínigo), "Paraguayan politics were intoxicating." With the loosening of political controls, parties participated in a number of plots and conspiracies to mobilize and strengthen their respective forces in an effort to overthrow the Morínigo government and seize power. Gradually, Morínigo's control slipped away, even as his coalition partners maneuvered against the president and each other. The social and political climate deteriorated rapidly as violence and lawlessness spread. In the meantime, the United States viewed the changes with great satisfaction despite the increasing levels of violence and uncertainty.

By late 1946 and early 1947 it was enough for Beaulac that Frente officers were gone and that the airport was open for U.S. commercial airlines. The State Department was pleased with the formation of the coalition government on the grounds that it would lead to the next phase of legislative elections; however, Beaulac quickly discovered that the Febreristas could not be trusted. He viewed them as "tending toward socialism—even Communist" and prone to demagogic outbursts. On the other hand, the Colorados, specifically party leaders Federico Chaves and Juan Natalicio González (the latter had strong Fascist inclinations), were "held in high regard by United States officials." Chaves was described by the State Department as "staunchly democratic in ideals and actuation," whereas González, who made no secret of his admiration and respect for U.S. leadership, patience, and compassion for its weaker neighbors, was equally viewed by the U.S. Embassy as "serious, thoughtful and decisive."[44]

The 1947 Civil War and the Seeds of Anticommunism

By December 1946 the Morínigo regime was near collapse from inter- and intraparty struggles and fissures within the government as Liberals and Communists strived to create an untenable social situation and precipitate a military overthrow of the coalition government. Political disputes and rallies degenerated into street fights. On 11 February 1947 the Febreristas resigned from the cabinet and called on the military to take over. The Colorados and Morínigo moved swiftly to join forces to form a military-Colorado government, arresting Febreristas while subjugating Liberals and Communists to an aggressive campaign of intimidation and repression. Paraguay was now polarized and at risk of a violent confrontation. In short order, a coalition of Communists, Liberals, and Febreristas launched an insurrection against the Asunción government. Ironically, U.S. pressures to democratize had unintentionally unleashed a destructive civil war that led to Washington's unobtrusive support for Morínigo against forces it perceived to be "suspicious and probably dangerous."

Once the Febreristas' challenge was neutralized, Colorado Party leaders, particularly Federico Chaves, began courting Ambassador Beaulac, trying to impress upon him the desirability of victory and the congruence of interests between Washington and the new government in Asunción: democratic government, inter-American cooperation, foreign investment, and, increasingly, anticommunism. Without the U.S. stamp of approval and access to considerable amounts of material assistance, the likelihood that the Colorados could entrench themselves in power and begin the "Coloradoization" of the regime would diminish. For the United States, Beaulac affirmed, the Colorados appeared to be Paraguay's best chance for democracy and stability.

At the outset of the civil war, the United States did not see communism as an immediate threat to Paraguay or the hemisphere and refused requests for military aid despite the government's constant "warnings" of Communist penetration. A CIA agent (Collins D. Almon) dispatched to Paraguay noted the presence of Communists but downgraded their influence and links to international communism. Nevertheless, government and Colorado Party officials exaggerated the presence of international communism in the rebel camp, which included a significant portion of the Paraguayan armed forces. The government also noted the capture of a Soviet agent who assisted the rebels during a naval uprising to persuade the United States to provide massive and immediate military and economic support to the government.[45]

At one point, Morínigo argued that hemispheric security was at risk if the United States and Brazil did not provide military equipment. The government further claimed that the rebels, whom it called the "triple alliance," were "servants of Moscow" determined to impose a Communist regime in Paraguay. Arms were needed to defend "hemispheric security against the bloody designs of Stalinist imperialism."[46] In a 13 June memorandum to Deputy Secretary of State Dean Acheson and Assistant Secretary of State Spruille Braden, Ambassador Beaulac spoke of a Communist conspiracy in South America determined to discredit Morínigo by using media outlets to accuse the president of being a "ruthless tyrant." The ambassador feared the campaign was having some success, as it seemed to be "influencing our government, making the State Department fearful of being seen as collaborating with the 'tyrant' Morínigo."[47]

Of parallel U.S. concern was the growing friendship between Perón and Morínigo.[48] Assistant Secretary of State Spruille Braden, former ambassador to Argentina and archenemy of the Argentine leader, was particularly dismayed at the prospect of such an alliance. For the Paraguayan government, reaching out to Buenos Aires reflected not only a shared ideological outlook but also a need for political and military support in light of rebel advances and U.S. and Brazilian refusals to intervene. Braden and Acheson refused to approve Ambassador Beaulac's recommendation that the United States provide Morínigo with arms; however, because the State Department had begun to take a more realistic and cautious approach to mending fences with Argentina, Washington was content to accept Argentina's military support of the Morínigo government. Subsequently, Perón funneled arms to the government at a critical moment in the conflict (August 1947) when a rebel assault on Asunción nearly overwhelmed government forces. If not for this decisive support from Buenos Aires, the Morínigo regime would have fallen.

The United States maintained a neutral position during the civil conflict; it had little desire to support a reactionary government while it promoted democratization elsewhere in the hemisphere. The Truman administration wanted to remain within the canons of the Good Neighbor Policy and therefore eschewed intervention. Mounting tensions with the Soviet Union and declaration of the U.S. cold war policy of containment (i.e., the Truman Doctrine) during the same month as the Paraguayan civil war began made the U.S. Embassy sensitive to rebel radicalism and Communist influence. Remaining true to the tenets of the Good Neighbor Policy while making sure the rebels were kept from defeating the Morínigo government required more indirect and discreet forms of intervention, that is, support for the present government. Washington did not object to Argentina supplying arms to the Paraguayan government and worked through diplomatic channels, particularly when the Morínigo government seemed close to defeat, to find a negotiated settlement of the conflict that would prevent a total takeover by the rebels. As Beaulac noted in his refusal to support a Brazilian proposal to create another coalition government with the rebels, "maintaining close relations will be beneficial to continue influencing Morínigo toward adopting constructive democratic reforms."[49]

As the civil war entered its final phase after the failed assault on Asunción by the rebels, the task of economic reconstruction required outside assistance. The Paraguayan government, particularly the Colorados, understood the importance of U.S. political, economic, and military support. In a meeting with Ambassador Beaulac, Minister of Economy Juan Natalicio González noted that in times of growing global uncertainty, "the cornerstone of Paraguayan foreign policy should be maintaining a close and friendly relationship with the United States." Foreign Minister Federico Chaves stated a more public expression of friendship and support for U.S. strategic goals at the historic signing of the Inter-American Treaty of Reciprocal Assistance or Rio Treaty in August 1947. Attempting to fuse Paraguay's national goals with those of the Colorado Party, he informed Secretary of State George Marshall that the Colorados were "a democratic party and a close friend and supporter of the United States." He requested that the United States continue providing much-needed assistance "in the fields of public health, economy and military training," assuring Marshall that in any conflict against communism, "Paraguay would unreservedly stand by the United States."[50]

U.S. Policy and the Roots of Stronismo

Once the civil war ended in a Colorado victory, U.S. attention to Paraguay lessened, increasingly subsumed by a broader containment policy. Washington, of course, was more preoccupied with security challenges in Europe and had little interest initially in devoting resources to Latin America. The Truman administration did favor political stability, of course, and considered the Colorados as the best placed to ensure Paraguay's internal peace. The administration believed that aid and investment would stabilize the economy and perhaps bring order to Paraguay's chaotic political situation. Under President Truman's Point IV program, whereby the United States provided economic and technical assistance to alleviate financial stress and the "lack of scientific advances" in developing countries, U.S. economic assistance between 1947 and 1953 reached $7.2 million, and loans from international organizations, over which the United States had overwhelming influence, came to $6.6 million. This was a considerable amount, given that annual U.S. aid to Latin America during this period averaged less than $30 million. This aid came in the form of technical and financial assistance (STICA) for agriculture, health, animal husbandry, educational programs, and public administration (civil service, budget, taxation, and land management). As Ambassador Howard Tewksbury noted in 1952, "the purpose of our contributions is to achieve a stable and developing economy so that a vacuum does not arise which would have unfortunate economic as well as political repercussions on our long and short term interests in the River Plate endangering the security of the hemisphere, and at the same time to combat any Communist penetration or extension of influence."[51]

But it was not to be. U.S. officials grew impatient and were increasingly exasperated by the highly erratic political environment in Paraguay caused by Colorado factionalism, infighting, and military conniving. The intraparty witch hunts and violence associated with this volatile period of Colorado rule led to the flight of capital and labor, which only exacerbated further Paraguay's unruly situation.[52] Despite their frustration, U.S. officials stuck by the Colorados largely because they feared the alternative was neither viable nor preferable.

By and large, Paraguay remained remote, small, and peripheral to U.S. policymakers. As a result, a comparatively small portion of U.S. effort, personnel, and assistance was channeled to it. Yet, what was minor for the United States was very important for Paraguay. As demonstrated by the government's constant courting of U.S. aid, the United States had acquired the leverage and deference it had been cultivating since the early 1940s. Expanding trade ties demonstrated the importance and pervading influence of U.S. and foreign capital flows during the 1947–54 period.[53] By the early 1950s, the United States had become the second-largest market for Paraguayan exports and the main supplier of its imports. In terms of foreign capital, the United States was second to Argentina as Paraguay's main source of capital, with 25 percent of the total. U.S. investments centered on Paraguay's most important economic sectors: cattle, tanning of leather, and petroleum exploration. Given the size of the Paraguayan economy and the fact that Paraguay had hitherto received little attention and no international aid or significant foreign investments, U.S. economic presence in Paraguay had a substantial impact on Paraguay's economy and government. As the cold war heated up in Korea, Washington increasingly looked for friends and allies in its global fight against communism.[54]

In the late 1940s and early 1950s, Washington's principal concern in Paraguay was not communism but Asunción's close economic and political ties with Perón's Argentina. When Federico Chaves became president after a coup in September 1949, several political leaders belonging to the president's *democrático* faction were admirers of Perón's labor-based, populist government. Against the background of civil war, factionalism, and militarism, Chaves managed to unify the party and bring some political order and stability to the country. However, soon after he was reelected (unopposed) in 1952, a rift began to appear between a pro-Argentine faction led by Epifanio Méndez Fleitas and Finance Minister Guillermo Enciso Velloso, and President Chaves, who was more sympathetic to the United States. In 1950 Chaves aggressively sought to expand relations with the United States and seek Washington's help in obtaining technical and financial assistance from multilateral development agencies. The United States responded reluctantly to the government's overture, suggesting to the president that pro-Argentine influence in his government could impinge on future cooperation and assistance.[55]

Almost as compensation, the United States agreed to establish in 1951 the Joint United States–Paraguayan Commission for Economic Development, one of only two in the hemisphere (the other was with Brazil), its objective being to provide a forum where loans and technical programs could be developed, requested, and supervised. Despite, and perhaps because of, concerns about Peronist influence in the cabinet, the United States used the commission to channel resources to Paraguay between 1950 and 1953, making Paraguay the third-largest recipient of technical assistance programs in Latin America, surpassed only by Brazil and Peru. During this time the Federal Reserve Board sent several technical missions to advise Paraguay on financial and monetary matters and strongly supported a World Bank loan of $5 million for the purchase of agricultural and road-building equipment.

By November 1953, however, Ambassador George Shaw, who in early January had lauded the commission for its "very effective work," expressed in a diplomatic cable to the State Department that the commission was "largely inactive . . . [and] has been considered by the Paraguayan government as little more than a body where requests may be presented with almost a certainty of approval." Ambassador Shaw recommended that the joint commission be downgraded and eventually disbanded. Besides the commission's ineffectiveness, the ambassador's opposition may have reflected other concerns. The U.S. Embassy was particularly displeased by Paraguay's August 1953 signing of a Treaty of Economic Union with Argentina, which President Chaves was forced to sign by the Peronist faction within the Colorado Party. The treaty raised fears in the embassy and Paraguayan army that Argentina would take over Paraguay's economy.

5 Our Man in Asunción: Anticommunism, 1954–1961

In 1954 Paraguay was still relatively unimportant to U.S. foreign policy considerations in Latin America, but it was not neglected. A pro-U.S. government in Asunción could serve as another strong partner supporting U.S. cold war policies and initiatives in Latin America, offering key votes in international organizations, and, if necessary, providing military bases.

The era of U.S. anticommunism in the region began in the early 1950s when Washington decided to make the issue of economic and social reform in Guatemala a test case for its Latin American policy. Arguing that the government of President Jacobo Arbenz not only had links to Soviet bloc countries but also was influenced by Communists committed to nationalizing private property and establishing a regime hostile to democracy and the security of the hemisphere, the United States organized a diplomatic and covert effort to overthrow Arbenz in 1954. From then on, Washington committed itself to eliminating real and imagined internal and external communist threats in the region it believed could threaten U.S. security interests, including access to strategic resources. This commitment was reinforced after the radicalization of the Cuban Revolution and establishment of a pro–Soviet Union, Marxist-Leninist regime in Havana.

Our Man: General Alfredo Stroessner Matiauda

In May 1954, as the United States successfully helped organize a plot to remove the Arbenz government, General Alfredo Stroessner in Paraguay staged a coup, without U.S. knowledge, against the government of President Federico Chaves. Not long after Stroessner's coup, relations between the United States and Paraguay entered an unprecedented phase of asymmetrical cooperation founded upon a convergence of cold war security interests.[1]

Perhaps no single individual or actor was more important in U.S.-Paraguayan relations during the course of the cold war than General Alfredo Stroessner Matiauda. Paraguay's long tradition of personalism and autocratic rule coupled with the semitotalitarian nature of the regime emphasized the role of the *caudillo* or executive in all public policy matters, including relations with the United States.

Stroessner was not a charismatic figure, as many caudillos of his time were. Unlike many of his flamboyant contemporaries, such as Perón, Castro, and Trujillo, he was reserved and mild mannered, which helped him get a long way in politics, as supposedly clever Paraguayan politicians constantly underestimated him until it was too late. He was well respected by his soldiers for his courage and professionalism, which also helped him in his military and political career, particularly at key crisis moments when he was most vulnerable. According to Richard Bourne and Anibal Miranda, Stroessner personified discipline and exemplified the qualities of the traditional Latin caudillo: courage, toughness, cunning, and boldness. He was an astute, devious, and calculating leader, often changing sides (or loyalties) or discarding political allies when they were no longer useful in his struggle to achieve and consolidate political power.

Born in Encarnación in 1912, son of a strict German immigrant father and a Paraguayan woman, Alfredo Stroessner entered the military at the young age of sixteen. Early in his military career he distinguished himself as an artillery officer in the Chaco War, fighting bravely, according to official biographies, in the battles of Boquerón, Nanawa, and El Carmen.[2] He received several medals for bravery, including the Chaco Cross medal for his performance at El Carmen. After the war, he continued to rise in the military hierarchy, dedicating himself to advanced training while staying out of the confusing politics of the Franco and Estigarribia regimes. In 1940 he reached the rank of major and was selected to attend special artillery training at the Brazilian Army College. According to his Brazilian instructors, Stroessner proved to be a capable student demonstrating persistence, discipline, and hard work. He gained an appreciation and respect for the Brazilian defense establishment and formed friendships with several key Brazilian military officers, some of them close to U.S. officers such as Captain Vernon Walters. These relationships with Brazilian officers and Rio de Janeiro's close alliance with the United States proved critical to Stroessner's military and political career and in shaping his strategic view of the world and Paraguay's place in the Southern Cone.

During much of the 1940s, Stroessner stayed largely out of Paraguay's chaotic politics, remaining "discreet and very circumspect." He dedicated himself to the military profession, advancing to the rank of colonel by 1948 after serving as an artillery instructor, student of the Superior War College, and commander of the General Brugez Regiment, Paraguay's chief artillery unit. By the time Stroessner became a lieutenant colonel in 1945, it was impossible for any high-ranking officer in Paraguay's highly politicized military to stay out of politics. Professional advancement and politics, particularly that associated with the Colorado Party, were closely intertwined.

In the 1947 civil war, Stroessner had to choose sides and, after much vacillation, threw his lot in with the government of General Higinio Morínigo. This was a risky decision since more than 75 percent of the officer corps had gone over to the rebel side, but his taste for order, hierarchy, authority, and respect for the chain of command prompted him to support the government. Also, there is some indication that Stroessner's decision was based on a calculated risk: if the government defeated the rebels, he would be in a position to participate in an extensive purging of the armed forces, allowing him to rise up the ranks quickly.

Stroessner's role in preventing the insurgents from taking control of Asunción helped the government overcome a massive offensive from a coalition of rebel forces made up of Liberals, Febreristas, and Communists. This event catapulted Stroessner to prominence within the military and Colorado Party. From that point on, Stroessner focused his attention and ambitions on politics. He proved to be an adept schemer, a skillful and ruthless Machiavellian, constantly plotting against every president under whom he served between 1947 and 1954. After a short period in exile in Brazil (1948) for conspiring, Stroessner returned to Paraguay to lead troops against his former patron General Raimundo Rólon. In 1949 he was promoted to brigadier general, and in 1951, after helping President Federico Chaves and the *democráticos* consolidate control over the Colorado Party and armed forces, he was promoted to commander in chief of the armed forces.

Between 1951 and 1954, Stroessner turned his attention to strengthening international ties while working within the government and military to undermine President Chaves. As with politics prior to 1947, there is no evidence that Stroessner showed much interest in or knowledge of international relations before 1951. Soon after becoming commander in chief, he began to express interest in being courted by Paraguay's neighbors. In 1951 he was invited by Juan D. Perón to visit Argentina to tour military facilities and visit with the president and the chiefs of the armed forces. He also attended a presidential inauguration in Uruguay as his government's representative and visited Brazil on two occasions, once as a guest of the Brazilian government and the other time invited by the military for "talks" and to participate in several official functions. In 1953 he was awarded with the Argentine Order of Military Merit and the Brazilian Order of Military Merit. Stroessner understood the importance of reaching out and establishing contacts with Paraguay's powerful neighbors, who often played a role in the country's rough-and-tumble politics. They in turn saw Stroessner as a force to be reckoned with, as someone who must be scrutinized and courted.

This reality was not lost on the United States. Beginning in the early 1950s, the United States, as it did with many Latin American general officers, began to cultivate a relationship with Stroessner. His most important contact of those years was with the U.S. military. Stroessner graduated from a general staff course at Ft. Leavenworth, and in May–June 1953, U.S. Army secretary Robert T. Stevens invited Stroessner to tour several military facilities in the United States. He was entertained and given the "royal" treatment by General Withers A. Burress, head of the First Army Corps, when Stroessner visited the headquarters on Governor's Island. He also visited the Panama Canal Zone and met with the general staff of the United States Caribbean and Southern Defense Command. Stroessner made great use of his visit to the United States, establishing contacts in the U.S. military and government that would be very useful in the future.

U.S. notice of Paraguay increased sharply after the coup of General Alfredo Stroessner in 1954. Like other cold war dictatorships—Somoza, Pinochet, and Central American militaries—Stroessner identified with the West and adopted the U.S. National Security Doctrine that emphasized the use of security and armed forces to counter all internal and external "communist threats"—the lever used by Latin American dictators to suppress all opposition, while ensuring U.S. political and economic support, as a means of extending the life of the regime. Between 1954 and 1955 it was not clear to Stroessner, as he navigated through the difficult and troubled waters of Paraguay's domestic politics and international relations, where he could get international support. However, once the United States seemed willing to offer much-needed political and material support, the regime expressed full support for the Truman Doctrine, showing unequivocal friendship and support for U.S. anticommunism and counterinsurgency policy in Latin America. General Stroessner also proved to be an effective military officer and political leader who could be relied upon to maintain stability in Paraguay and support for anticommunism abroad. His decision to reorient Paraguay's foreign policy away from the traditional preference and concentration of relations with Argentina and toward greater economic and strategic integration with Brazil, a U.S. ally and strategic partner in the Southern Cone, was most appealing to government and military officials in Washington.

The Stronato and Foreign Policy

Stroessner's personalist-authoritarian regime—the Stronato—was not an aberration of Paraguayan political history, but a more sophisticated, modern, and institutionalized form of autocratic rule in which the binding norms and relations of bureaucratic state administration are constantly subverted by the personal fiat of the ruler. Stroessner's regime emerged, survived, and prospered because of a unique conjunction of favorable domestic and international influences. When he came to power in May 1954, many Colorados and a segment of the armed forces welcomed and supported the coup in the belief that the young general would stabilize the country and end interparty fighting. Those who supported the coup thought they could buy time and manipulate Stroessner. They were mistaken. Stroessner skillfully penetrated and seized control of the two most powerful institutions in Paraguay at the time: the Colorado Party and the armed forces. Between 1954 and 1959, Stroessner consolidated his party base by purging many factional leaders who contested his power, such as the popular Méndez Fleitas (who was forced into exile), and transformed the institution into the official and domesticated party of the regime. Ultimately, the Colorado Party became a "highly effective political machine" with an "extensive network of branches (*seccionales*) throughout the country that served as a major system of patronage" as well as a mechanism for the surveillance of political opposition. In short, Stroessner converted the party into a "tool to legitimize his regime, an instrument to extend his own power and a mass-based party that could be used to mobilize support and repress opposition."[3]

Stroessner retained the post of commander in chief, which allowed him to intervene personally in promotions and placement and gradually purge the police and the armed forces of elements loyal or sympathetic to certain factions of the Colorado Party, particularly those aligned with Méndez Fleitas. He used increased military budgets, forced retirements, promotion, and access to economic privileges to bring the military under his control. Stroessner's intimate knowledge of the military's organization and personnel helped him make structural changes that discouraged cliques and conspiracies. Disloyal officers were persecuted, and loyalty was rewarded with professional advancement and economic privileges, such as control of lucrative sinecures in state monopolies and access to land and the contraband trade. In other words, the armed forces (and the Colorado Party) were neutralized and controlled by a system of persecution and repression, retirement, co-option, and patronage that ultimately allowed Stroessner to penetrate and politicize the military, transforming it into an instrument and pillar of his power.

Stroessner's support from significant elements of the Paraguayan population that he was able to garner in the period 1954–59 should not be discounted. Unlike many of his predecessors, Stroessner delivered on his promises for internal peace, greater financial stability, and infrastructure modernization financed by U.S. aid. His policies were particularly popular among elites, particularly the business sector and Paraguayan landowners, who were pleased and impressed with Stroessner's ability to restore political and economic stability and attract foreign investments. Finally, Stroessner was particularly adept at cultivating the countryside by strengthening the Colorado Party's hold over the rural areas, mostly through patronage and the utilization of the party symbols and sentiments to "recruit" adherents among the peasants.

Apart from the internal structures of power created by the regime of General Alfredo Stroessner over the span of three decades, another important component of the regime's consolidation and maintenance was the international system and the legitimacy and economic support provided by key external actors, namely Brazil and the United States. Stroessner's foreign policy approach is best described as benign isolation. This approach consisted of discriminating and diversifying economic and commercial relations with select states, necessary in overcoming Paraguay's underdevelopment and geopolitical prisonality, while deliberately maintaining a "low profile" in order to minimize criticism and pass unnoticed under the facade of "representative democracy."[4]

Although Stroessner did not plan a political alliance with the United States from the beginning, offers of material and political support from the superpower, coupled with the troubles and the eventual collapse of Argentine president Perón's government, provided the Paraguayan caudillo with few options other than to take advantage of what the United States and its anti-Communist partner, Brazil, were willing to offer. Stroessner and his close advisers, particularly Foreign Minister Raúl Sapena Pastor (1956–76) and Ezequiel González Alsina, understood that Washington's economic and diplomatic support could be counted on if Paraguay became a fearless defender of the U.S. containment policy.

Stroessner became a steadfast anti-Communist, following the U.S. position on all matters in return for aid and legitimacy. Nationalism and anticommunism characterized the Stroessner era, and Washington had no quarrel with his variety of nationalism. In defining Paraguayan foreign policy and the centrality of relations with the United States, Stroessner stated in a 1955 letter to President Eisenhower, "in this struggle between two types of lives and concepts of human values, my government gives its enthusiastic and spontaneous support to the United States for its correct and positive role in protecting civilization."[5] He repeated the same message twenty-two years later, stating that "in international policy, in general, the Government of Paraguay gives decided support to the United States, as leader of the free world in its fight against international communism, and we share with this great nation the ideals of justice, peace, rights and liberty so that the world in which we live in can be more secure and have a more collective and individual guarantees."[6]

Paraguay consistently voted with the United States in the United Nations and the Organization of American States. In 1955, Ambassador Guillermo Enciso, Paraguay's ambassador to the United States, informed Deputy Assistant Secretary of State for Inter-American Affairs Cecil B. Lyon "that the Paraguayan Delegation in the UN in New York looked to the United States Delegation for guidance in maintaining the Paraguayan position identical to that of the United States." In 1963, Stroessner emphasized Paraguay's commitment to follow U.S. leadership when he stated, "the identification of our foreign policy with that of this country (United States) allows the exercise of one allied action in international organisms, especially in that which concerns our anticommunist posture."[7] Beyond symbolic demonstration of support for U.S. foreign policy, Stroessner offered, as he said during a meeting with President Eisenhower in Panama (1956), "Paraguayans and land."

In 1965 Asunción supported and provided a unit of military police to the U.S. intervention in the Dominican Republic and in 1968 offered to provide the United States with troops to fight in Vietnam. In terms of "land," in 1955 Defense Minister Herminio Morínigo told State Department officials that the Stroessner government would sign an agreement permitting the United States to build an air force base in Paraguay for the continent's defense.[8]

In return for this almost unconditional support, the United States provided exactly what Stroessner had hoped for to prop up his repressive regime: aid and legitimacy. In addition to public and diplomatic pronouncements of support, which translated into legitimacy, Stroessner wanted the United States to express its appreciation by offering material rewards in the form of economic aid, technical assistance, loans, grants, foreign investments, military security assistance, and trade concessions. In turn, much of this economic assistance, invested to modernize Paraguay's infrastructure, was used as a political instrument by which the government procured a degree of legitimacy for itself. In other words, public works projects financed by the United States were skillfully publicized as "accomplishments" of the government. Therefore, the U.S. policy toward Paraguay was characterized by its willingness to serve the Stroessner regime's objectives (i.e., strengthen its domestic position) as long as Asunción remained a faithful bastion of anticommunism in South America. In the end, bilateral relations during the 1950s and 1960s were "conditioned by a complementarity of security interests, and Asunción's desire for development-military assistance and international legitimacy."[9]

The Critical Years: Ambassadors and Aid

Perhaps at no time in postwar U.S.-Paraguayan relations was the relationship so close and cordial as during the Eisenhower administration. Between 1954 and 1960, when Stroessner faced the greatest threat from internal and external enemies, Washington's economic, political, and military support proved central to the survival and consolidation of the regime. The density of the relationship is exemplified by the unprecedented number of conventions and agreements signed by both countries to enhance cooperation and U.S. assistance on programs of great importance to Paraguay's political stability and economic development, such as agriculture, health, livestock, educational training and exchange, modernization of infrastructure, financial stabilization, and military aid.[10] The United States supplied arms to Stroessner's Paraguay, expanded the presence of military advisers in Asunción, and welcomed Paraguayan officers to training facilities in the United States—all in the name of anticommunism and particularly for antisubversive purposes. Within the parameters of U.S. hemispheric security strategy, the armed forces of Paraguay (and Latin America) were privileged as the institution best suited to maintain stability and fend off Communist threats, making Paraguay a strong asset in the Southern Cone. Stroessner understood U.S. priorities and the importance of the northern protector in helping him maintain political power.

The Eisenhower administration sent a clear message when it chose three noncareer appointees, recognized for their anti-Communist credentials, as U.S. ambassadors to Asunción. Not since Ambassador Findley B. Howard in the late 1930s had a noncareer appointee been named ambassador to Asunción. The three ambassadors, Vice Admiral (Retired) Arthur A. Ageton (1954–57), William Ploeser (1957–59), and Harry F. Stimpson (1959–61), were not only pivotal in the expansion and strengthening of bilateral ties but also played important roles as domestic and international champions of the regime at a time when Stroessner faced so many challenges to his power, particularly from within the Colorado Party (i.e., Epifanio Méndez Fleitas) and from Argentina. These U.S. representatives seemed to be doing Stroessner's bidding in Washington as they often lobbied the White House and State Department to meet the regime's request for financial and military support. As a result, these diplomats exercised a tremendous amount of influence in Paraguay's domestic affairs, providing Stroessner with constant advice on all matters including the structure of the cabinet, economic policy, and military promotion. Stroessner often referred to Ageton or Ploeser as "the most influential member of my cabinet."

The U.S. Embassy took an interest in Méndez Fleitas. Many embassy reports stressed Méndez Fleitas's alleged association with Communists and Peronists. It did not help that Méndez Fleitas was constantly engaged in conspiring to destabilize Paraguay and overthrow the Stroessner regime. Ageton distrusted Méndez Fleitas, as Stroessner did, and often assured the Paraguayan dictator that the United States would not object to his efforts to purge the Colorado Party and military of *epifanistas*.[11] The year 1955 was a particularly critical and tense time in Paraguay. Intraparty infighting was intense, and rumors of military conspiracies were rampant. Stroessner was still relatively weak and vulnerable to the intense party infighting and attempts by factions to curry favor from sectors within the armed forces willing to overthrow the regime. The U.S. decision to stand unequivocally behind Stroessner, providing political support and security assistance, helped strengthen the dictator's position against his opponents within the party and military. Ambassador Ageton repeatedly warned the president that his political enemy Méndez Fleitas and his close ties to Argentine president Juan Perón and Argentina represented a threat to the regime and security of Paraguay and, in turn, a threat to U.S. interests in the region. The opportunity came when President Perón was removed from office in September by a military coup and was exiled for a brief time in Paraguay. In order to avoid tensions with the new Argentine government while eliminating a domestic political threat, Stroessner forced Perón to leave the country and pushed a politically debilitated Méndez Fleitas and his followers out of the party. By early 1956, Méndez Fleitas was exiled and his faction purged from the party along with elements within the military sympathetic to the *epifanistas*. Subsequently, dissident factions within the party were co-opted or eradicated, allowing Stroessner to gain control of the party.

The ambassador understood that obtaining economic and military assistance not only strengthened the position of Stroessner but also provided the U.S. Embassy with the leverage to influence domestic politics. The dictator accepted if not welcomed the ambassador's meddling, as it proved valuable to Stroessner's political objectives. During the ambassador's tenure, the embassy always offered its preferences for cabinet appointments and military promotion, helping to sow a network of political and military allies loyal to Stroessner and committed to U.S. objectives. One example of U.S. influence and Stroessner's deference to embassy preferences was when Stroessner decided to restructure the cabinet in May 1956; he presented the list of candidates to the embassy for its stamp of approval before announcing it publicly. In return, Washington reacted immediately to Stroessner's needs, such as the approval of a much-needed $7.2 million credit to Paraguay from the Export-Import Bank and Loan Development Fund in September 1954.[12] This credit was granted to provide financing to purchase U.S. equipment and supplies for the construction and operation of a water supply system. Just four months after the coup, the money came at a critical moment for the regime. As Anibal Miranda notes, for "cash-strapped Paraguay, withholding or granting a relatively large package—$7 million was a lot of money in those days—amounted to either toppling or effectively propping up a beleaguered government." The United States was acquiring significant leverage.

Washington was particularly interested in strengthening ties with the Paraguayan military and did so by providing military aid, training, equipment, and security assistance to the Paraguayan government. According to one account, soon after the coup Stroessner and some of his military cohorts held secret meetings with U.S. North American Strategic Command officers, the first in Lima, Peru (June), and the second (August) in Ft. Mariscal Estagarribia (Chaco region) with the presence of Brazilian general staff officers.[13] Also, several U.S. military delegations visited Asunción in the short period after Stroessner came to power, reinforcing the significance given to the military dimension of bilateral relations. In March 1955, Major General Robert Douglass, head of the U.S. delegation to the Inter-American Defense Board, met with several military officials, including Minister of Defense Higinio Morínigo and President Stroessner. According to an embassy cable informing the State Department of the visit, "Paraguayan military officials were deeply impressed and pleased with the visit and repeatedly expressed gratitude for the visit." In October 1955, the Program Committee for Military Defense Assistance, led by Colonel Neil

Wallace, visited Asunción to discuss the issue of military assistance. During the meeting, attended by Ambassador Ageton, the minister of defense, General Morínigo, reminded U.S. officials of the strategic importance of Paraguay and its firm support for United States security objectives in the region. He followed his request with an offer to build, with U.S. assistance, an air base in Paraguay for the defense of the continent. Ambassador Ageton responded that he would work hard to meet some of the government's requests. Finally, in July 1955, after several years of renegotiation and delay from some in the State Department who questioned the benefits of the program, the United States Military Mission (U.S. Army and Air Force) was extended and expanded. The appointment of Ambassador Ageton in July facilitated and accelerated approval of the program. In addition to training, the United States provided small arms, munitions, communications gear, three C-47 aircraft, spare parts, and security and police training.

In 1955 the United States helped create the Service of Political Intelligence within the Ministry of Interior, assigning a U.S. "expert in anti-communist affairs" who provided technical training and support. Paraguay also sent police officers to the International Police Academy in Washington, where they learned modern counterintelligence methods.[14] Cooperation between the embassy and military intelligence was particularly intense in 1954 and 1955 when Stroessner was maneuvering against factions within the party and armed forces to gain control. For example, during this period Lieutenant Colonel Esteban López Martínez, head of Paraguayan military intelligence, kept the U.S. Army mission constantly informed of Méndez Fleitas's efforts to undermine Stroessner's support in the military by catering to young officers with "favors and import permits" while he was president of the Central Bank.[15]

Chief of Police Edgar L. Ynsfrán, who subsequently became minister of interior, was a frequent visitor to the U.S. Embassy; he was effective in keeping the fires of anticommunism and anti-epifanismo alive and central to U.S.–Paraguayan relations during this period. Ynsfrán was one of the most skillful, energetic, and brutal subordinates Stroessner ever had. He also helped create a vast and effective internal security apparatus that exemplified his knack for vigilance, violence, and efficiency. The United States provided technical assistance and shared intelligence with Stroessner's able and influential adviser. Ynsfrán, in turn, provided what the embassy considered valuable information concerning domestic politics and internal security. For example, Law No. 294, "Defense of Democracy" (promulgated in October 1955), legalized searches and arrests without warrants and allowed the president to suspend other constitutional guarantees in case of threats to "representative democracy" from Communists (broadly interpreted). Finally, U.S. assistance helped Stroessner and Ynsfrán build coercive machinery that proved efficient in repressing, if not obliterating, competitors within the Colorado Party, in the military, and in the Liberal, Febrerista, and Communist parties.

Not long after Ambassador Ageton left his post on 10 April 1957, Roy Rubottom was sworn in as the new assistant secretary of state for inter-American affairs (June 1957). On 10–12 August he visited Asunción on the invitation of the Paraguayan government, stopping there en route to an economic conference in Buenos Aires. Rubottom knew Paraguay well; he had been U.S. naval attaché to Paraguay twelve years prior. During his time as attaché in Asunción, he established friendly relations with many Paraguayan leaders, including Stroessner's principal diplomat, Foreign Minister Sapena Pastor, whom he met at the Rotary Club of Asunción. Rubottom was known for his anticommunism, but unlike many in the administration, he did not necessarily believe that the answer to instability and communism was support for authoritarian rule. He learned quickly upon his arrival in Asunción that the Paraguayan government was not shy about asking for exorbitant amounts of economic aid. In a confidential memorandum about his visit to Paraguay, Rubottom expressed his near desperation and exhaustion with the Paraguayan government's substantial and unrelenting requests for aid. During his meeting with Stroessner, the Paraguayan caudillo provided a laundry list of projects requiring U.S. credits and loans, including completing the construction of the Trans-Chaco Road, finishing the asphalting of the highway from Coronel Oviedo to Puerto Presidente Stroessner, building an aircraft maintenance base, supporting Paraguayan applications for loans to the Export-Import Bank and the World Bank to build roads and purchase grain storage facilities and sugar-refining equipment; acquiring six hundred tractors for agricultural development; financing a pipeline and refinery; and additional PL-480 (Food for Peace) financial assistance. The total amount desired was more than $23 million. Rubottom offered little encouragement for approval, but Asunción continued to make its case for more assistance from the U.S. government.

When Ambassador Walter Ploeser arrived in November 1957, the issues confronting the Stroessner regime were more economic than political. Stroessner had largely penetrated and consolidated control over the Colorado Party and armed forces, though the work of transforming society and purging opposition elements from key organizations continued. But the critical issues challenging the regime were inflation, foreign exchange instability, and economic recession. Ambassador Ploeser's background and contacts were in business and politics, since he had served as a lobbyist and U.S. representative for the Twelfth Congressional District of Missouri (1941–49). Since World War II, when the USSR and United States were allies, Ploeser had always expressed a deep skepticism of the Soviet Union. The former congressman was also suspicious of Argentina and the Peronists who he believed were committed to challenging U.S. interests in the Southern Cone. Stroessner liked Ploeser. The ambassador often defended Stroessner against those in the State Department who were uncomfortable supporting a regime that was becoming increasingly tyrannical.

Immediately upon arrival in Asunción, Ambassador Ploeser went to work on stabilizing the economy. He delegated matters related to the military to the U.S. military mission in Asunción. Once the contract for the military mission was renewed and expanded in late 1958 (thanks to Ambassador Ploeser's lobbying), the U.S. defense attaché assumed a greater role in managing relations with the Paraguayan armed forces, while the ambassador concentrated on seeking development aid, loans, credits, and private investments for Paraguay. He believed that political stability, the key U.S. concern in Paraguay, was linked to economic development. He often worked closely with government economic officials, advising them and Stroessner on the need to take necessary policy measures. For instance, the ambassador played a central role in monitoring and advising the government on the implementation of the 1957 stabilization program. The ambassador and Stroessner even created an informal working group to discuss Paraguay's economic situation and determine appropriate measures to take, including requesting economic aid from the United States.

In fact, it is not an exaggeration to say that Ploeser worked as an unpaid lobbyist of the Paraguayan government. For example, during one of his trips to the United States he urged the World Bank to reduce its interest rates on loans to Paraguay and interested the institution in providing funds for the Paraguay Central Railway Company. He also contacted several U.S. investors, including Standard Oil of New Jersey, about investing in infrastructure projects in Paraguay. The ambassador was particularly successful in convincing the First National City Bank of New York to open a branch in Paraguay.

In early May 1958 Vice President Richard Nixon visited Asunción during his ill-received "goodwill" tour of eight South American countries. In Argentina, Bolivia, Peru, Uruguay, and Venezuela he was greeted by thousands of demonstrators protesting U.S. economic policy and support for dictatorships in Latin America. In Paraguay, on the other hand, the government and hundreds of Paraguayans lined the streets to welcome the vice president. There were no public protests or any expression of anti-Americanism in the press or political circles in Paraguay, unlike what the vice president experienced in other countries during his tour. Nixon clearly felt at home in Paraguay and appreciative of the country's hospitality and support for U.S. strategic objectives; he stated, "in the field of international affairs I do not know of any other nation which has risen more strongly against the threat of communism and this is one reason why I feel especially happy here." Nixon's visit and public statements were greatly valued by Stroessner, who faced growing opposition from labor, exiled Colorados and Liberals, and remaining dissident groups within the Colorado Party that were not pleased with the way the Paraguayan caudillo manipulated the party and imposed his will on the February general election, where he was elected for a full second term. Moreover, insurgent groups had begun to conduct hit-and-run operations across the border from Argentina, and Stroessner needed Nixon's stamp of approval to unite the Colorado Party and military against all real and imagined internal and external threats.

From a symbolic standpoint, the Nixon visit could not have come at a better time for the regime. By late 1959, when the new U.S. ambassador—Harry Stimpson—arrived, Washington's enthusiasm for Latin American dictators diminished. Stimpson proved less supportive of the regime but remained convinced that Stroessner was the best option available. This was particularly significant in the late 1950s when the regime faced criticism for its use of state violence against opponents. Stimpson expressed repeatedly that he considered the state of siege and the murder of political prisoners during the 1959–61 counterinsurgency an internal matter for which he had nothing to do or say. This new policy of nonintervention can be considered, at best, inconsistent.

Ambassador Stimpson faced a number of other challenges during his tenure, including government corruption and diversion of U.S. funds, specifically those provided for the 1959 stabilization program, to undisclosed "projects." The embassy also continued to closely monitor operations by small guerrilla groups that were crossing the border from Argentina and Brazil and attacking police stations and government posts in hit-and-run attacks. Ambassador Stimpson also inaugurated the new U.S. Embassy facility in 1960, located on a large lot on Mariscal López Street, across the street from Mburuvicha Roga, the presidential residence.

If anything, by the end of the 1950s, the United States and Paraguay had consummated a cold war "marriage of convenience." During the critical years between 1954 and 1961, when Stroessner was consolidating his regime, the total U.S. aid package (excluding military aid) plus loans via U.S.-controlled international banking institutions reached $53.2 million (representing 2.73 percent of GDP), an average of more than $6 million per year. This is a considerable amount when one considers that the total Paraguayan state budget for 1959 was $21 million.[16] Paraguay was among the top three recipients of U.S. aid in Latin

America during this period. In comparative terms, total U.S. aid to Paraguay before 1954 amounted to less than $10 million. The regime was skillful in the political use of U.S. aid. Through the use of effective propaganda, U.S.-financed projects (i.e., roads, airport, water, and sanitation) were transformed into government-delivered progress. Some of these projects financed by the United States were quite popular because of their immediate impact on people's lives. Paraguayans became quite accustomed to and grateful for the impact of U.S. aid, which Stroessner used to finance the patronage and corruption necessary to retain the loyalty of military and Colorado Party officials: the pillars of his patrimonial kleptocracy. In terms of military aid, during the 1954–59 period total aid amounted to close to $10 million. During 1959–61, when the regime faced several minor insurgencies, aid in the form of trucks, small arms, light artillery, munitions, and training amounted to nearly $5 million. It is hard to imagine how the Stroessner regime, after so many previous governments before were unable to overcome lesser political and economic challenges, could have survived and consolidated without the political, economic, and military support provided by Washington.

U.S. aid was significant and vital, but it was only 30–40 percent of the total requested by Paraguay during this period. According to an estimate of State Department documents, the total amount of economic assistance (loans, grants, credits) requested by the Paraguayan government between 1954 and 1959 was close to $120 million. Military aid requests amounted to approximately $75 million. In January 1959, even Ambassador Ploeser noted that "persistent requests from the Paraguayan government for United States assistance has reached a massive and unrealistic level." Repeatedly, U.S. officials expressed "exhaustion" at the constant requests and "frustration" at the limited financial and economic results of some U.S. aid programs. However, despite the squandering of some resources, the United States continued to provide the regime with loans and credits. In 1954–55 most aid requests were met, a decision the Paraguayans construed as not only unconditional but, as Ambassador Ageton noted alarmingly, "unrestricted in terms of available resources." It did not matter that many U.S. monies were being used for political reasons rather than for development and alleviating poverty.

Not all aid was squandered. Economic assistance programs directly managed by the United States or international lending institutions, such as internal construction and financial stabilization, were largely used for the expressed purposes. The guaraní was stabilized, and road building and modernization of Paraguay's infrastructure were important tangible results of these programs. Nonetheless, assistance programs managed by the Paraguayan government were mostly channeled into a vast prebendary system used by Stroessner to co-opt and corrupt key party and military officials who ultimately became the dictator's cronies. Therefore, obtaining U.S. financial assistance was so central to regime survival and consolidation that it practically turned the regime's interlocutors in Washington (and Paraguayan foreign ministry) into "addicts" of U.S. aid, as a Paraguayan desk officer at the State Department described.

On two separate occasions, Paraguayan officials made veiled threats that if U.S. aid were not forthcoming in the amounts requested, Paraguay would seek alternatives, including Soviet bloc countries. In 1958, Foreign Minister Sapena Pastor told Assistant Secretary Roy Rubottom that if the United States continued providing aid to Bolivia while rejecting requests from the Paraguayan government, this might force Paraguay to turn to Soviet bloc countries. In December 1959, Vice-Minister Luis Ramírez Boettner repeated the threat, informing Philip Burnett, first secretary of the U.S Embassy, that due to delays of promised aid from the United Nations and the United States, Paraguay would explore other sources, including an offer from the Soviets that all aid requested from Asunción would be provided without conditions.[17] The U.S. government's response was "to put forcefully to Paraguayan officials the position that efforts to play East vs. West were inappropriate." Despite these "misunderstandings," relations strengthened and expanded on the basis of an exchange of aid for alliance.

All the while, Stroessner used the "Washington connection" to strengthen his political control. His ambassadors in Washington during this period were largely powerful political figures within the Colorado

Party, sent to the United States, not so much because of their diplomatic talents or close ties to El Segundo Reconstructor, but as a way for the dictator to keep rivals and leaders of party factions away and distracted as he took control of the party. Stroessner sent many political opponents, particularly heads of factions, to diplomatic posts in Europe and Latin America, facilitating his efforts to unite and transform the party into an instrument of his power. The Colorado politicos quietly and graciously accepted being co-opted, if not exiled, to the comfortable and prestigious post of ambassador to the United States. They proved to be effective representatives of the regime in Washington, aggressively pursuing two key objectives as established by Asunción: first, aggressively seek economic, military, and political support; second, remind the U.S. government and public of Paraguay's friendship and commitment to U.S. cold war objectives. State Department documents reveal that the ambassadors were forceful and eloquent interlocutors of the Paraguayan government, each following the same blueprint in meetings with State Department officials: express gratitude for previous support, reiterate Paraguay's commitment to anticommunism and U.S. strategic objectives, and warn about, if not exaggerate, the Communist threat or influence in the country before making any request for economic or military assistance.

Stroessner cultivated President Eisenhower at the Commemorative Meeting of American Presidents in Panama (July 1956). A private exchange was critical because of the legitimacy it would bestow on Stroessner and his government at a time when he faced criticism at home and abroad. During the meeting Stroessner did much of the talking and fawning. He was obsequious in his tone and language. He placed Paraguay's two great resources—Paraguayans and land—at the disposal of the United States in its effort to defeat global communism. Stroessner described Paraguay's position in the world political situation as "one of open and decided support of the United States of America" in international relations and in its struggle against international communism. The Paraguayan president thanked Eisenhower for a technical assistance program that was of great help in the fields of health, education, and agriculture. Also, Stroessner politely brought up an issue that had been expressed by other Paraguayan officials concerning the inequity in assistance provided to Bolivia and Paraguay. President Eisenhower mentioned that Bolivia had several acute problems; Stroessner acknowledged this but said he would still like to see some parity. The meeting ended with each expressing his thanks for the meeting and each other's expression of support.

In a subsequent memorandum to President Eisenhower, Stroessner reiterated the same points made during the meeting, particularly anticommunism and parity in aid. In an effort to obtain more economic development aid, Stroessner stated that the way to combat communism was "by solving the problems and raising the standards of living of the peoples." He explained Paraguay's efforts to attain economic independence and described the Paraguayan economic development program. By linking communism to underdevelopment, Stroessner was shrewdly attempting to obtain economic aid from the United States by raising the specter of the Communist threat. Between 1954 and 1960, Eisenhower and Stroessner exchanged a total of three memoranda; in each Stroessner prefaced all requests for economic aid and/or military equipment, particularly aircraft, with reference to Paraguay's "friendship and invaluable support for the United States in all international matters." This was followed by an exaggerated emphasis on the nation's vulnerabilities to Communist penetration because of its underdevelopment and limited military resources and equipment. The Stroessner regime acquired a talent for subtle extortion and fear mongering.

Handshake and the Press

Elsewhere, the prospect for dictators did not appear promising. By the late 1950s, South America had entered what Tad Szulc described in 1959 as the "twilight of the tyrants."[18] Democratic governments replaced fraying dictatorships in Argentina (Juan D. Perón), Brazil (Getulio Vargas), Colombia (Gustavo Rojas Pinilla), Peru (Manuel Odría), and Venezuela (Marcos Pérez Jiménez), making Stroessner's Paraguay the sole dictatorship in South America. The economic recession of the post–Korean War period coupled with a loss of support from key political actors, namely military and economic elites, contributed to the wave of democratization. The United States played no significant role in pressuring these authoritarian regimes to leave but did welcome the rise of elected leaders in South America. Particularly during the Eisenhower administration, U.S. policy toward supporting and distinguishing between authoritarian and democratic regimes is best described by Vice President Richard Nixon's recommendation after his tumultuous visit to South America in 1958: extend a formal handshake to dictators and an "abrazo" to democrats.

By the "election" of February 1958, Paraguay was the only remaining dictatorship in South America and, as a result, was increasingly isolated and criticized by its neighbors and the international press for human rights violations against dissidents. Liberal and Colorado Party leaders in exile living in Argentina and Uruguay helped shape public opinion in those countries about the "evils" of the Paraguayan government. In August 1959, Father Ramón Talavera and moderate exiled leaders of the Liberal and Febrerista parties created the Unión Nacional Paraguaya (UNP), a political alliance committed to overthrowing the Stroessner regime through joint peaceful action. Specifically, the UNP sought to mobilize international public opinion to bring pressure on the Stroessner regime, including several formal requests, such as a February 1960 letter to President Eisenhower, pleading that Washington terminate all moral and material support to the dictatorship. Although Washington ignored these pleas, it was careful to avoid being too publicly supportive or critical of the regime.

In the late 1950s, the Eisenhower administration came under attack from democratic allies in the region and critics inside and outside the State Department who wanted a more active and democratic Latin American strategy. At least publicly in order to better reflect the sentiment of many in Congress and the State Department, the United States expressed "concern" about the political situation in Paraguay but never went so far as to demand democratization. Paraguay usually responded by implementing token measures to placate its critics in the United States. Stroessner also showered praise and expressions of unconditional support for the United States in his speeches to ameliorate any reaction to heightening of state repression.

For Stroessner's August 1958 inauguration, the United States sent a low-level delegation to Asunción to mollify the international press and South American democracies that were highly critical of U.S. policy, thus sending a message that Washington was unhappy with the intensification of repression in Paraguay. Stroessner took note and responded by easing repression against opposition groups but did not engage in any substantive liberalization. During brief periods, usually after crucial meetings with U.S. officials dealing with the question of repression, the regime eased the pressure on some members of the opposition by allowing some space for them to hold meetings. For instance, in 1958, not long after the March meeting with Ambassador Ploeser, Stroessner informed the Liberals that they could return to Paraguay and hold their first public convention since the 1940s. In 1959, the regime lifted the state of siege, allowing some Liberals and Febreristas to return. However, in each case, once the critics seemed satisfied and concerned with other matters, the regime would revert back to using its old ways of dealing with political opponents. As far as the regime was concerned, ephemeral gestures were enough to placate the U.S. government's unconvincing pleadings for human rights.

One important consequence of democratization and a free press in South America was the constant barrage of articles in Latin American and U.S. newspapers harshly attacking the only remaining dictatorship in South America. Dailies in Argentina and Uruguay were particularly critical, accusing the regime of assassination and of holding political prisoners in concentration camps. In the United States, the *New York Times*, *Time*, and the *New Republic* ran similar articles about the "totalitarian" nature of the regime; one piece argued that "torture and murder are common in Stroessner's Paraguay." Foreign Minister Sapena Pastor and Paraguayan ambassadors often called on U.S. officials to talk about the international conspiracy against the regime by Latin American and U.S. publications, hoping that somehow the United States could pressure the *New York Times* and other periodicals in Buenos Aires and Montevideo to stop the "hostile press from telling lies" about the

Paraguayan government. The Paraguayan government's reaction to this criticism was nothing short of frantic. On numerous occasions, President Stroessner, Foreign Minister Sapena Pastor, and Paraguayan ambassadors called on U.S. officials to express their dismay, frustration, and outrage, insisting that Washington put pressure on U.S. and South American newspapers to stop the "conspiracy of falsehoods." The usual U.S. response, as Ambassador Ploeser once said to President Stroessner, was that "it is best if Paraguayan government officials acquire a thicker skin against criticisms from the press."[19]

Counterinsurgency and the Final Purge

Soon after Stroessner's reelection, opposition political parties, student organizations, labor, and dissident groups within the Colorado Party realized that he planned on extending and institutionalizing his power and that of the armed forces. In the brief period after the election, social instability and political violence ensued that ultimately led to the "stroessnerization" of the Colorado Party and the Paraguayan Workers Confederation (CPT) and the obliteration of insurgency groups led by opposition political groups in exile. In February–March 1958 Father Ramón Talavera, a member of a wealthy family well known within the Colorado Party, openly criticized the regime for repression, corruption, human rights violations, and fraudulent elections. He called on all Paraguayans to rise up and demand their rights. Word of Talavera's defiance spread quickly throughout the Catholic Church and Paraguayan society. The regime reacted swiftly by going after what it believed was the source of the discontent. Talavera was kidnapped, brutally beaten, and expelled from Paraguay. This episode had a radicalizing and polarizing effect on Paraguayan society, exacerbated by the regime's reactionary retort to societal demands for change.

In addition to the Talavera episode, several factors contributed to the rise of insurgency groups committed not only to eliminating the Stroessner regime but also, in some cases, to the revolutionary transformation of Paraguay.[20] First, the urban-based Paraguayan Workers'

Confederation (the last stronghold of *epifanistas*) organized a general strike in August–September 1958 demanding a 30 percent wage increase. These political demands were unacceptable, and as a result, the Stroessner regime came down mercilessly on the confederation, closing its headquarters and arresting over two hundred of its militants. With all autonomous channels for articulation closed, many labor militants left the country believing that only violence could rid the country of the dictatorship.

Second, the success of the Cuban Revolution in January 1959 offered a model of armed struggle that many exiles believed could be replicated in Paraguay. The ability of Fidel Castro to overcome seemingly insurmountable obstacles to defeat a dictatorship created euphoria among Paraguayan youths in exile who believed that they could do the same. Third, several Latin American democratic governments and Cuba expressed a commitment to ridding the rest of the continent of military regimes. Venezuelan president Romulo Betancourt assumed a leadership role in providing moral and material support to opposition movements working to overthrow dictatorships. Venezuela provided money to the Liberals and Febreristas, and Argentina offered military support, training, and safe areas from which insurgencies could harass the Paraguayan government with sharp attacks across the border. Uruguay allowed the Paraguayan Communist Party and its armed wing to organize and plan its political-military campaign freely in Montevideo. In 1960 Cuba offered money, arms, and advisers to help Paraguayan exiles organize a military campaign against the regime. Therefore, thrilled by examples of democratization and revolutionary change coupled with a willingness from Argentina, Cuba, and Venezuela to provide arms, Paraguayan exiles were emboldened to embark on a campaign to remove Stroessner by force.

Another episode contributing to the polarization of Paraguayan society was the repression of high school and university students in May–June 1959 who rioted over the raising of bus fares. Brutal police repression and detention of several student leaders of the Paraguayan University Federation (FUP) led to street clashes between students, who occupied several university buildings, and units from the Fourteenth Infantry that were called in to support the police and cavalry forces. In the end, schools were closed, and students were jailed or exiled. The repression and weakening of student organizations constrained further available spaces for independent political participation. Finally, related to state repression against students, the *democrático* faction (also known as *civilista*) of the Colorado Party was purged and sent into exile after an attempt to gain control of the party. The *democrático* attempt to regain control of the party began when they condemned repression against student protestors and demanded prosecution of the minister of interior. This provided Stroessner with justification to close down Congress and arrest *civilista* leaders. In 1960 Colorado Party dissidents formed the Popular Colorado Movement (MOPOCO) in exile.[21]

As a result of the polarized domestic situation and the appeal of armed struggle among younger Paraguayan exiles (also disillusioned with the incompetence and appeasing attitude of opposition party leadership), several insurrectionist groups committed to overthrowing the regime through violence emerged.[22] In May 1958 a faction of the Liberal Party led by Benjamín Vargas Peña formed the Fourteenth of May Movement. It launched its first invasion on 1 April 1958 when it crossed the Upper Paraná and attacked the police garrison of Coronel Bogado in a hit-and-run operation. Then in May 1959 the Vanguardia Febrerista, headed by Arnaldo Valdovinos, merged with the Fourteenth of May Movement. Valdovinos used his contacts with social democratic parties and governments, particularly in Venezuela, to secure financial assistance. The guerrilla movement organized several other minor incursions, but the group was unable to stage a major operation because of internal infighting that ultimately led to a split between Vargas Peña and Valdovinos.

The other important insurgent group, called the United National Liberation Front (FULNA), was created in February 1959 in Montevideo, Uruguay. It was first established by a nucleus of Communists, Liberals, Febreristas, and dissident Colorados, but the Communists ultimately took control of the group's leadership and transformed it into a front organization of the Paraguayan Communist Party (PCP). The Cuban

Revolution provided the inspiration for the group. Ricardo Franco, a Febrerista and founding member of FULNA, visited Cuba and met with Che Guevara, who insisted that before any assistance was provided Paraguayan revolutionaries had to work together in a united front. Before sending any material support, the Cubans instructed José Iribar, an unofficial representative in Uruguay, to assist Paraguayans in their planning and organization. During much of 1959 FULNA engaged in planning and political activities in Uruguay.

Washington was attentive but largely untroubled by the emergence of guerrilla activities during the 1959–61 period. In fact, a February 1959 report by the Bureau of Intelligence and Research (BIR) of the U.S. State Department noted that Stroessner's government did not seem to be threatened by Cuba or the activities of Paraguayan exiles, but by elements within the armed forces concerned with the regime's use of Colorado Party militias (also known as urban guards) to combat the guerrillas. In February 1960, a couple of months after the 12 December attack by the Fourteenth of May Movement, the BIR issued another report suggesting that Stroessner's position had been weakened by the incursions; however, it did not believe that the regime was in any way threatened by what it considered a poorly organized and executed operation by the insurgency group. Nevertheless, Central Intelligence Agency stations in Uruguay and Argentina kept close tabs on these groups. CIA agents were quite successful in penetrating these groups and accumulating intelligence information that was forwarded to the station in Asunción.[23] Ultimately, the U.S. government was confident that the regime's effective and ruthless use of intelligence and repression against these groups, together with the guerrillas' poor military and ideological training and lack of organizational cohesion, funds, and equipment, was sufficient to prevent any destabilization even with Cuban support.[24]

Although the insurgency was far from threatening the regime, Stroessner sought to exaggerate the destabilizing effects of the attacks and overstate the influence of Communists and Fidel Castro in financing and organizing these guerrilla groups in order to raise fears in—and, consequently, funds from—the United States. The mere suspicion of a Communist link, however insignificant, was enough to instill panic in a few U.S. officials. Generally, Stroessner's fear tactics did not persuade most U.S. officials, but the U.S. government and international financial institutions did continue supporting the Stroessner regime with economic, financial, technical, and military-security support, but they were not pushed to do so by Stroessner's fear tactics. However, during this period, as the armed forces and police played vital roles in maintaining order, special attention was given to strengthening U.S. influence by providing technical and material aid. For example, the CIA maintained extensive contacts with Paraguayan security services, specifically sharing information with the intelligence division of the armed forces and the political section of the Ministry of Interior.

Economic and Cultural Links

Paraguay's macroeconomic situation was in shambles during 1954–57. Government expenditures increased as allocations for national defense and state security rose to 50 percent of the national budget. Government finances were always in deficit, and the inflation rate was one of the highest in Latin America. Gustavo Storm, the Central Bank president, asked the United States to convince the International Monetary Fund (IMF) of the need to provide an emergency loan to help Paraguay meet its immediate financial crisis. In the Stabilization Plan of 1956, the IMF, along with the U.S. Treasury, provided a standby loan and sent a technical commission to help Paraguay reform the country's finances. The austerity program consisted of tax reform, credit restrictions, and other measures to control the supply of money. However, spending and rampant corruption proved difficult to overcome for Storm and the IMF team. One source of U.S. frustration and tension during this period was the government's reluctance to implement many of the adjustment policies requested by the IMF and championed by the very pro-U.S. technocrat Storm. It was difficult for Storm to resist pressures from party and military officials who wanted to continue using the Central Bank as a favor-dispensing institution, regardless of the economic consequences or effect on relations with the United States and international financial institutions.

The nature of U.S.-Paraguayan economic relations during 1954–61 was largely a function of loans, grants, and credits provided by U.S. aid agencies and international financial institutions, such as the World Bank and IMF, to help Paraguay modernize its poor infrastructure, specifically transportation, communication, and water and sanitation systems. The United States also continued to provide technical assistance in the areas of vocational and elementary education, public administration, agricultural programs, livestock development, and health. The United States and Paraguay were concerned that the country's isolation, largely a function of an antiquated or nonexistent infrastructure, impeded its development and long-term stability. In terms of modernizing the infrastructure, the United States disbursed significant funds to pave roads, such as the highway linking Asunción and Brazil, and improve air transport. The United States provided funds to build a new airport in Asunción and also arranged a seven hundred thousand dollar loan from the Export-Import Bank in June 1955 to extend the runway in order to accommodate heavy jet aircraft that were in greater use.

Although Paraguay's share of U.S. investments and trade in Latin America was negligible, the amount was significant for Paraguay. U.S. investments had been increasing since the 1940s; however, a significant and impressive expansion (for Paraguay) occurred in the late 1950s and early 1960s. Direct foreign investments (DFI) began their quick and relatively impressive rise after President Stroessner promulgated Law No. 246 (February 1955), which actively encouraged foreign investments by offering import tax exemptions on imported machinery, a 25 percent reduction on revenues, and access to foreign exchange of up to 20 percent of the registered capital.[25] In the 1940s, the United States was Paraguay's third largest source of capital investment, with 23 percent of the total, after Argentina and Great Britain. By 1960 the United States became Paraguay's most important source of DFI, with nearly 39 percent of the total. There were about ten U.S. companies in 1960, with total capital amounting to $17 million, invested (in descending order) in oil-refining industries, meatpacking, banking, and tannin production.

One of the more important U.S. companies, the International Products Corporation (IPC), reopened its meatpacking house in 1956 with a credit of 60 million guaranís approved by the Central Bank. The IPC exerted considerable influence on the Stroessner regime because of the number of people it employed at its two plants and in cattle raising.[26] Taxes collected on cattle export and slaughter were also important for the Paraguayan treasury. Charles Koons, president and CEO of IPC, visited Paraguay frequently to meet with President Stroessner and other Paraguayan government and military officials.

In addition to IPC, key investments included the First National City Bank, which opened an office in Asunción in September 1958—the first U.S. bank to open a branch in Paraguay. In the early 1960s other banks opened offices, including the Chase Manhattan Bank and Bankers Trust. These financial institutions helped create a more stable and favorable financial environment for domestic and international investors. In the petroleum-refining industry in the mid-1950s Pure Oil, Hancock Oil, Signal Oil of California, Standard Oil of Ohio, and Williams Brothers of Oklahoma formed a private group whose aim was to explore the Chaco region.

Much like investments, trade between the United States and Paraguay was negligible for the former but relatively significant for the latter. Since the late 1930s bilateral trade, especially Paraguayan exports to the United States, had been growing at a rapid rate as a result of a U.S. effort to strengthen economic and strategic ties with Southern Cone countries. In 1946, trade with the United States represented 11.4 percent of Paraguay's total trade, up from 3.2 percent in 1933. By the early 1960s the United States was the second most important market for Paraguayan exports (24 percent), after Argentina, and the principal source of Paraguayan imports (20.3 percent). The principal Paraguayan exports during the period in question were tung oil, cattle products, timber products, and cotton. Once again, the United States in the late 1950s, unlike the 1930s, did not seek economic opportunities in Paraguay but did assess trade and economic links as a means of protecting and strengthening the regime and the Paraguayan economy against the evils of instability, underdevelopment, and communism.

Cultural and personal contacts between the United States and Paraguay during this period continued their steady growth but, by and large, remained marginal compared to the rest of South America. In 1957 Asunción, with fewer than 250,000 people, was the smallest capital in South America, a remote and largely unattractive city that reminded many Americans of a small town or outpost in the old American West. In the late 1950s about 650 Americans lived in Asunción, many of them family members of U.S. Embassy officials. It was still difficult and expensive for Americans to travel to Paraguay, largely because of the distance and Asunción's isolation. Braniff Airlines, the only U.S. carrier with service to Asunción, offered only two flights a week.

The depiction of a poor, unstable, and culturally backward country portrayed by the few visitors and U.S. diplomats did not incite much attention. A typical portrayal of Paraguay given in a 1956 U.S. Embassy despatch asserts that

> the cultural drags in this subsistence economy are tremendous. It is not overdrawing the picture of the culture in the central zone to say that it consists of a lot of Guaraní-speaking, barefooted mestizos walking around with their shirttails hanging out, selling feather dusters to each other. This mestizo culture represents a sixteenth-century Spanish colonialism, overlaid on an extremely primitive and poorly developed Indian culture that goes back thousands of years.[27]

Whether this was a correct characterization of Paraguayan society and culture did not matter. The perception that it conjured did. For example, in a 1956 article in the *Saturday Evening Post*, the Guaraní in the Chaco are depicted as barbaric and childlike. The article featured Bob and Dorothy Eaton (the latter born in Paraguay of English parents), who owned a 160,000-acre ranch in the Chaco—"the last shooting frontier in South America"—and "had about 328 Indians under their care." Paraguay and its people were portrayed as uncivilized, a place that only cowboys, adventurers, and fugitives could be interested in visiting.

However, among the 650 Americans living in Asunción at the time, there was a sense of fascination with the "charming" culture and people of Paraguay. Most were U.S. government employees and their families, families associated with business firms, and missionaries and their families. The small U.S. community was vibrant and quite interested in engaging Paraguayans. This community organized several institutions, including churches, schools, and a flourishing women's organization, known as Las Amigas Norteamericanas del Paraguay, which exemplified the U.S. fascination with Paraguayan customs and society. Members of the organization were mostly wives of U.S. diplomats and military officers attached to the military mission; the president of the organization in the late 1950s was the wife of the defense attaché. Las Amigas met regularly to hold cultural events at the Paraguayan-American Cultural Center and raise funds for local institutions. In 1958, as part of their fundraising activities, the organization published an "informal guide to Paraguay" titled *Land of Lace and Legend.*[28] Its targeted audience was Americans visiting or moving to Paraguay, and it was a guide for daily life, culture, shopping, customs, restaurants, and other relevant bits of information that might be of interest to Americans in Paraguay. Much of the guide is filled with advertisements from the principal U.S. companies in Paraguay, such as Pure Oil, Kaiser Engineers, Rader and Associate Engineers, Morrison-Knudsen Contractors and Engineers, IPC, and First National City Bank of New York.

The U.S. Embassy and U.S. community in Asunción were interested in disseminating U.S. culture while learning about Paraguayan history and culture. The Paraguayan-American Cultural Center was active in hosting cultural events; specifically the center screened U.S. movies (with Spanish subtitles) and invited Paraguayan dance and musical groups to perform regularly at the centrally located offices of the center on España 494. The center also provided English classes to over three thousand Paraguayans each year.

There was, however, interest growing in Paraguay by the U.S. scholarly community. After Professor Harris Gaylord Warren published his book *Paraguay: An Informal History* in 1949 and an article on the "political aspects of the Paraguayan Revolution, 1936–1949" in 1950, Dr. Elman Service, a cultural anthropologist from Columbia University and the University of Michigan, was the first to conduct field research in

Paraguay in the early 1950s. In 1951 he published an article on the *encomienda,* or mission, in Paraguay, and in 1954 he and his wife, Helen S. Service, completed a book titled *Tobatí: Paraguayan Town,* the first modern sociological study of rural Paraguay.[29] Based on nearly a year of field work, Service's study of a small town thirty-five miles from Asunción argued that there was hardly any Guaraní Indian cultural component in present-day Paraguayan life. Warren's and Service's scholarly contributions tentatively opened the way for a birth of interest in Paraguay among U.S. scholars that began to take off in the 1960s.

For Paraguayans, the United States was a much more recognizable and respected nation (thanks to the work of the Paraguayan-American Cultural Center), though still very distant and in some ways abstract. For 80 percent of Paraguayans who lived in the rural areas, U.S. power and culture were not tangibly relevant; however, in Asunción, U.S. movies and actors continued to grow in popularity. The gradual spread of U.S. culture coupled with the lessening of ties with Argentina and the expansion of Paraguay's political and economic ties with Brazil and the United States enhanced the U.S. presence and influence. Because of the profound asymmetries in power and wealth, the flow of capital, culture, and personal contact had a greater impact on Paraguay than the United States. As a result, the U.S. public remained largely aloof and disinterested, whereas Paraguayans (mostly Asunceños) were excited by their increasing exposure to U.S. products and people.

If it was difficult and expensive for Americans to visit Paraguay, it was incredibly so for Paraguayans to travel to the United States. Only diplomats and government officials had the resources, time, and inclination to make the trip. Most Paraguayans of means continued to study at Argentine and European universities. There was also no significant emigration of Paraguayans to the United States, so on a human level, interaction and cultural exchange in the United States were minimal. There were, however, a few important exceptions. Pablo Max Ynsfrán (1894–1972) was a distinguished professor who served in several government and diplomatic posts, including president of the Paraguayan State Bank (1933), member of the Chamber of Deputies (1924–28), secretary to the Paraguayan delegation at the Fifth Pan American

Conference in Chile (1923), chargé d'affaires of the Paraguayan Legation in Washington, D.C. (1929–33; 1938–40), and minister of economy, public works and colonization (1940). In 1940 Ynsfrán was exiled by General Higinio Morínigo and moved to the United States. In 1942 he arrived at the University of Texas, where he taught Romance languages, government, and economics until his retirement in 1963. There was perhaps no other Paraguayan at the time who understood and appreciated U.S. society, politics, and culture as well as Ynsfrán. His career as a diplomat, student at the School of Foreign Service at Georgetown University, and lecturer at the University of Texas and his more than three decades of living in the United States after his exile offered him an insight and understanding of the country that few Paraguayans possessed. Because of politics, Ynsfrán's expertise and talents were not exploited by Paraguay; however, his affable personality and commitment to education and research opened a window to many students and scholars interested in, if not captivated by, the happenings of that distant Guaraní nation.

In the 1950s the United States expanded its political, military, economic, and cultural presence in Paraguay and, as a result, strengthened its influence on domestic politics. Some interpreted this expansion and penetration of U.S. capital and political influence in Paraguay as "imperialistic," as it helped strengthen a dictatorship that was committed to turning Paraguay into a "satellite" of U.S. economic and strategic power.[30] There is no evidence to suggest that Washington was interested in "obtaining a colony" in South America. Though U.S. financial flows and trade were important for the Paraguayan economy and regime, the country offered little of economic value to the United States.

In terms of Paraguay's strategic value, there were some in Washington who believed the country could be an important asset, but there was certainly no concerted effort to explore the possibility of turning the country into the USS *Paraguay,* despite Asunción's invitation for the United States to do so. Stroessner understood well the value of U.S. political and material support to his regime and exploited it to its fullest. However, Stroessner did not necessarily have to pay a price for U.S. support. There was a clear convergence of interests (i.e., stability, development, and anticommunism) between the United States and Paraguay that facilitated the expansion of bilateral ties and, consequently, U.S. influence. Between 1954 and 1961, the United States amassed a significant amount of leverage that it would later try to use to obtain certain concessions from Asunción. In the end, U.S.-Paraguayan relations continued a trend in the late 1950s and into the next few decades that began in the 1930s and that can be described as a "constant two-way flow of mutual opportunism and reciprocal exploitation" that lay at the core of this inherently unequal, but mutually beneficial, partnership.[31]

6 Alliance for Progress and the Ricord Affair, 1962–1976

By the time of President John F. Kennedy's inauguration in January 1961, the Stroessner regime and its peasant supporters had not only crushed the "invasions" but were not far from completely dismantling Paraguay's ineffective revolutionary groups. Some members of the FULNA and the Columna Mariscal López (associated with the Paraguayan Communist Party) remained at large, but their capacity to operate inside Paraguay had ended. By mid-1963, guerrilla leaders had either fallen into police custody or had died fighting. Yet, the Stroessner regime refused to declare victory. In fact, the spokespeople of the dictatorship continued to insist that Cuban-oriented subversives were busily attempting to destabilize the country.

As the regime conducted several successful mopping up operations in the countryside between 1961 and 1963, it attempted to win favor with the new administration in Washington. The Kennedy administration provided economic and military aid to Latin America and the Caribbean under the rubric of the Alliance for Progress, hoping to eliminate the region's social and economic ills while simultaneously containing the Communist threat. Paraguay was not about to be left out of the new U.S. largesse and Washington's strategic approach to the security challenge in the Western Hemisphere. The Stroessner regime calculated that the Kennedy administration's profound concern with the Cuban example could funnel into support for Paraguay's economic development. Stroessner sought to obtain extensive economic and military-security aid with minimal concessions, specifically avoiding any political liberalization of the sort that the U.S. administration defined as a critical component of its policy. Stroessner's assessment was dead on; he received a great deal for very little in return.

Alliance for Progress

Even before the 1960 presidential campaign, Senator John F. Kennedy expressed concern about the spread of communism in Latin America. He believed that the region's poverty, underdevelopment, and lack of social justice and democratic rule resulted from U.S. support or tolerance of dictatorships. In December 1960, the president-elect ordered aides Adolf Berle, Richard Goodwin, and Lincoln Gordon (all members of a special task force on Latin American policy) to draw up a battle plan for the cold war in Latin America. The new U.S. administration felt it needed to design a bold plan to address both the sources and consequences of that vulnerability. This radicalizing convergence of the region's social and economic ills with communism, symbolized by the Cuban Revolution, made Latin America "the most dangerous area in the world" to the United States.[1]

Fidel Castro's commitment to exporting radicalism in the Western Hemisphere was sufficient to alarm Kennedy. It was, however, Soviet premier Nikita Khrushchev's lengthy speech of 6 January 1961 in Moscow that most concerned the president-elect. In the speech, Khrushchev promised to back "national liberation movements" in the Third World, which meant that the USSR intended to promote guerrilla warfare in the Western Hemisphere. For Kennedy and his advisers, Soviet initiatives required vigorous responses. Kennedy's Latin American advisers agreed with the new president; instability, agitation, and even revolution might flow from Latin America's "ancient heritage of poverty, widespread illiteracy, and grave social injustice"—fertile ground for Communist exploitation. Therefore, the United States needed to outline a development program to help Latin Americans transform their traditional social and economic institutions into vibrant, progressive agents of modernity and prosperity. The new administration concluded that progressive social change and democracy would undermine the appeal of radicals and prevent a second Communist outpost in the Western Hemisphere.

In March 1961, the president announced a long-range program to provide economic, technical, and scientific aid to assist the region in transforming and modernizing their societies in ways that would address the problem of poverty and injustice in the region. In August, the administration provided the specifics of the program at an inter-American conference in Punta del Este, Uruguay, where the charter of the Alliance for Progress was approved. Treasury Secretary C. Douglas Dillon, head of the U.S. delegation, assured Latin American delegates that they could count on receiving $20 billion in public and private capital from the United States, international lending institutions, and private U.S. investors over the next ten years. With this influx of foreign money coupled with additional funds from internal investment, Latin American nations would experience a real economic growth rate of 2.5 percent a year, enough to underwrite improvements in health, education, and infrastructure development.

The Alliance for Progress meant more than economic aid, however. Political freedom, social reform, and the strengthening of cultural relations had to accompany material progress if Latin America were to fulfill its promise of development, stability, and a robust relationship with the United States. Democracy and constitutional order accompanied by reform of Latin America's archaic and unjust social structure were the goals, with the specific intention of ridding the region of dictatorship, antiquated laws, and feudalistic systems of land tenure. The administration's "vision affirmed the attainability of freedom and progress within the context of democratic capitalism, a preferred and viable alternative to the Castro example."[2]

In the area of culture and propaganda, Adolf Berle, the head of the president's task force on Latin America, insisted that the Alliance for Progress lacked a fourth leg. Beyond democracy, economic development assistance, and social reform, the United States needed to mount a "psychological offensive" in Latin America. President Kennedy accepted Berle's proposal that the United States "fund friendly university professors, journalists, and media personalities. Students and military men should be brought to the United States for education, training, and indoctrination" as a means of socializing, if not co-opting, a new crop of Latin American leaders sympathetic to U.S. cold war policies in the region and across the globe.[3] According to Berle, the stakes justified using propaganda, particularly expansion of cultural contacts and propagation of U.S. values and policy goals through the use, if not ownership, of Latin American news and informational outlets.

With the help of the Pentagon and his brother, Attorney General Robert F. Kennedy, President Kennedy added a military and counter-insurgency component to the Alliance for Progress. Concerned with Communist-supported insurgency in the region, Kennedy instructed the Defense Department to formulate a plan "to increase the intimacy" between the United States and Latin American armed forces. Economic development and social reform took too long to deal with the existing threat from guerrillas in the region. Only an efficient military trained in counterinsurgency could confront this immediate threat. By the end of 1961, the Joint Chiefs of Staff and the Special Group, a committee headed by the attorney general to oversee counterinsurgency efforts, suggested to the president that "through the rapid provision of equipment, training, and materiel, the United States could shift the Latin American military's focus away from hemispheric defense and enhance the capability of indigenous forces to conduct counter-insurgency, anti-subversion and psychological warfare operations."[4] As a result, in addition to a sharp increase in military aid to the region, during 1962–66 thousands of Latin American officers, enlisted soldiers, and police received training and instruction at U.S. military schools and academies on such topics as civic action, communism and democracy, civil affairs, psychological operations, national development, and clandestine operations.[5]

The goal of the Alliance for Progress and U.S. policy during the 1960s, as outlined in the Kennedy Doctrine (May 1963), was the "absolute determination" to secure the hemisphere from Soviet influence. In short, as President Kennedy uttered, the Soviets and Latin Americans were now placed on notice that the "United States would use every resource at its command to prevent the establishment of another Cuba in this hemisphere."[6] The *stronistas* in Asunción could not have been more pleased with the strong anti-Communist rhetoric and the massive economic and military assistance that the administration promised. The regime could point to Paraguay's social and economic underdevelopment and ongoing struggle against Communist guerrillas to extract resources and support for the Stronato. There was no time to lose. Paraguay needed to make its case quickly and dramatically.

For the Kennedy administration, Paraguay presented a difficult problem. On the one hand, the Alliance for Progress's commitment to democratic government and social justice presumably mandated that the Stroessner regime liberalize its political system and reorganize Paraguay's social structure. However, Paraguay's severe underdevelopment and immediate need for economic assistance suggested that placing too much pressure on the regime (i.e., withholding aid until reforms were enacted), especially at a time when it faced a challenge from Communist rebel movements, might destabilize the government and undermine Washington's overriding national interests in the country. It was not clear how the administration was to address this dilemma, but it became evident that Washington was not about to push very hard. In the end, as Stroessner and Foreign Minister Raúl Sapena Pastor well understood, in Washington fear of communism always trumped the need for democracy and social reform.

Token Concessions and Material Rewards

Not long after his March 1961 speech in which he outlined the fundamentals of the Alliance for Progress, President Kennedy dispatched Arthur Schlesinger Jr. and U.S. ambassador to the UN Adlai Stevenson to conduct fact-finding tours of Latin America.[7] Their mission included assessing the region's financial needs in the face of Communist subversion. Ambassador Stevenson visited Paraguay to meet with President Stroessner.[8] Some within Stroessner's close circle, such as policy adviser Ezequiel González Alsina, were wary of the new administration's focus on pressuring regimes in the region to democratize. González Alsina, who also served as director of *Patria,* the Colorado Party official newspaper, feared that Stevenson's visit could turn into a propaganda nightmare if the U.S. ambassador publicly harangued Stroessner for the lack of democracy in the country. The Paraguayan intellectual suggested that Paraguay request assistance from "other countries" outside the West, carefully alluding to the socialist camp. Stroessner rejected the proposal not only because it was impractical for a committed anti-Communist to reach out to the Soviet bloc, but also because the Paraguayan caudillo felt that he could work with the Kennedy administration on the basis of their common stand against communism.

Before leaving Rio de Janeiro on his way to Asunción, Stevenson was asked about his trip to Paraguay to meet with a dictator. He responded with a willingness to work with authoritarian rulers: "we do not like tyranny in the hearts and minds of men. We do not like closed societies but we would like to offer help to societies in need." Stevenson arrived at the Presidente Stroessner International Airport on 13 June to great pomp. The entire cabinet, led by Foreign Minister Sapena Pastor, and the high command of the armed forces were there to receive the U.S. envoy. From the airport, the ambassador went directly to Palacio de López where President Stroessner had mounted a major propaganda spectacle that made the ambassador uneasy, especially when Stroessner practically embraced him as television camera crews and photographers took pictures.[9]

After brief pleasantries and Stroessner's repeated expressions of admiration for the new administration and gratitude for previous U.S. support, the conversation turned toward the business at hand: U.S. assistance to contain the Communist threat in Paraguay. As if reading from a script, the Paraguayan dictator argued that Paraguay needed much assistance to defend itself. Stevenson asked Stroessner about democratization and insisted that opposition representation in the parliament "by means of free elections" was a critical requirement for future U.S. support. According to Ambassador Stevenson's notes of the meeting, when it seemed that the Paraguayan president felt a bit dismayed by this talk of democracy, the U.S. envoy dropped the issue and began discussing aid amounts and the Communist threat in Paraguay.[10]

At the conclusion of the meeting, a quid pro quo was worked out that defined the nature of U.S.-Paraguayan relations: economic and military aid for opposition representation in the legislature. Even though Washington's public message to Asunción emphasized structural reforms,

Stevenson's visit really concerned a political cover, that is, token concessions to justify U.S. political, economic, and military support. In a speech at the airport before departing, with President Stroessner present, Stevenson stated that the "protection of civil rights, free elections and the democratic process will greatly help Paraguay's future development and prosperity. . . . The existing climate of political tension in Paraguay impedes economic cooperation with the United States. . . . President Stroessner has assured me that there will be national elections and that they will be free and fair where all Paraguayans will be able to participate." It was clear to Stroessner from his meeting with Stevenson that Washington had modest expectations for democratic reform.

The Kennedy administration's commitment to democracy in Latin America was conditional on the imminence of the threat from subversion, which required supporting Latin American regimes regardless of their democratic credentials. There was also growing realization among key administration officials, such as assistant secretary of state for inter-American affairs Edward M. Martin and National Security Council official Walt Rostow, that many countries lacked the capacity or experience to establish democratic rule.[11] As a result, the United States could not always dictate who held political office in the Americas nor could it expect to impose a government with democratic leanings. Stability continued to outweigh democracy and social reform as a goal of U.S. foreign policy in Latin America. In the end, U.S. policy toward dictators exhibited a pattern that was defined by President Kennedy in reference to the dictatorship of General Rafael Trujillo in the Dominican Republic: "There are three possibilities in descending order of preference: a decent democratic regime, a continuation of the Trujillo regime, or a Castro regime. We ought to aim for the first, but we really can't renounce the second until we are sure that we can avoid the third."[12]

The Kennedy administration often liked to showcase countries, such as Chile, Colombia, Uruguay, and Venezuela, that it considered models of democratic social development under the Alliance for Progress program. Paraguay never aspired to be one of those cases. In Paraguay the United States felt it had to be "pragmatic"; to hold the line against regime collapse and subversion and, if possible, to counter Argentine influence by helping Paraguay establish closer relations with the Brazilian generals governing in Brasilia after the 1964 military takeover. Pressuring the Stroessner regime to implement broad structural reforms was risky and unlikely to succeed. By the end of 1961, the State Department reported that Paraguay, along with several other South American countries, was threatened by internal subversion.[13] For the White House and the State Department, supporting an ally that faced unrepentant Communist forces was more important than trying to make Paraguay into a model of the Alliance for Progress.[14] The Kennedy administration concluded that too many demands could destabilize the regime and unintentionally promote the rebel movements and consequent repression.

U.S. Aid Arrives

Even before Stroessner agreed to any commitments for liberalization, the Kennedy administration demonstrated that the United States was not unwilling to make economic aid conditional on political pluralism and social reform. In 1961, the White House requested and received from the Congress over $17 million in loans for international lending institutions, and nearly $7 million was disbursed in PL-480 (Food for Peace program) funds, 40 percent of which was in grants. In December, the Palacio de López presented Ambassador William P. Snow with a detailed list of projects that it wished to finance through the Alliance for Progress. Paraguay was the first country in Latin America to make a request for aid under the alliance, and the regime was not modest in its requests. Paraguay asked for $80 million to support twenty-four projects, an enormous amount requested for a country of 1.8 million people and a GDP of $330 million. The request amounted to nearly 25 percent of its gross domestic product (GDP). Most of the projects listed focused on agriculture and infrastructure. However, about one-third of the amount was requested to finance the growing deficit caused by heavy spending for the armed forces. The Paraguayan government made similar requests every subsequent year, with the total amount solicited increasing every year until the mid 1960s.

As in the past, Washington largely ignored Paraguay's wish list, but it did not refrain from providing assistance in areas that technical experts and policymakers regarded as important to the country's development and political stability. During the critical years of the alliance (1962–66), the Stroessner regime received $41 million in U.S. public assistance, which, combined with soft loans from U.S. private banking institutions and U.S.-controlled international lending agencies, added up to $73 million. Military aid ($5.5 million) pushed the total amount of aid to more than 5 percent of Paraguay's GDP.[15]

This major injection of capital helped support Paraguay's budgetary and development needs, particularly agriculture, infrastructure, health, fiscal reform, and education. Specifically, the government spent large sums on schools, transportation, port facilities, and energy projects. In addition to a joint project with Argentina to build a dam on the Upper Paraná (Acaray Falls Dam), U.S. economic aid helped build an extensive road network, from less than 1,200 kilometers (744 miles), of which only 95 kilometers were paved in 1954, to over 1,800 kilometers (1,116 miles), with 261 paved kilometers, by 1968. Stroessner was especially proud of a 196-mile highway that connected Asunción to Brazil. The highway extended through the bush to a new town on the Paraná River named Presidente Stroessner. A bridge, known as the Friendship International Bridge, connected the two at this point. The new road gave Paraguay an alternate trade route to the Atlantic, helping to diminish Paraguay's former dependence on Argentina and increasing economic and political ties with Brazil's pro-U.S. regime. The highway and bridge, opened in March 1965, were built with substantial help from the leading U.S. aid entity charged with disbursing Alliance for Progress funds, the U.S. Agency for International Development (USAID).[16] Other specific USAID-funded projects included improving the navigability of the Paraguay River, research to enhance telecommunications links in the country, and a new water works plant that provided safe water to several villages. Assistance provided under the alliance contributed to the modernization of Paraguay's infrastructure and economy providing the base (i.e., road network) from which Paraguay's economic boom of the 1970s flourished.[17]

Though the regime was careful that Paraguayans' patriotic feelings were not offended by any hint of the country's increasing dependence on U.S. development aid, President Stroessner did use the highly visible projects, such as the road network and dam, to reaffirm the legitimacy of his presidency. In other words, effective propaganda turned the U.S.-financed projects into government-sponsored patronage. As important, U.S. aid subsidized the Stronato's efforts to grease the wheel of a vast network of patronage and corruption that helped ensure the support of the military and the rank and file of the Colorado Party.

Though Paraguay received less U.S. military aid than its South American neighbors, military-to-military contacts were enhanced as a result of interactions between U.S. and Paraguayan officers and noncommissioned officers who received counterinsurgency training at U.S. bases in the Panama Canal Zone or at the International Police Academy in Washington. Between 1962 and 1966 nearly four hundred Paraguayans participated in military educational programs in the Panama Canal Zone and the United States. The Paraguayan military did receive some counterinsurgency equipment—light arms and patrol boats—but the crux of military aid came in the form of training and contacts that Stroessner strongly cultivated and exploited. It was not uncommon for Stroessner to seek personal contacts at the Pentagon. In contrast, he kept contacts with the State Department to a minimum, preferring to interact with U.S. military personnel, particularly World War II veterans. For example, the Paraguayan president often sent messages and gifts to high-ranking military officers, among them Joint Chiefs of Staff chairman General Lyman L. Lemnitzer, who received a table cloth as a Christmas gift just before the Kennedy inaugural. General Lemnitzer wrote an extravagant letter of thanks to Stroessner in which he went out of his way to praise the Paraguayan dictator's "Christian qualities" and "moral might."[18]

The Stronato "Reforms"

What did the United States get in return for all of its material assistance to Paraguay? The regime kept its word. It upheld an unconditional support for U.S. anti-Communist policy in the hemisphere, as exemplified by its rhetoric and votes at international organizations and by doing exactly what Ambassador Stevenson requested—lift the ban on opposition representation in the parliament by "means of free elections." In the early 1960s when the conflict between the United States and Cuba intensified, Paraguay stood steadfast behind the Kennedy administration. For example, at the Eighth Meeting of Foreign Ministers of the Organization of American States (OAS) held in Punta del Este, Uruguay (January 1962), the Paraguayan delegation, led by Foreign Minister Sapena Pastor, vociferously insisted that Cuba be isolated and that, under Article 8 of the Rio Treaty, the OAS had the obligation to intervene in Cuba to ensure "defending the hemisphere against communist aggression."[19] In an organization with twenty-one members in the early 1960s, Paraguay's guaranteed vote in the OAS was not insignificant.

In 1962, Stroessner coaxed certain members of the traditional Liberal Party into a limited accommodation of his dictatorship. He thus showed a democratic facade without making any real concession. It was unusual for Ambassador Snow to forget to remind the Paraguayans of their promises to liberalize. He often insinuated that future allocations of aid under the Alliance for Progress were contingent on Stroessner fulfilling his promises to Stevenson. Two young Liberals, Carlos and Fernando Levi Ruffinelli, were more than willing to be of assistance. They organized a splinter group (the first of many fissures within the Liberal Party during the Stronato), known as Movimiento Renovacionista and petitioned the regime for recognition and permission to participate in the upcoming general election in 1963. The Renovacionistas, officially recognized as the Liberal Party, were allowed to publish newspapers, hold meetings, and criticize some government policy. The regime also granted the party one-third of the seats in the legislature, which allowed Stroessner to show his critics and the United States that he was committed to political liberalization now that Paraguay had a "two-party" system.[20]

In 1964, the Febreristas, wracked by internal dissension and generational shifts, petitioned for recognition, which Stroessner accorded without much hesitation. Many Febreristas, including Colonel Franco, returned from exile to participate in "supervised" elections. Finally, this period of relative liberalization continued in the second half of the decade when in 1967, as the regime was drafting the new Constitution of 1967 before the 1968 general election, another group within the traditional Liberal Party asked for legal recognition. As with the Renovacionistas, the new group was granted recognition, representation in the legislature, and participation in the drafting of the new constitution, if it renounced the left wing of the party that continued to reject the legitimacy of the Stroessner regime. The new Liberals were given the name the Radical Liberal Party.

It is important to note, however, that despite these "reforms," the Stroessner regime's physical and legal repressive machinery was kept intact. Not only was the state of siege maintained, but many dissenters continued to suffer from internal and external exile. For example, the city of Concepción remained an isolated and neglected area because of the number of oppositionists who lived in that community. Though Paraguay did experience a period of social stability during this period, the regime never did dismantle its repressive apparatus for fear that it could face political or violent challenges in the future. Their concern was well founded.

Both the Kennedy and Johnson administrations felt pleased with Stroessner's willingness to allow some freedom of action to the opposition. In the 1960s, he went beyond just allowing the opposition to hold meetings and publish newspapers; he felt confident enough of his grip on power that he allowed exiles to return with their families, open businesses, and recruit new members to their parties. With the suppression of the guerrilla groups in the early 1960s and guerrilla tactics, it became clear that Paraguay was not likely to be the next Cuba. The regime thus felt it could meet U.S. demands for reform without fear that this might undermine the dictatorship.

The Apex of an Anti-Communist Alliance

Kennedy's tragic death in November 1963 profoundly shook most Latin Americans. Paraguay was no exception. The dashing young president with a beautiful, Spanish-speaking wife had captured the imaginations and hearts of people rich and poor, young and old, opponents or supporters of the regime. No other political leader of the time could claim such support from virtually all Paraguayans, regardless of political parties and ideological inclinations. Nearly everyone in Paraguay mourned his death. It seemed, if for only a moment, that the tragic death of the U.S. president could cause Paraguayans to come together to resolve their political and personal differences. Kennedy was remembered in many ways. Streets and buildings received his name, but more importantly, Paraguayans credited JFK for some of the dramatic changes they were seeing in their country: the development and modernization of their infrastructure and economy, the technological advancements, the relative liberalization and peace, and the insertion of Paraguay into the greater international community. Perhaps Kennedy did not deserve all the credit for this, but the changes proved so tangible during his time that many automatically associated progress with Kennedy, even if they also acknowledged Stroessner's contributions.

During these years and throughout much of the decade, U.S. culture had a tremendous impact upon urban Paraguayan society. Paraguayans had grown fond of U.S. movies since the 1940s, but the number and prevalence of these big-screen productions increased considerably in the mid-1960s, as did U.S. television. Paraguayan youth, particularly the newly affluent middle class, were tantalized by much of what they saw in the movies and television, from blue jeans to rock and roll. They began to appreciate and assimilate much of these U.S. tastes. Significant numbers of offspring of the elite and new middle class first began to attend U.S. universities and professional schools, gradually turning away from traditional centers of higher learning in Argentina, Brazil, and Europe. Though Paraguay was still off the beaten track for U.S. tourists, the number of U.S. visitors increased in the 1960s. Better air connections and the new Hotel Guaraní, a showpiece building designed by the Brazilian architect Oscar Niemeyer, helped attract tourists. The intensity, speed, and breadth of the interaction and Paraguayan exposure to U.S. culture reached unprecedented levels. Much of the credit was given to the slain U.S. president. It was not uncommon to see his picture in every shop along Pettirossi Street. Paraguayans eulogized JFK for the prosperity, peace, and modernity that Paraguay enjoyed during the decade.

When Lyndon B. Johnson became president, many of the Kennedy advisers remained, particularly those working on Latin America and the Alliance for Progress. They presumed that the president would continue to support the programs they had established. Only a few days after Kennedy's assassination, President Johnson addressed Latin American ambassadors at the first official gathering in the White House to assure them that his commitment to the ideals of the Alliance for Progress was unconditional, and that he would do "everything in his power to expand the Alliance and make it work."[21] Despite these words, however, by December 1963 Johnson had appointed a skeptic of the alliance and of the Kennedy administration's policy of promoting social reform and democracy in the region to the post of assistant secretary of state for Latin America and coordinator for the Alliance for Progress. Fellow Texan Thomas C. Mann, a senior foreign service officer and ambassador to Mexico (prior to his posting in Mexico City, he served as assistant secretary in the Eisenhower administration), was appointed the president's chief Latin America adviser, a decision that ultimately pushed out several key Kennedy people (Arthur Schlesinger Jr., Richard Goodwin, and Ralph Dungan), all of them advocates of a policy of supporting democracy and of linking democracy and social reform to development aid. President Johnson demonstrated little interest in and knowledge of Latin American policy (unless a crisis situation presented itself, as in Brazil and the Dominican Republic), which provided Mann with great latitude to reshape the strategic U.S. policy and some tactical aspects of it.

The assassination of President Kennedy made some in the Stroessner regime nervous. As vice president, Johnson had kept a low profile, particularly in matters related to foreign affairs, as he much preferred the familiarity of his old stomping grounds in the Congress. As a result, once Johnson had assumed the presidency, Stroessner's advisers knew little about Johnson, who on the surface seemed quite different from the sophisticated and dashing Kennedy. Not long after the death of the young president, Ambassador Snow requested an audience with

Foreign Minister Sapena Pastor in which he reassured the Paraguayan government of continuity in U.S. foreign policy, which was later confirmed on 27 November when President Johnson met with Latin American ambassadors at the White House, putting many Latin American representatives, particularly the Paraguayan ambassador, at ease about the direction of U.S. policy under the new administration. In fact, relations seem to have intensified during the presidency of LBJ to a level reminiscent of the early years of the Stroessner regime.

If the Kennedy administration insisted on at least some token reforms as a condition for economic aid and political support, the Johnson White House seemed exclusively interested in stabilizing the regime and maintaining close security relations with Asunción. Never had relations reached such a high level of cooperation and unconditional U.S. support than under the Johnson administration. Reflecting the Mann Doctrine (i.e., support any government, including antidemocratic regimes, that opposed communism and remained open to U.S. business interests), Washington viewed Stroessner's Paraguay as a committed anti-Communist ally, an ardent supporter of U.S. counterinsurgency policy in the region and in other hot spots (such as in Southeast Asia). Support for the regime, moreover, was the only option in Paraguay. The Cuban-supported insurgencies and the Indochinese specter tipped the administration (and Latin American civil-military elites) toward predominantly supporting military regimes and responses and subordinating the requirements for democracy, civil liberties and rights, and political reform to the requirements of anticommunism and political stability. Asunción could not have been more enthusiastic about the changes in U.S. policy. Between 1964 and 1967 no one in the U.S. government was overly concerned about the repression of political opponents and blatant human rights violations by the regime, though this was a period of relative peace in the country.

U.S.-Paraguayan relations entered a new and more strategic phase after the Brazilian military toppled the populist government of João Goulart in late March 1964. Washington and Asunción both welcomed the advent of the pro-U.S. military regime. The United States and Paraguay immediately and almost simultaneously recognized the government. As they established closer security and economic ties with the military government of General Humberto Castelo Branco, Brazil provided a new avenue through which the United States and Paraguay strengthened their relations. The convergence of strategic interests among the three countries helped forge an informal alliance that helped expand and solidify relations on the basis of a common security imperative: anticommunism.

By the end of 1964 U.S.-Paraguayan security and defense cooperation had reached its highest level in ten years. Paraguay received the arms that the Kennedy government had promised, expanded the presence of military advisers in Asunción from three to six, and enhanced the previous administration's program of welcoming Paraguayan officers to training facilities in the United States. In the first fiscal year of the Johnson administration (1965), military aid increased by 25 percent, much of it in the form of equipment and training of Paraguayan officers. Between 1964 and 1968 more than three hundred Paraguayan officers, under the International Military Education and Training (IMET) program, were trained by the U.S. government at its bases in the Panama Canal Zone or in facilities in the continental United States—among the most in South America. According to one estimate, from 1964 to 1967, U.S. military assistance and sales programs accounted for 17 percent of Paraguay's total defense spending, a significant amount that helped the regime alleviate mounting fiscal difficulties.[22]

Development aid did not lag behind the security and defense assistance and cooperation offered by Washington during this period. Economic assistance in the form of credits, grants, PL-480, Point 4 and other Alliance for Progress subventions expanded from $5.4 million in 1964 to nearly $8 million in 1965.[23] One critical project financed by USAID in 1965 was the establishment of SANOS, the National Potable Water Authority, which not only expanded access to water but also helped stamp out the waterborne diseases endemic to many places in Paraguay. The Johnson administration's efforts were reciprocated by the Stroessner regime; it not only continued to support U.S. interests without cavil in the UN and OAS but became much more aggressive in its rhetoric and actions in support of the Mann Doctrine.

The Dominican Republic crisis of 1965 and the passing of the Selden Resolution in September by the U.S. Congress helped solidify U.S.-Paraguayan relations, particularly in the area of security and defense. U.S. military occupation of the Dominican Republic represented a distinct break from the nonintervention pledges associated with the Good Neighbor Policy and was a clear expression of the Mann and Johnson Doctrines' principal tenet—stability was a top priority in order to protect the hemisphere from subversion.

The Johnson administration sought to obtain the cover of OAS involvement to legitimize U.S. actions, but most member nations felt reluctant to become involved in peacekeeping ventures and on a number of occasions criticized the United States for its partiality and heavy-handedness in Santo Domingo. After intense pressure from the Johnson administration, however, the OAS supported the creation of the Inter-American Peace Force (IAPF) providing a token Latin American presence during the summer of 1965; most of the troops were from many of the region's most repressive dictatorships, including two hundred soldiers and officers from Paraguay. During the Tenth Meeting of Consultation of the OAS, convoked in 1965 to deal with the Dominican civil conflict, the Paraguayan delegation adamantly supported the U.S. position, explicitly calling for international action to bloc "communist aggression in the Caribbean."[24]

Stroessner quickly organized and dispatched the Paraguayan contingent of the IAPF under the command of a trusted officer, Colonel Roberto Cubas Barbosa. Colonel Cubas, a U.S.-trained career army officer attached to the First Cavalry Division, was one of Stroessner's favorite officers. He was likewise well known and respected by the U.S. military officers who organized the Dominican intervention, having trained with some of them in the Panama Canal Zone. He also had close ties to the Brazilian military, including General Hugo Panasco Alvim, the Brazilian commanding general of the multinational force. Paraguayan participation in the IAPF consisted largely of military police duties, but it was another indication of the regime's commitment to support its key foreign policy priorities: anticommunism and stronger ties with the United States.

The U.S. link became further institutionalized in September 1965 when the U.S. House of Representatives passed a resolution that authorized the "unilateral intervention of United States troops on Paraguayan territory in the event of what was vaguely described as the threat of international communism, directly or indirectly."[25] The Selden Resolution, a nonbinding House resolution but codified by the Paraguayan government, affirmed the Stroessner regime's unconditional support for the Johnson administration's Latin American policy.

The strong reciprocity that characterized U.S.-Paraguayan relations during the Johnson administration continued until the end of President Johnson's tenure in the Oval Office in January 1969. In each of the fiscal years from 1967 to 1969, economic and development assistance to Paraguay increased by about 5 percent and military aid, specifically IMET and military equipment purchases, expanded by almost as much; in the three years more than a hundred Paraguayan officers received training in U.S. military facilities. Much of the USAID assistance went to road construction and maintenance (25 percent), public administration (20 percent), and agricultural productivity and institutional development (40 percent).[26]

This financial and technical assistance proved critical to the regime in the prelude to the Constitutional Assembly of 1967 and the general elections of 1968. The principal objective of the new constitution was to enable General Stroessner to extend his rule for an additional two five-year terms as president. The regime's hold on power along with U.S. political and economic support and a return to economic stability and development brought a period of relative peace to Paraguay. By early 1967, the old Liberals realized the futility of their struggle against Stroessner and petitioned for official recognition. Feeling confident, Stroessner granted their request and allowed the new Radical Liberal party to participate in the drafting of the new constitution and in the general election of 1968. Perhaps at no other time since it came to power in 1954 had the regime felt so secure and popular as it did in the late 1960s.

In exchange for U.S. support, Stroessner offered more than the United States expected. With problems in Southeast Asia mounting, he took the occasion of an official visit to Washington in March 1969 to offer to send Paraguayan troops to Vietnam.[27] Washington, frankly surprised, respectfully declined the offer. Nevertheless, the message that Asunción wanted to transmit—that Paraguay was an unconditional ally of the United States in its struggle against communism—was acknowledged and appreciated by the Pentagon and White House. Finally, during the 1968–69 sessions of the UN Security Council, Paraguay served as one of the Latin American representatives. No other country on the council voted as often with the United States as Paraguay did, especially on critical issues in the Middle East, Eastern Europe (i.e., Czechoslovakia), and Southeast Asia.

U.S. Companies: Investments and Trade

In the 1960s, U.S. investments and bilateral trade in Paraguay remained relatively insignificant for the United States; however, as with other aspects of this highly asymmetrical relationship, what was marginal for the United States was of some importance to Paraguay. Paraguay's political and social stability in the second half of the decade provided a more favorable climate for some U.S. investors. Moreover, a new law and agreement with the United States (Investment Guaranty Agreement, 1966) guaranteeing low taxes and easy repatriation of profits brought direct investment from the United States to record levels in 1966 and 1967. Consequently, U.S. companies began to enhance their exposure in the banking, beverages, meatpacking, and oil-refining industries, surpassing Argentina as Paraguay's most important source of private capital. The twenty-five major U.S. companies in Paraguay had a total of about $20 million invested in the economy by 1968, approximately 20 percent of all foreign direct investments in the country.[28] Some of the more important investors included the Bolivian Oil Company International, which in 1962 built and managed a pipeline and the largest petroleum refinery in the country. The U.S. soft drink industry (and by extension another trademark of U.S. culture) arrived in the mid-1960s when the Coca-Cola Company and Pepsico established their subsidiaries in Paraguay.

Similar trends characterized bilateral trade. During the decade, the United States was the second most important market for Paraguayan exports (24 percent average), after Argentina, and the largest source of imports (20 percent average). Given that agriculture accounted for nearly 40 percent of GDP and 55 percent of the economically active population, it is unsurprising that Paraguay's exports to the United States consisted principally of tobacco, wood, vegetable oils, and livestock.[29] Paraguay received much-needed capital and intermediate goods from the United States that, along with U.S. investments and markets, contributed significantly to Paraguay's 4.2 percent average growth rate during the decade, helping establish a strong base for the economic boom of the 1970s.[30]

In the 1970s U.S. investors and banks paid even more attention to Paraguay and took advantage of the new finance opportunities in that nation accompanying the boom of the decade with the construction of the great hydroelectric project of Itaipu. However, as a percentage of the total foreign investment, U.S. capital experienced a gradual but noticeable decline as the Brazilians began to replace Argentina and the United States as Paraguay's principal source of capital and technology. Law 550 of 1975 (Promotion of Investments for Economic and Social Development), which removed the distinction between foreign and domestic investment and included an exemption from taxes on capital transfers and on imports of capital goods, as well as a 50 percent reduction of income tax liability, provided an attractive environment for investors from Brazil, Europe, and the United States. In addition to First National City Bank of New York, which expanded its lending and branches in Paraguay, Bank of America, Chase Manhattan Bank, and Bank of Boston established subsidiaries and greatly expanded their commercial lending, specifically in the construction sector. Banking witnessed the largest U.S. investments during the decade.

In addition to construction, investment opportunities expanded in the agricultural sector as a result of an increase in the international demand for goods such as cotton, grains, and soybeans and the opening, thanks to improved infrastructure, of Paraguay's agricultural frontier in the Alto Paraná region, which enabled the country to boost its agricultural exports. Some of the most important agricultural investments were made by Continental Grain (cotton, vegetable oil, and agricultural processing), Cargill (cotton and soybeans), and American Farms. However, Gulf and Western, with no previous experience in the Southern Cone, made one of the single most important purchases when in 1975 it bought sixty thousand hectares in Alto Paraná for the installation of an agro-industrial complex devoted to the large production of soybeans, maize, and other crops. Gulf and Western made similar investment in 1979.[31] Investments by Continental Grain, Cargill, and Gulf and Western helped bring not only jobs and technology but also U.S. culture and brand names to previously remote and isolated parts of Paraguay. Other industries that experienced growth in U.S. capital were consulting and auditing (Arthur Young, Harza, and Price Waterhouse), mining (Chesapeake, Pecten, and United Nuclear), and office equipment (IBM and Xerox).[32] From 1974 to 1979, U.S. capital amounted to 8 percent of the total investments in Paraguay, fourth after Argentina, Brazil, and Japan. Despite the growth of U.S. capital, the diversification and expansion of foreign investments gradually lessened the weight of U.S. economic ties and influence in Paraguay.[33]

With the expansion of diplomatic, commercial, and infrastructure links with Paraguay as well as the large-scale migration of Brazilian colonists into the eastern region in the 1970s, Brazil rapidly assumed a commanding economic presence in Paraguay. The upsurge of foreign investments in the 1970s, mostly in construction (i.e., Itaipu), banking, and agriculture, led to a substantial decline in the importance of Argentina and the United Kingdom, a moderate increase in U.S. investments, and an exponential expansion in capital from Brazil and, to a lesser extent, Japan. As far as the United States was concerned, the replacement of Argentine economic influence in Paraguay with that of Brazil aroused little concern for policymakers who continued to have suspicions of Argentine governments.

Trade between the United States and Paraguay experienced the same patterns as investments; the volume increased, but because of the expansion and diversification of products and trading partners during the decade, the U.S. percentage of Paraguay's total trade declined. On average, trade with the United States represented 11.8 percent of Paraguay's exports and 12.7 percent of imports, a sizeable downturn from the over 20 percent of the previous decade. The United States went from being Paraguay's first or second most important trading partner in the 1960s to fourth, behind Argentina, Brazil, and the European Economic Community.

The economic transformation and the "Brazilianization" of Paraguay considerably enhanced Asunción's ties and dependence on Brasilia. It helped offset Buenos Aires' traditional political influence and hold over the Paraguayan economy, without excessively antagonizing Argentina, while contributing to the impressive Itaipu-led economic boom of the 1970s (average yearly growth rate of 8 percent).

Peace Corps and Kansas-Paraguay Partnership

Despite the decline in some of Washington's tangible or material sources of influence during the 1970s and the intensification of ties and dependence on Brazil, there was no indication that U.S. leverage had subsided as a result. In fact, during much of the decade, other mechanisms of influence and periodic crises in the relationship enhanced the visibility and understanding of U.S. power in Paraguay.

Early in his administration, President Kennedy called on young Americans to serve their country in the cause of peace by living and working in developing countries "to help break the bonds of mass misery." Another goal was to promote a better understanding of Americans on the part of the peoples of the Third World. Paraguay must have seemed a perfect candidate for the Peace Corps.

When the program began in 1961, however, Paraguay was not among the first countries in Latin America to receive volunteers. The first director of the Peace Corps, Sargent Shriver, the energetic and high-spirited brother-in-law of President Kennedy, had reservations about sending volunteers to Paraguay (and Nicaragua) because, he said, "those are governments totally opposed to every principle the Peace Corps stands for."[34] Shriver's attitude seemed inconsistent with the program's mission—helping interested countries meet their need for trained men and women, while promoting a better understanding of Americans throughout the world. Regardless of host-country politics and U.S. policies toward the country, the focus of the Peace Corps volunteers was to assist the poor, helpless, and marginalized climb out of poverty and underdevelopment. Shriver felt that the beneficiary would be the Stroessner regime. The Paraguayan government was not exactly excited about having volunteers spread throughout the country working with (and perhaps empowering) peasants in the vast countryside, but by the mid-1960s Asunción had made several inquiries and a request for assistance.

Jack Vaughn became the second director of the Peace Corps in 1966 and served until 1969. Vaughn was a true Latin Americanist. After serving as the Peace Corps' first Latin America director, he was appointed U.S. ambassador to Panama in 1964 and later served as assistant secretary of state for inter-American affairs, before returning to the Peace Corps as its director. Perhaps better than Shriver, Vaughn understood not only the mission of the Peace Corps and the challenge of poverty in the region but also the overall foreign policy objective of the program as expressed by President Kennedy—to help the United States by helping other nations grow stronger. Vaughn focused his attention where the Peace Corps was weak or absent. For this director, Paraguay proved exactly the place where volunteers needed to be sent.

In January 1967, two months after the signing of the joint agreement, the first U.S. volunteers arrived in Asunción. After several weeks of language training and cultural orientation in New Mexico, about thirty Peace Corps volunteers made their way to Paraguay, and without much delay (but not before a welcoming reception hosted by President Stroessner), many were sent into the interior of the country on mostly agricultural extension projects, but also programs in health and education. Richard Griscom was the first country director. Griscom was a true Kennedy foot soldier, extremely energetic, friendly, and committed to the president's foreign policy goals in Latin America. After Harvard Law School, he joined the Peace Corps and became the first country director in many new host countries in Latin America, where, as in Paraguay, he helped organize the program and establish necessary contacts with the U.S. Embassy and host government officials and agencies. Griscom was succeeded in 1969 by Jim Sherman, who was fortunate to have Tony Belloti, Griscom's able deputy, as his number two in Paraguay.

Each of the first three volunteer groups had about thirty members and served for about two years. A new group arrived in January of every year so that there were fifty-five to sixty volunteers serving at any time in Paraguay. Though most participated in agricultural extension, some taught language and literature at the university, directed health education and maintenance programs, and worked in co-ops and credit unions. Many who went into the campo felt they had gone back in time to the nineteenth century because of the poverty and lack of development in Paraguay's countryside. As one volunteer noted, "Paraguay seem to epitomize the small, rural backwater country that many people imagined Latin American to be."

Despite the isolation that some felt, all were pleased to see the warmth and friendliness with which they were received. Even Colorado Party and government officials behaved with great hospitality and openness. There were a few minor incidents. For example, Rick Smith was picked up as part of the government's Operación Tijeras (individuals with long hair, perceived by the government to be a sign of subversive attitudes, were taken to a barbershop to have their mane cut to an acceptable length), but there were no actions directed at the volunteers. In fact, the government was careful not to let any incident damage the future of the program or its relations with the United States. By the same token, the volunteers, despite feeling great disdain for the regime, refrained (under orders) from participating in anything political.

Paraguayans of all backgrounds and political affiliations welcomed the volunteers and were always willing to accept their help and advice. Starting with the second group, Peace Corps volunteers received training in the Guaraní language that was reinforced and perfected when they reached the campo. This was greatly appreciated by the campesinos and others. No other foreigner had taken the time and interest to learn the Paraguayan language; to a large extent, the success of the program in the campo had much to do with the volunteers' language skills. As a result, close bonds were forged between volunteers and Paraguayans. The success of the early years institutionalized a relationship between the Peace Corps and Paraguay that flourished for years to come (despite the Nixon administration's antipathy to the Kennedy-inspired program), making it one of the largest and most successful Peace Corps programs in Latin America.

A complementary facet of the Alliance for Progress proposed the establishment of a special relationship between individual states in the United States and selected Latin American nations or regional states for "a more productive human relationship." The concept of Partners of the Americas was born in 1963 when President Kennedy called for a new alliance of friendship and cooperation between communities, local governments, and citizens of the United States and Latin America. Through these partnerships, volunteer committees would work together on self-help projects in community and economic development, while fostering inter-American friendship and cooperation. As the National Association of the Partners of the Americas summarized, "the treasure of the program is to be found in that body of intangible value which comes from the citizens of the Americas working together in the spirit of the Alliance for Progress."[35]

Not long after the partners program was established Paraguay came to the attention of civic, religious, and government officials in Kansas. After several initial attempts to establish partnerships with the Brazilian state of Santa Catarina and the Colombian state of Santander, the Governor's Committee on the Alliance recommended that Kansas explore opportunities in Paraguay for partnership. An important factor in forming the partnership unique to the Kansas-Paraguay association was the vital role played by the Mennonite Church and its long established ties with the Paraguayan Mennonite community. For several years, the Mennonite community in Kansas had visited Paraguay, offering technical and financial assistance to this largely agricultural society. This level of cooperation and the role played by several church leaders, such as Dr. Elmer Ediger, Lyle Yost, Frank Wiens, Marianne Beach, and Representative E. F. Steichen, proved instrumental in the early phase of the program. The initial argument made in favor of establishing the partnership stressed the strong similarities between the partners—landlocked (about the same size), cattle-producing and agricultural economies, and the close ties that Kansan Mennonites maintained with their brethren in the Paraguayan Chaco. Paraguay and Kansas seemed natural partners.

A flurry of activity helped expand and consolidate the partnership during 1968 and 1969. Delegations from Kansas and Paraguay exchanged numerous visits. These led to some important tangible benefits for Paraguay. One Kansas delegation observed how public and private organizations in Paraguay worked at the local, regional, and national levels. Another delegation made up of university professors served as consultants at Paraguayan universities, while several other delegations visited health care facilities (mainly treating mental disorders) to provide assistance. One important Kansas delegation, led by Lyle Yost, president of the Hesson Corporation, traveled to Paraguay in 1969 to evaluate the general agricultural needs and help establish the San Juan Bautista agricultural training center. A few Paraguayan delegations visited Kansas and other parts of the United States; one group made up of mostly journalists visited to observe the role of the media in the 1968 U.S. presidential election.

All this culminated with the largest visit up to that time. In 1969 Kansas governor Robert Docking led a delegation of twenty-four Kansans from all walks of life. The purpose of the trip was to "sustain and increase the level of involvement in the Partners program at the highest echelon of government while assessing the existing programs."[36] Governor Docking and his delegation arrived during a bone-chilling Asunción winter in July carrying thirty thousand dollars appropriated by the Kansas legislature for start-up costs for the partnership and other programs, a large supply of antibiotics and other medicines for distribution to the Peace Corps, and four scholarships for Paraguayan students to study at any of several Kansas state universities. A John Deere tractor was also presented to the San Juan Bautista Center. It was not often that Paraguay received an important official from the United States; it was the second visit by a U.S. governor, one month after New York governor Nelson Rockefeller's stop in Asunción. As a result, not only were Governor Docking and his delegation given the royal treatment, but the Stroessner regime made every effort to politicize the visit and remind the governor of Paraguay's long and committed friendship to the United States. The governor, known for his cold warrior credentials, appreciated Stroessner's comments when he said during a personal interview that because of Paraguay's geopolitical position it was a "target for Castro-communism . . . the Paraguayan people know how to resist whatever new attempts that will be made to convert Paraguay into a fountainhead of international communism in this hemisphere." However, the governor grew bored with and wary of the dictator's obsessive repetition of the anticommunism mantra. As the visit concluded, many in the Kansas delegation felt quite distressed with the Paraguayan government's attempts to politicize the visit because they believed it diverted attention from the real objective—strengthening the partnership and providing technical and financial assistance to Paraguay's educational, health, and agricultural sectors.

In the end, however, the delegation achieved its purpose. It solidified a relationship and program that saw exchanges between the partners expand exponentially throughout the 1970s. It forged an alliance of farmers and teachers, doctors and engineers, students and scientists, homemakers and businesspeople. No other program intensified bilateral relations more than the Kansas-Paraguay Partnership (KPP).

Nixon Administration and the Ricord Affair

Not surprisingly, the Paraguayan government expressed delight at the 1968 election of Richard M. Nixon, who had visited Paraguay as vice president during his 1958 tour of South America. At that time, he spoke highly of Stroessner and the Paraguayan people, saying that perhaps the United States had no stronger ally in the struggle against communism. Some in the Paraguayan government, such as Foreign Minister Sapena Pastor, Interior Minister Sabino Montanaro, and Stroessner propagandist Ezequiel González Alsina, could not contain their enthusiasm in announcing a "new era" in U.S.-Paraguayan relations characterized by a "friendship stronger than any in the hemisphere."[37]

What confirmed the initial Paraguayan view of the new administration's friendship was the decision by the White House to send its special envoy, New York governor Nelson Rockefeller, head of a commission charged with conducting a study of U.S.–Latin American relations, to Paraguay as one of his first stops in the region.[38] Rockefeller arrived in Asunción on 19 June 1969 for a brief thirty-six-hour visit. As expected, he was received with all the pomp and circumstance imaginable. On meeting Stroessner, Rockefeller echoed remarks made by Nixon a decade earlier: "Stroessner did more for Paraguay than what had been done fifty years prior to his coming to office."[39]

All the enthusiasm, however, was dashed by the unexpected student protests that the Rockefeller delegation encountered not long after its arrival. Prior to the governor's arrival, the Paraguayan government arrested several hundred university students and others in opposition to the Stroessner government. The regime's preemptive measure did not work. Near the Pantheon of Heroes, over a hundred university students protested against the U.S. government's support for the Stroessner regime. Never before had anyone demonstrated against the United States. The regime quickly responded by unleashing its Colorado Party enforcers against the students, some of whom were badly injured. The Paraguayan government was embarrassed, but more importantly, the protests and subsequent repression clearly affected the findings of the commission, which in its August 1969 report made several references to Paraguay when describing the disturbing social and political situation in the region that had fostered radicalism and anti-U.S. sentiment. It was not clear if Stroessner was more embarrassed and frustrated by the protest or the report.

Soon after Rockefeller's visit and presentation of the report, relations between the two countries went sour, reaching their lowest ebb since General Stroessner came to power. The tension had nothing to do with Rockefeller or the regime's continued denial of political and civil rights to its citizens, but with Paraguay's links to international drug traffic and its unwillingness to heed the Nixon administration's call for cooperation in the new war on drugs. Because of growing domestic concern with crime and drug consumption in the United States, in a July 1971 speech President Nixon called on all friendly governments to cooperate with the United States in combating this new threat. Known for being at the heart of contraband trade in South America, Paraguay appeared as a major player in the drug trade. The Nixon administration accused Asunción of allowing Paraguay to be used as a transit point for drugs destined for the United States and Europe; specifically, Paraguay was accused of offering protection to one of the largest drug-smuggling rings in Latin America. Government complicity, coupled with the immediacy of the drug issue at home and the easing of the cold war as a result of détente, brought a major confrontation between Washington and Asunción.[40]

Paraguay's notoriety as a major drug entrepôt started in the early 1960s, when evidence emerged that linked military and Colorado Party officials to the drug trade, either as traffickers or facilitators. However, it was not until August 1967, when Frenchman August (André) Ricord arrived in Asunción to coordinate the transport of heroin to the United States via Paraguay that narcotics became the focus of relations. Ricord used Paraguay as a privileged haven and transit point for running a lucrative heroin-smuggling business worth an estimated $2.5 billion a year.[41]

According to U.S. federal agents, Ricord's organization, known as the French Connection by some and the Latin Connection by others, was responsible for 50–75 percent of all the heroin smuggled into the United States. This kind of operation necessarily required the participation or consent of Paraguayan government officials. Ricord almost certainly received protection and was offered pilots, aircraft, and landing strips by a high-ranking military officer, namely General Andrés Rodríguez, then second in command of the armed forces and related to Stroessner by marriage. Two other backers of the Ricord operation were General Patricio Colman, one of Stroessner's oldest and closest friends, who commanded the counterinsurgency unit, Fourteenth Infantry Cerro Corá, and Pastor Coronel, head of the secret police. These men and some of their underlings had already made their fortunes in the alcohol- and tobacco-smuggling racket of the 1960s and now profited from their association with Ricord. In addition to turning their ranches into clandestine landing strips (charging twenty-five thousand dollars per plane), General Rodríguez, a major stockholder in Taxi Aéreo Guaraní, offered pilots and aircraft to the French Connection.[42]

Despite some attention given by the U.S. news media, much of the evidence that the U.S. government compiled about Paraguayan government complicity was kept under wraps (largely because of the uncertainty among U.S. federal officials about Paraguay's involvement) until December 1970, when over two hundred pounds of heroin were seized at Miami International Airport on a plane from Paraguay piloted by an employee of Taxi Aéreo Guaraní.[43] Suddenly, narcotics came to dominate U.S.-Paraguayan relations. The topic was always paramount in all discussions between Ambassador J. Raymond Ylitalo and Paraguayan government officials.

After much intelligence work and political pressure, U.S. narcotics agents penetrated the smuggling operation in April 1971 and asked that Ricord be arrested and extradited to the United States. The indictment and extradition request stipulated that Ricord "was accused by the United States government of masterminding the smuggling of 5,000 kilos of heroin to the United States between 1965 and 1970, equivalent to 50 percent of the total inflow during that period."[44] The Paraguayans detained Ricord but refused to hand him over to U.S. federal agents, a decision that led to the most serious rift in relations since the 1940s. The incident created a crisis within the government. Interior Minister Montanaro and Foreign Minister Sapena Pastor wanted to avoid a confrontation with the United States, while generals Rodríguez and Colman were determined to protect Ricord. In December 1971, a Paraguayan court ruled that the extradition requested by the United States did not meet the requirements of the 1913 treaty between the two countries and ordered Ricord's release. The embassy responded by expressing its "profound disappointment and concern with the decision of the court. Let us not forget that the accused is one of the heads of the international heroin trafficking industry, who has brought misery and death to thousands of youths in the United States and around the world."[45]

In January 1972, President Nixon threatened to cut off aid to Paraguay if Stroessner did not extradite Ricord. The U.S. president sent his Paraguayan counterpart a personal note reminding him that under the 1971 Foreign Assistance Act, the president was authorized to suspend economic aid to any nation that failed to cooperate in fighting international drug trafficking. In one of his few demonstrations of defiance, perhaps out of loyalty to Colman or fear of how Rodríguez might respond, Stroessner refused to hand over Ricord on the grounds that a president could not intervene in the proceedings of a Paraguayan court.[46] The United States cancelled Paraguay's sugar quota, and nearly $5 million in credit lines were suspended, as was military aid. Washington also threatened to suspend $11 million in additional aid if Paraguay maintained its intransigence.

Just as relations went from bad to worse, two developments helped deter what might have been a disaster for Paraguay. In August, General Colman died at Walter Reed Hospital of old bullet wounds, thus releasing Stroessner from his commitment to an old friend. Then on 8 August, the deputy assistant secretary of state for international narcotics matters, Nelson Gross, arrived in Asunción to deliver a personal ultimatum to Stroessner from President Nixon, threatening economic sanctions to the Paraguayan economy if Ricord was not extradited. Within forty-eight hours a Paraguayan court reversed the lower court decision, and the French heroin trafficker was immediately extradited to the United States, where he was sentenced to twenty years of imprisonment.

With the extradition of Ricord, the smuggling of hard drugs from Paraguay declined, and U.S.-Paraguayan relations returned to their earlier status. Asunción went out of its way to heal the wounds by taking measures that explicitly demonstrated its commitment to the U.S. counternarcotics effort. After ratifying the 1961 UN Single Convention on Narcotics in December 1971, the Paraguayan government signed and ratified several multilateral and bilateral conventions, accords, and protocols, such as the South American Accord on Drugs and Psychotropic Substances (1973), a treaty of extradition with the United States in 1973 (ratified by Law 399), and a 1972 accord with the United States "to combat the unauthorized use and illicit traffic of narcotics and other dangerous drugs" (ratified by Law 379). In 1972 Stroessner also signed Law

357, Paraguay's antidrug legislation; it committed the government to repressing "the illicit traffic in narcotics and dangerous drugs and other related crimes and establishes the means for the prevention and rehabilitation of drug dependency." Finally, in 1973, upon the request of Interpol and the Drug Enforcement Administration, and with their assistance, Paraguay agreed to establish an antinarcotics unit, known as the Dirección Nacional de Narcóticos (DINAR).[47]

Relations improved between the two countries, but Paraguay's negative international image was damaged beyond repair. News reports and feature magazine articles were published describing the role of Paraguay and its government in the drug trade. For example, Jack Anderson, a well-known and prizewinning U.S. journalist, published an article in 1973 that was picked up by many outlets in the United States and Europe. He published a list of names based on a CIA memo that revealed the major Paraguayan players, offering a detailed description of the drug-related activities of General Andrés Rodríguez, Pastor Coronel, and General Germán Martínez. And in March, *Reader's Digest*, the periodical with the largest circulation in the world, published an exposé ("The Hunt for Andre") by Nathan Adams that linked the "stronista connection" to the thriving global drug trade. It accused high civil and military officials in the Stroessner government of protecting Ricord. The article appeared in *Selecciones* (the Spanish version of *Reader's Digest*) and was read by many throughout Latin America. Paraguayan authorities sought to prevent its circulation in the country by confiscating the issue, but it was smuggled in anyway and widely reproduced for many to read. To Asunción's consternation, the resolution of the Ricord affair did not end the bad press. More importantly, though relations with the United States normalized, they never fully returned to their previous status quo.

The Nixon and Ford administrations subscribed to some of the key recommendations of the Rockefeller report, meaning that despite evidence of Paraguayan government involvement in the narcotics trade, Washington provided quiet support or remained indifferent to the absence of political and civil rights in Paraguay, so long as Asunción cooperated on the issue of drugs and continued to be a bastion of anticommunism in the heart of South America. For example, in the early 1970s peasant and religious groups joined together to form the Ligas Agrarias Cristianas (LAC), an effort to organize and empower peasant cooperatives and grassroots communities to challenge state repression and government agricultural policies. The regional networks ("leagues") were brutally repressed (most severely in Caaguazú) by the regime that felt these organizations were undermining the Colorado Party's base of support in the countryside. Neither Washington nor the U.S. Embassy expressed a bit of concern over the torture and imprisonment of peasant and religious leaders. The repression reached its peak in April–May 1976 when the government arrested nearly two thousand members of the Organización Primero de Marzo (OPM), an embryonic guerrilla movement consisting mainly of radical university students, and Ligas activists who had joined the armed struggle against the regime.[48] Several dozen members of the OPM died in police custody, including its top two leaders, Juan Carlos Da Costa and Mario Schaerer. Others were imprisoned and tortured at the Emboscada prison camp, a ghastly detention center that was reopened, but never reconditioned, for members of the OPM. Also during this period, the Paraguayan Communist Party leadership was decapitated after a vicious raid in San Bernardino. Once again, the Ford administration remained mute to the brutality of the regime.

7 Human Rights and "Democracy by Pressure," 1977–1989

Though it is frequently forgotten today, the U.S. government tried to make the protection of human rights an important component of its foreign policy soon after the end of World War II. After the UN General Assembly approved the Universal Declaration of Human Rights in December 1948, many in the United States and around the world assumed that human rights had become the cornerstone of U.S. foreign policy and the new international order. Unfortunately, the cold war and its attendant focus on national security quickly dampened expectations, and only with the development of widespread opposition to the Vietnam War in the late 1960s did human rights reappear in the policy discourse. Though human rights never completely vanished as a concern, it could not balance the emphasis placed on national security and the stability of friendly regimes regardless of their human rights record.[1]

President Richard Nixon never discussed human rights directly. When he did refer to human rights, he always placed his comments in the context of other potentially competing values, particularly the stability of existing relationships. In 1971 he stated, "we hope that governments will evolve toward constitutional procedures but it is not our mission to try to provide except by example, the answers to such questions. . . . We deal with governments as they are." Although both the president and his secretary of state, Henry Kissinger, felt reluctant to address the issue, attitudes in Congress and public opinion dramatically shifted so as to favor placing human rights at the top of U.S. foreign policy priorities. Alarmed by U.S. silence regarding the systematic violations of human rights committed by pro-U.S. authoritarian regimes in Asia and Latin America, activists organized a campaign to pressure Congress to make this humanitarian consideration an integral part of U.S. foreign policy. As a result, Congress passed legislation between 1973 and 1975 that made human rights one of the conditions under which the United States grants economic assistance, supplies military weapons, or supports loans by multilateral development banks.

In mid-1975 the Ford administration began to propose a change in the importance of human rights in U.S. foreign policy. Secretary of State Kissinger warned some Latin American dictatorships that there were limits to which the United States could accept friendly relations with governments engaged in systematic repression. Although Kissinger consistently voiced his belief that human rights concerns remain secondary to the maintenance of peace and world order, in his last eighteen months in office he and President Ford attempted to appease a vocal human rights constituency in the United States. In June 1976 Kissinger gave a speech at the Organization of American States (OAS) entitled "Human Rights and the Western Hemisphere," where he noted that "one of the most compelling issues of our time, and one which calls for the concerted action of all responsible peoples and nations, is the necessity to protect and extend fundamental rights of humanity." The message sent to U.S. diplomats and military dictatorships in the region was clear: the value of human rights in U.S. policy toward Latin America was now firm and irrefutable.

Meanwhile, although human rights awareness was growing in the United States and the international community, in Paraguay the Stroessner regime was expanding and intensifying its repression of journalists, peasants, students, priests, and Catholic Church organizations. Tensions between the regime and some key groups within the Catholic Church hierarchy were particularly intense during the first part of the 1970s.[2] Church organizations, such as the Ligas Agrarias Cristianas (Christian Church Leagues; LAC), empowered by the new social encyclicals of Pope John XXIII and angered by Brazilian land colonization, began setting up organizations (i.e., cooperatives and grassroots communities) among workers and peasants in the 1960s in an effort to *conscientizar*—create a social and political consciousness through a series of educational and welfare programs. Sectors of the Catholic Church began to assume a more activist pastoral role. As the church openly challenged the regime's traditional base of support in the countryside, it was impossible for the government to ignore the "rebelliousness." Church-state relations reached their lowest point when Minister of Interior Sabino Montanaro and Chief of Police Francisco Brítez were excommunicated as a result of their role in repressing students, priests, and nuns who peacefully demonstrated against the deportation of a Paraguayan priest, the first of eight priests expelled by the government between 1969 and 1973. The growth of the LAC and the emergence of a radicalized university student movement combined to offer the most serious threat to Stroessner since the early 1960s.

After several strikes and demonstrations at Asunción's two universities peaked in 1969, the regime mounted a campaign to stifle all forms of political activism. Student and church leaders were imprisoned, tortured, and deported; base communities were destroyed. The government also launched a media campaign denouncing Communist infiltration of the university and church. In September 1970 it enacted a piece of "anti-subversive" legislation titled "Law in Defense of Public Peace and Personal Freedom" (Law 209), which prohibited practically all forms of political activities, including public meetings and dissemination of information.

At first, the progressive elements within the Catholic Church refused to back down. The LAC went beyond preaching social justice to peasants to condemning repression and corruption and occupying churches and other facilities in small rural towns. The regime responded viciously when peasants, encouraged by Ligas leadership, occupied churches in Caaguazú and Coronel Oviedo. The more the LAC tried to mobilize supporters in the countryside, the more intense the regime's repression became. One incident was particularly brutal. On 8 February 1975 an army antiguerrilla detachment, led by Colonel Joaquín Grace, entered the northern village of Jejuí, which boasted a peasant commune. The troops fired on the inhabitants, killing eight, and then beat survivors, raped women, and destroyed homes.

After the discovery of an assassination plot against President Stroessner in November 1974, the regime unleashed a new wave of arrests, beatings, and violence against real and imagined opponents on a scale unseen since Stroessner's rise to power. The police arrested and interrogated thousands of peasants, students, priests, and opposition party officials. Some were tortured by the feared Departamento de Investigaciones de la Policía Central (Department of Investigations of the Police), headed by Pastor Coronel, and its Dirección de Vigilancia y Delitos (Division of Crime and Vigilance), a center known for conducting extreme torture. State repression peaked in April–May 1976 when an incipient urban-based guerrilla movement, established in the early 1970s by radical university students and known as the Organización Primero de Marzo or the Organización Político-Militar (First of March Organization or Politico-Military Organization; OPM), was nearly decimated after several violent armed confrontations between the guerrillas and Paraguayan security services.[3] Over a hundred OPM fighters were captured and about thirty-five were killed, including several leaders who died in police custody. Another component of this wave of repression was unleashed against church organizations and leaders, peasants, and students throughout the country. Nearly two thousand suspects were detained and kept at the Emboscada prison.

Before 1976, Stroessner's effective low profile foreign policy allowed his regime and its dismal human rights record to pass largely unnoticed by the international community. Only sporadically did the international press report on repression in Paraguay. Some argued that a "silent international plot" either purposely ignored Paraguay's human rights situation or simply accepted the regime's contention that Paraguay was a "democracy without communism." Clearly, no "international conspiracy" existed against democracy in Paraguay; the coverage simply reflected the country's irrelevance in international affairs.

By the mid-1970s, however, a new generalized international consciousness of human rights began to expand. The Stroessner regime's systematic violations of the most basic constitutional guarantees became a focus of international concern. The U.S. Congress, pressured by several nongovernmental groups, began to take notice of the wave of repression that engulfed Paraguay in the 1970s. On 28 July 1976 a subcommittee of the House of Representatives Committee on Foreign Affairs held hearings on the human rights situation in Paraguay in which a number of domestic and international human rights activists testified to the mass arrests and beatings. As never before, Paraguay was singled out as one of most despotic regimes in the Western Hemisphere. Relatively negligible U.S. interests in Paraguay allowed Washington to make a strong commitment to human rights without fear of losing anything of importance. In short, pushing hard in Paraguay was largely cost free.

This and other efforts by Congress and human rights groups in the United States to focus attention on Paraguay's human rights situation were, in part, a result of the high-profile case involving the torture and murder in March 1976 of Joelito Filártiga, the seventeen-year-old son of a prominent dissident and medical doctor. The teenager's mutilated body was found in the Asunción home of Americo Peña-Irala, the capital's police inspector. The regime alleged a crime of passion, but as Peña-Irala made abundantly clear to the victim's sister, Dolly, Joelito was murdered in retaliation for his father's political activities and, supposedly, for the father and son's involvement in the OPM. With no recourse for justice in Paraguay, the family asked the U.S. government for help; the U.S. Embassy became directly involved in the case, working behind the scenes to assist the family with their request for justice. It was not, however, until the family filed a civil suit in U.S. courts that the case and Paraguay's dismal human rights situation garnered worldwide attention, particularly from U.S. legislators and the new U.S. administration.

Under Jimmy Carter, human rights promptly assumed an unparalleled prominence in foreign policy decision making. Even before entering the White House, Governor Carter was a committed defendant of human rights. In a speech in September 1976, he noted that Americans "cannot look away when a government tortures people, or jails them for their beliefs. . . . We should begin by having it understood that if any nation deprives its own people of basic human rights, that fact will help shape our own people's attitudes toward that nation's government." President Carter would later say, "our commitment to human rights must be absolute . . . human rights is the soul of our foreign policy."[4] The message sent by Washington and carried by U.S. diplomats was that the United States would no longer ignore human rights in the name of national security. Dictatorships in Argentina, Brazil, Chile, Paraguay, and Uruguay could no longer expect even a "firm handshake" from Washington but, instead, would receive a slap in the form of reduced aid if human rights were not respected.

Confrontation

U.S.-Paraguayan relations changed dramatically as a result. Between 1954 and 1977 U.S. policy actively served the regime's interests. In addition to the internal power structure created by the regime during a span of more than two decades (support from the military, Colorado Party, business circles, and, until the 1970s, peasantry), another key pillar of the regime that sustained it during this period was the firm and continuous political and economic support provided by five successive U.S. administrations. However, in 1977 there appeared a clear break with the past. Two new issues were suddenly infused into U.S.-Paraguayan relations: human rights and democracy. The pressure placed on the Stroessner regime by the Carter administration to respect human rights, at a time when state repression was perhaps at its height, caught Asunción by surprise, transforming the U.S. government from an unconditional ally to a vehement opponent of the regime.[5] On a more pragmatic policy level, in 1977 "Paraguay must have appeared as a 'safe bet' for the Carter administration to show its concern with democracy and human rights . . . the threat from the left was weak." Hence, the United States felt it could afford to push the regime hard without fearing that Paraguay would fall to the "communists."[6]

Washington immediately began criticizing the Stronato, holding it up to international public opinion as one of the most egregious violators of human rights, along with Argentina's and Uruguay's military rulers, the Somoza dictatorship in Nicaragua, and the Pinochet regime in Chile. Instructions were sent to Ambassador George Landau to demand that some three hundred political prisoners be released and that the regime end its violent campaign against dissidents. In short order, Washington "declared war" on a regime it described as a "military, unipersonal, and reactionary dictatorship." Never had such words been used before to describe the regime. The administration also announced that it was dramatically cutting military and economic assistance by 50 and 70 percent, respectively. For the first time in the history of bilateral relations, the United States was distancing itself publicly from the Paraguayan dictatorship.

As relations deteriorated, a meeting between Presidents Carter and Stroessner was arranged for early September 1977 when most heads of OAS member states were in Washington for the historic signing of the Panama Canal treaties.[7] For months, Ambassador Landau had insisted that Paraguay allow the OAS Human Rights Commission to visit Paraguay. Stroessner dragged his feet. As the administration prepared for the one-hour meeting with Stroessner, the president's briefing book indicated to all of his advisers, including Ambassador Landau, that President Carter would urge President Stroessner to permit the OAS mission to visit Paraguay. President Carter also requested that Paraguay release its political prisoners. Many of the president's aides were a bit anxious as to how a meeting between a dictator and human rights champion would work out, but they were confident that Stroessner would agree to the OAS mission if Carter so requested. After hearing the presidents share pleasantries and Stroessner's customary expressions of solidarity with the United States and anticommunism, U.S. officials were shocked when President Carter failed to broach the issue of the OAS mission and human rights with the Paraguayan strongman. As some in the meeting speculated, this pleasant, nonconfrontational president from the South did not feel it appropriate to make demands of a guest. It would be up to others to do the president's bidding.

Ambassador Landau pressed hard on the issue of human rights, but it was not until Robert White, an outspoken and strong advocate of civil liberties and democracy, became ambassador that the confrontation with the regime came to a head. Not long after presenting his credentials in November 1977, Ambassador White went on the offensive. He threatened the Paraguayans with isolation and sanctions if they failed to release political prisoners. Thanks to White's determined efforts, Stroessner freed hundreds of political prisoners, many of whom might have died were it not for the ambassador. According to one estimate, by the end of the ambassador's tenure, the number of political prisoners dropped to fewer than twenty-five. Ambassador White also played a pivotal role in helping the opposition establish the Acuerdo Nacional (National Accord), the first coalition of opposition parties created during the Stroessner regime, established in January 1979. To the regime's deep consternation, White offered National Accord leaders the ambassador's residence to strategize and coordinate efforts with opposition organizations in and out of the country as well as with the U.S. government.

The administration's point man on human rights and close aide to the president, Deputy Secretary of State Warren Christopher, headed an interagency committee charged with the goal of ensuring the incorporation of human rights criteria into U.S. foreign policy and foreign aid decisions. With respect to Paraguay, the committee urged that all economic and military aid be suspended (a recommendation viewed positively by the White House) and that the United States vote against loans for Paraguay in international lending institutions, where the United States had sufficient voting power to deny approval of loans. Much debate ensued on this last suggestion. Some argued that denying development loans from the World Bank and the Inter-American Development Bank would hurt Paraguayans more than the regime. In the end, the administration decided to send a signal by voting against or abstaining from voting on development loans that did not directly benefit the Paraguayan people. In 1978–79, the United States opposed seven of nineteen loans from multilateral development banks destined for Paraguay. The cost to the regime might have been limited, but the message was heard loud and clear.

The weight of U.S. pressure stemmed not only from the embassy and the White House, but from the Congress, which in early 1978 suspended all military aid and hardware deliveries to Paraguay and insisted that the White House pull its military advisory group from Asunción to protest human rights violations, child prostitution, and drug smuggling. The White House heeded the advice of Congress and closed the military advisory group office, while continuing to reduce requests for economic aid. By 1980, after an appeal by several senators, no military aid was requested for Paraguay.

Individual representatives and senators took on the issue of human rights in Paraguay. For example, in July 1978 after the arrest of opposition leader Domingo Laíno by Paraguayan security forces, Senator Edward Kennedy came out publicly denouncing the Stroessner regime and threatening that "if Dr. Laíno remained under arrest or was falsely implicated, the United States should consider terminating all economic assistance to Paraguay."

The Defense Department, through its military group (milgroup) in Asunción, also got into the fray, if only in an informal and unofficial manner. U.S. military officers in the 1970s and into the next decade were disdainful of the regime and Paraguay's military officers. Officers in the military group, many of them having received medals for their service in Vietnam, viewed their Paraguayan counterparts as repressors and parasites who were more interested in enriching themselves than in serving their country and profession. It was not uncommon, therefore, in the late 1970s for many of these officers to help the cause of human rights in Paraguay by serving as facilitators or liaisons for Paraguayan human rights activists. In order to circumvent police monitoring of mail, milgroup officers allowed Paraguayan democrats to use U.S. official military or diplomatic channels to send their correspondence abroad. According to one account, U.S. officers also provided some Paraguayan opposition activists with information about regime efforts to quell opposition activities.

The Carter administration's foreign policy priority not only mobilized the government but also roused nongovernmental organizations and the OAS to focus their attention on Paraguay's worsening human rights situation. In January 1978, the Inter-American Human Rights Commission of the OAS issued a scathing report accusing the Stroessner regime of torture and kidnapping. It was the first time that an international organization publicly scorned the Paraguayan government for "violating practically every human right recognized by the American Declaration of Rights and Duties of Man. . . . The application of physical and psychological cruelty to extract confessions and to intimidate is a common practice in Paraguay."[8] The United States, in an unprecedented move, voted in favor of approving the report. Another entity that exposed abuses of the Stroessner regime was Amnesty International. In 1977, encouraged by the U.S. State Department, Amnesty International issued two reports detailing cases of torture and murder committed by the regime against students, church officials, and peasants. The reports also noted continued restrictions to freedom of the press and academic life, limitations to organizing unions, intimidation of human rights activists, and repression and corruption committed against indigenous groups.

Thanks in large part to the forces unleashed by the Carter administration, the Stroessner regime could no longer attempt to pass unnoticed by the international community. By the late 1970s, Paraguay was in the crosshairs of every government and nongovernmental organization in the country committed to exposing human rights violations. Stroessner now faced a hostile international community led by a U.S. administration committed to isolating and, ultimately, undermining his regime.

Under such an assault, even from its long-standing patron in North America, President Stroessner could not afford to be indifferent. The regime believed its survival was at stake. As far as Stroessner was concerned, historical precedent abounded of "pro–United States allies" (i.e., dictators), especially in the Caribbean and Central America, being undermined by the partial withdrawal of crucial support from the United States. Despite his resistance to liberalize, Stroessner was adroit enough to appease the United States by offering concessions, such as releasing political prisoners and allowing for the first National Human Rights Congress to be held in Asunción in December 1978. He also granted legal recognition to "purified" opposition parties and, to some extent, tolerated activities of the National Accord. The Carter administration deemed these concessions "an acceptable improvement," but when Washington or Ambassador White insisted that more be done, the regime loudly condemned the "interventionist character of the United States." The regime would never accept any U.S. demand that could result in its demise.

The Paraguayan government's perception of the United States

changed markedly. The U.S. government, once regarded as a close ally in the struggle against communism, was now held in angry disdain. In the late 1970s, Paraguayan government officials, like their military counterparts in Argentina, began to use the language of interventionism and sovereignty, terms usually employed by leftist anti-U.S. regimes. President Stroessner, during the Third Congress of the Latin American Anti-Communist Confederation held in Asunción in March 1977 (hosting the Congress was viewed as an act of defiance by Paraguayan government officials), stated, in reference to U.S. pressures, that "the administration of the United States should refrain from continuing to use demagogically the theme of Human Rights in order to intervene in the internal politics of each country of Latin America."[9] Then, in April 1979, at the Twelfth International Congress of the World Anti-Communist League (WACL) that Paraguay hosted, several cabinet and government officials expressed outrage and "profound umbrage" at the U.S. ambassador's "illegal interventions" in Paraguay's domestic affairs. During the Congress, the Paraguayan government established a national chapter of the WACL and created a study center to investigate and monitor "communist infiltration" in the Americas. Several cabinet members, acting as the regime's spokespeople, and the government-controlled press, led by Stroessner speechwriter Ezequiel González Alsina, were the most vocal and confrontational in expressing their outrage at U.S. policy. For example, Alberto Nogues, foreign affairs minister, and Sabino Montanaro, interior minister, often stated, when U.S. pressure was felt most intensely, the theme that "Paraguay would remain anti-Communist with or without the support of the United States," while Colorado Party officials and the government-controlled press described U.S. foreign policy as "Carter-Communism."

Colorado Party officials reserved their strongest condemnation, however, for Ambassador White, whom they accused of being a Communist and a drunk. They constantly berated the ambassador in the press. The Ministry of Interior organized anti-U.S. demonstrations outside the embassy, particularly when the ambassador held meetings with the National Accord and other opposition leaders. Sabino Montanaro often threatened to declare the ambassador persona non grata if he failed to refrain from intervening in Paraguay's domestic affairs. The minister was also quoted as saying, "Robert White thinks our country is an *estancia,* and he the *capitaz.*"

By 1980, U.S.-Paraguayan relations had reached their lowest point since the time of Washburn and Solano López. Believing there were no costs to pressuring the regime to liberalize because of the weakness and incapacity of the radical left to threaten a takeover, the Carter administration exhausted most of its leverage and influence in trying to force the Stroessner regime to respect Paraguayans' basic political rights. By the same token, though Stroessner made some concessions, he had no intention of accepting all of Washington's demands since doing so threatened the survival of his regime. As a result, in 1980 total U.S. aid to Paraguay reached its lowest figure since 1958: $3.7 million. All military assistance was suspended. The tone and content of the rhetoric also deteriorated as each side amplified its verbal attacks on the other.

By 1981 bilateral trade and investments also declined significantly, an important variable in explaining the Carter administration's failure to encourage the Stroessner regime to reform. Paraguayan exports to the United States declined to 2.6 percent of the country's total exports, a significant drop from the 21.5 percent average of the 1966–70 period. Paraguayan imports from the United States underwent a similar decline: down to 7.5 percent of the total in 1981 from an average of 19 percent in 1967–70. In investments, the United States placed fourth behind Brazil, Argentina, and Japan with 7 percent of the total, a 50 percent plunge from the early 1970s when U.S. investments placed second with nearly 16 percent of the total.[10] This waning in economic links began in 1973, when the United States imposed economic and commercial sanctions during the Ricord affair and accelerated during the Carter administration, when the Stroessner regime, in an attempt to reduce Paraguay's trade and capital dependence on the United States and to reverse Washington's leverage over the regime, took great pains to diversify Paraguay's trade partners, focusing on Brazil, Europe, South Africa, and Asia.[11] It is important to note, however, that although there were political reasons for these sharp declines in trade and investments, the phenomenon also reflected the Itaipú boom that brought extensive

Brazilian and German capital into Paraguay. This diversification gave Paraguay a growing degree of economic and political autonomy in its international economic and political contacts and helped the regime weather pressures from its long-time benefactor.[12]

Throughout the 1970s, the United States successfully exerted, then exhausted, nearly all the hard power leverage it had at its disposal, trying to pressure the Stroessner regime into a broader respect for human rights. By the 1980s, it had pushed and pressured the regime so much that it had run out of traditional hard power levers needed to continue swaying the regime. The bases upon which U.S.-Paraguayan relations had operated since the 1950s were gone. More important, Paraguay's relevance in the east-west struggle had waned. The Stroessner regime became a victim of the cold war's decline and of the U.S. preoccupation with human rights, democracy, and drug trafficking. Despite its best efforts to diversify economic and political contacts (expanding ties with other pariah nations such as Taiwan and South Africa), the regime found itself increasingly isolated in a changing international system.

Reagan Administration: Exercising Soft Power

Less than two months before the U.S. general election, the former Nicaraguan dictator Anastasio Somoza Debayle was assassinated in his Paraguayan exile on 17 September 1980 by an Argentine guerrilla group. Stroessner's security forces responded with a wave of repression that featured the arrest and torture of over a hundred political prisoners, mostly journalists, students, and opposition political figures. The decline in the number of arrests and political prisoners thus reversed. The Carter administration's preoccupation with the Iranian hostage crisis brought little sustained attention to Paraguay. Moreover, since January the United States was without an ambassador and a voice in Paraguay to continue White's crusade. Ambassador Lyle Franklin Lane presented his credentials less than a week before the Somoza assassination and was ill prepared to handle the fast-paced developments of the post-assassination period. Ambassador Lane had rushed to Asunción from his previous post in Uruguay not because of any human rights imperative but, as he said, "large United States companies engaged in the bidding for the Yacyretá hydroelectric project brought considerable pressure in Washington to have an ambassador named. The companies included Brown and Root, Allis-Chalmers and Westinghouse."[13] Business interests, the U.S. general election, crises in the Middle East, and "speculation in Washington about an imminent political transition in Paraguay due to persistent questions about President Stroessner's health" led to a considerable drop in U.S. criticisms of Paraguay's human rights situation.

The election of an ideologically conservative Republican administration was enthusiastically received by the Paraguayan regime. Some of the more powerful and loyal supporters of the Stroessner regime even boasted they had donated funds to the campaign of Ronald Reagan.[14] The vigor of Reagan's cold war rhetoric made Asunción hopeful that relations would return to the standards of the past. The more that President-elect and later President Reagan heightened the tone of his administration's strong anti-Communist discourse, the more Paraguayan officials believed that Carter's human rights policy was inexorably buried and forgotten. As Ambassador Lane noted, "clearly the Paraguayan government now believed that it had more United States friends at court."

The Reagan administration maintained the global focus that characterized the previous administration's foreign policy; however, its orientation proved radically different. The framework of the new U.S. foreign policy emphasized geo-strategic factors, the ideological struggle between the United States and the Soviet Union, and an explicit desire to "roll-back" communism. In short, the human rights and north-south emphasis of the Carter administration was replaced by the geopolitical exigencies of the cold war. In this context, Latin America was considered a key strategic area in which to test a new policy of containment. With respect to authoritarian regimes in the region, during and after the presidential campaign, Ronald Reagan insisted that "friends be treated as friends and enemies as enemies." He suggested that his administration would once again privilege its relations with dictatorships that identified themselves as U.S. allies. Jeanne Kirkpatrick, Georgetown University professor and subsequent U.S. ambassador to the United Nations, made the analytical distinction between authoritarian regimes (friends) and totalitarian ones (enemies), indicating that the former were both strategic allies and more susceptible to U.S. influence.[15] Totalitarian regimes, on the other hand, were "lost" in their alliance with the Soviet Union and were incapable of reform. Needless to say, Ambassador Kirkpatrick's analytical essay and robust cold war rhetoric that buttressed the new administration were well received in Asunción.

Paraguayan government officials soon found that President Carter's policies could not be so easily reversed; however, during its first term, the Reagan administration's policy toward Paraguay was one of "quiet diplomacy," characterized by private negotiations and application of mild pressures in an attempt to "persuade" the regime to democratize. The objective was to avoid open confrontations and deemphasize the regime's violations of human rights, while avoiding open identification with Stroessner. Ambassador Lane, who served until May 1982, stressed that Washington wanted to retain human rights as an issue, but it wanted to definitely tone down the public rhetoric as it pursued a broader array of U.S. interests. Initially, the Paraguayan government reacted well to Washington's approach. The United States seemed indifferent to the issue of human rights. After reinstating military training funds, the Reagan administration asked Congress to increase funding from $50,000 to $75,000 (for the 1982–83 fiscal year). This position received much criticism from members of Congress and human rights groups, but the State Department defended the request, arguing the funds "are for a training program that the United States gets as much out of as Paraguay because it wins the friendships of young Paraguayan officers." The Reagan administration also voted in favor of more than $420 million in multilateral development bank loans to Paraguay. The Stroessner regime, therefore, felt no compunction to respond in any way to Washington's silent persuasions.

However, the new U.S. ambassador, Arthur Davis, a Denver, Colorado, shopping center developer and friend of Joseph Coors, the influential conservative Republican and Colorado beer maker, seems not to have heeded some of Washington's general policy directions that he keep a low profile and engage in "silent diplomacy." In fact, Ambassador Davis "maintained relations with opposition sectors while insisting that the State Department take a more forceful posture with respect to free press and human rights in Paraguay." His pro–human rights position was more out of conviction than based on his instructions. "I didn't go down there with the idea of being a human rights activist," Davis said. "But I realized that if I didn't represent what the United States stood for, I wouldn't have their respect."[16]

Though government officials warmly received him when he arrived in August 1982, not long had passed before Ambassador Davis began to irritate Stroessner's cronies. In addition to his meeting with the opposition, Ambassador Davis also maintained a critical posture, though more subdued than Ambassador White, with respect to political and civil rights in Paraguay and, increasingly, the growing problem of drug trafficking in the country.

By 1983 change was engulfing many authoritarian regimes as a democratic tide began sweeping across South America. This contributed to the progressive international isolation and ostracism of Paraguay and a concomitant change in U.S. policy. As new democratic regimes emerged in Argentina, Bolivia, Ecuador, and Peru, Stroessner remained committed to the status quo, insisting that his national security doctrine regime was the best way of defending Paraguay's interests.

In 1983, Stroessner was elected president for the sixth consecutive time with over 90 percent of the vote. In his inaugural address he warned that Paraguayans would never deviate from the "stable and prosperous path" he had taken when first elected in the 1950s. Thirty years later, as pressure from below began to build as a result of the social transformation and modernization spawned by the Itaipú boom of the 1970s, the expansion of the agro-export industry, and a period of economic recession, the regime responded by intensifying the repression. In March 1984, *ABC color,* an independent newspaper that was investigating corruption, was permanently closed down. Radio Ñandutí, another outspoken source of criticism, was consistently harassed; its director, Humberto Rubin, was detained on numerous occasions.

Meanwhile, by 1985 Brazil and Uruguay had also joined the democratic states in South America. The growing democratic trend in the region and intense external pressures and ostracism from Paraguay's democratic neighbors, particularly the Raúl Alfonsín administration in Argentina, began to expose and weaken the Stronato. As more of Paraguay's neighbors became democratic and U.S. tolerance for Paraguay's lack of political liberalization ebbed, Stroessner's ability to shield his regime was undermined by the very international system that had so long protected it. In other words, Paraguay was dragged willy-nilly from its isolation and placed on the bench of the accused by its democratic neighbors and a less indulgent United States. Suddenly, as two Paraguayan analysts aptly described, the country now found itself "an authoritarian island surrounded by a sea of democracies."[17]

Ambassador Davis became more forceful and outspoken in his criticisms, not only of the regime's resistance to liberalization but also of drug trafficking and allegations that government and military officials were involved in the illicit trade. Davis's response to the quashing of *ABC color* was to cancel a planned appearance by the U.S. Southern Command's band and parachute team at Paraguay's May 15 Independence Day parade—a symbolic gesture that "caused a greater reaction than any other thing we've done in Paraguay," the ambassador noted. The U.S. Embassy also sent a strong letter of protest to the Paraguayan government that was made public by the U.S. Information Service (USIS). Another protest was issued after police arrested five members of a joint Americas Watch–Human Rights Committee of Lawyers delegation in April 1984 and forced them to leave the country on the next available flight. Many Paraguayan officials wondered if Davis was any better than White.

In 1985, Washington issued a scathing and unequivocal attack on Paraguay in the State Department's annual human rights report that was received with shock and anger by Stronista officials. The report and rapidly changing regional context seemed to embolden Davis to demand that the regime respect the press and other rights in Paraguay.

As government and military officials expressed outrage, many dissidents and members of opposition parties, particularly members of the Popular Colorado Movement (MOPOCO), a Colorado Party dissident faction, recognized Davis's "invaluable" contribution to reform in Paraguay.[18] Sara Lara Castro, a Liberal and president of the Human Rights Commission of Paraguay, noted, "without Davis here, I fear that we would be completely at the mercy of the regime."

As in the past, the regime's response to this kind of challenge was to go on the offense—detain opponents, harass the press, and snub or issue ad hominid attacks on representatives of foreign governments and organizations. The low point in Davis's relations with the Palacio de López came in September 1984 when Paraguayan custom officials confiscated more than a hundred thousand liters of ether, acetone, and hydrochloric acid—enough to produce eight tons of cocaine. U.S. officials demanded that the precursor chemicals be destroyed. After Paraguay refused to do so, Ambassador Davis requested a meeting with President Stroessner, who, in an unprecedented move, publicly rebuffed the shocked ambassador. It was the first time that Stroessner had refused to receive an ambassador from the United States.

U.S. Media Take Notice

Before 1984, the U.S. media paid little attention to Paraguay. Even during the Carter administration when Ambassador White and the Paraguayan government were at loggerheads, newspapers and other media outlets rarely reported on political, social, and economic developments in Paraguay. An occasional essay or reportage on Paraguayan culture or the Itaipú project appeared, but for the most part, this faraway land and its despotic government only garnered interest among a few journalists and travelers captivated by its "exotic" character. As a result, the repression and corruption went largely unnoticed for the first thirty years of the Stronato's existence. This was partly by design. As described above, the regime purposely sought to maintain a low profile in international affairs so as not to attract much attention. However, it is also true that the security imperative of the cold war and the prevalence of authoritarian regimes in South America, many of which engaged in brutal "dirty wars" against their own citizens, allowed Paraguay, which experienced no real threat from Communist insurgents and which was never accused of torturing and disappearing its citizens on the scale of its neighbors, to be overlooked by the press.

It was not until the hated military dictatorships in South America disappeared and Stroessner's harassment of the Paraguayan media intensified, particularly after the closing of *ABC color*, that the media "discovered" Paraguay's "democracy without communism" regime. The sensationalism surrounding the Josef Mengele case—the Nazi war criminal who for a period of several months was protected by Asunción—also brought Paraguay to the attention of news outlets in the United States, Europe, and Latin America.

By 1984–85 all of South America, except Chile and Paraguay, was democratic. Both of these pariah states now came into focus as the only countries resisting the tide of democratization and human rights in the region. In the 1984–87 period the U.S. media embarked on a massive and nearly concerted effort to expose the Paraguayan government, warts and all. Between May 1984 and September 1985, more articles on Paraguay were published in U.S. newspapers than in the previous thirty years combined.[19] Most newspaper articles dealt with the issue of corruption and contraband trade. For example, on 6 June 1984 the *Los Angeles Time*s ran a piece that detailed the kleptocratic nature of the Stroessner regime, emphasizing how the military had been transformed into a "band of depraved hustlers." Within the category of corruption, many articles, playing off a growing concern about the problem of drug trafficking, examined the role of Paraguayan government and military officials in the drug trade. A 30 January 1985 piece in the *New York Times* titled "United States Aides Suspect Paraguay Officials of a Narcotics Link" broke the story of the confiscated precursor chemicals and Stroessner's snub of Ambassador Davis.[20] Another important piece of reporting that was the subject of much discussion and irritation in Paraguay was Tina Rosenberg's "Smuggler's Paradise" published in the *New Republic* on 8 June 1987. The article was somewhat sensationalist; it was effective, however, in raising awareness in the United States and indignation among Paraguayan officials, particularly from those named in the essay.

Two reportages, however, had an even greater impact by informing the U.S. Congress and general public about corruption and despotism in Paraguay. The first was an exposé by *New York Times* reporter John Vinocur titled "A Republic of Fear: Thirty Years of General Stroessner's Paraguay" (23 September 1984). Vinocur described a semitotalitarian government ruled by a strongman, obsessed with detail, punctuality, and arrogance, and a group of corrupt and incompetent sycophants who dared not move without the dictator's permission. The article also detailed specific brutal acts taken against opponents as well as the corruption that ran rampant throughout the government, military, and society. Without a doubt, this long exposé was the hardest-hitting and most damaging piece of reporting to the regime's image up to that point. In the United States, the article became a key reference during a Senate committee hearing as well as a must-read among scholars and journalists covering Latin America. In Latin America, a translation of the article appeared in several dailies, some of which were "smuggled" into Paraguay where they were widely read. It became the topic of much discussion and irritation within government and military circles.

Then on 6 January 1986, the CBS News documentary program *60 Minutes* began its television broadcast with its best-known journalist, Mike Wallace, stating, "What is the price of freedom? That is the question we asked when several months ago we visited Paraguay, a Third World country governed during the last thirty-one years by this man, who outside of Paraguay, is perhaps the most despised, most hated dictator in the world today, Alfredo Stroessner." Much like Vinocur's exposé, Mike Wallace told the story of a brutal, corrupt, and perverse dictatorship led by a ruler ("with a preference for sycophants . . . and girls") determined to stay in power at whatever costs. No other report, because of its medium, had a greater impact on U.S. public opinion and on the regime's sense of betrayal and harassment. Not long after the *60 Minutes* program was aired, a siege mentality evolved within the Stroessner regime that lasted until its downfall. More importantly, the media attention received by Paraguay contributed to a gradual but significant change in the Reagan administration's policy toward the Stronato.

Ambassador Taylor and Democracy by Pressure

By the beginning of Reagan's second term in 1985, his administration had reached the conclusion that its policy toward Paraguay had failed. More importantly, it realized that in order to find an accommodation with the Congress on its Nicaraguan policy, it had to balance its opposition with a policy that opposed right-wing dictatorships like that of General Stroessner. The second Reagan administration thus gravitated toward using economic and diplomatic pressure to induce the Stroessner regime to cede power, an approach the Americans called "democracy by pressure."[21] Total U.S. aid amounted to less than $2.5 million a year during the second half of the 1980s. Similarly, military assistance remained under $100,000 a year during this period. The administration also closed its Agency for International Development (AID) office in 1985 and in less than two years suspended Paraguay's access to trade benefits under the Generalized System of Preferences (GSP).

Trade with the United States, however, made up less than 6 percent of Paraguay's total trade, and nothing truly vital was bought or sold in either economy. In short, the amount of economic aid and the extent of commercial and financial ties had so diminished during the 1980s that the United States no longer could exercise hard power leverage against the Stroessner regime. As Mladen Yopo noted, "the lack of vital levers of pressure . . . explains the limits of the Reagan administration's leverage."[22] Consequently, the United States used, with relative success, its soft power tools to pressure the Stroessner regime to meet, voluntarily or involuntarily, United States demands for democracy.

The sources of U.S. "soft" power leverage over Paraguay consisted of a number of political and inertial factors. First, a certain amount of "inertial or residual leverage" came as a result of the regime's political and aid dependence on the United States and of the lingering hard power relationship. Strong opposition from the United States had a definite psychological impact, especially since Stroessner saw U.S. support as a pillar of his regime's legitimacy. Second, the status of the United States superpower had a symbolic impact and influence in terms of leadership in the promotion of democracy and economic reform. Third, the United States continued to exercise leadership and influence in international institutions, particularly lending and development entities. Fourth, Washington proclaimed itself the author of Latin America's wave of democracy in the mid-1980s. This trend increasingly isolated Asunción from its democratic neighbors. By the late 1980s, the United States began to shape and establish international norms, such as democratic rule and economic neoliberalism, as conditions for normal bilateral relations and insertion into the new and emerging international economy. Finally, the U.S. ability to pressure the regime by supporting such opposition forces as the National Accord impaired the international indifference and U.S. support from which the Stroessner regime benefited for so long. For example, the National Endowment for Democracy carried out a number of small assistance projects in Paraguay from 1985 to 1988, including providing support for Radio Ñandutí, Women for Democracy, the Center for Democracy, and several other such civil society organizations. The wielding of these forms of "soft" power leverage allowed Washington to effectively isolate Asunción in the late 1980s in ways that contributed to its downfall.

By 1985, the United States and Paraguay had reached the point of no return in their relationship. There were six reinforcing variables that prevented the Reagan administration from continuing its policy of quiet diplomacy in Paraguay. First, the Carter administration's human rights policy had become an essential component of U.S. foreign policy that could not now be abandoned. Moreover, a number of international governmental organizations, particularly the OAS, and nongovernment organizations such as Amnesty International and Human Rights Watch were too strong and vocal in their reporting of human rights violations in Latin America to be dismissed. The OAS and human rights organizations issued critical reports on Paraguay's dismal conditions that neither Washington nor Asunción could ignore. Next, Washington realized that Paraguay was not on the Soviet Union's "hit list," and, therefore, the United States could afford to pressure the regime without fear of Communists taking over. Another key variable, the spread of democratic rule throughout South America, made it politically difficult for Washington to support a dictatorship unwilling to concede anything to liberalization. Next, growing evidence had come to light that suggested that Paraguayan government and military officials had become involved in the drug trade, particularly in the trafficking of precursor chemicals for use in manufacturing cocaine. The media's focus on corruption and drug trafficking in Paraguay was unrelenting, making it a critical issue in for many in Congress from both parties.

But perhaps the most important factor contributing to a change in policy was the need for the administration to criticize and pressure authoritarian regimes such as Paraguay and Chile so as to balance and legitimize its anti-leftist policy in Central America. In other words, the price for obtaining congressional support for the anti-Sandinista guerrilla force (i.e., Contras) was a commitment to seek democratic change elsewhere in South America. Finally, no important U.S. economic and security interests would be risked by a change in policy. The Reagan administration, therefore, because of circumstances that diminished the importance of cold war ideology and economic interests in U.S.-Paraguayan relations, had no choice but to advance, in a more vociferous and confrontational fashion, the cause of democracy, human rights, and the war on drugs in Paraguay.

Reagan administration officials became openly harsh in their verbal attacks on the regime. Again, the State Department was concerned with being evenhanded in its overall democracy policy and was increasingly annoyed by the dictator's unwillingness to join his neighbors in permitting a transition to elected civilian rule and by his tolerance of government and military involvement in the drug trade. When President Reagan, speaking before the Spanish parliament in May 1985, referred to Paraguay "as one of the last remaining dictatorships in Latin America," the policy of quiet diplomacy had clearly vanished. In December 1985, not long after the president's unexpected but potent comments, the implacable cold war warrior Elliot Abrams, assistant secretary of state for inter-American affairs, referred to the political system in

Paraguay as "one of the forgotten dictatorships of the world." He went on to insist that Paraguay join the democratic wave, because if repression continued it could "portend to more tensions with the United States."

Despite these wounding statements by the president and his chief Latin American policy adviser in the State Department, it was perhaps the new U.S. ambassador, Clyde Taylor, a career foreign service officer, who had the greatest impact on bilateral relations and on Paraguayan democratization. Before arriving in Paraguay in early November 1985, Taylor had been given clear instructions "to aid and abet the development of democracy, to be very alert to human rights abuses, to offer within our normal historical bounds encouragement to those who were trying to open up a pluralistic society, and to use some of our organizations, such as both the Democratic and Republican Institutes, the National Endowment for Democracy, and other apolitical organizations, to try to maintain and develop our ties."[23] Taylor understood that like ambassadors before him, he enjoyed a tremendous amount of leeway. In Paraguay "we had no strategic interests, but because of what I just said about the need for policy balance [i.e., Central America], it gave the ambassador in Asunción a lot of discretion. It meant that he or she could put a lot of stamp on how they did things."[24] That he did.

Ambassador Taylor's previous post had been acting assistant secretary of state for international narcotics matters. Though his appointment as ambassador had little to do with Paraguay's continued complicity in the drug trade, it was interpreted as such by many in the country as well as U.S. journalists, academics, and some State Department officials. The new ambassador wasted no time exploiting this perception and carrying out his instructions. He played an "activist role in trying to encourage the growth of a pro–United States democratic opposition . . . [his] activities aroused intense suspicion."[25] He immediately began publicly challenging and chastising the regime, meeting with National Accord leaders (in the offices of the banned Febrerista Party), and accusing the government of failing to join in the war on drugs.

The Paraguayan government refused to sit idly by. Government officials, who normally would have been eager to improve relations with the United States, treated Taylor as if he were a maverick pursuing his own agenda irrespective of Washington's wishes. Through the official and pro-government press (*La Tarde, Patria,* and *El Diario de Noticias*), the regime lambasted U.S. Embassy officials. After President Reagan's 1985 speech, *Patria,* the official newspaper of the Colorado Party, categorized the president's comments as "a grave error that deserved a failing grade in any elemental test of constitutional or international law." Assistant Secretary Abrams was labeled a "fool" and a "drunkard" by the same daily after his comments about the state of democracy in Paraguay.

Ambassador Taylor became the chief target of most Paraguayan censure, however. In January 1986, Minister of Interior Sabino A. Montanaro (also vice president of the Colorado Party's governing board) summed up what many government and party officials said about the ambassador's actions and behavior:

> With emphasis we categorically reject Clyde Taylor's intervention in domestic political matters. . . . We do not accept his attempts to create or encourage irregular groups that have no representation, nor do we acknowledge his intentions of becoming the godfather or protector of the *acuerdistas.* We will defend the principles of authentic representative democracy in our country and reject all efforts, regardless of whether they are ambassadors, technical experts or international commissioners, at undermining our sovereignty, freedom and justice with which General Alfredo Stroessner and the Colorado party govern.[26]

Ambassador Taylor noted that these attacks would go on for as long as two weeks. Even if U.S. criticism emanated from Abrams, Secretary of State George Shultz, or other State Department officials, the blame was almost always placed on Taylor.

Similar reactions were registered after Senator Edward Kennedy criticized measures taken by Asunción to impede the return of such exile leaders as Domingo Laíno and Luis Alfonso Resck. Kennedy also announced in a January 1986 press conference that he would meet with National Accord leaders. The Paraguayan government's response, provided by Juan Ramón Chávez, president of the Colorado Party, was that "Senator Kennedy is misguided . . . [and] his comments are in direct violation of Paraguayan sovereignty . . . Paraguay has had a democratic regime for decades."

In order to mitigate further deterioration of relations between Taylor and the Paraguayan government, Washington dispatched Deputy Assistant Secretary of State Robert Gelbard to Asunción in July 1986 with instructions to normalize the situation but also to insist that Stroessner begin a process of political liberalization. In an effort to dismiss the perception that Taylor had acted as a maverick, Gelbard also emphasized that the ambassador had the full support of the White House. Gelbard's visit failed to impress Sabino Montanaro, but a cooling-off period did ensue, though the Palacio de López continued to resist U.S. pressures. During this time, Paraguayan government and military functionaries repeatedly claimed that the United States had abandoned Paraguay—a terrible betrayal given Paraguay's pro-U.S. votes in the United Nations and the OAS. In part, this was meant to convince Paraguayans that their government had been victimized by the United States after decades of steadfast support. The hope was that Paraguayans would rally around their offended government during a time of crisis. It did not work, however. According to Ambassador Taylor, "I feel comfortable saying that when I was there, it [Paraguay] was the most pro-American society maybe in the world, but certainly in the hemisphere. They [Paraguayan officials] desperately wanted approbation from any country, and so they would go at this issue [abandonment] to curry favor from society and other states." Admiration for the U.S. Embassy and the U.S. people and society, a product of decades of economic and technical assistance at the grassroots level, was widespread throughout Paraguayan society, from Asunción streets and universities to the countryside.

Cultural Links in Difficult Times

In the late 1970s and throughout the decade of the 1980s cultural exchanges reflected the political climate of U.S.-Paraguayan relations. As relations deteriorated so did efforts at enhancing bilateral interaction below the level of diplomatic relations. Were it not for the Kansas-Paraguay Partners (KPP) program, it would be difficult to point to many exchanges, other than to a slow growth in the number of U.S. scholars studying Paraguay. The Paraguayan-American Cultural Center (CCPA) continued to teach English and organize cultural events, which expanded during Ambassador Taylor's tenure, and the Peace Corps program remained a vibrant and growing mechanism for deepening understanding between the two countries. The Amigos de las Américas, a U.S. private development and health assistance outfit from Houston, Texas, organized several missions to Paraguay in the 1970s to conduct vaccination programs (tetanus, polio, smallpox) in the countryside, which, like the Peace Corps projects, contributed to expanding bilateral interaction and a positive image of the United States in Paraguay. More importantly, many Paraguayans, particularly in the countryside, continued to associate Americans, as they had since the Alliance for Progress, with positive achievements and a sincere commitment to improving the quality of life of Paraguayans long neglected by the government and Paraguay's two wealthy neighbors. Another factor contributing to this positive image of Americans is that Peace Corps volunteers and other U.S. visitors, unlike other foreigners, made a serious effort to learn Guaraní, which convinced Paraguayans that the United States really cared about Paraguay and its culture. Finally, this view of the United States was reinforced and bolstered in Asunción by reruns of the television program *Mission Impossible,* which made many residents in the capital believe the United States was omnipotent. The expansion of U.S. culture and technology in the 1970s and 1980s gave the United States more apparent influence in Paraguay than it had any tangible right to enjoy. In short, image was a critical variable in the expansion of U.S. soft power influence.

The KPP program, however, was the most active of all programs in intensifying contacts between the two countries. This partnership organized a number of programs, everything from musical, educational, and sports exchanges to art exhibits in Paraguay and the United States, agricultural missions, Special Olympics, and health care programs. The period between 1979 and 1983 was known as the "Years of Sustained

Growth for Partners" in terms of the number of exchanges and amount of funds raised from the U.S. government, foundations, and corporate sponsors.

Some of the more successful programs with the greatest impact on cultural, individual, and technical exchanges included Paraguayan guitarist Carlos Vásquez's well-received concerts in January and February 1977. David Suderman, a pianist and music educator, visited Paraguay and conducted several musical education seminars in Asunción that led to the development of music curriculum. Concert pianists Valerie Valois and Larry Walz were warmly received in Paraguay in 1978 and 1979, respectively. Paraguayan sculptor Herman Guggiari conducted workshops at various Kansas universities. In February 1981 KPP sponsored the Escuela Alegría, an integrated preschool for disabled children in Asunción. Medical doctors, particularly psychiatrists, and dentists visited Paraguay throughout the 1980s, helping set up clinics and health care centers in rural areas. One of the most successful KPP programs was the Special Olympics that began in 1977 and continued for a number of years. The number of athletes participating grew from two hundred in 1977 to almost four hundred by 1985.

What is arguably the most significant and enduring program contributing to exchange and mutual understanding was the university exchange program signed between Kansas state universities and the Catholic University and National University of Paraguay. Lower-level talks began in 1977 between Professor Charles Stansifer, professor of history and director of the Center for Latin American Studies at the University of Kansas (and also member of the KPP executive committee), and representatives of the two universities. In 1979 and 1980, the Catholic and National Universities, respectively, signed brief and general accords whereby Kansas and Paraguay institutions agreed to a program of cultural and student exchange. Paraguayan students paid the same tuition as residents of Kansas. Initially, the agreement included only the University of Kansas and Kansas State University, but it was not long before other Kansas state universities joined the program. No other university in the United States has negotiated an exchange relationship of this nature with either of the two Paraguayan universities.[27]

This exchange program grew dramatically in the number of Paraguayan students studying in Kansas. By the late 1980s nearly a hundred Paraguayan students were studying in Kansas, and about two hundred had gone through the program since its inception. Though it was meant to be reciprocal, no Kansas student had taken advantage of the program as of 1988.

Beyond Kansas, cultural and educational exchanges were largely limited to individuals, specifically scholars, journalists, and scientists, mostly Americans. There were, however, some Paraguayan scholars, such as Hugo Rodríguez Alcala, who spent numerous years in U.S. universities making Paraguayan culture and literature known in academic circles.[28] Scholarly work on Paraguay in the United States, on the other hand, had some notable accomplishments. Historians and anthropologists continued to make valuable contributions, but political science mostly ignored Paraguay until Paul Lewis, a political scientist from Tulane University who had published a book on Febrerismo in 1968, came out with *Paraguay under Stroessner* (1980). The difficulty of conducting political science research in Paraguay, considered a subversive activity by the regime, impeded the development of political science as a field of study and research in the country. Hence, when Lewis's book was first published, it became a bestseller among journalists, scholars, and even policy wonks interested in Paraguay. *Paraguay under Stroessner* was the first systematic attempt to study the Stroessner regime in the context of Paraguay's authoritarian political culture. This important book was translated and read widely in Latin America, including Paraguay.[29]

The United States and the Origins of Collapse

When 1987 began, no one expected bilateral relations to reach a point of open hostility between the Palacio de López and the U.S. Embassy, especially after nearly six months of détente. Conflict was inevitable, however, as the United States focused on bringing an end to the regime. According to Ambassador Taylor, by 1987, "the goal was to try and build for the future, for the post-Stroessner period, to try and uphold principles of pluralism and democracy; yet maintain correct relations so that we could have access."

In late 1986, Ambassador Taylor invited General John Galvin, commander in chief (CINC) of Southern Command (SOUTHCOM) and a personal friend of the ambassador, to visit Asunción and speak with Stroessner and some of Paraguay's key generals, such as Andrés Rodríguez, commander of the First Army Corps, about the need for democracy. Taylor believed that since the president respected military figures much more than civilians, he would pay much more attention to Galvin than to a diplomat. Assistant Secretary Abrams was reluctant to approve the visit at first, but Taylor convinced the State Department that Galvin's access to Stroessner would allow him to stress democracy and human rights in a way that Taylor or other U.S. diplomats could not. When General Galvin arrived for a two-day visit in January, the Paraguayan government and press warmly received the four-star general. The regime sought to portray the visit as the beginning of a rapprochement and an expression of support for President Stroessner. The Palacio de López, however, reacted with surprise and irritation when General Galvin repeated on several private and public occasions that "the United States believes that the best defense against communism was democracy and human rights"—an obvious slap against the regime. Galvin followed these comments with a direct reference to the need for change: "I expect conditions in Paraguay to evolve in a way that will allow the United States to assume its traditional support for economic development and security in Paraguay."[30] Finally, as Deputy Assistant Secretary Gelbard had done before, the general reiterated in no uncertain terms Washington's absolute support for Ambassador Taylor's actions in Paraguay. Stroessner felt so disappointed and annoyed with the general that the next time he visited Paraguay in 1988, the president snubbed Galvin by taking members of his cabinet and military on a visit to Brazil.

The lowest point in relations came in February 1988 when the ambassador and his wife were invited by a nonpolitical organization called Mujeres para la Democracia (Women for Democracy) to a dinner to honor the U.S. diplomat and his spouse. Before they arrived, the National Police had cordoned off a six-block area around the private home where the event was held. Thirty minutes after Taylor's arrival, the police lobbed tear gas canisters onto the patio where the guests were meeting. The ambassador and his wife, choking on the smoke, were promptly escorted out of the residence. Taylor and the State Department presented a letter of protest demanding an apology. The Palacio de López never formally apologized. The State Department later learned that President Stroessner had called the head of the National Police to order the teargassing. Years later, Ambassador Taylor called the event unique: "I don't know of another occasion when a head of state directed that the American ambassador accredited to him be tear gassed." Needless to say, the U.S. Embassy–Palacio de López conflict intensified once again. The pro-government press took to name calling again, labeling Taylor a "treacherous and caustic big-mouth" and a "defamer and blasphemer with diplomatic sinecure." Worse things were said about the ambassador on Voz del Coloradismo, the Colorado Party radio station.[31]

This event, along with persistent human rights violations and refusal to reform the system, led the United States to impose economic sanctions. In March, the United States announced that Paraguay would no longer enjoy trade benefits under the Generalized System of Preferences (GSP) because of continued violations of workers' rights. This represented a loss of 2.2 percent in the value of Paraguayan exports, but, more importantly, it had a tremendous impact on potential U.S. private investments in Paraguay and on development loans from private and international lending institutions. More than its quantitative or hard power impact, the psychological effects on Paraguayan society were profound. The regime attempted to alleviate the tensions by taking measures, specifically in the area of counternarcotics cooperation, to appease the U.S. government on an issue that did not weaken the regime. The Drug Enforcement Administration's office in Asunción reopened in early 1988, and several successful joint operations led to drug seizures and the destruction of several dozen hectares of marijuana. The Paraguayan government also redrafted, at U.S. insistence, an antidrug penal code, and Paraguayan drug enforcement officers received training from U.S. instructors.[32] It was the lifting of the state of siege in April 1987, in force in Paraguay almost continuously since 1929, that had the greatest impact, not so much on bilateral relations but on the political situation in Paraguay.

Despite these steps, the regime remained intransigent, especially after the August 1987 Colorado Party congress when the *militants* (an extremist political faction within the party that wanted, with the post-Stroessner era looming, to continue the Stronato with the dictator's son, Gustavo, as the leader) took control of the party hierarchy from the more proliberalization faction, the *traditionalists.* Stroessner's growing senility and detachment from daily political matters allowed the *militants* to influence and convince the aging dictator of the need to expel the "disloyal" *traditionalists.*[33] The dictator was increasingly prone to bask in flattery and to listen to anyone who agreed with him or pleased his every physical, emotional, or psychological need. The highest level of the regime seemed to be deteriorating, and the *militants* moved quickly to fill the vacuum and ensure that Stroessner's senility and growing inability to retain his grasp of affairs did not affect the continuation of the Stronato. The *militant* victory polarized the political situation and generated growing problems with the United States. The key militants, known as the *cuatrinomio de oro* (Golden Foursome), included Montanaro, Mario Abdo Benítez (Stroessner's private secretary), José Eugenio Jacquet (minister of labor and justice), and Adán Godoy Jiménez (minister of health and social welfare). These individuals, along with the regime's principal ideologue and intellectual, Ezequiel González Alsina, insisted that President Stroessner resist U.S. and other external pressures. Montanaro and González organized the public campaign through the pro-government press to discredit the U.S. ambassador and express Paraguay's commitment to anticommunism and "real democracy."[34] The militants tried to deal with the United States by separating Taylor from Washington, by heightening the confrontation with the ambassador while attempting to appease Washington by issuing public statements of support for its policy in Central America, and by implementing some token counternarcotics measures. When this failed, the Stronistas turned to reducing the material and political dependence on the United States by expanding ties with regimes with which it had some ideological affinity—South Africa, Taiwan, and South Korea—and others that still maintained normal economic links with Asunción, such as Brazil, Germany, and Japan.

The U.S. Embassy watched with great concern as the extremists took control of the party and government. The Americans feared that Paraguay's increasingly polarized situation could contribute to intraparty and societal violence. During the second half of 1987, Ambassador Taylor kept a lower profile as the situation clarified. He attempted to maintain "correct relations" under very irregular conditions. He made a special effort to develop apolitical vehicles of interaction, such as promoting and expanding the Peace Corps program and enhancing the number of activities at the Paraguayan-American Cultural Center, such as inviting U.S. and Paraguayan artists to perform or exhibit their work, as a way of "getting our message across." The number of Peace Corps volunteers increased from 110 to 200, and a second binational cultural center, located in San Lorenzo, was rejuvenated while construction began on a third center in Ciudad President Stroessner. During this time, the embassy also focused on seeking greater counterdrug cooperation. J. Mark Dion, deputy assistant secretary of state for international narcotics, visited Paraguay in September to warn the government of the "boom" in marijuana production, money laundering, and the transiting of cocaine through the country. Believing that counterdrug measures offered the most economical way of improving relations, the Palacio de López gave its approval to U.S. demands on this issue.

In early 1988, U.S. diplomatic pressure on the regime turned pugnacious once again. On 7 January 1988, Ambassador Taylor, in an extensive interview published in *Ultima Hora,* characterized relations as "problematic" and full of "potholes." As in the past, the Paraguayan government sought to separate the ambassador's statements from the White House, believing that Taylor was somehow speaking without Washington's authorization. On 2 February, Vice Foreign Minister Elpidio Acevedo affirmed that "the deterioration of relations with

Washington is not due to a difference in interests or common principles, but to the distorted view United States embassy representatives present of the Paraguayan government." In responding to the foreign minister's comments, Assistant Secretary Abrams, a day before the February general elections, characterized the militant sector in the party and government as "extremists" and "out of control." He also described the elections as "irrelevant" because of the absence of competition.

Then on 10 March, Taylor accused the military and government officials of collusion with narcotics traffickers. That same day in Washington, Congressman Larry Smith of the House Foreign Affairs Committee presented an amendment to close off all economic aid and trade benefits to Paraguay. The Paraguayan government's furious response was unprecedented. Foreign Minister Carlos Saldívar demanded that the ambassador name names. Silvio Meza Brítez, member of the party's governing board, called the ambassador "irresponsible" and cautioned Taylor that "he will have to face the consequences." Minister Montanaro threatened to declare the ambassador persona non grata. The name-calling and personal attacks continued for weeks until it was announced that Vernon Walters, U.S. ambassador to the United Nations and a retired general officer well known in Latin American military circles, would visit in April. Both the regime and the opposition believed the retired general was coming to Asunción to provide succor to the beleaguered president. Both were wrong.

Ambassador Taylor invited Walters, who had a long history with Paraguay and Stroessner from the time he was defense and army attaché in Brazil. Ambassador Walters met several Paraguayan officers during his tenure in Brazil and maintained acquaintances with many of them, who were now general officers. Taylor believed there was no better U.S. official to talk seriously about the need for political reform to the Paraguayans than General Walters. When the general arrived on 22 April, the daily *Patria*, mouthpiece of the Colorados, greeted Walters with an attack on the State Department: "the current misunderstandings between the United States and Paraguay were the fruit of the anti-Stroessner passions and interests of Taylor, Gelbard and Abrams." The newspaper article went on to say, "Walters's long-standing friendship with Paraguay and President Stroessner will clarify and strengthen bonds between our two nations."

Though officially the purpose of Walter's visit was to consult with the Paraguayan government on matters related to the United Nations, the not-so-discreet goal was to tell the Paraguayan president, in no uncertain terms, that the public positions of Taylor, Gelbard, and Abrams faithfully reflected the opinion of the Reagan administration and the Republican-Democrat consensus on Paraguay. Though the opposition felt irked by some of Ambassador Walters's comments that stressed U.S. interest in "stability and prosperity," concepts that Stroessner claimed he had provided for Paraguay, in his private meetings with the Paraguayan dictator Walters was adamant that Stroessner respect human rights and make strides toward democratic transition. At one point, President Stroessner got so irritated with the portly Walters that in an effort to change the subject while conspicuously humiliating the U.S. representative, he asked Walters how a former officer could be so out of shape. Acting as if he did not hear Stroessner's comment, Walters turned to the president and asserted, once again, that Ambassador Taylor had the full confidence of the White House. The meeting ended soon after.

By May, relations seem to be spiraling out of control. Not long after Walters left the country, character assassinations against Taylor resumed. Meanwhile, the regime attempted to counteract the effects of the deterioration of relations by strengthening its contacts with influential individuals, such as Enzo De Chiara, a member of the Republican National Committee. In September 1988, De Chiara met with Stroessner and other regime officials in Asunción; the Republican promised to introduce into the party's platform a resolution calling for a normalization of relations between the United States and Paraguay.[35] De Chiara also proposed to invest in Paraguay's cotton industry and organize a business transaction that consisted of exchanging dozens of buses for soybeans. Clearly, De Chiara made promises that he never intended to keep. De Chiara's plan was to offer the resolution as bait for the business deal. Only the most narcissistic of the Stronistas could delude themselves into believing Paraguay was so important to the United States and Republican Party that it merited a resolution in the party's platform. Once again, President Stroessner felt surprised and disappointed when his diplomatic efforts failed to bear fruit.

When September arrived, a momentary sense of relief settled into the Palacio de López as Taylor's tenure came to an end. He was replaced by Timothy Towell, a diplomat who had served as a consular officer in Paraguay in the late 1960s when relations were very close, and before assuming his post in Asunción served as a protocol officer in the State Department. The Paraguayans believed that they could work with and even cultivate a strong relationship with a U.S. diplomat who knew Paraguay well. The regime began romancing Towell, and the ambassador seemed to reciprocate. The relationship got so cozy that Assistant Secretary Abrams, in a meeting with Towell in Washington, told the ambassador to stay focused on democracy and avoid seeming too close to Stronistas.[36] Despite Towell's efforts to convince Abrams of the need to talk to government officials in order to achieve U.S. objectives, the assistant secretary repeated his instruction: do not establish a friendly or normal relationship with the regime. Abrams's final instruction was to "prepare for a post-Stroessner regime."

During the rest of 1988, Ambassador Towell heightened his contacts with the opposition—particularly in the weeks leading up to the November visit to Asunción by General Fred Woerner, commander in chief of SOUTHCOM, to meet with Paraguay's military high command. What was publicized as a visit to enhance military-to-military cooperation became another embarrassment for the regime. During an event at the embassy, General Woerner met with National Accord leaders. After the meeting, Domingo Laíno, a key opposition leader whom Towell distrusted, gave a press conference where he informed the public that he and General Woerner had a private meeting to talk about "major issues." Laíno misrepresented his meeting with Woerner; at best, they shared pleasantries. Ambassador Towell was infuriated with Laíno's attempt to gain political points by using the embassy as his platform, implicitly suggesting that he had U.S. backing. Needless to say, Stroessner was extremely unhappy. He had Foreign Minister Acevedo contact Ambassador Towell to express the government's discontent with

Laíno's showmanship. Towell tried to limit the damage, but his instructions from Abrams kept him from going too far to appease the regime.

By the end of 1988, the political situation deteriorated further as the militants began their campaign of purging the military of traditionalists or officers unsympathetic to a Gustavo Stroessner succession. Meanwhile, anxiety and uncertainty within the regime intensified as, once again, rumors of Stroessner's ill health spread. For many in the government, particularly the armed forces, the future leadership of Paraguay was now in doubt. For the first time in decades, leadership change was the subject of open conversation, speculation, and worry. The U.S. Embassy knew with certainty about the dictator's condition. It so happened that Dr. Fred Peabody, a close friend of Towell's, received Stroessner's full medical history and file from the dictator's personal physician (a professional acquaintance). Dr. Peabody then forwarded the medical file to the ambassador, giving the United States knowledge of a critically important element of the succession drama. The embassy understood that if news of Stroessner's prostate cancer leaked out, the political situation could unravel quickly, leading to violence and social chaos. Despite Ambassador Towell's attempt to keep the report a secret, the speed with which the militants moved to purge the military suggests that they knew of the president's condition and rapidly shifted to fill key military and government posts with allies before his death or incapacitation, in order to preempt the military from gaining power.

For decades, the Stroessner regime celebrated U.S. backing as the mainstay of its political survival. It was the threat of losing the legitimacy confirmed by this support—an example of U.S. soft power leverage—that forced the regime to yield, even if it did so while showing utter contempt for U.S. officials. When it resisted, it weakened the Stronato. The United States was changing its foreign policy priorities as the cold war waned, from security to the consolidation of market democracies. National Security Doctrine regimes were no longer welcomed. U.S. leadership and influence in key international organizations and norms helped it isolate Paraguay when, for its own reasons, it came to see the Stroessner dictatorship as dispensable. This made it difficult for Asunción to garner support from any nation-state or international institution after this. As Ambassador Timothy Towell stated, "the United States played a part in isolating Paraguay, to the point of making it the Mongolia of Latin America." Finally, the U.S. ability to indirectly pressure the regime by supporting opposition forces, such as the National Accord, not only shook the foundations of the Stronato's domestic legitimacy but also deprived Stroessner of the international legitimacy he had cultivated for so long. In sum, U.S. power and its role in the decomposition of the regime, though not dominant, cannot be easily dismissed, for it was by this form of leverage (soft power) that Washington effectively pressured and isolated Asunción during the second Reagan administration and continued to be the main form of U.S. influence in the post-Stroessner, post–cold war period.

8 Safeguarding Democracy in Paraguay, 1989–2000

By late 1988 the international and domestic environment that had long been so well manipulated by Stroessner no longer assured his uninterrupted continuance in power. By November it was clear that the United States had shifted toward encouraging, if only through subtle gestures and messages, an outright change of government. After General Woerner's visit in December, when he met with General Andrés Rodríguez and the National Accord, avoiding any serious contact with political leaders close to the regime, the militants within the Colorado Party took an openly xenophobic attitude toward Washington and other external actors who favored an end to the Stronato. As pressures intensified, the regime found itself isolated and fearful that the ruler's failing health (i.e., senility, prostate cancer), the growing split within the Colorado Party, economic crises, and international condemnation could very well bring its collapse.

It appeared that as the Berlin Wall fell and the cold war ended in 1989, so would the Stroessner regime. The growing irrelevance of the East-West conflict and the division and fissures within the regime, along with an increasingly independent and organized civil society, robbed the regime of its remaining legitimacy. This occurred within an environment that favored change coming from within and without. Not surprisingly, domestic factors and processes ultimately proved more important in explaining the end of the Stronato than international pressures.[1]

Several factors were at work. First, Stroessner had named no successor, and his son Gustavo, an air force colonel, was unacceptable to many in the military high command. Second, there was much concern among senior officers that the militants were planning to purge them from the military and appoint promilitant, pro-Gustavo officers. Efforts to isolate and remove the traditionalists from the army were considered an attack on the integrity and unity of the armed forces unacceptable to General Rodríguez and his cadre of loyal colonels. Finally, the economic recession of the mid-1980s, after a decade of high growth rates, resulted in high inflation, unemployment, and debt, producing the conditions for social discontent and upheaval. In the end, "As the old power arrangement crumbled, several factors—the decline of the dictator, division among the elites, economic discontent, dispute over succession, calls for liberalization—combined to sap the ability of the Stronato to repress the escalating disarray and discontent."[2]

By mid-January 1989, the domestic situation and the regime's relations with Washington had become untenable. Asunción was immersed in intrigue, rumors, and uncertainty about the fate of the traditionalists and the regime. The U.S. Embassy was sending signals (though still relatively discreet) to the traditionalists that Stroessner could no longer expect Washington's patronage in the absence of a liberalizing change. Press releases from the embassy began to openly address charges of abuse and human rights violations in Paraguay, and a number of critical U.S. newspaper articles had U.S. government officials on the record about the need for democracy in Paraguay.

The regime, in turn, led by the most obstinate and militant stronistas, the Gang of Four or the Golden Foursome, embarked on a campaign to discredit and threaten Colorado Party dissidents, the opposition, and the United States. With the help of the regime's two most influential and vocal journalists and ideologues—José Caceres Almada and Ezequiel González Alsina—the cuatrinomio used discreet propagandistic means and references in speeches to discredit the traditionalists and condemn U.S. policy and maneuverings while attempting to bolster the regime's nationalist credentials and record of stability and prosperity.[3] However, they were careful not to heighten the level of polarization in the media. In an effort to depoliticize the situation, the Paraguay public was given a heavy dose of soap operas and beauty contests on television.

Meanwhile, in November–December 1988, as the crisis within the Asociación Nacional Republicana (ANR) intensified, General Rodríguez and a group of loyal colonels concluded that Stroessner had to be removed if Paraguay and the military were to be saved, but some were concerned that Washington might not support a coup.[4] Until 1988, the U.S. government had avoided any contact with Rodríguez, convinced that the general was either the boss of drug-smuggling operations in Paraguay or at least had greatly benefited from them. By September 1988, however, priorities changed. The United States was concerned about stability, human rights, and the polarization of politics in Paraguay. Drug trafficking, the number one issue in bilateral relations, seems to have declined in importance, at least until the political crisis was resolved.

In an effort to appease Washington, the Stroessner government enhanced the level of counternarcotic cooperation. For example, on 22 January 1989, the antidrug penal code Law 1340/88 went into effect; it included every counternarcotic measure that Washington had requested from Asunción since the early 1980s, including the creation of an antidrug agency, the National Directorate of Narcotics (DINAR).[5] Asunción also allowed the reopening of the Drug Enforcement Administration (DEA) office in January.

After General Woerner's December visit, contacts between the embassy and the armed forces escalated. The regime feared the United States was encouraging dissent within the military. In late January the government announced the retirement of dozens of colonels believed to be loyal to Rodríguez and the traditionalists. General Rodríguez was also informed that he would be "promoted" to the relatively powerless and ceremonial position of defense minister.

By January, General Rodríguez and his comrades could no longer wait. The U.S. Embassy seemed to want change, but it was still unclear whether embassy officials would support a coup. Nonetheless, the situation reached an intolerable level for Rodríguez and the traditionalists. Time was of the essence. On the night of 2 February 1989, armored vehicles from the First Army Corps headquarters were mobilized by General Rodríguez, as were assets from the navy and the air force to overthrow President Stroessner. Meanwhile, on the civilian side, Edgar Ynsfrán and Juan Ramón Chávez (pushed out as party president in

1987 by the militantes) worked behind the scenes to bolster support for the coup and unify antimilitant forces within the Colorado Party. Ambassador Towell and the embassy were caught off guard but made no move to impede Rodríguez's forces from occupying Asunción. By the morning of 3 February, after some artillery fire and bombardments from rebel forces and resistance from the Presidential Escort Regiment, General Rodríguez announced that government forces had surrendered. By the end of the day, Rodríguez was sworn in as interim president, and on Sunday, 5 February, Alfredo Stroessner boarded an airplane that flew him into exile in Brazil.[6]

Mending Ties and Obtaining Legitimacy

For about a week after the coup, the U.S. press was filled with articles detailing the events of 2–3 February in Paraguay. A number of newspaper reports examined the domestic factors that contributed to Sroessner's downfall as well as allegations that linked his successor to the drug trade. Never before, not even during the Chaco War, had Paraguay received such robust attention in the U.S. media.[7] As reported in the media, Washington reacted cautiously to the coup, concerned with Rodríguez's commitment to democratic rule and counternarcotics, particularly in light of his corrupt, antidemocratic past. Charles Redman, the U.S. State Department spokesperson, reiterated for several days after the putsch that relations with United States hinged on establishing a democracy, respect for human rights, and an active policy against drug trafficking.

Despite public apprehension, it was clear, however, from private exchanges that Washington welcomed the coup and applauded the reassuring public statements made by President Rodríguez and the quick measures taken by the interim government toward elections, democracy, and civilian rule. On 9 February, three days after the interim government announced elections, the United States recognized the new government. Ambassador Towell had just finished meeting with the new foreign minister, Luis María Argaña, after which Towell announced "the reestablishment of diplomatic relations between Paraguay and the United States. [Argaña and I] spoke about the new government's plan and its policy to bring democracy to Paraguay, respect human rights international norms and its commitment in the struggle against the scourge of drug trafficking."[8] A few days later, the government affirmed its commitment to fight drugs when Foreign Minister Argaña promised Ambassador Towell the eradication of all marijuana fields and the end of Paraguay's role as a transshipment point for drugs destined for Europe and the United States.[9]

General Rodríguez had to obtain international support for his government through an aggressive public relations campaign to change his and Paraguay's poor image. He considered outside support vital to the regime's domestic legitimacy. He focused on breaking Paraguay's international isolation and reinserting the country into the regional and global community of democratic states.[10] By showing his commitment to democracy and economic reform, Rodríguez hoped to obtain much needed access to foreign investments, trade concessions, economic aid, and credit. For instance, a few days after assuming power, he ratified the Pact of San José (American Convention on Human Rights) and consistently repeated, particularly at international forums, his vow to strengthen democracy. He assured the international community that he would not seek reelection after his term ended in 1993.[11]

Repairing the image of Paraguay and General Rodríguez depended on an open commitment to democracy. Just as important, however, was demonstrating the will and capacity to suppress corruption and drug trafficking. The government immediately sought to dispel allegations that the president and others in the administration had been involved in the drug trade. They ardently denied involvement and promised to aggressively tackle the problem. Rodríguez affirmed that the Paraguayans "would wage a firm and intransigent struggle against drug trafficking, and will make the laws even stricter and stronger in order to repress it." At the United Nations he reiterated this commitment: "My Government will not permit Paraguayan land to be used as a road for the transit of drugs and drug trafficking, and within economic limits, will arrange the resources to prevent and eradicate this situation."[12]

Improving relations with the United States was a key priority in Rodríguez's foreign policy plan. Asunción understood that U.S. approval was an essential condition for Paraguay's reinsertion into the international system. The fact that the United States stood as the only superpower in the post–cold war period and as leader of the "free and democratic world" had tremendous symbolic meaning for a regime desperately seeking to translate international support into domestic gain. The Bush administration, in turn, understood its privileged position and sought to take advantage of its leverage to insist that Rodríguez maintain his pledge to the three "Ds"—*democracia, derechos humanos, y drogas* (democracy, human rights, and drugs).[13] Asunción was more than happy to oblige if at times it seemed its actions, particularly on the issue of drugs, were not as resounding as its rhetoric. Nevertheless, the United States did respond in kind by giving President Rodríguez what he most wanted—Washington's stamp of approval.

During the three years following the coup, contacts between the United States and Paraguay expanded more than at any other time in the history of the relationship. A few days after recognition, a large delegation of U.S. politicians, former diplomats, and academics arrived in Asunción to "evaluate political changes and establish contact with government officials, members of the opposition and civil society organizations." The delegation included former ambassador Robert White, Connecticut congressman Bruce Morrison, former Arizona governor Bruce Babbitt, and political analyst Douglas Sosnik. The delegation met for an hour with President Rodríguez during which Congressman Morrison expressed full support for the new government. On returning to Washington, Morrison noted with approval that Rodríguez had promised to "change the reputation of Paraguay as a haven for smugglers and criminals" and highlighted his commitment to combating drug trafficking.[14] This delegation was followed by a number of visits from nongovernmental groups, such the National Endowment for Democracy (NED) and the Latin American Studies Association (LASA), many of which came to provide civil society support, technical assistance, and observers for the 1 May general elections.

In 1989 alone there were six high-level visits by U.S. government and military officials to Paraguay. In March, Robert Howard, deputy assistant secretary of state, met with President Rodríguez and other officials to talk at length about human rights. Howard was followed by a delegation led by Dorothy Bush Leblond, daughter of President George Bush, and Senator Paul Coverdale of Georgia, who traveled to Paraguay for the inauguration of Andrés Rodríguez. The absence of a high government official at the inauguration indicates a diplomatic slap or warning, but at the time it was not interpreted as such by Asunción. In August, Senator Richard Lugar—an influential member of the Foreign Relations Committee—spent a few days on an "assessment visit." After the Paraguayan government requested in August the renewal of Generalized System of Preferences (GSP) benefits, Senator Lugar affirmed his commitment to getting GSP benefits and other trade concessions restored as soon as possible. In the second half of the year, Rodríguez received several visits from U.S. military personnel, including the new Southern Command head General Maxwell Thurman.

During this time, the United States offered limited tangible benefits other than increasing Paraguay's sugar quota and providing only slight increases in economic and counterdrug assistance. Paraguay, on the other hand, made every effort to meet all of Washington's demands. This asymmetry, however, brought no frustration in Asunción. For Rodríguez, U.S. diplomatic efforts to strengthen ties with the new government was exactly what he hoped for.

Tennis Diplomacy: Rodríguez's Second Foreign Minister?

The Rodríguez government had no better advocate and adviser during the first two critical years after the coup than U.S. ambassador Timothy Towell. Before the 3 February putsch, Rodríguez and Towell became friends first as a result of a shared love for the game of tennis, but later, once Rodríguez came to power, both found they could trust and help one another get their message across.[15] Towell often used the venue of a tennis court to communicate U.S. policy objectives in Paraguay to Rodríguez and others in and out of the Paraguayan government. Rodríguez used these occasions to communicate his views to

Washington through the ambassador, trusting that Towell would act as an advocate, if not a lobbyist, for the new Paraguayan government. Towell did not disappoint. He wielded such considerable influence that he once told a Paraguayan analyst that "he was practically Rodríguez's foreign minister," an assertion that many Paraguayans could confirm.[16] No previous foreign ambassador in Asunción had made such an assertion.

Ambassador Towell worked hard to get what Rodríguez wanted most—U.S. political and economic support for his government. More than a "foreign minister," the ambassador was virtually an unpaid agent of the Paraguayan government (he would later become a paid lobbyist for Paraguayan interests). In return, however, Towell received what the United States most demanded from Paraguay—respect for democratic rule and human rights and an unrelenting effort to fight drugs in Paraguay. Towell understood the value of symbolism or what he referred to as "diploteatro," or good diplomatic theater.

In Paraguay that meant getting high U.S. government officials to visit Paraguay and meet with Rodríguez. Each visit was widely reported by the media. The Americans publicly praised President Rodríguez for his commitment to democracy and human rights. The intent was clearly to show Paraguayans and the international community that this general, the long-time defender of the Stroessner regime and allegedly a former drug trafficker, had the blessings of the U.S. government. In this spirit, Ambassador Towell arranged to have Vice President Dan Quayle visit Paraguay during his South America tour in March 1990 in an effort to "showcase" Paraguay's new democratic credentials. Paraguay's decision to be the first Latin American country to recognize the new government of Panama installed after the U.S. invasion of December 1989 did not go unnoticed by Washington.

Bilateral military and economic ties improved markedly, thanks, in large part, to a commitment from both sides to normalize and strengthen relations. Several high-ranking military officials visited Asunción, most of them to observe a number of joint military exercises held between 1989 and 1991.[17] In one instance that exemplified statements made by high-ranking U.S. military officers, Vice Admiral

Theodore Lockhart stated, during a visit to Asunción to assess an ongoing joint military exercise, that "this combined training work, while the country [Paraguay] is in transition to democracy, facilitates wider cooperation and, through these contacts, strengthens relations."[18]

More than just providing symbolic political support, Asunción sought to get some economic benefits restored. After serious delays and some concern by Paraguay, the Bush administration restored GSP in February 1991 and reinstated Paraguay into the Overseas Protection Insurance Corporation (OPIC) in July of the same year. It was perhaps no coincidence that these trade and investment concessions were granted not long after a telephone conversation between Presidents Bush and Rodríguez in January in which the U.S. president requested that Paraguay support U.S. policy in the Persian Gulf. Paraguay supported all UN resolutions and U.S. measures to liberate Kuwait. Only 2.5 percent of Paraguay's exports benefited from GSP trade concessions, but the measure was interpreted by the Paraguayans as a sign of how far bilateral relations had developed.

Also in 1991, the United States signed the "Rose Garden Agreement" with the Southern Cone Common Market (Mercosur) countries—Argentina, Brazil, Uruguay, and Paraguay—which set up a framework for talks that the signatories hoped would lead to a free trade agreement. Ambassador Towell stated the agreement was in part "recognition of the positive changes registered in Paraguay." In 1992 the United States also increased its technical and material assistance to Paraguay from less than $150,000 in 1991 to nearly $2 million in 1992—still a small commitment but a gesture perceived by many as indicative of U.S. support.[19] With the budget deficit debate in full gear in Washington coupled with the strategic irrelevance of Paraguay, one is hard-pressed to explain why U.S. foreign assistance to Paraguay increased while that to most countries in the region declined.

In the area of antidrug assistance, once Rodríguez vowed to combat trafficking in Paraguay, the United States increased amounts allocated from $300,000 in 1990 to $1 million in 1991 and $2.2 million in 1992. The Paraguayan reciprocated by destroying an unprecedented number of marijuana fields and enhancing the government's capacity to interdict the flow of cocaine through the country. In May 1991, upon the recommendation of the U.S. State Department and DEA, Paraguay established a special joint police and military task force, the National Antidrug Secretariat (SENAD), to govern and coordinate all government and nongovernment bodies that work in prevention, rehabilitation, and repression of drugs. General Marcial Samaniego became the first executive secretary of this new executive and coordinating agency that reported directly to the president. He was an officer with impeccable professional credentials and a graduate of West Point who enjoyed the complete confidence of the State Department and the Pentagon.[20]

Bilateral relations broadened and deepened during the administrations of George H. W. Bush and Andrés Rodríguez. The honeymoon seems to have had no end during the first few years after the coup. However, relations would never be the same once Jon D. Glassman replaced Towell and Paraguay faced a difficult hurdle, the 1993 election campaign.

Economic Ties Remain Stagnant

Save for trade and investments, the level of interaction and cooperation between the United States and Paraguay improved significantly. More U.S. tourists and academics visited Paraguay in the early 1990s than at any other time. The Peace Corps became more robust and more visible (i.e., attention given to the program by the government) as the Rodríguez government viewed it as an instrument to enhance cooperation and regime legitimacy. Official U.S. assistance increased during the first few years after the 1989 coup, but trade and capital flows remained stagnant through the early 1990s despite U.S. reinstatement of GSP benefits and other trade and investment concessions.[21] Not long after coming to power, the Rodríguez administration initiated a unilateral process of economic liberalization that brought some important dividends to the economy, though it had negligible impact on trade with the United States. Between 1988 and 1994 Paraguayan exports to the United States fluctuated between 4 and 5 percent of total exports. Imports did not change, with 14 percent of the total amount in 1988 and 1994. Much of this is due to the deepening of economic ties between Paraguay and its two large neighbors, but also the lack of complementarity between U.S. and Paraguayan markets limited commercial possibilities. The size of the Paraguayan market and the distance from the United States continued to be a hindrance. Also, the problem of intellectual property and lack of antipiracy enforcement in Paraguay continued to frustrate U.S. companies and investors.

In terms of U.S. capital flows to Paraguay, in the first five years after the fall of the Stroessner regime, U.S. investment never surpassed $14 million. Reinstating benefits under the Overseas Protection Insurance Corporation (OPIC) in 1991 and the 1990 Investment Law in Paraguay had an insignificant impact on U.S. investments. For example, the total number of U.S. companies in Paraguay increased negligibly from 63 in 1987 to 65 in 1994. Moreover, with the establishment of Mercosur in 1991, Paraguayans believed that their economic future was better served by relations with Brazil and Argentina, and so little effort was put into cultivating the U.S. market.[22]

During the honeymoon period (1989–92), there seemed to be no end to the level of cooperation and U.S. support for the Rodríguez government and Paraguay's democratic transition. The United States found itself in a unique position to exercise leverage over Paraguay's government, despite the relatively small amounts of trade, aid, and U.S. investments in the country. The fact that the United States stood as the only superpower in the post–cold war period and as leader of the free and democratic world had tremendous symbolic meaning and influence. During this period and for years to come, the influence of the United States in Paraguay's political process was notable. One need only to consider the anxiety and ire that the State Department's Human Rights and International Narcotics Reports produced in Paraguay to notice the import of U.S. policy and opinion on Paraguay's transition and public opinion.[23]

The Bush administration understood President Rodríguez's political needs and used them as leverage to gain influence over Paraguayan domestic politics, obtaining a commitment from Asunción to do more in the fight against drug trafficking and not deviate from the path of democratic transition. Such an approach proved more effective than suspension of economic assistance and trade concession as its most effective instrument in encouraging Asunción's adherence to U.S. policy interests.

Turmoil in Bilateral Relations and Paraguayan Democratization

The new ambassador, Jon Glassman, arrived in August 1991 to a warm welcome from Paraguayan government officials. Before his appointment, Ambassador Glassman worked on national security matters in the office of Vice President Quayle. In 1989 he had closed the U.S. Embassy in Kabul, Afghanistan, in the midst of a major civil war. The appointment of a "high government official" with close ties to the vice president reinforced the impression that Paraguay had come of age. The rumors in Asunción held that Glassman had a direct line to the White House that might be used to obtain more tangible concessions. It did not take long, however, before the Paraguayans became disappointed and exasperated by what they perceived as the arrogance, meddling, and heavy-handedness of Glassman's undiplomatic behavior. Some in the media referred to the ambassador as the "American Pro-consul."

Ambassador Glassman became a kind of "guard dog" against those seeking to undermine Paraguay's democracy and commitment to counternarcotics. His steadfastness in support of democratic rule was unequivocal and commendable, especially when Paraguay's democracy came under attack by a faction within the military led by General Lino Oviedo, but as one Paraguayan journalist noted, the ambassador took Paraguayan democratization "too personally."[24] Perhaps the personalization of his duties was a result of his outstanding knowledge of Paraguayan history and politics. He seemed to understand Paraguay better than most U.S. ambassadors, but as some indicated, he went too far. Glassman was particularly vocal and critical of democratic reversals, real or imagined, and openly criticized politicians for Paraguay's slow-moving democratic transition, at times raising the ire of legislators and officials who accused him of meddling in Paraguay's internal affairs.

He understood the value of soft power leverage, often warning Paraguay of the severe "consequences of any attempt at usurping Paraguayan democracy such as international isolation." He also made reference to the importance of "image and credibility," which he considered to be fundamental in attracting trade, credit, and investments. In a 1992 interview Glassman stressed the "potential benefits" Paraguay could obtain from the United States and international financial institutions, where Washington had much influence, if Paraguay behaved in relation to democracy, corruption, and counternarcotics.[25] The persistent intrusion of the U.S. Embassy during Ambassador Glassman's tenure (1991–94) was visible and pressing.

Weeks after presenting his credentials, Glassman publicly responded to unfounded rumors that President Rodríguez was planning to extend his tenure in office. He threatened the government with sanctions and international isolation if Rodríguez failed to hand over power to an elected successor in 1993. The threats continued even after President Rodríguez repeatedly denied the allegation. What seemed most confusing is that while Glassman was issuing warnings, the Bush administration was lauding President Rodríguez and announcing that Paraguay was well into consolidating its democracy.[26] Paraguayan government officials felt perplexed and insulted by the ambassador's zeal and statements, which rapidly contributed to a cooling of ties, especially with the embassy.

By the end of 1991 the degree to which the ambassador interfered in Paraguay's domestic affairs, including appointments to the cabinet and key leadership positions in the military and bureaucracy, embarrassed the government as the media began to report that Rodríguez was not up to confronting the abrasive diplomat. Bilateral relations, nonetheless, remained cordial throughout 1992 despite Glassman's periodic warnings that militarism and corruption were antithetical to the development of a modern state.

The first real test for both Paraguay's democracy and Washington's commitment to safeguarding the country's democratic institutions came at the end of 1992. During the ANR primary, Luis María Argaña was pitted against businessman Juan Carlos Wasmosy, President Rodríguez's candidate—and, many believed, Washington's as well. As the country geared up for the May 1993 election, Ambassador Glassman warned First Army Corps commander general Lino Oviedo and his antidemocratic allies within the ruling Colorado Party that severe consequences would follow any break in democratic practices. Rumors ran rampant about the intentions of General Oviedo if Argaña won the primary against his candidate, Wasmosy. It was clear that Oviedo was a central figure in the months leading to the December 1992 primary.

During this time, Oviedo worked behind the scenes, with the tacit support of President Rodríguez, to negotiate a Colorado candidacy that would be amenable to the general's interests.[27] After some jockeying and support from the Palacio de López, Oviedo endorsed the candidacy of Wasmosy as president and Angel Roberto Seifert as vice president against the Luis María Argaña–Carlos Ibañez team. On primary election day the exit polls indicated a victory for Argaña-Ibañez with 48 percent of the vote against Wasmosy-Seifert's 42 percent. Before the official results were announced, the Electoral Tribunal postponed the process because of a "series of irregularities." Oviedo's allies in the party managed to postpone the results, and as a result, a crisis ensued within the Colorado Party that threatened Paraguay's young democracy. Reports arrived at the U.S. Embassy that General Oviedo was preparing a coup, probably for New Year's Eve. As Ambassador Glassman described, "he had an itch and we needed to make sure that he didn't scratch it."[28]

The U.S. Embassy and Ambassador Glassman immediately went into action, warning the insubordinate general and other commanders that any attempt to subvert the democratic process by manipulating election results would bring sanctions and international recriminations against specific individuals. In the end, General Oviedo and his men stood down. A weakened Paraguayan democracy survived the test but just barely. It is difficult to ascertain whether Glassman's admonitions contained Oviedo and the military. After all, Wasmosy received the nomination of the party and ultimately won the general election in May; it is undeniable, however, that the embassy's warnings played an important role. In an interview, Ambassador Glassman signaled Washington's role in confronting the threat, insisting that the United States "helped save Paraguayan democratization."[29]

The legacy of the 1992 crisis and enduring structural obstacles to deepening democratization coupled with the weakness and corruption of Wasmosy and his administration and a deterioration in the financial and social situation (i.e., banking crisis, labor strikes, social protests) undermined and delegitimated many of Paraguay's democratic institutions. As institutions proved unable to mediate political disputes that intensified with the 1993 campaign, *la embajada,* as many Paraguayans referred to the U.S. Embassy, began to act as a domestic political actor and unofficial arbitrator resolving political disputes. Also, being seen entering the embassy or meeting with the ambassador conferred a degree of legitimacy that politicians desperately sought, as this enhanced their political position before the public, particularly in Asunción. Political leaders and institutions delegated greater authority and responsibility to the United States for the survival of Paraguay's democracy. After the inauguration of President Juan Carlos Wasmosy, Ambassador Glassman and the embassy did not refrain from using the growing U.S. influence to play a larger role in Paraguay's domestic affairs.

The inauguration of Democrat Bill Clinton in January 1993 did not modify U.S. policy priorities in Paraguay, nor did it alter Ambassador Glassman's activist approach to dealing with Paraguayan authorities. The White House strongly urged the incoming administration of Juan Carlos Wasmosy to deepen democratic and economic reforms and strengthen its commitment to counternarcotics, antipiracy, and improving the foreign investment climate in the country.[30]

Between the May general election and August, when Wasmosy moved into the Palacio de López, Glassman's admonitions and abrasive behavior intensified with every passing day. As a result, relations deteriorated between the Rodríguez government and the U.S. Embassy. The Argaña faction within the ruling party accused Glassman of having engineered its candidate's loss in the primary. In order to discredit and weaken the incoming president, Arganistas also claimed that the U.S.

ambassador was the power behind the Wasmosy throne. It was not uncommon to hear from some political circles Glassman referred to as the "viceroy" and "Washington's man in the Palacio de López." The opposition—in and out of the Colorado Party—stepped up efforts to get Glassman removed.

Not long after Wasmosy came into office, tensions appeared between the new government and Glassman over the issue of drugs. Upon returning from the United States in late September, where he had an "excellent meeting" with President Clinton, Wasmosy announced that relations with the United States had improved dramatically. Increases in antidrug assistance and other programs, he felt, would soon be forthcoming. However, the U.S. ambassador was quick to frustrate expectations, at least in terms of the rhetoric. Consequently, relations proved cordial and cooperative with Washington but conflicted and tense with the embassy.

Glassman often used the media and meetings with the interior minister and the National Police commander (without official permission from the Palacio de López) to get his point across that the government had not done enough to combat drug trafficking.[31] Problems came to a head with the new government when General Mario Escobar, director of the National Antidrug Secretariat (SENAD), was removed from his post. The embassy had regarded Escobar as extremely competent and honest. The ambassador believed that he had been relieved because SENAD's investigations into money laundering had revealed involvement by high-ranking military and government officials. The ambassador said publicly that it was a "disgrace" to replace honest officials with dishonest ones. President Wasmosy, in turn, felt angered by the ambassador's accusations and insinuation that the United States should expect a say in SENAD's new appointments. The Paraguayan president responded forcefully by reminding Glassman that "he [the president] was in charge of the country's antidrug policy and not the ambassador."[32]

By January 1994 the relationship between the Palacio de López and the U.S. Embassy had become so poisonous that even small matters took on aspects of crises. For example, a confrontation surfaced over a U.S.

offer to send six hundred soldiers to build schools and health centers in the Paraguayan interior. Observers immediately denounced the project, known as Fuertes Caminos, as a cover for the United States to gather intelligence and pursue drug traffickers. The government ultimately rejected the offer on nationalist grounds, arguing that the United States placed "unacceptable demands," such as absolute freedom of movement for U.S. forces and no participation by Paraguayan troops.

Finally, the 1994 State Department report on human rights, which was highly critical of Paraguay, infuriated Wasmosy, who dismissed it as being "out of touch with reality."[33] As his official letter of protest indicated, the report "seemed to be more interested in damaging the image of Paraguayan democracy."[34] As far as Paraguayans were concerned, Glassman was at the center of a sinister effort to introduce U.S. troops into Paraguay while damaging the country's carefully constructed image.

Although it seemed that relations had reached a low point, bilateral ties remained strong on many different levels, particularly in terms of antidrug cooperation, culture, and the expanding presence of U.S. government and nongovernment organizations. The number of Americans visiting the country continued to increase, and the flow of private and public resources into the country did not slow down because of the clash between the Palacio de López and the U.S. Embassy. As far as President Wasmosy was concerned, the only thing standing in the way of a more robust relationship between the two countries was the U.S. representative in Asunción. Wasmosy seemed to have reached this conclusion after a meeting in Chile on 19 March 1994 with Alexander Watson, assistant secretary of state for inter-American affairs. Watson acknowledged "points of friction" between the two countries but insisted that they would be overcome. The Paraguayan media reported that Wasmosy asked Watson to replace Glassman. Wasmosy did interpret Watson's promises of better relations and cooperation, specifically in the area of economic and social development, as a slap at the U.S. ambassador.

In the first few months of 1994, the Paraguayan government twice sent senior officials to Washington to press for Glassman's removal.

According to a news report in the *Washington Post*, the State Department "quietly yanked" Glassman from his job a few months before the end of his three-year tenure. Because of his undiplomatic style, "he had simply stepped on too many toes too often" in Washington and Asunción.[35] In fact, the report asserts the ambassador was "summarily bounced by Assistant Secretary Watson and principal deputy Michael Skol around mid-February and was given until April 30 to leave." An unidentified administration source added that "we simply lost confidence in his reporting . . . [his departure] has been a long time coming." One can only imagine the excitement with which the news of Glassman's exit was received in the Palacio de López and by many Paraguayan politicians and observers. President Wasmosy viewed the incident as a political victory. As irony would have it, however, in two years it was that same embassy, albeit under different management, that saved his administration and Paraguay's democracy from General Lino Oviedo.

Ambassador Service and the Constitutional Crisis of 1996

At least for the Paraguayans, an unusually long time passed after Jon Glassman left Asunción on 3 May until the new ambassador, Robert Service, presented his credentials on 18 November. During the nearly six months without a U.S. ambassador in Asunción there were some noticeable improvements, due, in large part, to the able leadership of the chargé d'affaires, Gerald McCullough. Certainly the tenor of the relationship between the embassy and the Palacio de López improved markedly; yet by October things seemed to unravel once again in the aftermath of the assassination of SENAD director General Ramón Rosa Rodríguez. The embassy alleged that Paraguayan military and government officials were involved, while President Wasmosy countered by suggesting that the Drug Enforcement Administration had a hand in the killing and in propagating corruption in Paraguay.[36] Senator Elena Recalde, chair of the bicameral parliamentary committee investigating the incident, went as far as to accuse the United States of introducing drugs into Paraguay so as to justify intervention in Paraguay's internal affairs. As many noted, relations had become too "narcotized"—embassy officials talked of nothing but antidrug policy. The Paraguayan government expressed deep frustration at how narrow the bilateral agenda had become.

When Ambassador Service assumed his duties in November, he made every effort to broaden the relationship, without ignoring the issue of drugs. He maintained a low profile to allow things to calm down. He much preferred the one-on-one discussion with government officials than the much less effective approach of dealing with issues in public through the sensationalist media. Once again, it is important to note that U.S.-Paraguayan relations during this time existed on two levels. For example, between 1994 and 1996 bilateral trade increased for the first time in years by an average of 4.5 percent a year, and according to Paraguayan sources, the number of U.S. visitors also climbed by 7 percent from 1993 to 1995. For one thing, the number of Americans traveling to Asunción to adopt Paraguayan babies, described as a "boom" by the media, was impressive, although the corruption associated with the process became the subject of much news coverage in the United States.[37]

In other words, although diplomatic troubles persisted, cultural, economic, academic, and other private forms of interaction were unaffected by the spat. Even so, the sensationalist Paraguayan press gave the impression that Washington and Asunción remained at loggerheads.

During the first eighteen months of his tenure, Service did much to gain the respect, admiration, and good will of President Wasmosy. Even though Service insisted that Wasmosy needed to do more to combat corruption and cooperate in counternarcotics if Paraguay were to obtain the benefits of a modern state (Paraguay was decertified without waiver in the March 1995 State Department drug report), his style and language were much less confrontational and threatening, and, therefore, he was relatively successful in getting the Paraguayans to listen and act. The political capital and personal relations Ambassador Service built during his first year and a half in Asunción proved critically important in Paraguay's constitutional crisis of April 1996.

Ever since 1989, Paraguay's democracy had been under tremendous stress and pressure from authoritarian enclaves—specifically within the ruling Colorado Party and the armed forces—resulting in socioeconomic deterioration, labor protests, corruption, and weak and ineffective institutions and leadership, all of which eroded the credibility of the regime. During the administration of President Wasmosy, General Oviedo was an influential political actor, intervening, to the great consternation of the U.S. Embassy, in the internal affairs of the party and in other government or policy initiatives. After all, Wasmosy owed his presidency to an Oviedo-led antidemocratic alliance of civilian and military officials that had reversed results of the 1992 primary election in Wasmosy's favor. However, by 1996 Oviedo's constant intrusions in government decisions and party politics "constituted a direct challenge to the president's authority and a serious threat to Paraguay's fragile democracy." It was clear to President Wasmosy that "his position had become untenable . . . [he] understood that his survival as president depended on his ability to remove the commander of the army."[38]

By late March, many in Asunción sensed that a conflict between President Wasmosy and General Oviedo was coming to a head. On 14 April, Wasmosy summoned Ambassador Service to his residence (just across the street from the embassy) and, in the presence of Jorge Prieto, Paraguay's ambassador to the United States, expressed his deep frustration and fear that Oviedo harbored *golpista,* or coup, inclinations and was preparing to overthrow the government if Wasmosy challenged the general on key political issues, specifically the upcoming Colorado Party internal elections that Oviedo was attempting to control. Then came the reason for the meeting. President Wasmosy announced his intention to remove the general from his post and "wondered whether the United States would support Paraguay [i.e., his government] in the event of a coup."[39] It is not known exactly what Service said, but if subsequent developments were any indication, the ambassador gave his government's unequivocal support to President Wasmosy's stand on Paraguayan democracy.

On 17 April, while Wasmosy informed anti-Oviedo military commanders that he would ask the general to resign and needed their support in case of an attempted coup, the U.S. Embassy and State Department were busy preparing to contain Oviedo, working with South American countries to send a clear signal that an interruption of the democratic process was unacceptable. Finally, on 20 April, the Palacio de López informed the U.S., Argentine, and Brazilian embassies that President Wasmosy intended to relieve Oviedo of his duties in two days.

When he received the orders on the 22nd, however, General Oviedo adamantly refused to obey and returned to his headquarters, warning that the president's actions would result in "rivers of blood." Wasmosy immediately informed foreign ambassadors of the general's insubordination. Rumors ran rampant as no official statement was released until 6:30 pm, when the U.S. Embassy issued a strongly worded communiqué stating that the United States "recognized President Wasmosy's constitutional right to dismiss Army Commander General Lino Oviedo." The statement continued, "General Oviedo's refusal to accept the President's decision constitutes a direct challenge to the constitutional order in Paraguay and runs counter to the democratic norms accepted by the countries of this hemisphere." The communiqué ended with a warning, that if the general usurped power, his actions would "be met with the appropriate response from the international community. We will continue to monitor the situation in Paraguay and, in consultation with our OAS partners, will review the full range of necessary actions."[40] This communiqué issued by the United States at this early point in the crisis did much to bolster democratic forces and galvanize support for President Wasmosy.

On the evening of 22 April, Service and the Argentine and Brazilian ambassadors appeared at Oviedo's command, but the general refused to see them. He refused to bow to what he considered a weak and ungrateful president and the meddling of outsiders. By midnight Oviedo issued an ultimatum to the president that if he did not resign, the general's forces would attack the president's residence. The crisis escalated. Wasmosy began to wonder about the many deaths that would come about if Oviedo carried out his threat. The president seemed prepared to resign, but Ambassador Service urged him to take more time to consider his response. He offered the president the safety of the embassy compound. The president accepted the offer and came to the embassy with his sons in the ambassador's car.

Ambassador Service and the president's sons urged President Wasmosy to resist Oviedo's threats and not draft a letter of resignation. He did so any way. Upon the Brazilian ambassador's recommendation, a second letter was drafted in which the president offered a temporary leave of absence. The letter was presented to Oviedo, but it was rejected. Nothing short of an unconditional resignation was acceptable to the rebellious general. Meanwhile, support for the government grew from the international community and the Paraguayan Navy and Air Force. On the morning of 23 April, President Wasmosy received several calls from Assistant Secretary of State for Inter-American Affairs Jeffrey Davidow, who, along with Ambassador Prieto, spent the night at the State Department. Davidow urged the president to stand firm and not sacrifice the future of the country. The president was also heartened by the calls he received from OAS Secretary General César Gaviria, who promised to rally international support in favor of Wasmosy's government.[41]

The Paraguayan Air Force and Navy were determined not to let Oviedo get his way. Air force general Rafael Cramer maintained close contact with U.S. military and State Department officials as he prepared his aircraft to attack Oviedo's forces if they moved on Asunción. General Cramer received several calls from Washington requesting information on developments and encouraging him to defend the government. He was also called by Lieutenant General James Record, commander of the U.S. Southern Command Air Forces, who unequivocally reiterated U.S. support for Paraguay's endangered democracy. General Cramer, a well-respected and self-confident officer, believed he had all the authority and support he needed to challenge Oviedo. Domestic and international forces were building into a coalition that was increasing the political costs on Oviedo.

Meanwhile, in Washington the U.S. government and the Organization of American States continued to rally international support from the European Union and Latin American states. Assistant Secretary Davidow and Deputy Secretary of State Strobe Talbott kept abreast of all developments while supporting OAS Secretary General César Gaviria's efforts to invoke Resolution 1080, which would consider specific actions if the constitutional order were interrupted. By 23 April, anti-Oviedo forces had coalesced into a force that the general understood he could not defeat. On the morning of 24 April the crisis concluded with General Oviedo's resignation. Despite several missteps by Wasmosy, a potential constitutional crisis was averted by an "internal correlation of forces in Paraguay, coupled with the strong diplomatic response from abroad."[42] At critical moments loyalist forces in the armed forces, and the U.S. Embassy, played a decisive role in defending democracy in Paraguay.

Before the crisis, President Wasmosy had been a weak, ineffective, and increasingly illegitimate leader beholden to a coalition of antidemocratic forces led by Oviedo. He was indecisive and incompetent, and he was unable or unwilling to confront Paraguay's massive political, social, and economic challenges. Infighting among factions within the ruling party had paralyzed the pace of reform. As a result, a vacuum appeared with the absence of mediating institutions. The U.S. Embassy seemed like the only actor capable of mediating political disputes. Dependence on the United States for resolving domestic disputes was exemplified when the crisis erupted, and President Wasmosy sought refuge, assistance, and advice from Ambassador Service. As Arturo Valenzuela points out, "Ambassador Service not only strengthened President Wasmosy's resolve, he provided the president with a safe haven, making it difficult for Oviedo to contemplate a direct move against the president."[43] For many Paraguayans, particularly political leaders of the country's major parties, the key lesson learned from the 1996 crisis was that the United States could shape any, perhaps all, political outcomes in Paraguay. The legitimacy of the U.S. role in domestic matters seemed to grow, while protestations of interference or violations of sovereignty seemed to dissipate in light of the weakness and vulnerability of Paraguay's institutionally deficient democracy.

U.S. Soft Power and the Constitutional Crisis of 1999

Although Paraguayan democracy and the Wasmosy government survived the 1996 crisis, the country began to spiral out of control after several years of poor economic performance, increasing poverty, rising unemployment, failing banks, increasing crime rates and corruption, and weak and corrupt political leadership leaving many Paraguayans disillusioned. President Wasmosy could do nothing more in the remaining time in office than to muddle through and try to survive what seemed to many as a period of permanent crisis. In the aftermath of the 1996 crisis, his relationship with the U.S. Embassy deepened in ways that can only be described as unhealthy to the institutionalization of Paraguay's democracy. In other words, the more that Wasmosy and other political leaders entrusted the fate of the government and Paraguay's democracy to *la embajada,* the less legitimate and effective the institutions became. Delegating what was the authority and responsibility of institutions such as political parties, the judiciary, and the legislature to the U.S. Embassy only made Paraguay's democracy more dysfunctional and illegitimate, though during Paraguay's constant crisis mode the United States (and some of Paraguay's neighbors) could be counted on to safeguard Paraguay's fragile democracy.

Paraguay's political-psychological dependence was best exemplified by the actions and attitudes of the media and some political leaders. Being seen meeting with the ambassador or coming out of the embassy provided an instant shot of credibility. An invitation to the embassy could be of great importance to the political future of any Paraguayan and was often the subject of much speculation among the small circle of rumormongering politicians, journalists, and intellectuals.

It was not unusual to find journalists and photographers across the street from the two entrances to the U.S. Embassy keeping a watchful eye out for Paraguayan politicians and intellectuals. At no other foreign embassy in Asunción did journalists camp out to see similar activities. Sometimes impromptu press conferences were held outside the embassy, where political leaders answered questions and commented as to the nature of their visit. For political leaders of all stripes seeking to enhance their credibility and profile, it was almost compulsory to be seen on television or in the newspapers coming out of the embassy after a meeting and answering reporters' questions. If a public appearance with the ambassador could be arranged, better still. Needless to say, the U.S. ambassador remained in high demand. More important, the ambassador understood the impact and effectiveness of his symbolic or soft power and often used it to promote U.S. interests and defend Paraguayan democratization.

In the end, the source of U.S. influence had more to do with the weakness of Paraguay's democracy and the symbolism of U.S. superpower status than with leverage associated with trade, investments, or economic and military assistance. In fact, starting in 1996, bilateral trade declined and U.S. investments halted, while aid remained at very low levels. In short, despite the loss of traditional leverage, U.S. influence skyrocketed in the late 1990s.

Paraguay's abysmal political, social, and economic situation in the late 1990s made another constitutional crisis nearly inevitable. Conditions were ripe for an antidemocratic populist leader such as Lino Oviedo to play a destabilizing role.[44] During the eighteen months following his resignation, Oviedo overcame efforts by the courts and the legislature to jail him for sedition. Not only did he avoid conviction, but with the support of the mostly rural poor and disenfranchised Paraguayans who sought a strong savior, he won the presidential nomination of the Colorado Party on 7 September 1997 in a very close and disputed election. The U.S. Embassy made no secret of its opposition to Oviedo. Ambassador Service and his successor, Maura Harty, refused to meet with the former general, which sent a clear signal that an Oviedo presidency would find no support in Washington. Oviedo, offended and irritated by the U.S. rebuff, tried to exploit it by playing the nationalist card to expand and mobilize popular support.

Fearing the consequences of an Oviedo victory, the military and opposing factions within the ruling party led by Luis María Argaña and President Wasmosy intensified efforts to get Oviedo behind bars. On 8 January 1998, a military tribunal sentenced Oviedo to a ten-year prison term for sedition. The conviction and sentence were upheld on appeal by the Supreme Court. Between January and April, when the Supreme Court issued its decision, Ambassador Harty made numerous statements in support of the court and met with some of its members at a time when the institution was under attack by Oviedistas. Harty's actions provided the cover and protection that the court needed to make its decision under perilous circumstances.

As a result of his conviction, Oviedo was disqualified from holding office. His running mate, Raúl Cubas, became the Colorado Party candidate, and Argaña joined the ticket as the vice presidential candidate, uniting the party. The Cubas-Argaña ticket won the 10 May general elections with 54 percent of the votes. Many believed that Cubas would take advantage of his position and Oviedo's misfortunes to consolidate his own authority before releasing his friend and mentor. These observers were immediately disappointed. In his first act as president, Cubas signed Decree 117 releasing Oviedo from prison. This led to a firestorm of protest from Oviedo's opponents within the ANR, especially Vice President Argaña, opposition party leaders, and anti-Oviedo military officers who feared that Cubas would reinstate Oviedista officers. Once again, the Supreme Court intervened, ruling that Cubas acted unconstitutionally and ordering Oviedo back to jail. When President Cubas refused to respect the court's authority, the crisis escalated. The Congress was now committed to impeaching the president. Meanwhile, Oviedo issued threats and used violence to intimidate his opponents. Many Paraguayans began to talk of "implosion" and "civil war."[45]

In the first few months of 1999, politicians flocked to the U.S. Embassy seeking support or some sign or guidance regarding Washington's expectations. In one highly public meeting, Ambassador Maura Harty met with Vice President Argaña on 15 February. Immediately, many saw the meeting as a show of support for Argaña and the embattled Supreme Court, which was the subject of the meeting. Although the official press release from the embassy was that Harty "routinely meets with party leaders to further her understanding of the country," it was hard to believe the embassy misunderstood the impact that such a meeting would have on Paraguay's desperate political situation. As one Colorado Party official who attended the meeting commented, "what is very obvious after the ambassador's visit is that the United States wants to know what Argaña's eventual government would look like." Whether true, it was certainly the overwhelming perception among most Paraguayans, once again reflecting the great influence of the United States on Paraguay's fragile democracy.[46]

In March the impeachment proceedings ensued rapidly. A vote was scheduled for 7 April, and according to most observers, the opposition had gathered the necessary votes to impeach the president. Consequently, tensions increased considerably. Finally, the constitutional crisis came to a climax on 23 March when several men dressed in military fatigues ambushed and killed Vice President Argaña in a well-orchestrated attack. It was the first time since the death of President Juan Bautista Gill in 1877 that a president or vice president was killed in Paraguay. Inevitably, the public accused Cubas and Oviedo of the attack and called for the removal of Cubas as president and the arrest of Oviedo on the charge of murder. Popular support for impeachment intensified as people poured into the square in front of the Congress, demanding that the legislature act immediately. Social groups, particularly striking labor unions, peasant associations, and a democratic youth movement, mobilized to support Cubas's removal and the institutionalization of Paraguayan democracy.

On the morning of 24 March, the Chamber of Deputies impeached the president, but not without a response from Oviedo supporters. The general's followers congregated and moved against the prodemocracy supporters, carrying clubs and weapons. Meanwhile, events were moving too quickly for the United States to respond. At first, the United States seemed to want to avoid Cubas's resignation, fearing that a constitutional breakdown under such stressful and uncertain circumstances could lead to utter chaos. Some evidence suggested that elements within the military were planning a coup that could split the armed forces. Members of the opposition in Congress, specifically Senators José Félix Estigarribia, Euclides Acevedo, and Bader Rachid Lichi, lobbied the U.S. ambassador (and other diplomats) to support anti-Oviedo forces to ensure the survival of the democratic system under a new government headed by Senator Luis González Macchi, president of the Senate and first in line of succession.[47]

As the situation spiraled out of control, the United States became convinced that order and the future of democracy hinged on Cubas's exit from power. On the evening of 26 March, pro-Oviedo supporters began to fire on the demonstrators from rooftops and windows in nearby buildings. By the end, 8 prodemocracy demonstrators had been killed and 150 wounded, but the young anti-Oviedo protestors remained in firm control of the area. Washington and the U.S. Embassy quickly became convinced that Cubas had to go. On 28 March, Ambassador Harty brokered discussions between Cubas and key legislators, informing both parties that further bloodshed was unacceptable.[48] By late afternoon, Brazilian president Fernando Henrique Cardoso telephoned Cubas, asking that he resign and leave the country. A few hours later Cubas left for Brazil, where he was granted asylum. Oviedo left the country for Argentina moments before Cubas's televised resignation address to the nation.

Earlier in the evening of the twenty-eighth, Senator González Macchi, the president-in-waiting, and more than a half-dozen other key legislators went to the U.S. Embassy. They met with Ambassador Harty for more than ninety minutes to work out the details of the transition of power and the makeup of the new cabinet. As had become almost customary in recent years, the U.S. stamp of approval was needed before moving forward. At least as far as the Paraguayans were concerned, the ultimate domestic arbiter had to bring the parties together and support the arrangement before achieving consensus. As one U.S. official recognized, "we didn't necessarily put ourselves in the middle, but that's the way it often happens in this country."[49]

As in 1996, though democracy survived the 1999 crisis, it was deeply scarred by the experience. Throughout González Macchi's presidency (1999–2003) Paraguay continued to be plagued by weak leadership, corruption, poverty, dismal economic performance, and constant threats to the stability of its fledgling democracy. Paraguay's democracy grew weaker and more illegitimate as greater numbers of citizens began to question the viability and utility of democratic rule. Consequently, as crises grew in quantity and intensity during the González Macchi administration, the United States was always there to offer warnings, advice, and a neutral site or institution for political leaders to resolve their dispute, if only temporarily. The United States, of course, was willing to use its soft power influence not only to safeguard democratic rule but also to enhance its leverage over the Paraguayan government on issues of national interest to the United States, such as counternarcotics, copyrights and patents, piracy, and cooperation on a range of hemispheric matters. As long as Paraguay's democracy remained tenuous, the United States was sure to play a central role in protecting it against all threats, even as sources of U.S. hard power leverage declined.

Epilogue

During the first few years of the twenty-first century much did not change in U.S.-Paraguayan relations. The terrorist attack on the United States on 11 September 2001 did make counterterrorism cooperation a more important component, if not a requirement, in the relationship, but it did not subsume the other more traditional issues, particularly support for democracy, counternarcotics, and intellectual property. In fact, in the last two years of President Luis Ángel González Macchi's government (2001–3), Washington could not find a way to engage Asunción on a broad range of issues because of the government's weakness and the overall state of permanent political crisis engulfing the country. The United States feared the consequences of another presidential resignation or impeachment.

During the administration of President González Macchi, Paraguay's democracy limped along at best, crippled by profound administrative incompetence and rampant corruption that led to a number of parliamentary investigations and attempts to impeach the president (the last being in February 2003). Washington sought to dissuade Paraguayan political leaders from pursuing impeachment for fear that such action would create greater turmoil. The weakness of democratic institutions coupled with slow growth and an encumbering poverty rate seems to keep bilateral relations narrowly focused on safeguarding democracy in Paraguay. As in the past, Washington, along with Paraguay's neighbors, worked behind the scenes to ensure that Paraguay's democracy survived until the next election in April 2003.

After the terrorist attack of 11 September 2001, the United States became greatly concerned with activities in Ciudad del Este and the lawless triborder area that connects Argentina, Brazil, and Paraguay. The region has long been known as Latin America's contraband capital, an entrepôt for the smuggling of arms and drugs, document fraud, money laundering, and the manufacture and movement of contraband.

Described by one U.S. intelligence officer as "one of the most important financing centers for Islamic terrorists outside the Middle East," the triborder area with its large population of Arab descent became the focus of an intensive, U.S.-supported law enforcement effort soon after the 11 September attacks in which Washington solicited and received the full cooperation of Paraguay's security and intelligence services.[1]

Even prior to the terrorist attack, the United States had been concerned with terrorism-related activities in the region. U.S. apprehension about the area intensified after a November 1996 incident in Paraguay in which a Lebanese-born man arrested in Ciudad del Este was linked to an alleged Islamic terrorist plan to bomb the U.S. Embassy in Paraguay. According to U.S. ambassador Robert Service, "there was enough corroborating information to suggest that there was a plan against the U.S. Embassy."[2] Also, in two separate incidents in October 1999, suspected members of Hizballah were arrested in Asunción reconnoitering the U.S. and Israeli embassies. According to the intelligence report, one of the suspects began working with authorities, providing "invaluable" information on the activities of Hizballah and Hamas in the triborder area.[3] In November 2000 Paraguayan authorities arrested Salah Abdul Karim Yassine, a Palestinian with links to Hizballah, who allegedly threatened to bomb the U.S. and Israeli embassies in Asunción. Finally, in April 2001 the U.S. State Department temporarily closed its embassies in Paraguay after receiving information of a terrorist threat.

After 11 September, despite protests and pressure from influential leaders of the Arab community in the area, Paraguay's police did not back off from moving aggressively against real and perceived associates of terrorist organizations. Under U.S. pressure, Paraguayan commandos raided homes and places of businesses believed to be laundering money for the Lebanese-based Hizballah movement. The sweeps resulted in more than twenty arrests on false passport and visa charges, and a half-dozen suspects were investigated before the end of the year for links to radical Islamic groups.

Since then cooperation has continued to be productive. In 2002, at the invitation of Paraguay, Argentina, and Brazil, the United States joined in the "3+1 Group on Triborder Area Security" to improve capabilities and cooperation against cross-border crime and potential terrorist fundraising activities. Although counterterrorism and anti-money-laundering legislation remain stalled in the Paraguayan legislature (despite considerable pressure from the U.S. Embassy), the government has taken steps to combat terrorism financing. Washington has assisted Paraguay with antiterrorism training, particularly through the Counter-Terrorism Fellowship program, which has not only enhanced U.S.-Paraguayan security cooperation but has also contributed to building a strategic partnership.

Since the inauguration of President Nicanor Duarte Frutos in August 2003, Paraguay's democracy and economy have stabilized. The Duarte government immediately focused on attacking corruption and enhancing the quality of governance. Duarte resolved many of the internal conflicts within the Colorado Party and was effective in working with the opposition-controlled Congress to enact major tax reform and in removing six Supreme Court justices suspected of corruption. Although many social issues remain unresolved (poverty and unemployment), the Duarte administration improved the country's macroeconomic performance and governance.

Not since the end of President Andrés Rodríguez's administration in 1993 did Washington believe there was a government in Asunción that it could seriously and effectively engage on a range of issues. The new government's actions and rhetoric indicated that there was a leader in the Palacio de López with whom Washington could work. The defining moment for post-2003 U.S.-Paraguayan relations came only a month after the inauguration of President Duarte when he visited Washington for a working visit and met with President George W. Bush in the Oval Office. The two connected on a personal level as they shared their experiences and views as Christians. A level of trust was quickly established that would have positive consequences for bilateral relations.

A shift to a new engagement with Paraguay would be in line with historical precedent. For much of the 160 years of relations, U.S. involvement in the Upper Plata was characterized by periods of significant interest, followed by lulls of almost indifference. With no geographical closeness and relatively slight economic interest, the United States has sought stronger relations only when Paraguay might play a role in the "large picture." Paraguay, on the other hand, has learned well how to profit from changing trajectories of U.S.-Paraguayan relations. And in 2004 it appeared that such a change might serve the interests of both parties. It seemed to the U.S. Embassy in that year that the Paraguayan government had made a strategic decision to align Paraguay with the United States. Problems with Brazil and Argentina over a number of economic issues within Mercosur and U.S. willingness to increase security cooperation and potentially negotiate a free trade agreement led Asunción to test U.S. receptiveness. Paraguayan exports to the United States remained low, however, increasing from only $32 million in 2001 to $51 million in 2005. Imports, however, climbed significantly, which contributed to a trade deficit that escalated from $363 million in 2001 to $844 million in 2005. The trade imbalance and U.S. ambassador Jim Cason's suggestion in 2005 of a possible free trade agreement heightened interest and speculation in Asunción.

In other key economic areas the relationship strengthened. In July 2004 the United States and Paraguay signed a Memorandum of Understanding that called for Paraguay to enhance its intellectual property laws and enforcement capabilities. Washington provided $320,000 in assistance to implement intellectual property reforms. This was the first time for the signing of an agreement and financial assistance of this nature on an important bilateral issue. During the first half of the decade, U.S. Agency for International Development (USAID) assistance averaged $8 million a year on programs to help solidify democratic institutions and integrate environment and reproductive health initiatives into the overall democracy program. Though not significant in terms of total amount, USAID programs continued to have great impact and exposure in Paraguay and are still an important source of U.S. influence in the country. However, the most significant aid program, in terms of amount and impact, came in 2004–5 when Paraguay was deemed eligible to participate in the Millennium Challenge Corporations (MCC) Threshold Country Program (TCP), "which helps countries improve governance, levels of investment in their citizens and economic freedom, so they can qualify for the MCC's principal program."[4] Under this program, in May 2006 Paraguay received $37 million of Millennium Challenge Account funds to help the country combat corruption and achieve greater economic growth. No other country in South America has received funds under any MCC program. The Peace Corps presence in Paraguay remains strong, as do U.S. cultural programs. The small number of U.S. academicians interested in Paraguay is steadily growing, as are U.S. scholarly publications on this region.

In the area of security and defense, bilateral ties have been enhanced but not to the extent that the Paraguayans would like. An important military-humanitarian medical assistance exercise called the Medical Readiness Training Exercise (Medretes) has provided medical care to over a hundred thousand Paraguayans since 2000. There has also been a robust Joint Combined Exercise Training (JCET) program where U.S. Special Forces train along with their Paraguayan counterparts in a number of unconventional warfare training exercises. Since 2002 some forty-six U.S. military operations have been conducted in Paraguay, including visits, special exercises, and humanitarian missions.

Military cooperation has not been without its controversy, however. Many Paraguayan politicians and activists noticed the increase in security and military cooperation after the 2004 kidnapping and subsequent murder of Cecilia Cubas, the daughter of former president Raul Cubas. Alfredo Boccia Paz, a political analyst, journalist, and human rights activist, noted, with other analysts and some Paraguayan politicians, "a clear shift of Paraguayan foreign policy in the direction of the United States."[5] In July 2005 Vice President Luis Castiglioni visited the United States and was received by Vice President Dick Cheney. Many interpreted the visit and access given to Castiglioni as part of a strategic plan by the United States not only to forge a closer tie with the Duarte government, but to possibly install a U.S. military base at the Mariscal Estigarribia Airfield in the Paraguayan Chaco. Such rumors were consistently denied by the U.S. Embassy, but it did not seem to quell the allegations. The embassy also had to dispel rumors that the United States had an interest in the Guaraní aquifer, one of the largest reserves of fresh water in South America. All this came on the heels of the Paraguayan Congress's decision to grant immunity from prosecution for eighteen months to U.S. soldiers participating in thirteen missions—each up to 45 days—between July 2004 and December 2006.

The speculation and controversy continued when the media in Argentina and Brazil interpreted the courtesy visit by Defense Secretary Donald Rumsfeld to Paraguay in August 2005 as part of Washington's "secret agenda" to establish a foothold in the Chaco, close to Bolivia's natural gas reserves. It did not help Washington's effort to dispel the rumors when Brazilian foreign minister Celso Amorim denounced a "secret agreement" to install a U.S. Marine Corps base in the Chaco. Nevertheless, despite these political challenges, security cooperation has continued as Paraguay has sought greater help with counterterrorism assistance. The 2006 Bolivian election of Evo Morales, and his closeness to Hugo Chávez of Venezuela, heightened both Washington's and Asunción's concerns about political stability in the Upper Plata and will probably strengthen the drive toward security cooperation between Paraguay and the United States.

It is unlikely that bilateral relations will be impaired by the normal practice of Paraguayan politics. As Paraguayans begin to question the benefits of closer relations with its two larger neighbors, particularly in the context of Mercosur, closer economic and security ties with the United States, the largest consumer market and provider of security assistance in the world, may reach levels not seen since the 1960s. It is highly probable that the more than three thousand U.S. citizens residing in the country and some seventy-five U.S. businesses with agents or representatives in Paraguay will continue to be welcomed, and that one can expect those numbers to increase in the years to come.

Notes

Preface

1. John Gunther, *Inside South America* (New York: Harper & Row, 1966), 238.
2. There is no good, up-to-date single volume of the history of Paraguay—in English or Spanish. However, still readable but lacking results of modern research and carrying the reader only to the late 1940s is Harris Gaylord Warren, *Paraguay: An Informal History* (Norman: University of Oklahoma Press, 1949). The two volumes by Efraím Cardozo are also well written but suffer from the same limitations as does the Warren work. Efraím Cardozo, *El Paraguay colonial: Las raices de la nacionalidad* (Asunción: Ediciones Nizza, 1959) and *Paraguay independiente,* 1st Paraguayan ed. (Asunción: Carlos Schauman Editor, 1987). These works should be supplemented by Paul Lewis, *Paraguay under Stroessner* (Chapel Hill: University of North Carolina Press, 1980), and Richard Scott Sacks and Riordan Roett, *Paraguay: The Personalist Legacy* (Boulder, Colo.: Westview Press, 1991).

Introduction

1. For the colonial era see Cardozo, *El Paraguay colonial;* and Warren, *An Informal History,* 3–141. Two works are useful for the economic, political and social changes in the final years of the colonial period: Edberto Oscar Acevedo, *La intendencia del Paraguay en el virreinato del Río de la Plata* (Buenos Aires: Ediciones Ciudad Argentina, 1996); and Jerry W. Cooney, *Economía y sociedad en la intendencia del Paraguay* (Asunción: CPES, 1990).
2. Independence and early nationhood are well treated in John Hoyt Williams, *The Rise and Fall of the Paraguayan Republic, 1810–1870* (Austin, Texas: Institute of Latin American Studies, 1979), 19–42. Also see Luis Vittone, *El Paraguay en la lucha por su independencia* (Asunción: Imprenta Militar, 1960). An interesting view of Paraguay by Scottish merchants in the early days of independence is J. P. and W. P. Robertson, *Letters on Paraguay comprising an Account of Four Years' Residence in that Republic under the government of the*

Dictator Francia, 3 vols. (London: J. Murray, 1838–39). Much has been written about Dr. Francia, but perhaps still the best, though somewhat dated, is Julio César Chaves, *El Supremo Dictador: Biografía de José Gaspar de Francia,* 4th ed. (Madrid: Atlas, 1964).

3. R. Antonio Ramos, *La política del Brasil en el Paraguay bajo la dictadura del Dr. Francia,* 2nd ed. (Buenos Aires: Nizza, 1959).
4. Still a good overview of the U.S. policies with regard to Latin American independence is Charles C. Griffin, *The United States and the Disruption of the Spanish Empire, 1810–1822* (New York: Columbia University Press, 1937).
5. C. A. Rodney to Secretary of State John Q. Adams, Washington, 5 November 1818; and John Graham to Secretary of State John Q. Adams, Washington, 5 November 1818. Both in C. A. Rodney and John Graham, *The Reports of the Present State of the United Provinces of South America; drawn up by Messrs. Rodney and Graham, commissioners sent to Buenos Ayres by the government of North America, and laid before the Congress of the United States* (New York: Praeger, 1969), 63–113 and 114–35, respectively.

1. A Troubled Beginning

1. There is no biography of Carlos Antonio López in English. A standard one in Spanish is Julio César Chávez, *El Presidente López: Vida y gobierno de don Carlos,* 2nd ed. (Buenos Aires: Ediciones Depalma, 1968). Also see Williams, *Rise and Fall,* 101–94. For a brief and positive view of the foreign policy of Carlos Antionio López, see José Luis Simón G., "El autoritarismo de Carlos Antonio López y su exítoso pragmatismo diplomático," *Propuestas Democráticas* (Asunción) 2, no. 7 (July–September 1995): 107–57.
2. During this visit Gil made a tentative approach to the U.S. consul in Buenos Aires about recognition of Paraguay's sovereignty. Amory Edwards, U.S. consul at Buenos Aires, to Daniel Webster, U.S. secretary of state, Buenos Aires, 1 April 1843, in William R. Manning, *Diplomatic Correspondence of the United States: Inter-American Affairs, 1831–1860,* vol. 10, *The Netherlands, Paraguay, Peru* (Washington: Carnegie Endowment for International Peace, 1938), 51–52. Much of the diplomatic correspondence between Paraguay and the United States in the period 1843–60 is found in this work.
3. While the direction of this chapter is the relationship between the United States and Paraguay in the 1840s and 1850s, Paraguay faced other international problems, both from neighbors and European powers in this era. For

an overview of the cautious approach of Paraguay to the outside world in the early 1840s and the resultant difficulties, see Williams, *Rise and Fall*, 139–75.

4. Juan Bautista Rivarola Paoli, *Historia monetaria del Paraguay: Monedas, bancos, crédito público* (Asunción: El Gráfico, 1982): 81–87.
5. That passage of American merchantmen was bitterly attacked by a special agent to Paraguay who considered it to be playing into the hands of the interventionist British and French by displaying a lack of U.S. resolution in face of the European powers. Edward A. Hopkins, special agent of the United States to Paraguay, to James Buchanan, U.S. secretary of state, U.S. sloop *Saratoga* at sea, February 1846, in Manning, *Diplomatic Correspondence*, 10:80–85. Needless to state, Rosas was also angered at the American presence in that merchant fleet.
6. James Buchanan, U.S. secretary of state, to Edward A. Hopkins, special agent of the United States to Paraguay, Washington, 10 June 1845 in Manning, *Diplomatic Correspondence*, 10:29–32.
7. Somewhat dated but still useful for Hopkins are Harris Gaylord Warren, "The Hopkins Claim against Paraguay and 'The Case of the Missing Jewels,'" *Inter-American Economic Affairs* 22, no. 1 (1968): 23–44; and Harold F. Peterson, "Edward A. Hopkins: A Pioneer Promoter in Paraguay," *Hispanic American Historical Review* 22, no. 2 (1942): 245–61.
8. Edward A. Hopkins, special agent of the United States to Paraguay, to James Buchanan, U.S. secretary of state, Asunción, 31 (sic) November 1845, in Manning, *Diplomatic Correspondence*, 10:63–76. No study of the course of U.S.-Paraguayan relations between the visit of Hopkins to Asunción in 1845 and the very early 1860s is complete without reference to the well-researched and detailed two-volume work by Pablo Max Ynsfrán, *La expedición norteamericana contra el Paraguay, 1858–1859* (México/Buenos Aires: Editorial Guaranía, 1954/1958). This work has been extremely useful in the preparation of this chapter.
9. James Buchanan, U.S. secretary of state, to Edward A. Hopkins, special agent of the United States to Paraguay, Washington, 30 March 1846, in Manning, *Diplomatic Correspondence*, 10:32–34.
10. Consideration of recognition had clearly been in the process for at least a year before the official act inasmuch as Hopkins received an appointment as consul to Asunción in 1851, although it was not officially announced until the next year.
11. A good source for the business enterprise of Hopkins in Paraguay, as well as his attitudes toward Paraguayans, and theirs to him, is John Bassett

Moore, "Claim of the United States and Paraguay Navigation Company: Commission under the Convention between the United States and Paraguay of February 4, 1859," in *History and Digest of the International Arbitrations to which the United States has been a Party* (Washington: GPO, 1898), 2:1485–1549.

12. Edward A. Hopkins, U.S. consul at Asunción, to William L. Marcy, U.S. secretary of state, Asunción, 22 August 1854, in Manning, *Diplomatic Correspondence,* 10:120–33.

13. Decree of President López, Asunción, 1 September 1854, in *Semanario* of 2 September 1854, 1; and "Motivos de esta providencia," in ibid., 1–2. The Paraguayan government does not appear to have been informed of Hopkins's resignation as consul.

14. The political aspects of this era of naval exploration and scientific investigation are discussed in John P. Harrison, "Science and Politics: Origins and Objectives of Mid-nineteenth Century Government Expeditions to Latin America," *Hispanic American Historical Review* 35, no. 2 (May 1955): 175–202. For general background of the activities of the U.S. Navy in this period, see "An Empire of Trade," in Robert W. Love Jr., *History of the U.S. Navy, 1775–1941* (Harrisburg, Pa.: Stackpole Books, 1991): 221–43.

15. A good work on the *Water Witch* expedition is Robert D. Wood, *The Voyage of the Water Witch: A Scientific Expedition to Paraguay and the La Plata Region (1853–1856)* (Culver City, Calif.: Labyrinthos, 1985). Also, Clare V. McKanna, "The Water Witch Incident," *American Neptune* 31, no. 1 (January 1971): 7–18; and Thomas Jefferson Page, *La Plata, the Argentine Confederation, and Paraguay; Being a Narrative of the Explorations of the Tributaries of the River La Plata and Adjacent Countries During the Years 1853, 54, 55, and 56, Under orders of the United States Government* (New York: Harper, 1859): 567. While a very interesting work, this account by Page must be used with great care.

16. The most detailed account of this expedition is found in vol. 2 of Pablo Max Ynsfrán, *La expedición norteamericana contra el Paraguay, 1858–1859.*

17. For an account giving great credit to Urquiza for the settlement of the dispute, see Harold F. Peterson, *Argentina and the United States, 1810–1960* (New York: State University of New York, 1964), 172–78. A corrective to Peterson, giving much more credit to the astute diplomacy of Bowlin, as well as the common sense of both Bowlin and López, and analyzing other factors that led the United States and Paraguay to a solution is Thomas O. Flickema, "The Settlement of the Paraguayan-American Controversy of 1859: A Reappraisal," *Americas* 25, no. 1 (July 1968): 49–69.

18. Treaty of Friendship, Commerce, and Navigation between the United States and Paraguay, at Asunción, 4 February 1859 in *Treaties and Other International Acts of the United States of America,* ed. Hunter Miller (Washington, D.C.: GPO, 1942), 8:189–201. One difference from the 1853 unratified treaty was now American merchantmen were allowed to pass completely through Paraguayan territory and enter the Brazilian Mato Grosso.
19. Convention Relating to Claims of the United States and Paraguay Navigation Company against the Government of Paraguay, Asunción, 4 February 1859 in Miller, 8, 259–64.
20. Award of the Paraguayan Claims Commissioners Cave Johnson and José Berges, Washington, D.C., 10 August 1860, in Moore, "Claim of the United States and Paraguay Navigation Company against the Government of Paraguay . . . . ," 2:1501.
21. The charge by the U.S. minister to Paraguay in the 1860s, Charles Ames Washburn, that Cave Johnson was inordinately prejudiced against New England, and thus against Hopkins's claims, can be dismissed in light of the evidence presented before the Commission on Claims. The same holds true for the claim that Samuel Ward, secretary of the commission, unduly influenced its deliberations in favor of Paraguay. See Charles A. Washburn, *The History of Paraguay, with Notes of Personal Observation and Reminiscences of Diplomacy under Difficulties,* 2 vols. (Boston: Lee and Shepard, 1871), 1:385 and 2:179; Pablo Max Ynsfrán, "Sam Ward's Bargain with President López of Paraguay," *Hispanic American Historical Review* 34, no. 3 (August 1954): 313–31; and Thomas O. Flickema, "'Sam Ward's Bargain': A Tentative Reconsideration," *Hispanic American Historical Review* 50, no. 3 (August 1976): 539–42.
22. For Charles Ames Washburn's seven-year tour of duty in Paraguay, see vol. 2 of his *History of Paraguay*. The reader is cautioned, however, that it is an intemperate and prejudiced account.
23. For a well-researched and judicious history of the Triple Alliance War, see Thomas L. Whigham, *The Paraguayan War,* vol. 1, *Causes and Early Conflict* (Lincoln: University of Nebraska Press, 2002).
24. Washburn to Secretary of State William H. Seward, Buenos Aires, 16 January 1866, in Norlands Library, Norlands, Maine. Washburn to his brother Elihu, Corrientes, 1 June 1866, in Norlands Library. Rear Admiral S. W. Godon, acting commander of the U.S. Brazil Squadron, to Secretary of the Navy Gideon Welles, Montevideo Harbor, 23 January 1866, in U.S.

House of Representatives, Committee on Foreign Affairs, *Paraguay Difficulties,* 40th Cong., 3rd sess., Exec. Doc. no. 79, 1–3. This executive document is a fine source for the navy's justification of its conduct in the war, especially in relation to problems of getting U.S. diplomats to and from Asunción.

25. Harold F. Peterson, "Efforts of the United States to Mediate in the Paraguayan War," *Hispanic American Historical Review* 12, no. 1 (1932): 2–16.
26. Washburn's description of López in "Deposition of Charles A. Washburn," Edinburgh, Scotland, 29 September 1869, in Norlands Library.
27. Washburn to Secretary of State Seward, Asunción, 14 October 1867, in U.S. Senate, Committee on Foreign Relations, *Presidential Message communicating Correspondence concerning recent transactions in the La Plata region affecting political relations of United States with Paraguay, Argentine Republic, Uruguay, and Brazil,* 40th Cong., 3rd sess., Exec. Doc. no. 5, 94–96.
28. Seward to Washburn, Washington, 11 January 1868, in ibid., 98–99.
29. "Private" letter of Charles A. Washburn to minister resident in Paraguay General M. T. McMahon, Buenos Aires, 11 November 1868, in Norlands Library.
30. The tension and danger felt by Washburn from about June 1868 until his evacuation by the United States a few months later is best described by the minister himself. Washburn, *History of Paraguay,* 2:328–437.
31. U.S. House of Representative, Committee on Foreign Affairs, *Memorial of Porter C. Bliss and George F. Masterman,* 41st Cong., 2nd sess., Misc. Doc. no. 8, pt. 2, 3. For the "confessions" of those foreigners arrested and interrogated by Paraguayan officials, see U.S. House of Representatives, Committee on Foreign Affairs, 40th Cong., 3rd sess., Exec. Doc. no. 5, pt. 3.
32. Robert Conrad Hersch, "American Interests in the War of the Triple Alliance, 1865–1870" (PhD diss., New York University, 1974), 323–43.
33. U.S. House of Representatives, Committee on Foreign Affairs, *Paraguayan Investigation,* 41st Cong., 2nd sess., report no. 65, xiii.
34. Washburn, *History of Paraguay,* 2:104.
35. For McMahon's service in Paraguay, see Lawrence Robert Hughes, "General Martin T. McMahon and the Conduct of Diplomatic Relations between the United States and Paraguay" (master's thesis, University of Colorado, 1962), 30–33. This thesis is the best single work on McMahon's mission to Paraguay. Also see Arthur H. Davis, *Martin T. McMahon: Diplomático en el*

estridor de las armas (Asunción: Editora Litocolor, 1985). This work, penned by a U.S. ambassador to Paraguay, contains (in Spanish) all the official communications to and from McMahon during his mission, as well as much of the correspondence between McMahon and the Paraguayan government.

36. Seward to McMahon, Washington, 3 September 1869 (sic) in U.S. Senate, Committee on Foreign Relations, *Presidential Message communicating Correspondence concerning recent transactions in the La Plata region affecting political relations of United States with Paraguay, Argentine Republic, Uruguay, and Brazil*, 40th Cong., 3rd sess., Exec. Doc. no. 5, 102–3.
37. U.S. minister to Brazil General J. Watson Webb to McMahon, Boa Viagem, 23 October 1868, in Hughes, "General Martin T. McMahon," 36.
38. Ibid., 39.
39. "Private" letter of Charles A. Washburn to U.S. minister resident in Paraguay General M. T. McMahon, Buenos Aires, 11 November 1868, in Norlands Library.
40. For instance, see Martin T. McMahon, "Paraguay and Her Enemies," and "The War in Paraguay," both in *Harper's New Monthly Magazine*, 40 (February 1870): 421–29, and 40 (April 1870): 633–47, respectively.
41. "Donación a Elisa Alicia Lynch," Francisco S. López, Cuartel General de Pykysyry, 23 December 1868, and accompanying note of López to General McMahon, both in Davis, "Martin T. McMahon," 443.
42. Hughes, "General Martin T. McMahon," 51–53.
43. Gideon Welles, *The Diary of Gideon Welles, Secretary of the Navy under Lincoln and Johnson*, 3 vols. (Boston: Houghton Mifflin, 1911), 3:510.
44. Unless otherwise stated, this account of the 1869 investigation of Paraguayan affairs is drawn from U.S. House of Representatives, Committee on Foreign Affairs, *Paraguayan Investigation*, 41st Cong., 2nd sess., report no. 65.
45. Shortly after the Paraguayan investigation Charles Ames Washburn published his prejudiced, self-serving, and polemical work *The History of Paraguay, with Notes of Personal Observations of Diplomacy under Difficulties*, 2 vols. (Boston: Houghton Mifflin, 1871). It has been used, though with much care, by historians interested in Washburn's actions as minister to Paraguay. The tragedy of this publication is that for better than half a century it was the only work in English on Paraguay provided to North Americans interested in that republic, and it undoubtedly contributed to many erroneous assumptions about Paraguay.

46. The visits of Benites and the young López to the United States in 1869 and 1870 are well handled in Hersch, "American Interest in the War of the Triple Alliance," 323–43.

2. A Distant Relationship

1. The traditional view of a great population disaster has been solidly confirmed by Thomas L. Whigham and Barbara Potthast, "The Paraguayan Rosetta Stone: New Insights into the Demographics of the Paraguayan War, 1864–1870," *Latin American Research Review* 34, no. 1 (1999): 174–86. For the economic and even spiritual destruction suffered, see Harris Gaylord Warren with the assistance of Katherine F. Warren, *Paraguay and the Triple Alliance: The Postwar Decade, 1869–1878* (Austin, Texas: Latin American Monographs, no. 44, Institute of Latin American Studies; 1978).
2. The normal course of diplomatic relations between Paraguay and the United States after the War of the Triple Alliance until the early 1900s is well handed in Benedict J. Dulaski, "Diplomatic Relations between the United States and Paraguay, 1845–1914" (master's thesis, George Washington University, 1966): 54–131 passim. Unless otherwise cited, we have employed Dulaski for this era.
3. Decree of Provisional Government, Asunción, 28 September 1869, in República del Paraguay, *Registro Oficial* (Asunción: n.p., 1871): 22–23.
4. General Emilio Mitre to the Provisional Government of Paraguay, 17 November 1869, in Robert Conrad Hersch, "American Interest in the War of the Triple Alliance, 1865–1870" (PhD diss., New York University, 1974), 457–58.
5. That charge was probably correct. John Bassett Moore, chapter 46, "The Middle Chaco Arbitration: Treaty between the Argentine Republic and Paraguay of February 3, 1876," in *History and Digest of the International Arbitrations to which the United States has been a Party . . .* (Washington: GPO, 1898), 2:1935.
6. Warren, *Paraguay and the Triple Alliance,* pp. 58–59, 241–61; and "The Middle Chaco Arbitration: February 3, 1876," in John Bassett Moore, *History and Digest of the International Arbitration to which the United Treaty between the Argentine Republic and Paraguay of States has been a Party . . .* (Washington: GPO, 1898), 2:1923–44.

7. President Rutherford B. Hayes, Washington, 12 November 1878, in *Index to the Executive Documents of the House of Representative for the Third Session of the Forty-fifth Congress, 1878–1879,* vol. 1, *Foreign Relations* (Washington: GPO, 1870), 711.
8. Enrique Finot, *The Chaco War and the United States* (New York: L & S Printing, 1934): 6–8.
9. Unless otherwise stated, material for the postwar revival of the Hopkins claims and the problem of the jewel box is taken from Harris Gaylord Warren, "The Hopkins Claim against Paraguay and 'the Case of the Missing Jewels,'" *Inter-American Economic Affairs* 22, no. 1 (Summer 1968): 23–44; and Victor C. Dahl, "The Paraguayan 'Jewel Box,'" *Americas* 21, no. 3 (January 1965): 223–42.
10. Washburn, *History of Paraguay,* 2:422–44.
11. A curious aspect of Hopkins's efforts in the 1880s was his secret attempt to use a "front" to gain a Paraguayan railroad concession at the same time as he demanded a settlement of the earlier claims. The concession was granted, but financial backing failed. Victor L. Johnson, "Edward A. Hopkins and the Development of Argentine Transportation and Communication," *Hispanic American Historical Review* 26, no. 1 (February 1946): 19–37. For other interests of Hopkins in Paraguay in the 1870s and 1880s, see his "My Life Record," appendix 2 in Ynsfrán, *La expedición norteamericana,* 1:251–55.
12. Rafael Calzada, *Rasgos biográficos de José Segundo Decoud* (Buenos Aires: n.p., 1913): 48–51.
13. Harris Gaylord Warren, with the assistance of Katherine F. Warren, *Rebirth of the Paraguayan Republic: The First Colorado Era, 1878–1904* (Pittsburgh: University of Pittsburgh Press, 1985): 104.
14. The U.S. consul in Asunción, John N. Ruffin, some forty-five years later, claimed that the *Temerario*'s purpose in the Río de la Plata was to prey upon U.S. commerce. He also claimed that the USS *Oregon,* then engaged in its famous race from the Pacific Northwest around Cape Horn to join the blockading squadron off Santiago de Cuba, had a mission to destroy the Spanish gunboat. The latter claim is dubious. The *Oregon* had a more important mission in Cuban waters than any diversion to hunt down the errant gunboat. John N. Ruffin, "*Temerario* at Asunción," *American Foreign Service Journal* 21, no. 11 (November 1944): 636.
15. For a brief discussion of these points on the responsibility of neutrals as they then existed, see Daniel Chauncey Brewer, *Rights and Duties of Neutrals:*

A Discussion of Principles and Practices (New York: G. P. Putnam's Sons, 1916): 166–75.

16. Dulaski, "Diplomatic Relations," 78–81.
17. Andrés de Belmont, *Situación internacional del Paraguay* (Asunción: La Colmena, 1912): 5–11.
18. E. Bradford Burns, *The Unwritten Alliance: Rio-Branco and Brazilian-American Relations* (New York: Columbia University Press, 1966).
19. Ibid., 152.
20. Quoted in Dulaski, "Diplomatic Relations," 127.
21. The standard biography of Percival Farquhar is Charles A. Gauld, *The Last Titan: Percival Farquhar, American Entrepreneur in Latin America* (Stanford, Calif.: Institute of Hispanic and Luso-Brazilian Studies, Stanford University, 1964). Unfortunately, this work is rather weak on Farquhar's machinations in Paraguay.
22. Juan Carlos Herken, *Ferrocarrilles, conspiraciones y negocios en el Paraguay, 1910–1914* (Asunción: Arte Nuevo Editores, 1984): 19–28. Herken's work is indispensable for the operations of the syndicate in Paraguay during the brief era of its economic dominance. Unless otherwise stated, this study follows the account of Herken.
23. For the status and description of the International Products Corporation after the liquidation of the Farquhar Syndicate, see W. L. Shurz, *Paraguay: A Commercial Handbook,* Department of Commerce, Bureau of Foreign and Domestic Commerce, Special Agent Series no. 199 (Washington: GPO, 1920), 72–75, 80–81. Also see Jan M. G. Kleinpenning, *Rural Paraguay, 1870–1932* (Amsterdam: CEDLA , 1992): 189, 271–72.
24. Diego Abente, "Foreign Capital, Economic Elites and the State in Paraguay during the Liberal Republic, 1870–1936," *Journal of Latin American Studies* 21, no. 1 (February 1989): 61–71.
25. Victor C. Dahl, "A Montana Pioneer Abroad: Granville Stuart in South America," *Journal of the West* 4 (July 1965): 356–59.
26. Gauld, *Last Titan,* 221.
27. Ibid.
28. Karen Holiday Tanner and John D. Tanner Jr., *Last of the Old-time Outlaws: The George West Musgrave Story* (Norman: University of Oklahoma Press, 2002): 201–59.
29. A good analysis of the international economy of Paraguay in this period is Miguel Angel González Erico, "Estructura y desarrollo del comercio

exterior del Paraguay: 1870–1918," in *Pasado y presente de la realidad social paraguaya,* vol. 1, *Historia social* (Asunción: CPES/RPS, 1995): 185–215.

30. Max Winkler, *Investments of United States Capital in Latin America,* no. 6 in vol. 11, World Peace Foundation Pamphlets (Boston: World Peace Foundation, 1928): 893.
31. Ibid., 895–96.
32. See, for instance, M. D. Carral, "Paraguay and Its Possibilities as a Market," *Bulletin of the Pan American Union* 40 (May 1915): 651–56; and especially Schurz, *Paraguay: A Commercial Handbook,* 72–76, 143–70. Schurz's work is still a useful resource for economic conditions of the republic in this era.
33. Percy Alvin Martin, *Latin America and the War* (Baltimore: Johns Hopkins Press, 1925): 480–81.
34. Manuel Gondra, "El Paraguay ante la guerra" (1919), manuscript in the Manuel E. Gondra Manuscript Collection, Nettie Lee Benson Latin American Collection, University of Texas, Austin MG 1988. Hereinafter cited as MG 1988.
35. Foreign Minister Manuel E. Gondra to U.S. minister to Paraguay Daniel F. Mooney, Asunción, 12 February 1917, in MG 1988.
36. See, for instance, the article by Cecilio Báez in *La Tribuna* (Asunción), 27 July 1917, quoted in Martin, *Latin America and the War,* 481–82. Also see Cecilio Báez et al., *En favor de los aliados: Discursos pronunciados en la ocasión de la gran demostración en favor de los aliados readizada en Asunción (Paraguay) el 11 de julio de 1917* (London: Hayman, Christy & Lilly, 1917); and Antolín Irala, *La causa aliada en el Paraguay* (Asunción: Talleres Zamphirópolis, 1919).
37. Theodore Roosevelt, *Through the Brazilian Wilderness* (New York: Charles Scribner's Sons, 1914), 38–48.
38. Frank G. Carpenter, *Along the Paraná and the Amazon* (Garden City, N.Y.: Doubleday, Page, 1925).
39. William Spence Robertson, *Hispanic-American Relations with the United States,* ed. David Kinley (New York: Oxford University Press, 1923), 303. Harris Gaylord Warren, *Rebirth of the Paraguayan Republic: The First Colorado Era, 1878–1904* (Pittsburgh: University of Pittsburgh Press, 1985), 296.
40. Clement Manly Morton, *Paraguay: The Inland Republic* (Cincinnati: Powell & White, 1926), 143–65. Arthur Elwood Elliott, *Paraguay: Its Cultural Heritage, Social Conditions, and Educational Problems,* Columbia University Contributions to Education, no. 473 (New York: Bureau of Publications, Teachers College, 1931): 129–46.

41. For the activities and impressions of a U.S. missionary in Villarrica and Concepción in the 1920s, see the Papers of Hazel Chamberlain, Special Collections, University of Oregon Library, Eugene.
42. Fred L. Soper, "Treatment of Hookworm Disease . . . ," *American Journal of Hygiene* 4, no. 6 (November 1924): 708.
43. Elliott, *Paraguay,* 18–31. Kleinpennig, *Rural Paraguay,* 343–44.
44. Pan American Society of the United States, "Paraguay and the United States of America. Address by Mr. Manuel Gondra, Envoy Extraordinary and Minister Plenipotentiary of Paraguay," Bankers Club, New York, 30 January 1919. Also see Juan José Soler, *Pacifismo international del Paraguay* (Asunción: Imprenta Ariel, 1924), 12–15.
45. Roberto A. Romero, *Manuel Gondra: Un intelectual ejemplar* (Asunción: Intercontinental Editora, 1989): 126–28.
46. See, for example, [Juan F. Pérez], *El Instituto Paraguayo y su representación en el Congreso Panamericano de Washington . . .* (Asunción: La Mundial, 1917).
47. An interesting reflection of this desire not to antagonize the United States unduly is seen in the very brief discussion of the 1928 Havana Conference by an important Paraguayan diplomat. Cecilio Baéz, *Historia diplomática del Paraguay* (Asunción: Imprenta Nacional, 1931–32), 2:295. Also see Foreign Policy Association, "The Sixth Pan American Conference, Part I," *Foreign Policy Association. Information Service* 4, no. 4 (27 April 1928): 61–72. The U.S. position at the Havana Conference on the difficult question of intervention is briefly summarized in Betty Glad, *Charles Evans Hughes and the Illusion of Innocence: A Study in American Diplomacy* (Urbana: University of Illinois Press; 1966): 258–63.

3. War and the Search for Peace

1. The historical literature on the Chaco question is immense. Any investigator of the origins of the war, the war itself, and the eventual peace settlement between the two combatants will discover that polemics, nationalistic bombast, special pleadings, and deliberate bias abound. The diplomatic history of this conflict is no exception. Space precludes an in-depth analysis of the diplomacy of this war, but those interested should explore the bibliographies of the works the authors have employed as guides and sources in this matter. Several general studies have received recognition for their judicial consideration of various aspects of the Chaco conflict. For a discussion of

the diplomatic background to the Chaco War, as well as the complex negotiations that terminated the war, see Leslie B. Rout Jr., *Politics of the Chaco Peace Conference, 1935–1939*, Institute of Latin American Studies, Latin American Monographs, no. 19 (Austin: University of Texas Press, 1970). Also useful for the Chaco War are David Zook, *The Conduct of the Chaco War* (New York: Bookman Associates, 1961); and Bryce Wood, *The United States and Latin American Wars* (New York: Columbia University Press, 1966). The authors relied heavily upon these works in the preparation of this chapter. The Chaco Boreal is the major portion of the region known as the Gran Chaco. Technically the Bolivian-Paraguayan dispute was solely over ownership of the Chaco Boreal, but it became the custom to speak of the region in dispute solely as the "Chaco." We follow the general custom in this chapter.

2. To be sure, Bolivia did have a minor enclave upon the Paraguay River, north of Paraguayan-claimed territory, opposite the Brazilian Mato Grosso. For reasons of river flow and terrain in that region, it was not then considered a useful port area on the Paraguay River.
3. An excellent contemporary analysis of Paraguay's vital economic need for the Chaco is Ronald S. Kain, "Behind the Chaco War," *Current History* 42 (1935): 468–74.
4. The diplomacy of the nineteenth century between Bolivia and Paraguay over ownership of the Chaco is well described in Ricardo Scavone Yegros, *Las relaciones entre el Paraguay y Bolivia en el siglo XIX* (Asunción: Servilibros, 2004).
5. Among the oddities of this fervent nationalism were the "doctores en Chaco"—historians of both sides who ransacked national, foreign, and colonial archives to bolster their respective nation's claims to that territory. Certainly, the work of these historians illuminated much of the colonial history of the Chaco, but the reader is warned this "title" controversy is a quagmire. Whether, as the Bolivians claimed, title to the Chaco proceeded from the colonial Audiencia of Charcas that theoretically exercised an overall legal and administrative power over this vast unknown area, or, as the Paraguayans claimed, from the de facto administration the Intendentes of Paraguay exercised along the Chaco littoral in the late colonial era, most of this forbidding region had never really experienced Spanish rule.
6. An excellent discussion of preparations for war by both Bolivia and Paraguay may be found in Mathew Hughes, "Logistics and the Chaco War: Bolivia versus Paraguay, 1932–1935," *Journal of Military History* 69, no. 2 (April 2005): 411–37.

7. The views of Post Wheeler relative to his Paraguayan tour of duty and the Chaco dispute are found in Post Wheeler and Hallie Rives (Mrs. Post Wheeler), *Dome of Many-Colored Glass* (New York: Doubleday, 1955): 767–802. The book describes the normal functions of a U.S. diplomat in Asunción and includes interesting vignettes of Asunción life and the diplomatic circle of the era. Wheeler was an experienced diplomat and quite observant. He well illuminates Paraguayan fears and apprehensions, particularly in the period just prior to the Chaco War. Nonetheless, his account must be used with care as it is extremely one sided, and Wheeler had a definite animus toward Francis White.
8. Although the Paraguayans believed that White favored Bolivia, it is probable that his actions sprang from a belief that Paraguay had little chance in the face of Bolivia's armed might. Other Americans with a greater understanding of Paraguay's military tradition and knowledge of the Chaco, such as the U.S. military attaché in Buenos Aires, were not so dismissive of Paraguay's chances in a war with Bolivia. They, however, were not in policymaking positions.
9. Rout, *Politics of the Chaco Peace Conference,* 39.
10. Cordell Hull, *The Memoirs of Cordell Hull* (New York: Macmillan, 1948), 1:336–38.
11. Some violations of the embargo did occur in the United States, most notably by Curtis-Wright as it supplied Bolivia with spare parts for military airplanes. That company was fined for its transgression.
12. A concise and well-reasoned exposition of the "Guerra del Standard" argument is found in Rout, *Politics of the Chaco Peace Conference,* 45–52.
13. An intriguing, and amusing, example of the longevity of the myth on the left was the Paraguayan Communist Party's scorn for Dr. Thomas Whigham in the 1990s. The respected North American historian of Paraguay was termed a "bisoño" (whippersnapper) for daring to doubt the "Guerra del Standard."
14. Unless otherwise noted, material on Senator Huey Long's involvement in the Chaco dispute is extracted from Michael L. Gillette, "Huey Long and the Chaco War," *Louisiana History* 11, no. 4 (Fall 1970): 293–311.
15. Even today there are reputable Paraguayan historians who are convinced that Long's assassination in late 1935 was not a result of sordid Louisiana politics but rather was due to a conspiracy to silence his revelations about the Chaco War.

16. Enrique Finot, "The Chaco War and the United States," 11–15.
17. Gillette, "Huey Long and the Chaco War," 311. Also see Kain, "Behind the Chaco War," 474.
18. The Chaco Peace Conference lasted two years, handled a multitude of issues, and generated an immense amount of documentation. For obvious reasons, the authors' account of this conference and the eventual peace barely covers even the most important events.
19. "Protocol of June 12, 1935," U.S. Department of State, *The Chaco Peace Conference: Report of the Delegation of the United States of America to the Peace Conference Held at Buenos Aires July 1, 1935–January 23, 1939,* Department of State Publication 1466, Conference Series 46 (Washington, D.C.: GPO, 1940), 49–52.
20. Spruille Braden, *Diplomats and Demagogues: The Memoirs of Spruille Braden* (New Rochelle, N.Y.: Arlington House, 1971), 144–47. This work is essential for an "insider's" view of U.S. participation in the Chaco peace process. It is a candid, sometimes vitriolic, account of people and problems faced by U.S. diplomats and others in the long negotiations that led to the Chaco Peace Treaty. The authors have utilized this work, as well as that of Rout, in their narration of the peace conference. However, it must be emphasized that Braden is stating a U.S. viewpoint of the conference.
21. Braden, *Diplomats and Demagogues,* 160–63.
22. The La Paz visit by Braden is described in Braden, *Diplomats and Demagogues,* 183–86.
23. Efraím Cardozo to Leslie Rout, Asunción, 22 March 1966, in Rout, *Politics of the Chaco Peace Conference,* 211n.
24. "Treaty of Peace, Friendship, and Boundaries between the Republics of Bolivia and Paraguay," Buenos Aires, 21 July 1938, in Department of State, *Chaco Peace Conference,* 148–51.

4. Civil War and Hemispheric Security, 1939–1954

1. For a discussion of Fascist pro-German and Italian influence in South America prior to World War II, see Alton Frye, *Nazi Germany and the American Hemisphere, 1933–1941* (New Haven: Yale University Press, 1967); Stanley Hilton, *Brazil and the Great Powers, 1930–1939: The Politics of Trade Rivalry* (Austin: University of Texas Press, 1965); Irwin Gellman, *Good Neighbor*

Diplomacy: United States Policies in Latin America, 1933–1945 (Baltimore: Johns Hopkins University Press, 1979), chap. 6; Michael Grow, *The Good Neighbor Policy and Authoritarianism in Paraguay* (Lawrence: University of Kansas Press, 1981), chap. 3.

2. R. A. Humphreys, *Latin America and the Second World War, 1939–1942* (London: Athlone, 1981), 1.
3. Unless otherwise stated, material for this section is taken from Grow, *Good Neighbor Policy;* Alfredo Seiferheld, *Nazismo y Fascismo en el Paraguay: Vísperas de la II Guerra Mundial, 1936–1939* (Asunción: Editorial Histórica, 1985; Frank O. Mora, "The Forgotten Relationship: United States–Paraguay Relations, 1937–1989," *Journal of Contemporary History* 33, no. 3 (1998): 451–73.
4. Riordan Roett and Richard S. Sacks, *Paraguay: The Personalist Legacy* (Boulder, Colo.: Westview Press, 1991), 147.
5. Roett and Sacks, *Paraguay,* 147.
6. Grow, *Good Neighbor Policy,* 65.
7. Ibid., 54.
8. Ibid., 53.
9. The highway contract was awarded to a U.S. engineering company.
10. Grow, *Good Neighbor Policy,* 55.
11. Argentina clandestinely aided Paraguay during the Chaco War and expected payment in the form of political influence in consequence. Many Paraguayans, including Liberals, were willing to follow Argentina even if it was down a pro-Nazi path.
12. Grow, *Good Neighbor Policy,* 57.
13. Much of this discussion on the Paraguayan military and Morínigo government is taken from Paul Lewis, "Paraguayan Political Parties and the Military, 1935–1954," paper presented at the 1995 Latin American Studies Association Conference, 28–30 September 1995; Paul Lewis, "Paraguay since 1930," in *Latin America since 1930: Spanish South America,* ed. Leslie Bethel (New York: Cambridge University Press, 1996), 8:233–66.
14. Grow, *Good Neighbor Policy,* 62.
15. U.S. Legation memorandum is taken from Grow, *Good Neighbor Policy,* 66.
16. FRUS (1941) 7:480; Grow, *Good Neighbor Policy,* 69.
17. Grow, *Good Neighbor Policy,* 68.
18. Ibid., 70.
19. Augusto Ocampos Caballero, *Testimonios de un presidente: Entrevista al General Higinio Morínigo* (Asunción: El Lector, 1983), 120.
20. Grow, *Good Neighbor Policy,* 68.

21. Ocampos Caballero, *Testimonios de un presidente,* 122.
22. This discussion of Minister Findley Howard is taken from Ocampos Caballero, *Testimonios de un presidente,* 130–32; Grow, *Good Neighbor Policy,* 66–69; Luis González, *Paraguay: Prisonero geo-politico* (Asunción: Instituto de Estudios Geopolíticos e Internacionales, 1990), 172–73; John Neill, "A Nebraska Diplomat in Paraguay," *Life* 10 (14 April 1941): 17–20.
23. Grow, *Good Neighbor Policy,* 76. Probably exaggerating to gain Washington's attention, Ambassador Frost described further how desperate the situation was when he telegraphed Welles that "police-army fanatics . . . are resolute to reverse Paraguay's course and actually have plans to assassinate Argaña, Andrada and myself."
24. Grow, *Good Neighbor Policy,* 76.
25. This quotation is taken from Claude Curtis Erb, "Nelson Rockefeller and United States–Latin American Relations, 1940–1945" (Ph.D. dissertation, Clark University, 1982), 119. However, not all U.S. films were welcomed in Paraguay. In one incident, Tiempistas and Frente officers in Morínigo's government fought to keep Charlie Chaplin's *The Great Dictator,* a parody of Europe's Fascist regimes, from being shown in the country. Many Paraguayan intellectuals and military officers argued that the movie not only insulted Paraguay's friends in Europe, but it demeaned "ideological and intellectual tenets" of Paraguay's government. After several failed attempts to bring the movie into the country from Buenos Aires (it was confiscated by the Paraguayan government), Chaplin's movie was finally featured in Asunción on 6 May 1942. The direct intervention of Rockefeller and several State Department officials was decisive in persuading the government to screen the movie in Paraguay.
26. U.S.-Paraguayan educational and cultural exchange programs and list of grantees is provided in J. Manuel Espinosa, *Inter-American Beginnings of United States Cultural Diplomacy, 1936–1948* (Washington, D.C.: State Department, Bureau of Educational and Cultural Affairs, 1976).
27. For a review of this program, see Robert Triffin, *Monetary and Banking Reform in Paraguay* (Washington, D.C.: Board of Governors of the Federal Reserve System, 1946).
28. Grow, *Good Neighbor Policy,* 88–89.
29. Much of this information on investments is taken from Reineiro Parquet, *Las empresas transnacionales en la economía del Paraguay* (Santiago, Chile: CEPAL, 1987).
30. Grow, *Good Neighbor Policy,* 80.

31. Ibid., 117.
32. Ocampos Caballero, *Testimonios de un presidente,* 120.
33. Much of this discussion on U.S. pressure to expel Nazi sympathizers from positions of influence is taken from Seiferheld, *Nazismo y Fascismo en el Paraguay.*
34. See Max Paul Friedman, *Nazis and Good Neighbors: The United States Campaign against the Germans of Latin America in World War II* (New York: Oxford University Press, 2003), 226.
35. Much of this discussion on U.S. policy during Beaulac's tenure is taken from his biography; see Willard L. Beaulac, *Career Ambassador* (New York: Macmillan, 1951).
36. Grow, *Good Neighbor Policy,* 102.
37. Beaulac, *Career Ambassador,* 217.
38. Grow, *Good Neighbor Policy,* 102.
39. Ibid., 103.
40. Ibid., 103.
41. Ibid., 104.
42. Another reason given as to why Morínigo chose to loosen political control and form a coalition government was fear that if he did not reform he would possibly meet the fate of Colonel Gualberto Villaroel, the pro-Fascist leader of Bolivia who was hanged from a lamppost by a revolutionist in July 1946 after he sought to withstand the forces of political liberalization.
43. Much of this analysis of the events leading up to the 1947 civil war is taken from Alcibiades González Delvalle, *El drama del 47: Documentos secretos de la Guerra civil* (Asunción: Editorial Histórica, 1988), and Saturnino Ferreira Perez, *Proceso político del Paraguay, 1936–1949* (Asunción: El Lector, 1987–89).
44. Grow, *Good Neighbor Policy,* 107.
45. See Edgar Ynsfrán, *La irrupción muscovite en la Marina Paraguaya* (Asunción: n.p., 1947).
46. Grow, *Good Neighbor Policy,* 146.
47. González Delvalle, *El drama del 47,* 259.
48. Luis Fernando Beraza, "Perón, Braden y la Guerra civil en el Paraguay (1947)," *Ñe-engatu* 10, no. 60 (September 1992): 35.
49. Fernando Masi, "La Doctrina Truman y al Guerra Civil del 1947," in González Delvalle, *El drama del 47,* 321–27; Beraza, "Perón, Braden y la Guerra civil," 38.
50. Grow, *Good Neighbor Policy,* 110.
51. FRUS, 1952–54, 4:1469.

52. There were seven presidential changes between 1947 and 1954.
53. Werner Baer and Melissa Birch, "The International Economic Relations of a Small Country: The Case of Paraguay," *Economic Development and Cultural Change* 35 (April 1987): 602.
54. The Paraguayan government made a contribution of ten thousand dollars to the Korean conflict, but to the apparent disappointment of Ambassador George Shaw, "it consistently refused to make a definite statement as to whether Paraguayan troops might be available to service abroad, even if they were equipped, trained, transported, and armed by a friendly nation or nations." See FRUS, 1952–54, 4:1477.
55. For a documented analysis of U.S.-Paraguayan relations in the early 1950s leading to the downfall of the Chaves government, see Alfredo Seiferheld, *La caida de Federico Chaves: Una vision documental norteamericana* (Asunción: Editorial Histórica, 1987).

5. Our Man in Asunción: Anticommunism, 1954–1961

1. Much of the discussion in this section is taken from Anibal Miranda, *United States–Paraguay Relations: The Eisenhower Years,* Working Paper 183, Latin American Program, Woodrow Wilson International Center for Scholars, 1990. For documentation and views of U.S. government officials during the 1950s, see Anibal Miranda, *EEUU y el regimen militar paraguayo, 1954–1958* (Asunción: El Lector, 1987); Anibal Miranda, *Argentina, Estados Unidos e insurrección en Paraguay* (Asunción: RP Ediciones, 1988).
2. Some sources have indicated that Stroessner's war record was undistinguished. There are no serious biographies of Alfredo Stroessner, only official and opposition descriptions of his life and career. Much of the discussion provided here is taken from Richard Bourne, *Political Leaders of Latin America* (Harmondsworth, U.K.: Pelican Books, 1969), 98–130; Julio José Chiavenato, *Stroessner: Retrato de uma ditadura* (São Paulo: Brasilense, 1980); Paul Lewis, *Socialism, Liberalism and Dictatorship in Paraguay* (New York: Praeger/Hoover Institution, 1982); Paulo Rafael Trinidad Alderete, *El Stroessner desconocido: Intimidades de su inmenso poder* (Asunción: published by author, 1993).
3. Peter Lambert, "The Regime of Alfredo Stroessner," in *The Transition to Democracy in Paraguay,* ed. Peter Lambert and Andrew Nickson (New York: St. Martin's Press, 1997), 5. For sources on the Stroessner regime, see Paul

Lewis, *Paraguay under Stroessner* (Chapel Hill: University of North Carolina Press, 1980); Carlos Miranda, *The Stroessner Era: Authoritarian Rule in Paraguay* (Boulder, Colo.: Westview Press, 1990); Fatima M. Yore, *La dominación stronista* (Asunción: BASE, 1992); Peter Lambert, "Mechanisms of Control: The Stroessner Regime in Paraguay," in *Authoritarianism in Latin America*, ed. Will Fowler (Westport, Conn.: Greenwood Press, 1996), 93–108.

4. Research on Paraguayan foreign policy during the Stroessner era includes Hans Hoyer, "Paraguay," in *Latin American Foreign Policy Analysis*, ed. Harold E. Davis and Larman C. Wilson (Baltimore: Johns Hopkins University Press, 1975), 294–305; José Félix Estigarribia and José Luis Simón, *La sociedad internacional y el estado autoritario del Paraguay* (Asunción: Aravera, 1987); Fernando Masi, *Relaciones internacionales del Paraguay con y sin Stroessner*, Working Paper 3 (Asunción: Instituto Paraguayo para la integración de America Latin, March 1991); Mladen Yopo, *Paraguay-Stroessner: La política exterior del regimen autoritario* (Santiago: PROSPEL, 1991); Frank O. Mora, *Política exterior del Paraguay, 1811–1989* (Asunción: CPES, 1993).
5. Alfredo M. Seiferheld and José Luis de Tone, eds., *El asilo a Perón y la caída de Epifanio Méndez* (Asunción: Editorial Historica, 1988), 110–11.
6. Alfredo Stroessner, *Política y estrategia del desarrollo* (Asunción: Biblioteca Colorada, 1977), 211.
7. Frank O. Mora, "The Forgotten Relationship: United States–Paraguay Relations, 1937–1989," *Journal of Contemporary History* 33, no. 3 (1998): 460; Anibal Miranda, *Lucha armada en Paraguay* (Asunción: Miranda & Asociados, 1989), 17.
8. Anibal Miranda, *EEUU y el regimen military Paraguayo*, 45, 72.
9. Frank O. Mora, "From Dictatorship to Democracy: The United States and Regime Change in Paraguay, 1954–1994," *Bulletin of Latin American Research* 17, no. 1 (1998): 60.
10. For all agreements during this period, see Enrique Bordenave and Leila Rachid de Racca, eds., *Tratados y actos internacionales del la República del Paraguay*, vol. 6 (Asunción: Instituto Paraguayo de Estudios Geopoliticos e Internacionales, 1990). During this period, Paraguay signed more agreements with the United States than with any other country.
11. Much of this material is taken from Alfredo Seiferheld and José Luis Tone, *El asilo a Peron y la caida de Epifanio Méndez: Un visión documental norteamericana* (Asunción: Editorial Historica, 1988).
12. U.S. economic and technical aid was administered through the United States Operations Missions to Paraguay.

13. James Painter, *Paraguay in the 1970s: Continuity and Change in the Political Process* (London: Institute of Latin American Studies, 1983), 3.
14. Lewis, *Paraguay under Stroessner,* 172.
15. Anibal Miranda, *United States–Paraguay Relations,* 20.
16. Diego Abente, "Constraints and Opportunities: Prospects for Democratization in Paraguay," *Journal of Interamerican Studies and World Affairs* 30, no. 1 (Spring 1988): 82; R. Andrew Nickson, *Historical Dictionary of Paraguay,* revised ed. (Metuchen, N.J.: Scarecrow Press, 1993), 607.
17. Anibal Miranda, *Argentina, Estados Unidos e insurrección en Paraguay,* 187.
18. Tad Szulc, *Twilight of the Tyrants* (New York: Holt, 1959).
19. Anibal Miranda, *Argentina, Estados Unidos e insurrección en Paraguay,* 168.
20. This analysis is extrapolated from Nickson, *Historical Dictionary of Paraguay,* 275.
21. See Paul Lewis, "Paraguay since 1930," in *The Cambridge History of Latin America: Latin America since 1930; Spanish South America,* ed. Leslie Bethell (New York: Cambridge University Press, 1992), 254.
22. Material on Paraguayan insurgency and state responses is taken from Anibal Miranda, *Argentina, Estados Unidos e insurrección en Paraguay;* Anibal Miranda, *Lucha armada en Paraguay;* Yore, *La dominación stronista: Origenes y consolidación,* 202–30; and Cristina Teherne, *The Guerrilla War of the Paraguayan Communist Party* (Portsmouth, U.K.: Prensa Libre, 1982).
23. Philip Agee, *Inside the Company: CIA Diary* (New York: Stonehill, 1975). According to Agee, a CIA operative who worked in Montevideo, Uruguay, FULNA and the Paraguayan Communist Party were successfully dismantled thanks in part to the penetration of the organizations' leadership and the intelligence collected. This same source indicates that in the early 1960s one of the key sources recruited by the agency was Epifanio Méndez Fleitas, who, according to Agee, was a paid informant of the CIA.
24. The guerrilla strategy also failed because the peasants, who the insurgents believed would support armed struggle against a regime that was expropriating land, not only refused to cooperate but actually became an integral part of the state's repressive and counterinsurgency apparatus. The insurgents grossly underestimated the Colorado Party's strong presence in the countryside.
25. In 1955, the U.S. Department of Commerce published a report titled *Investment in Paraguay: Conditions and Outlook for United States Investors;* it provided an overview of the opportunities and challenges for U.S. investors in Paraguay.

26. In the late 1950s former ambassador Arthur Ageton worked as a lobbyist for IPC, often visiting Asunción on business.
27. This excerpt from an embassy despatch is taken from Anibal Miranda, *United States–Paraguay Relations,* 16.
28. Las Amigas Norteamericanas del Paraguay, *Land of Lace and Legend: An Informal Guide to Paraguay* (Asunción: La Colmena, 1958).
29. Elman Service, "The Encomienda in Paraguay," *Hispanic American Historical Review* 31, no. 2 (May 1951): 230–52; Elman and Helen S. Service, *Tobatí: Paraguayan Town* (Chicago: University of Chicago Press, 1954). Elman Service also published a 106-page study titled "Spanish-Guaraní Relations in Early Colonial Paraguay," *Museum of Anthropology,* Anthropological Papers no. 9, 1954.
30. Epifanio Méndez Fleitas, *Psicologia de colonialismo: Imperialismo Yanqui-Brasilero en el Paraguay* (Buenos Aires: Instituto Paraguayo de Cultura, 1971).
31. This characterization of the relationship is taken from Michael Grow, *The Good Neighbor Policy and Authoritarianism in Paraguay* (Lawrence: University of Kansas Press, 1981), 117.

6. Alliance for Progress and the Ricord Affair, 1962–1976

1. Much of this discussion of U.S. Latin American policy during the Kennedy administration is taken from Stephen Rabe, *The Most Dangerous Area in the World: John F. Kennedy Confronts Communist Revolution in Latin America* (Chapel Hill: University of North Carolina Press, 1999); Federico Gil, "The Kennedy-Johnson Years," in *United States Policy in Latin America: A Quarter Century of Crisis and Change, 1961–1986,* ed. John D. Martz (Lincoln: University of Nebraska Press, 1988), 3–27; and Edwin McCammon Martin, *Kennedy and Latin America* (Lanham, Md.: University Press of America, 1994).
2. Mark T. Gilderhus, *The Second Century: United States–Latin American Relations since 1889* (Wilmington, Del.: Scholarly Resources, 2000), 173.
3. See Rabe, *Most Dangerous Area in the World,* 25.
4. Ibid., 129.
5. See Willard F. Barber and C. Neale Ronning, *Internal Security and Military Power: Counterinsurgency and Civic Action in Latin America* (Columbus: Ohio State University Press, 1966).

6. Kennedy's statement quoted in Rabe, *Most Dangerous Area in the World,* 98.
7. William O. Walker, "Mixing Sweet with the Sour: Kennedy, Johnson, and Latin America," in *The Diplomacy of the Crucial Decade: American Foreign Relations during the 1960s,* ed. Diane B. Kunz (New York: Columbia University Press, 1994), 47.
8. Unless otherwise indicated, this discussion on Stevenson's visit to Paraguay is taken from Anibal Miranda, *Lucha armada en Paraguay* (Asunción: Miranda & Associates, 1989).
9. The day before Stevenson's visit, in order to avoid embarrassment and hopefully convince the ambassador of Paraguayans' strong support for Stroessner, the regime arrested hundreds of students and other opposition activists who were planning antigovernment demonstrations during the visit. The regime also exiled several opposition leaders. These actions did not go unnoticed by Stevenson and his delegation.
10. John Bartlow Martin, *Adlai Stevenson and the World: The Life of Adlai E. Stevenson* (Garden City, N.Y.: Doubleday, 1977), 434. Stevenson noted in his diary how surprised he was at the hospitality and kindness of Paraguayans. He was particularly impressed with Foreign Minister Sapena Pastor, who convinced him that "repression in Paraguay was not as bad as I thought."
11. There were six *golpes,* or coups, in 1962–63 alone, most of which the administration either tolerated or imposed symbolic sanctions against.
12. Quoted in Arthur M. Schlesinger Jr., *A Thousand Days: John F. Kennedy in the White House* (Boston: Houghton Mifflin, 1965), 769.
13. Walker, "Mixing the Sweet with the Sour," 55.
14. At a speech at the National Press Club (26 June 1961) after his tour of Latin America, Stevenson said that although he was hopeful that Stroessner would enact some reforms, he understood why Stroessner had reservations about fulfilling his promises to democratize. Not only was there popular sympathy for the proclaimed objectives of the Cuban Revolution in Paraguay, but also "most observers seem to have underestimated the strength of subversive, or at least communist forces in Paraguay." See Adlai Stevenson, "Problems Facing the Alliance for Progress in the Americas," *Department of State Bulletin* 95, no. 1152 (24 July 1961), 139.
15. Joseph Pincus, *The Economy of Paraguay* (New York: Praeger, 1968), 508; Diego Abente, "Constraints and Opportunities: Prospects for Democratization in Paraguay," *Journal of Inter-American Studies and World Affairs* 30, no. 1 (Spring 1988): 83.

16. Paul Lewis, "Paraguay since 1930," in *The Cambridge History of Latin America: Latin American since 1930,* vol. 8, ed. Leslie Bethell (New York: Cambridge University Press, 1991), 260; John Gunther, *Inside South America* (New York: Harper and Row, 1967), 246.
17. Werner Baer and Melissa Birch, "The International Economic Relations of a Small Country: The Case of Paraguay," *Economic Development and Cultural Change* 35 (April 1987): 607.
18. Schlesinger, *Thousand Days,* 200. In the early 1960s, relations between respected Chaco War veterans and U.S. military officers assigned to the military group in Asunción remained strong and focused on counterinsurgency, but by the early 1970s, the Chaco War veterans were replaced by a cadre of corrupt and highly politicized senior officers who changed the dynamic of military-to-military relations between the United States and Paraguay. U.S. military officers perceived their Paraguayan counterparts as sleazy and not worthy of any professional respect.
19. Anibal Miranda, *Lucha armada en Paraguay,* 19.
20. Lewis, "Paraguay since 1930," 256–57.
21. Much of this discussion of the Johnson administration's policy toward Latin America is extrapolated from Joseph Tulchin, "The Promise of Progress: U.S. Relations with Latin American during the Administration of Lyndon B. Johnson," in *Lyndon Johnson Confronts the World: American Foreign Policy, 1963–1968,* ed. Warren I. Cohen and Nancy Bernkopf Tucker (New York: Cambridge University Press, 1994), 211–44; Walker, "Mixing the Sweet with the Sour"; Gil, "Kennedy-Johnson Years"; Rabe, *Most Dangerous Area in the World,* 173–94.
22. Brian Loveman, *For la Patria: Politics and the Armed Forces in Latin America* (Wilmington, Del.: Scholarly Resources, 1999), 171.
23. Pincus, *Economy of Paraguay,* 510.
24. G. Pope Atkins, *Encyclopedia of the Inter-American System* (Westport, Conn.: Greenwood Press, 1997), 266–68.
25. House Resolution 542, "International Communism in the Western Hemisphere" (28 August 1965). See R. Andrew Nickson, *Historical Dictionary of Paraguay,* 2nd ed. (Metuchen, N.J.: Scarecrow Press, 1993), 537.
26. Leo B. Lott, *Venezuela and Paraguay: Political Modernity and Tradition in Conflict* (New York: Holt, Rinehart and Winston, 1972), 370.
27. It was during this visit that Stroessner "was quoted in the United States press as saying that he considered the United States ambassador

to be a member of his cabinet." See Nickson, *Historical Dictionary of Paraguay*, 607.

28. Hoyer, "Paraguay," 299.
29. Werner Baer and Melissa Birch, "Expansion of the Economic Frontier: Paraguayan Growth in the 1970s," *World Development* 12 (August 1984): 785; Baer and Birch, "International Economic Relations of a Small Country," 604.
30. Baer and Birch, "Expansion of the Economic Frontier," 785.
31. James Painter, *Paraguay in the 1970s: Continuity and Change in the Political Process* (London: Institute of Latin American Studies, 1983); Reinerio Parquet, *Las empresas transnacionales en la economía del Paraguay* (Santiago de Chile: Comisión Economica para America Latina y el Caribe, 1987), 57.
32. Ricardo Rodríguez Silvero, *Las mayores empresas brasileñas, alemanas y norteamericanas en el Paraguay* (Asunción: El Lector, 1986), 161–67.
33. Ricardo Rodríguez Silvero, *Las transnacionales en el Paraguay* (Asunción: Editorial Histórica, 1985), 23–25.
34. Terrence Smith, "Peace Corps: Alive but Not So Well," *New York Times Magazine* (25 December 1977), 9.
35. Quotation and much of the material on the Kansas-Paraguay Partnership is taken from Bruce Fritz, "Historical Overview, 1968–1988," unpublished monograph, University of Kansas, 1988. Other primary materials related to the partnership (several boxes of original documents) were consulted. The documents are housed at the Kansas Historical Society in Topeka.
36. Fritz, "Historical Overview, 1968–1988," 4.
37. Frank O. Mora, "The Forgotten Relationship: United States–Paraguay Relations, 1937–1989," *Journal of Contemporary History* 33, no. 3 (July 1998): 464.
38. So as to set the tone for Rockefeller's visit, just prior to the governor's arrival Colonel Thomas Meredith Waitt, commander of the U.S. military group, stated during a ceremony in which twelve helicopters were donated to Paraguay, "I have never seen in any other country, with the exception of the United States, the discipline, morality and combative sprit of Paraguay and . . . my good friend General Alfredo Stroessner." See Domingo Laíno, *Paraguay: Represión, estafa y anticomunismo* (Asunción: Ediciones Cerro Corá, 1979), 88.
39. Ibid., 88.
40. Unless otherwise indicated, this analysis of the impact of Paraguay's role in international drug trafficking on U.S.-Paraguayan relations is taken from Frank O. Mora, "Paraguay and International Drug Trafficking," in *Drug*

Trafficking in the Americas, ed. Bruce M. Bagley and William O. Walker (Coral Gables, Fla.: North-South Center, 1994), 351–62; Julio José Chiavenato, *Stroessner: Retrato de uma ditadura* (São Paulo: Brasilense, 1980), chapter 3; Evert Clark and Nicholas Horrock, *Contrabandista!* (New York: Praeger, 1973).

41. Riordan Roett and Richard Scott Sacks, *Paraguay: A Personalist Legacy* (Boulder, Colo.: Westview Press, 1991), 149.
42. Paul Lewis, *Paraguay under Stroessner* (Chapel Hill: University of North Carolina, 1980), 136; Nathan Adams, "The Hunt for Andre," *Reader's Digest,* March 1973, 238–39.
43. Nickson, *Historical Dictionary of Paraguay,* 508.
44. Ibid., 508.
45. Laíno, *Paraguay,* 142.
46. During this series of events, Stroessner took a trip to Japan to explore the possibility of securing assistance to compensate for any loss of U.S. aid. He was not successful.
47. For a review of the antidrug conventions and agreements signed by Paraguay, see José Luis Simón, "Drug Addiction and Traffic in Paraguay: An Approach to the Problem during the Transition," *Journal of Interamerican Studies and World Affairs* 34, no. 3 (Fall 1992): 155–200.
48. For more on the Ligas, the OPM, and the state's response, see Alfredo Boccia Paz, *La decada inconclusa: Historia real de la OPM* (Asunción: El Lector, 1997); Guido Rodríguez Alcala, *Testimonio de la represión política en Paraguay, 1975–1989* (Asunción: Comite de Iglesias, 1990); José Luis Simón, *Testimonio de la represión política en Paraguay, 1954–1974* (Asunción: El Comite de Iglesias, 1991).

7. Human Rights and "Democracy by Pressure," 1977–1989

1. For an excellent discussion of human rights and U.S. policy, see Lars Schoultz, *Human Rights and United States Policy toward Latin America* (Princeton: Princeton University Press, 1981).
2. For an exhaustive review of Paraguay's human rights situation in the 1970s, see José Luis Simón, *La dictadura de Stroessner y los derechos humanos* (Asunción: Comite de Iglesias, 1990).

3. For a history of the establishment and repression of the OPM, see Alfredo Boccia Paz, *La decada inconclusa: Historial real de la OPM* (Asunción: El Lector, 1997).
4. Carter's statements are quoted in Schoultz, *Human Rights and United States Policy toward Latin America,* 33–35.
5. Unless otherwise indicated, information on U.S.-Paraguayan relations during the Carter presidency is taken from Jorge Castro, "Las relaciones Estados Unidos—Paraguay bajo la administración Carter," *Revista CIDE* 6 (1979): 33–47; James Painter, *Paraguay in the 1970s: Continuity and Change in the Political Process* (London: Institute of Latin American Studies, 1983); Frank O. Mora, "Relaciones EEUU-Paraguay: Conflicto y cooperación," *Perspectiva Internacional Paraguaya* 2, no. 3 (1990): 79–94; Diego Abente, "Constraints and Opportunities: Prospects for Democratization in Paraguay," *Journal of Inter-American Studies and World Affairs* 31, no. 1 (Spring 1988): 73–104.
6. Painter, *Paraguay in the 1970s,* 21.
7. This information concerning the planning and actual meeting between Carter and Stroessner is taken from the authors' personal interview with Ambassador George Landau, 8 March 2002, Miami, Fla.
8. Inter-American Commission on Human Rights, *Report on the Situation of Human Rights in Paraguay* (Washington, D.C.: General Secretariat—Organization of American States, 1978), 2, 6.
9. Stroessner's statement is quoted in Domingo Laíno, *Paraguay: Represión, estafa y anticomunismo* (Asunción: Ediciones Cerro Corá, 1979), 60.
10. Ricardo Rodrígez Silvero, "Empresas transnacionales en el Paraguay: Tipos, formas de accion y origen," in *Las transnacionales en el Paraguay,* ed. Ricardo Rodríguez Silvero (Asunción: Editorial Histórica, 1985), 22–26.
11. Mladen Yopo, *Paraguay Stroessner: La política exterior del regimen autoritario, 1954–1989* (Santiago, Chile: PROSPEL, 1991), 63.
12. Werner Baer and Melissa Birch, "Expansion of the Economic Frontier: Paraguayan Growth in the 1970s," *World Development* 12 (August 1984): 783–98.
13. Correspondence with Ambassador Lyle Franklin Lane, 21 March 1998.
14. Yopo, *Paraguay Stroessner,* 68; Riordan Roett, "Paraguay without Stroessner," in *Friendly Tyrants: An American Dilemma,* ed. Daniel Pipes and Adam Garfinkle (New York: St. Martin's Press, 1991).

15. Jeanne Kirkpatrick, "Dictatorships and Double Standards," *Commentary* 68 (November 1979). See also "United States Security and Latin America," *Commentary* 71 (January 1981).
16. Quotation in Robert S. Greenberger, "Unlikely Ambassador Puts Indelible Mark on the Job in Paraguay," *Wall Street Journal*, 10 September 1984, 1, 27.
17. José Félix Fernández Estigarribia and José Luis Simón, *La sociedad internacional y el estado autoritario del Paraguay* (Asunción: Aravera, 1987), 64; José Luis Simón, "Aislamiento político internacional y desconcertación: El Paraguay de Stroessner de espaldas a America Latina," *Revista Paraguaya de Sociología* 25, no. 73 (September 1988): 185–236.
18. Ambassador Davis was instrumental in having MOPOCO deleted from the State Department's list of international terrorist groups, a measure that infuriated Stroessner.
19. This information on U.S. media coverage is taken from Yopo, *Paraguay Stroessner*, 70–72; Fernandez Estigarribia and Simon, *La sociedad internacional y el estado autoritario del Paraguay*, 100–102; Mladen Yopo, "Paraguay: Transición o reacomodo?" *Cono Sur* 6, no. 3 (1987): 1–6.
20. Many journalists pursued this story and published many articles on the drug trade in Paraguay, particularly after the U.S. government made drug trafficking one of its key priorities in Paraguay. Another important piece of investigative reporting on the topic was published in *Newsweek* (14 May 1985).
21. Thomas Carothers, *In the Name of Democracy: United States Policy toward Latin America in the Reagan Years* (Berkeley: University of California Press, 1991).
22. Yopo, *Paraguay Stroessner*, 74.
23. Correspondence with Ambassador Clyde Taylor, 28 March 1998.
24. Ibid.
25. Riordan Roett, "Paraguay without Stroessner," 295.
26. Montanaro statement quoted in Fernandez Estigarribia and Simon, *La sociedad internacional y el estado autoritario del Paraguay*, 119.
27. For a review of KPP programs and the university exchange agreement, see Bruce Fritz, *Kansas-Paraguay Partnership: An Historical Overview, 1968–1988*, unpublished manuscript (Lawrence: University of Kansas, 1988); and Charles Stansifer, *Establishing an Exchange Program between the State Universities of Kansas and the Universities of Paraguay*, paper prepared for presentation at the Conference on American Academic Programs Abroad, Omaha, Nebraska, November 1980.

28. Professor Rodríguez Alcala taught for many years at the University of California, Riverside.
29. The book, however, was broadly criticized in Paraguay for its "errors of detail."
30. *Ultima Hora,* "Galvin: 'Espero la evolucion de condiciones en el Paraguay,'" 31 January 1987.
31. Roett, "Paraguay without Stroessner," 295.
32. Frank O. Mora, "Paraguay and International Drug Trafficking," in *Drug Trafficking in the Americas,* ed. Bruce M. Bagley and William Walker (Coral Gables, Fla.: North-South Center Press, 1994), 351–62.
33. Analyses of domestic factors contributing to regime collapse are provided by Diego Abente, *Stronismo, Post-Stronismo and the Prospects for Democratization in Paraguay,* Working Paper no. 119, Kellogg Institute for International Studies, University of Notre Dame (March 1989); Fernando Masi, *Stroessner: La extinction de un modelo politico en Paraguay* (Asunción: Intercontinental Editora, 1989).
34. See Ezequiel González Alsina, *Paraguay ante el mundo: Verdad, democracia y derechos humanos* (Asunción: Colección Biblioteca Republicana, 1989).
35. This information is taken from Yopo, *Paraguay-Stroessner,* 76.
36. Phone interview with Ambassador Timothy Towell, 30 October 2001.

8. Safeguarding Democracy in Paraguay, 1989–2000

1. For analyses of the causes of the regime's deterioration and collapse, see Benjamin Arditi, *Adios a Stroessner: La reconstrucción de la política en el Paraguay* (Asunción: RP Ediciones, 1992); Fernando Masi, *Stroessner: La extinción de un modelo político en Paraguay* (Asunción: Intercontinental Editora, 1989).
2. Paul Sondrol, "The Emerging New Politics of Liberalizing Paraguay: Sustained Civil-Military Control without Democracy," *Journal of Interamerican Studies and World Affairs* 34, no. 2 (1992): 134.
3. For a compilation of articles defending Stroessner against "domestic and international enemies" in late 1988, see Ezequiel González Alsina, *Paraguay ante el mundo: Verdad, democracia y derechos humanos* (Asunción: Colección Biblioteca Republicana, 1989). González was director of *Patria,* the official daily newspaper of the Colorado Party, since 1956, and Caceres Almada served as editor of *Patria,* head of the state-owned *Radio Nacional,* and host of the radio program *La Voz del Coloradismo.*

4. For an analysis of the conflicts and tensions within the military that ultimately led to the putsch of 1989, see Virginia Bouvier, *Decline of a Dictator: Paraguay at a Crossroads* (Washington, D.C.: WOLA, 1988); Marcial Riquelme, *Stronismo, golpe militar y apertura tutelada* (Asunción: RP Ediciones, 1992); and Paul Sondrol, "The Paraguayan Military in Transition and the Implications for Civil-Military Relations," *Armed Forces and Society* 19, no. 1 (Fall 1992): 105–22.
5. José Luis Simón, "Drug Addiction and Trafficking in Paraguay: An Approach to the Problem during the Transition," *Journal of Interamerican Studies and World Affairs* 34, no. 3 (Fall 1992): 162.
6. For a journalistic account that reconstructs the steps that led to the successful coup, see Liz Varela and Roberto Paredes, *Los Carlos,* 2nd ed. (Asunción: QR Producciones Grafícas, 1999). "Carlos" was the code name used by the leading conspirators. The reported death toll ranged from dozens to more than three hundred.
7. A short list of articles includes Alan Riding, "Paraguay Coup: Battle for Succession," *New York Times,* 4 February 1989, 4; James Smith, "Military Coup Topples Paraguay's Stroessner," *Los Angeles Times,* 4 February 1989, 1, 12–13; "Paraguayan Ruler Tied to Drugs," *Ft. Lauderdale Sun-Sentinel,* 5 February 1989, 17A; "Coup Leader Denies Drug Link, Schedules Election," *Washington Times,* 7 February 1989, A7; Alan Riding, "Paraguay Leader Denies Ties to Drugs," *New York Times,* 7 February 1989, 5.
8. The ambassador's statement is taken from José Luís Simón, "Del aislamiento a la reinsercion internacional: El Paraguay de la inmediata transicion poststronista," *Perspectiva Internacional Paraguaya* 1, no. 1–2 (1989): 172.
9. Frank O. Mora, "Relaciones Estados Unidos-Paraguay: Conflicto y cooperacion," *Perspectiva Internacional Paraguaya* 2, no. 3 (January–June 1990): 92.
10. Fernando Masi, *Relaciones internacionales del Paraguay con y sin Stroessner,* Working Paper 3 (Asunción: Instituto Paraguayo para la integración de America Latina, March 1991).
11. Rodríguez's foreign policy is discussed in Antonio Salum Flecha, "Una nueva proyeccion de la politica internacional del Paraguay," *Perspectiva Internacional Paraguaya* 1, no. 1–2 (January–December 1989): 157–61; Fernando Masi, "Foreign Policy," in *The Transition to Democracy in Paraguay,* ed. Peter Lambert and Andrew Nickson (New York: St. Martin's, 1997), 174–84; Frank O. Mora, "Paraguay: The Legacy of Authoritarianism," in *Latin American and Caribbean Foreign Policy,* ed. Frank O. Mora and Jeanne A. K. Hey, 309–27 (Boulder, Colo.: Rowman and Littlefield, 2003).

12. Rodríguez's statement is taken from José Félix Estigarribia, "Perspectiva de cambio de la politica exterior paraguaya," *Sintesis* 10 (January–December 1990): 332.
13. Fernando Labra, "Paraguay: Un nuevo perfil internacional," *Perspectiva Internacional Paraguaya* 2, no. 4 (July–December 1990): 33; Frank O. Mora, "From Dictatorship to Democracy: The United States and Regime Change in Paraguay, 1954–1994," *Bulletin of Latin American Research* 17, no. 1 (January 1998): 71.
14. The visit by the delegation is reported in José Luís Simón, "Del aislamiento a la reinserción internacional," 182–83.
15. Much of this section is based on a telephone interview with Ambassador Towell (30 October 2001).
16. Fernando Masi, "Paraguay: Hasta cuando la 'diplomacia presidencialista'?" unpublished mimeo, Asunción, 1991.
17. In 1990 alone, there were five high-level military visits; each had as its objective to strengthen antidrug cooperation.
18. José Luís Simón, "La politica exterior paraguaya en 1991: Modernizacion insuficiente, carencia de una vision global y condicionamiento de un estado prebendario en crisis," unpublished mimeo, Asunción, 1992.
19. Ibid. See also Thomas Bruneau, *The Political Situation in Paraguay Two Years after the Coup,* Naval Postgraduate School, Monterey, Calif., November 1991.
20. José Luís Simón, "Drug Trafficking and Abuse in Paraguay," in *Drug Trafficking in the Americas,* ed. Bruce M. Bagley and William O. Walker (Coral Gables, Fla.: North-South Center; New Brunswick, N.J.: Transaction, 1994), 333.
21. Much of the data for this section comes from Dionisio Borda and Fernando Masi, *Paraguay–Estados Unidos: Posibilidades de un acuerdo de libre comercio,* Centro de Analisis y Difusion de Economía Paraguaya (January 1994); Frank O. Mora, "From Dictatorship to Democracy: The United States and Regime Change in Paraguay, 1954–1994," *Bulletin of Latin American Research* 17, no. 1 (January 1998): 59–79.
22. Fernando Masi, "Paraguay y el Mercosur: Posibilidades en un mercando ampliado," *Propuestas Democraticas* 2, no. 7 (July–September 1995): 23.
23. Mora, "From Dictatorship to Democracy," 71.
24. José Luís Simón, "Ni el cielo ni en el infierno: En el Paraguay de 1994," *Hoy,* Asunción, 13 February 1994, 8.
25. Santiago Trias Coll, "E.E.U.U. y Paraguay, una luna de miel? Entrevista con el embajador Glassman," *Diario de Noticias,* Asunción, 19 April 1992, 10–11.

26. *Analisis del Mes,* August 1991, 6.
27. Much of the discussion related to the 1992–93 crisis is drawn from issues of *Analisis del Mes* (September 1992 to February 1993). The information and analysis is also derived from Frank O. Mora, "Paraguayan Democratization from Abroad: External Determinants of Regime Survival and Democratic Deepening," *South Eastern Latin Americanist* 19, no. 3 (Winter 2001): 23–40.
28. Jon D. Glassman, interview with author, Asunción, 11 May 1993.
29. Ibid.
30. This message was offered in a letter from President Clinton to President-elect Wasmosy in June 1993. It was also relayed during a July visit by Donald Planty, State Department director for Southern Cone Affairs. See *Analisis del Mes,* July 1993.
31. Much of this information is taken from media accounts in *Diario de Noticias, Hoy,* and *Ne-engatu* between September and November 1993.
32. *Diario de Noticias,* "Sorpresivo incidente entre Wasmosy y Glassman, Asunción, 24 November 1993, 8–9.
33. José Luís Simón, "Ni en el cielo ni en el infierno: En el Paraguay de 1994," *Hoy,* Asunción, 13 February 1994, 8.
34. Luís María Ramírez Boettner, "Nota a Glassman fija la posicion de la Cancilleria," *Hoy,* Asunción, 4 February 1994, 19.
35. Al Kamen, "Diplomat Loses Latitude," *Washington Post,* 3 June 1994, 21.
36. *Analisis del Mes,* Asunción, October 1994, 9; *Miami Herald,* "A Shaky Start for a New Democracy," 7 November 1994, 16A.
37. See, for example, Katherine Ellison, "Paraguayan Adoptions Spur Pathos amid Chaos," *Miami Herald,* 6 June 1996, 1A, 14A.
38. Arturo Valenzuela, "Paraguay: The Coup That Didn't Happen," *Journal of Democracy* 8, no. 1 (January 1997): 47. Other important sources used here include Arturo Valenzuela, *The Collective Defense of Democracy: Lessons from the Paraguayan Crisis of 1996* (New York: Report of the Carnegie Commission on Preventing Deadly Conflict, December 1999); Jorge Aiguade, ed., *El ocaso del jinete: Cronica de un intento de golpe de estado en el Paraguay* (Asunción: abc color, 1996); José María Costa and Oscar Ayala Bogarin, *Operacion Gedeon: Los secretos de un golpe frustrado* (Asunción: Editorial Don Bosco, 1996).
39. Valenzuela, *Lessons from the Paraguayan Crisis of 1996,* 8.
40. Ibid., 10.
41. For an analysis of the role of international actors during the crisis, see Frank O. Mora, "Paraguay y el sistema interamericano: Del autoritarismo y la

paralysis a la democracia y la aplicación de la Resolución 1080," in *Sistema interamericano y democracia: Antecedentes históricos y tendencias futuras,* ed. Arlene Tickner (Bogota: CEI-Ediciones Uniandes, 2000), 248–56.

42. Valenzuela, *Lessons from the Paraguayan Crisis of 1996,* 19.
43. Valenzuela, "Paraguay," 53.
44. Unless otherwise cited, this section is extrapolated from Diego Abente Brun, "People Power in Paraguay," *Journal of Democracy* 10, no. 3 (1999): 93–100; Valenzuela, *Collective Defense of Democracy;* Peter Lambert, "A Decade of Electoral Democracy: Continuity, Change and Crisis in Paraguay," *Bulletin of Latin American Research* 19, no. 3 (2000): 379–97.
45. Observations made by author Frank Mora during January 1999 visit.
46. Latin American Institute–Latin American Database, "Paraguay: President Raúl Cubas Faces Impeachment," *NotiSur—South American Political and Economic Affairs* 9, no. 10 (12 March 1999).
47. José del Puerto, "Presión popular y diplómatica, una combinación perfecta," *El Dia* (Asunción), 23 April 1999, 66–67.
48. Katherine Ellison, "Ruler's Ouster a Hollow Victory for Paraguayans," *Miami Herald,* 30 March 1999, 12A.
49. Katherine Ellison, "Paraguay's President Resigns," *Miami Herald,* 20 March 1999, 10A.

Epilogue

1. Anthony Faiola, "U.S. Terrorist Search Reaches Paraguay: Black Market Border Hub Called Key Finance Center for Middle East Extremists," *Washington Post,* 13 October 2001, A21.
2. Andres Oppenheimer, "Terrorist Threat Feared on South America Borders," *Miami Herald,* 22 December 1997, 1A, 16A.
3. Stratfor.com, "Terrorist Networks Being Broken in South America," *Global Intelligence Update,* 2 February 2000.
4. The description of MCC and TCP comes from U.S. Department of State, "Background Note: Paraguay," www.state.gov/r/pa/ei/bgn/1841.htm.
5. Alejandro Sciscioli, "Paraguay: Rights Activist Sees Foreign Policy Shift toward U.S." *Global Information Network,* 4 August 2005, 1.

Bibliographical Essay

No adequate history of Paraguay exists in English. The old standard, Harris Gaylord Warren, *Paraguay: An Informal History* (Norman: University of Oklahoma Press, 1949), is not only dated but also lacks the extensive research of the past sixty years. Much the same can be said about the two works by Efraím Cardozo, *El Paraguay colonial* (Asunción: Ediciones Nizza, 1959) and *Paraguay independiente* (Asunción: Carlos Schuman Editor, 1987). A recent two-volume publication, Jan Kleinpenning, *Paraguay 1515–1870: A Thematic Geography of Its Development* (Frankfurt am Main: Ibero-Vervuert, 2003), is much broader than its title may suggest and is a wide synthesis of the colonial and early national period. It certainly can be used with profit to complement the older works. Nonetheless, a general history of Paraguay utilizing the historical investigation of the past half-century is vitally needed.

In the narrow arena of Paraguayan-U.S. relations, no comprehensive study has heretofore been attempted, either by U.S. or Paraguayan historians. Even so, there do exist monographic and article studies of many of the episodic difficulties between the two nations that can contribute to the construction of a general history. The lack of such a history should not be surprising. Paraguay did not play a significant role in the foreign relations of the United States until the second half of the twentieth century, and the same can be said for the United States in the eyes of Paraguayans. This lack of reciprocal interest prior to the 1950s is reflected in the paucity of serious studies on foreign relations. Since that decade, however, both Paraguayan and U.S. historians have delved into relations between the two republics, and their efforts have greatly benefited the authors of this work.

For the first thirty years of Paraguayan independence, no relationship at all existed between the two nations. Nonetheless, basic views of Paraguayan goals in regard to the outside world coalesced during that era. For an understanding of Paraguay from 1810 to the 1840s see the important biography by Julio César Chaves, *El Supremo Dictador: Biografía de José Gaspar de Francia*, 4th ed. (Madrid: Atlas, 1964), and the well-researched and well-reasoned work by John Hoyt Williams, *The Rise and Fall of the Paraguayan Republic, 1800–1870*, Latin American monographs, no. 48, Institute of Latin American Studies, University of Texas at Austin (Austin: University of Texas Press, 1979).

After the death of Dr. Francia in 1840, Paraguay eventually fell into the hands of the second great dictator of the republic, President don Carlos Antonio López. For Paraguay in the 1840s and 1850s one is directed to Julio César Chaves, *El presidente López: Vida y gobierno de don Carlos*, 2nd ed. (Buenos Aires: Ediciones Depalma, 1968), and again, John Hoyt Williams, *The Rise and Fall of the Paraguayan Republic, 1800–1870* (1979).

In the era of Carlos Antonio López, much of the difficulties between the two nations can be laid at the feet of Edward A. Hopkins. Unfortunately this American lacks a biographer, and his thirty-year career as a diplomat and promoter in both Paraguay and Argentina must be pieced together from a variety of sources, the most important for our purposes being William R. Manning, ed., *Diplomatic Correspondence of the United States: Inter-American Affairs, 1831–1860*, vol. 10, *The Netherlands, Paraguay, Peru* (Washington, D.C.: Carnegie Endowment for International Peace, 1938); Harris Gaylord Warren, "The Hopkins Claim against Paraguay and 'the Case of the Missing Jewels,'" *Inter-American Economic Affairs* 22, no. 1 (Summer 1968): 23–44; Harold F. Peterson, "Edward A. Hopkins: A Pioneer Promoter in Paraguay," *Hispanic American Historical Review* 22, no. 2 (May 1942): 245–61; and John Bassett Moore, "Claim of the United States and Paraguay Navigation Company: Commission under the Convention between the United States and Paraguay of February 4, 1859," in *History and Digest of the International Arbitration to which the United States has been a Party* (Washington, D.C.: GPO, 1898), 2:1485–1549.

Other U.S.-Paraguayan difficulties in the 1850s are addressed in Hunter Miller, ed., "The Unperfected Treaty with Paraguay of March 4, 1853," in *Treaties and Other International Acts of the United States of America* (Washington, D.C.: GPO, 1942), 4:231–40; Robert D. Wood, *The*

Voyage of the Water Witch: A Scientific Expedition to Paraguay and the La Plata Region (1853–1856) (Culver City, Calif.: Labyrinthos, 1985); Clare V. McKanna, "The Water Witch Incident," *American Neptune* 31, no. 1 (January 1971):7–18; and Thomas Page, *La Plata, the Argentine Confederation, and Paraguay: Being a Narrative of the Exploration of the Tributaries of the River La Plata and Adjacent Countries During the years 1853, 54, 55, and 56, Under orders of the United States Government* (New York: Harper, 1859). One must use Page for the *Water Witch* problem, but be careful about his obvious bias.

All these problems—the Hopkins Claim, the Unperfected Treaty, and the *Water Witch* incident—culminated in the 1858–59 U.S. naval expedition against Paraguay. That expedition and its peaceful conclusion are best described in the two-volume work by Pablo Max Ynsfrán, *La expedición norteamericana contra el Paraguay, 1858–1859* (Mexico/Buenos Aires: Editorial Guaranía, 1954/1958). Ynsfrán's professional study is the first detailed monograph of relations between the two nations and, regardless of its title, covers the entirety of the 1850s. Also of use in this context are Harold F. Peterson, *Argentina and the United States, 1810–1860* (New York: State University of New York, 1964); Pablo Max Ynsfrán, "Sam Ward's Bargain with President López of Paraguay," *Hispanic American Historical Review* 34, no. 3 (August 1954): 313–31; and the two articles by Thomas O. Flickema, "The Settlement of the Paraguayan Controversy of 1859: A Reappraisal," *Americas* 25, no. 1 (July 1968): 49–69; and "'Sam Ward's Bargain': A Tentative Reconsideration," *Hispanic American Historical Review* 50, no. 3 (August 1976): 539–42. Finally, resolving the differences of this era was the "Treaty of Friendship, Commerce and Navigation between the United States and Paraguay, at Asunción, February 4, 1859," in *Treaties and Other International Acts of the United States of America,* ed. Hunter Miller (Washington, D.C.: GPO, 1942): 189–201.

For most of the decade of the 1860s Paraguay was concerned with preparation for war and then the War of the Triple Alliance (1864–70). The historical literature of this era is voluminous, but unfortunately too much is just polemical. However, a recent work by Thomas L. Whigham, *The Paraguayan War,* vol. 1, *Causes and Early Conflict* (Lincoln:

University of Nebraska Press, 2002) offers a well-researched and disinterested account. Williams, *The Rise and Fall of the Paraguayan Republic,* again should be consulted. Charles J. Kolinski, *Independence or Death: The Story of the Paraguayan War* (Gainesville: University of Florida Press, 1965), is not as strong as the first two but does give an account of the latter years of the war.

Any scholar of U.S.-Paraguayan relations during this war decade must resort to Charles Ames Washburn, *History of Paraguay, with Notes of Personal Observations and Reminiscences of Diplomacy under Difficulties,* 2 vols. (Boston: Lee and Shepard, 1871). That scholar will find, however, that the account of the U.S. minister to Paraguay from 1861 to 1868 must be used with extreme care as Washburn exhibits a fierce hatred for the wartime leader of Paraguay, President Francisco Solano López. In the same vein, "Paraguay Investigation," U.S. House of Representatives, 40th Cong., 3rd sess., Executive Document no. 79 (1869), was as much a justification for Washburn's actions in Asunción as it was an investigation into U.S. policy toward Paraguay. More balanced is Harold F. Peterson, "Efforts of the United States to Mediate in the Paraguayan War," *Hispanic American Historical Review* 12, no. 1 (February 1932): 2–17, and an exhaustive study by Robert Conrad Hersch, "American Interest in the War of the Triple Alliance, 1865–1870," PhD diss., History Department, New York University, 1964.

The controversial and short mission of General Martin T. McMahon to Paraguay is best described by Lawrence Roberts Hughes, "General Martin T. McMahon and the Conduct of Diplomatic Relations between the United States and Paraguay," MA thesis, History Department, University of Colorado, 1962. Also worthy of notice is Arthur H. Davis, *Martin T. McMahon: Diplomático en el estridor de las armas* (Asunción: Editora Litocolor, 1985). Finally, much of what Paraguayan historians have written about relations with the United States during the war is greatly biased against Washburn and as polemical as was Washburn himself. Nonetheless, for a good account of Paraguayan diplomacy in the United States near the end of the war and Paraguay's view that it was championing the case of "republicanism" in the Western Hemisphere by opposing the Empire of Brazil, see Gregorio Benítez, *Anales diplomáticas y militares de la Guerra del Paraguay* (Asunción: Muñoz Hermanos, 1903).

Perhaps no other individual contributed more to Paraguayan studies in the United States and to inspiring a generation of scholars interested in studying the history, anthropology, and politics of the Guaraní nation than Professor Harris Gaylord Warren. Until the late 1940s and early 1950s, U.S. scholars largely ignored Paraguay as a field of study. Professor Warren's early works became the conduit through which Americans and Paraguayans began to interact and learn more about each other on an intellectual level never seen before. He helped pave the way for the birth and growth of U.S.-Paraguayan scholarly relations.

Dr. Warren first arrived in Asunción in 1928 as a State Department civil servant assisting U.S. minister George L. Kreeck as a translator and speechwriter. During his time in Paraguay, he traveled extensively throughout the country meeting peasants as well as intellectuals of the time, such as Cecilio Báez, Pablo Max Ysnfran, Efraím Cardozo, and Julio César Chaves, historians who became lifelong friends and mentors. He returned to the United States to pursue other endeavors, including a PhD from Northwestern University (1937) and a teaching position at Louisiana State University before entering the army as an intelligence officer and historian during the Second World War. After the war, he began to focus on Paraguay when his wife, Katherine, suggested that he use all the legation letters, copies of which he kept, and other documents to write a history of Paraguay, *Paraguay: An Informal History*. It was "informal" because it was not based on much original research, but it became the seminal work on Paraguayan history in the United States, not only withstanding the test of time but also becoming the foundation upon which he and other historians would flesh out his interpretations. Professor Warren continued to work on Paraguay, publishing an article (1950) in the *Hispanic American Historical Review* on the "political aspects" and consequences of the Febrerista Revolution, but career paths and lack of resources impinged on his ability to continue writing and retrieving Paraguayan history from its scattered archives. When he arrived at the University of Mississippi he realized that the library did not offer the resources to continue his work on Paraguay. He did publish several important articles on the War of the Triple Alliance, the Paraguay Central Railway, and the Hopkins claim, but it was not until after his retirement that he made his greatest contributions to the study of Paraguayan history. During this time he published over a dozen articles and two major books covering the period from 1869 to 1904, *Paraguay and the Triple Alliance: The Postwar Decade, 1869–1878* (Austin: University of Texas Press, 1978) and *Rebirth of the Paraguayan Republic: The First Colorado Era, 1878–1904* (Pittsburgh: University of Pittsburgh Press, 1985). In these studies, Professor Warren endeavored to elevate his subject above anecdote and uninformed description, and in so doing, he produced excellent accounts of Paraguayan railroads, the Febrerista Revolution, the foundations of the Liberal and Colorado parties, banking in the late nineteenth century, immigration, and much more. His last effort, *Rebirth of the Paraguayan Republic: The First Colorado Era (1878–1904),* was the first comprehensive treatment of this period based on archival materials.

Professor Warren passed away in April 1988 short of completing another volume on Paraguayan history (1904–54) and long before he had begun to work on other projects of interest, such as a history of foreign aid to Paraguay. The rigor and meticulousness of his archival work contributed to our knowledge, and it became the standard by which outstanding historians and disciples of Warren, such as John Hoyt Williams, James Saeger, Jerry W. Cooney, and Thomas L. Whigham, would continue to contribute to our understanding of Paraguay's complex and fascinating past. More on Professor Warren is available in Jerry W. Cooney and Thomas Lyle Whigham, "An Interview with Harris Gaylord Warren: From the Borderlands to Paraguay," *Americas* 45, no. 4 (April 1989): 443–60, from which much of the above information on Warren is taken.

For the general history of the period 1870–1930, there are two excellent contributions by Harris Gaylord Warren with the assistance of Katherine F. Warren, *Paraguay and the Triple Alliance: The Postwar Decade, 1869–1878,* Institute of Latin American Studies, Latin American Monographs no. 44 (Austin: University of Texas Press, 1978), and *Rebirth of the Paraguayan Republic: The First Colorado Era (1878–1904)* (Pittsburgh: University of Pittsburgh Press, 1985). Also important are Jan Kleinpenning, *Rural Paraguay, 1870–1932* (Amsterdam: CEDLA, 1991); Juan Carlos Herken Krauer, *El Paraguay rural entre 1869 y 1913: Contribución a la historia económica regional del Plata* (Asunción: CPES, 1984); and Ricardo Caballero Aquino, *La segunda República Paraguaya, 1869–1906: Política-economía-sociedad* (Asunción: Arte Nuevo Editores, 1985).

For Paraguayan-U.S. relations in this period, Benedict J. Dulaski, "Diplomatic Relations between the United States and Paraguay, 1845–1914," MA thesis, History Department, George Washington University, 1966, presents a good overview. The Chaco Arbitration is well handed by John Bassett Moore, "The Middle Chaco Arbitration: Treaty between the Argentine Republic and Paraguay of February 3, 1876," in *History and Digest of the International Arbitrations to which the United States has been Party* (Washington, D.C.: GPO, 1898). For the Bolivian and Paraguayan assessment of those arbitrations see Ricardo Scavone Yegros, *Las relaciones entre el Paraguay y Bolivia en el siglo XIX* (Asunción: SERVILIBRO, 2004); and Leon M. Loza, *El laudo Hayes: Su ineficacia en el litigio boliviano-paraguayo* (La Paz: Editorial "Renacimiento," Flores, San Roman y cia., 1936). Revival of the Hopkins claims and the interminable case of the missing "Jewel Box" are exhaustively analyzed in Harris Gaylord Warren, "The Hopkins Claim against Paraguay and 'the Case of the Missing Jewels,'" *Inter-American Economic Affairs* 22, no. 1 (Summer 1968): 23–44; and Victor C. Dahl, "The Paraguayan 'Jewel Box,'" *Americas* 21, no. 3 (January 1965): 223–42. The first American interest in the possibilities of stock raising in Paraguay is addressed by Victor C. Dahl, "A Montana Pioneer Abroad: Granville Stuart in South America," *Journal of the West* 4 (July 1965): 345–66.

Although rather weak on the Paraguayan involvement, Charles A. Gauld, *The Last Titan: Percival Farquhar* (Stanford, Calif.: California Institute of International Studies, 1964) supplies background to American involvement in the Paraguayan cattle industry prior to World War I. And Juan Carlos Herken Krauer, in his thoroughly researched *Ferrocarrilles, conspiraciones y negocios en el Paraguay, 1910–1914* (Asunción:

Arte Nuevo Editores, 1984) analyzes the Farquhar syndicate's railroad machinations in Paraguay of the same era. Although there is an unfortunate gap between 1914 and the late 1930s in the study of relations, several works deal with Americans in Paraguay. Karen Holiday Tanner and John D. Tanner, in *Last of the Old-time Outlaws: The George West Musgrave Story* (Norman: University of Oklahoma Press, 2002), detail the life in Paraguay of an old-time desperado of the American West who fled to Paraguay in the 1910s and there found opportunities for his nefarious actions for the next thirty years. On the brighter side, Arthur Elwood Elliott, in *Paraguay: Its Cultural Heritage, Social Conditions and Educational Problems,* Contributions to Education no. 473 (New York: Bureau of Publications, Teachers College, Columbia University, 1931), discusses the action of American church groups in advancing education in Paraguay as well as the hookworm eradication program of the Rockefeller Commission.

For Paraguay the 1930s was a decade of preparation for war against Bolivia, the war itself (1932–35), a truce and a long Chaco Peace Conference, and internal political turmoil after the conclusion of the truce. The United States found itself involved in several diplomatic aspects of the war. An excellent introduction to war preparations of both Bolivia and Paraguay, as well as the war itself, is David Zook, *The Conduct of the Chaco War* (New York: Bookman Associates, 1961). Also of note are Ronald S. Kain, "Behind the Chaco War," *Current History* 43 (1935): 468–74, and Mathew Hughes, "Logistics and the Chaco War: Bolivia versus Paraguay, 1932–1935," *Journal of Military History* 69, no. 2 (April 2005): 411–37.

An intriguing account of the U.S. minister to Paraguay who disagreed with his country's foreign policy toward the impending Chaco conflict is Post Wheeler and Hallie Rives (Mrs. Post Wheeler), *Dome of Many-Colored Glass* (New York: Doubleday, 1955). The interjection of Senator Huey Long into the Chaco War policy of the United States is quite well described in Michael L. Gillette, "Huey Long and the Chaco War," *Louisiana History* 11, no. 4 (Fall 1970): 293–311, while the answer to Senator Long by the Bolivian minister to the United States was Enrique Finot, *The Chaco War and the United States* (New York: L. & S. Printing, 1934).

After a truce was obtained in mid-1935, the Chaco Peace Conference dragged on for more than three years. A good account of the diplomacy of this conference—both by the United States and the other parties involved—is Leslie B. Rout Jr., *Politics of the Chaco Peace Conference, 1935–1939,* Latin American Monographs no. 19, Institute of Latin American Studies, University of Texas at Austin (Austin: University of Texas Press, 1970). More focused on the American participation is Spruille Braden, *Diplomats and Demagogues: The Memoirs of Spruille Braden* (New Rochelle, N.Y.: Arlington House, 1971)—a most readable account but somewhat one sided. Finally, the results of the successful conference may be found in U.S. Department of State, *The Chaco Peace Conference: Report of the Delegation of the United States of America to the Peace Conference Held at Buenos Aires, July 1, 1935—January 23, 1939,* U.S. Department of State, Publication 1466, Conference Series 46 (Washington, D.C.: GPO, 1940).

Not long after the rise of fascism in Europe, similar ideological trends began to emerge in South America, especially in Paraguay. Ideology was followed by rapidly increasing ties between Nazi Germany and Southern Cone states. Some of the better-documented works on the subject include Alton Frye, *Nazi Germany and the American Hemisphere, 1933–1941* (New Haven: Yale University Press, 1967), and Stanley Hilton, *Hitler's Secret War in South America, 1939–1945: German Military Espionage* (Baton Rouge: Louisiana State University Press, 1981). One seminal study on the rise of fascism in Paraguay and on Paraguayan-German and U.S.-Paraguayan relations during this period is Michael Grow, *The Good Neighbor Policy and Authoritarianism in Paraguay* (Lawrence: Regents of Kansas Press, 1981). Grow provides much data on trade relations and investments between Paraguay and the two competing powers as well as interesting analyses, based on State Department despatches, of U.S. strategy toward undermining fascism in Paraguay, gaining support from the Morínigo dictatorship during the war, and pressuring for democratization.

The Paraguayan historian and journalist Alfredo Seiferheld provides an outstanding account of Paraguayan history during 1936–45 where in two volumes he traces the ideological and political emergence of fascism and nazism in Paraguay, giving special treatment to the Frente

Guerra and the Morínigo dictatorship. In both books—*Nazismo y fascismo en el Paraguay: Vispera de la II Guerra Mundial, 1936–1939* (Asunción: Editorial Historica, 1985), and *Nazismo y fascismo en el Paraguay: Los anos de la guerra, 1939–1945* (Asunción: Editorial Histórica, 1986)—Seiferheld also spends considerable time analyzing U.S. responses to fascism and dictatorship in Paraguay. A good historical treatment of Paraguay's tumultuous political development between 1936 and the end of the 1940s to include the Revolution of 1947 is Saturnino Ferreira Perez, *Proceso político del Paraguay, 1936–1949* (Asunción: El Lector, 1989).

One critical component or instrument of U.S. policy during the Good Neighbor era, promoted and led by Nelson Rockefeller to enhance U.S. influence in the region, was propaganda. Important cultural and educational programs were developed in Paraguay, some of which are examined in J. Manuel Espinosa, *Inter-American Beginnings of United States Cultural Diplomacy, 1936–1948* (Washington, D.C.: State Department, Bureau of Educational and Cultural Affairs, 1976); Claude Curtis Erb, "Nelson Rockefeller and United States–Latin American Relations, 1940–1945" (PhD diss., Clark University, 1982); and Louis J. Halle, *Significance of the Institute of Inter-American Affairs in the Conduct of United States Foreign Policy* (Washington, D.C.: State Department, Office of Public Affairs, 1948).

The economic agreement signed between the United States and Paraguay in June 1939 brought financial and technical assistance to Asunción. Several technical delegations arrived to provide help to Paraguay's financial and agricultural sectors, enhancing U.S. presence and leverage in the country. This development as well as the state of Paraguayan monetary system and agriculture is examined in Robert Triffin, *Monetary and Banking Reform in Paraguay* (Washington, D.C.: Board of Governors of the Federal Reserve System, 1946), and Emma Reh, *Paraguayan Rural Life: Survey of Food Problems, 1943–1945* (Westport, Conn.: Greenwood Press, 1975).

During this period of intense bilateral relations, much was written on the role and idiosyncrasies of key U.S. diplomats in Asunción. For example, Minister Findley Howard's difficulties with the Paraguayan government and his unusual behavior and outbursts are effectively captured in John Neill, "A Nebraska Diplomat in Paraguay," *Life* 10 (14 April 1941): 17–20, and in a book-length interview of General Morínigo in Augusto Ocampos Caballero, *Testimonios de un presidente: Entrevista al General Higinio Morínigo* (Asunción: El Lector, 1983). Luís González, *Paraguay: Prisonero geo-político,* 2nd ed. (Asunción: Instituto Paraguayo de Estudios Geopolíticos Internacionales, 1990), spends a better part of a chapter exploring U.S. policy and the pivotal role played by Washington's ambassadors during the war. Another important and forceful U.S. diplomat of the time was Willard Beaulac, who had the lead in pressuring Morínigo to liberalize the regime at the end of World War II. In his memoirs, *Career Ambassador* (New York: Macmillan, 1951), Beaulac argues that he always believed that pushing Paraguay hard on democratization would lead to instability.

The 1947 Revolution that ultimately led to Colorado Party dominance has been treated by Paraguayan authors, most of them participants in the conflict and therefore writing from a partisan standpoint, such as Enrique Volta Gaona, *La revolución del 47* (Asunción: Editora Liticolor, 1982), and Alfredo Ramos, *Concepción 1947: La revolución derrotada* (Asunción: Editorial Histórica, 1985). One interesting account of the events leading to and during the conflict is Alcibiades González Delvalle, *El drama del 47: Documentos secretos de la Guerra Civil* (Asunción: Editorial Histórica, 1988). The author examines developments during this turbulent conflict and U.S. reaction through the lens of declassified U.S. diplomatic despatches, reports, and transcripts of conversations. Other published works attempt, with mixed results, to place the conflict in an international dimension (cold war), such as Edgar Ynsfrán, *La irrupción muscovita en la Marina Paraguaya* (Asunción: n.p., 1947); and Fernando Masi, "La Doctrina Truman y la Guerra Civil del 47," in Alcibiades González Delvalle, *El drama del 47: Documentos secretos de la Guerra Civil* (Asunción: Editorial Histórica, 1988).

For the early 1950s, a highly erratic period in Paraguay, Alfredo Seiferheld, *La caída de Federico Chaves: Una visión documental norteamericana* (Asunción: Editorial Histórica, 1987), resorts to Delvalle's highly effective method of examining political developments leading to the fall of President Federico Chaves and the rise to power of General Alfredo

Stroessner through the analyses and observations provided by declassified U.S. documents. U.S. views of key Paraguayan political figures and concerns about Argentina's role in the country's turbulent and vulnerable political process are offered in this useful resource.

The thirty-five-year regime of Alfredo Stroessner was of such consequence in Paraguay's postwar political development and its relations with the United States that it engendered much interest among scholars and journalists in the United States and Paraguay. No one captured the pivotal period of regime consolidation and the U.S. role in the 1950s better than Anibal Miranda. His research remains the mainstay of U.S.-Paraguayan relations literature for the period between 1953 and 1965. His invaluable contributions include *United States–Paraguay Relations: The Eisenhower Years,* Working Paper 183 (Washington, D.C.: Latin American Program, Woodrow Wilson International Center for Scholars, 1990); *EE.UU y el regimen militar Paraguayo, 1954–1958* (Asunción: El Lector, 1987); and *Argentina, Estados Unidos e insurrección en Paraguay* (Asunción: RP Ediciones, 1988). Like Seiferheld, Miranda uses an extensive amount of declassified diplomatic and intelligence documents to dig deeper into the intricacies of the relationship through the lens of U.S. analysts and policymakers.

Alfredo Seiferheld and José de Tone made their contribution to this period by analyzing bilateral relations and Stroessner's machinations against his number one political enemy, Epifanio Méndez Fleitas, in *El asilo a Perón y la caída de Epifanio Méndez: Una visión documental norteamericana* (Asunción: Editorial Histórica, 1988). Once again, the editors used U.S. declassified documents to reveal the extent of U.S. support for Stroessner's anti-Méndez strategies.

Studies on Stroessner and his regime are not as extensive as one might think. However, there are some volumes that do an effective job of capturing the essence of this authoritarian-personalist regime; interestingly, none of these devote much time to discussing U.S. support of or ambivalence to the regime. The most important of these works include Paul Lewis, *Paraguay under Stroessner* (Chapel Hill: University of North Carolina Press, 1980); Julio José Chiavenato, *Stroessner: Retrato de uma ditadura* (São Paulo: Brasilense, 1980); Carlos Miranda, *The Stroess-*

ner Era: Authoritarian Rule in Paraguay (Boulder, Colo.: Westview Press, 1990); and Peter Lambert, "Mechanisms of Control: The Stroessner Regime in Paraguay," in *Authoritarianism in Latin America since Independence,* ed. Will Fowler (Westport, Conn.: Greenwood Press, 1996): 93–108. Fatima Yore's comprehensive study *La dominación stronista: Orígenes y consolidación, seguridad nacional y represión* (Asunción: BASE-IS, 1992) argues that from the moment he came to power Stroessner adopted with U.S. help Washington's National Security Doctrine as the ideological foundation upon which to consolidate his regime through repression.

Despite the paucity of work on Paraguay's foreign policy and international relations since Stroessner's rise to power, there has been some good research on the topic by José Luís Simón, Fernando Masi, and Mladen Yopo. Much of the focus is on Paraguay's relations with its neighbors, but some recent studies have much more in-depth research on U.S.-Paraguayan relations, such as Mladen Yopo, *Paraguay-Stroessner: La política exterior del regimen autoritario* (Santiago: PROSPEL, 1991); Frank O. Mora, *Política exterior del Paraguay, 1811–1989* (Asunción: CPES, 1993); Fernando Masi, *Relaciones internacionales del Paraguay con y sin Stroessner,* Working Paper no. 3 (Asunción: Instituto Paraguayo para la Integracion de America Latina, 1991); José Luís Simón, ed., *Política exterior y la relaciones internacionales del Paraguay contemporaneo* (Asunción: CPES, 1990). Other important works in this field that provide less in terms of bilateral relations include Hans Hoyer, "Paraguay," in *Latin American Foreign Policy Analysis,* ed. Harold E. Davis and Larman C. Wilson (Baltimore: Johns Hopkins University Press, 1975), 294–305; and Frank O. Mora, "Paraguay: The Legacy of Authoritarianism," in *Latin American and Caribbean Foreign Policies,* ed. Jeanne A. K. Hey and Frank O. Mora (Boulder, Colo.: Rowman and Littlefield, 2003), 309–27.

It was not until relatively recently that U.S.-Paraguayan relations were analyzed as a specific research topic. The first published work focused on bilateral relations during the administration of President Jimmy Carter: José Castro, "Las relaciones Estados Unidos–Paraguay bajo la administración de Carter, *Revista CIDE* 6 (1979): 33–47. Frank Mora's work has taken a much broader and analytical examination of relations from the 1930s to the 1990s—"Relaciones EEUU-Paraguay: Conflicto y cooperación," *Perspectiva Internacional Paraguaya* 2, no. 3 (1990): 79–94; "The Forgotten Relationship: United States–Paraguay Relations, 1937–1989," *Journal of Contemporary History* 33, no. 3 (July 1998): 451–73; "From Dictatorship to Democracy: The United States and Regime Change in Paraguay, 1954–1994," *Bulletin of Latin American Research* 17, no. 1 (1998): 59–79; and "Poder duro y poder blando: La influencia en la relaciones Estados Unidos-Paraguay," *Foro Internacional* (Mexico City) 35, no. 2 (April–June 1995): 219–61. Epifanio Méndez Fleitas, perhaps with an axe to grind, published a scathing book on Stroessner and United States–Brazilian neocolonialism in Paraguay, *Psicología de colonialismo: Imperialismo Yanqui-Brasilero en el Paraguay* (Buenos Aires: Instituto Paraguayo de Cultura, 1971). In this volume, Méndez claims the Stronato is largely an extension of United States and Brazilian imperialism.

With respect to the economic dimensions of the relationship during the early years of the Stronato, once again, the quantity of works was nearly non-existent. In 1955 the United States Department of Commerce published a report titled *Investment in Paraguay: Conditions and Outlook for United States Investors* that examined macroeconomic data relevant to potential U.S. investors in Paraguay. Other more minor reports gave only a brief look at trade relations and changes in U.S. investments in the country. Ricardo Rodríguez has made important contributions to understanding the nature and structure of foreign investments in Paraguay. In his two books—*Las transnacionales en el Paraguay* (Asunción: Editorial Histórica, 1985) and *Las mayors empresas brasleñas, alemanas y norteamericanas en el Paraguay* (Asunción: El Lector, 1986)—he provides a detailed examination of the structure and trends of U.S. investments. Parquet Reineiro in *Las empresas transnacionales en la economía del Paraguay* (Santiago, Chile: CEPAL, 1987) also provides much data and analysis of specific U.S. companies and amounts invested in Paraguay. Finally, very useful data and analysis, though much less focused on the United States, is provided by Werner Baer and Melissa Birch, "The International Economic Relations of a Small Country: The Case of Paraguay," *Economic Development and Cultural Change* 35 (April 1987): 601–27.

The quantity and quality of the literature on U.S.-Paraguayan relations during the 1960s and 1970s did not match the expansion and deepening of ties between both countries. Not even major works on the Kennedy administration and the Alliance for Progress make much reference to Paraguay at all, including Stephen Rabe, *The Most Dangerous Area in the World: John F. Kennedy Confronts Communist Revolution in Latin America* (Chapel Hill: University of North Carolina Press, 1999), and Edwin McCammon Martin, *Kennedy and Latin America* (Lanham, Md.: University Press of America, 1994). One has to consult *Foreign Relations of the United States* and disparate sources, such as John Bartlow Martin's biography on Adlai Stevenson, Arthur Schlesinger's *A Thousand Days,* and Miranda's *La lucha armada* to piece together key developments and interactions during this period.

The Peace Corps and the Partners for the Americas programs, pivotal components of the Alliance for Progress era, were and continue to be important programs in the relationship. The Kansas-Paraguay Partnership housed several boxes of original documents, including newsletters, correspondence, programs, and budgets, at the Kansas Historical Society in Topeka. A useful unpublished essay on the history of the Kansas-Paraguay Partnership program can be found in the collection: Bruce Fritz, *Kansas-Paraguay Partnership: Historical Overview, 1968–1988* (Lawrence, Kansas: unpublished manuscript, 1988). Among the documents, material on the Peace Corps program in Paraguay during the 1960s and 1970s can also be found. Other original documentation on the program and its development (i.e., members and projects) since the 1960s is available at the Peace Corps office in Washington, D.C.

An important piece of comparative scholarship of the time that not only examined Paraguay's political and economic system but also delved into issues related to foreign policy and relations with the United States was Leo B. Lott, *Venezuela and Paraguay: Political Modernity and Tradition in Conflict* (New York: Holt, Rinehart and Winston, 1972). Lott's book was the authoritative study on Paraguayan politics and foreign relations until the early 1980s when Paul Lewis's *Paraguay under Stroessner* and James Painter's *Paraguay in the 1970s: Continuity and Change in the Political Process* (London: Institute of Latin American Studies, 1983) were published. In 1979 Paraguayan opposition leader

Domingo Laíno authored *Paraguay: Represión, estafa y anticomunismo* (Asunción: Ediciones Cerro Cora), in which much of the corruption associated with the Stroessner regime in the 1970s is discussed in the context of deteriorating relations with the Nixon administration over the issue of drug trafficking.

Drug trafficking and the Ricord affaire were the subject of much journalistic reporting in the 1970s. The most important and widely read piece on the subject was Nathan Adams's controversial article, "The Hunt for Andre," *Reader's Digest,* March 1973, 223–59. Subsequently, a more extensive treatment of the collusion between Ricord and Paraguayan government officials in the drug trade and its impact on relations with the United States is provided by Evert Clark and Nicholas Horrock, *Contrabandista!* (New York: Praeger, 1973). Nearly two decades later, as part of a larger study on drug trafficking in the Americas, two scholars analyzed corruption, drug trafficking, and U.S.-Paraguayan relations since the late 1960s through the collapse of the Stroessner regime: José Luís Simón, "Drug Addiction and Traffic in Paraguay: An Approach to the Problem during the Transition," *Journal of Interamerican Studies and World Affairs* 34, no. 3 (Fall 1992): 155–200; and Frank O. Mora, "Paraguay and International Drug Trafficking," in *Drug Trafficking in the Americas,* ed. Bruce M. Bagley and William O. Walker (Coral Gables, Fla.: North-South Center, 1994): 351–69.

In the 1980s, as Paraguay came to the attention of more journalists and academics, more reporting and analyses were published, but most of these works focused on the regime's human rights violations, with little attention to U.S.-Paraguayan relations. One important exception, published after the downfall of the regime, that closely examined the academic and journalistic literature of the regime in the 1980s and U.S. policy is José Luís Simón, *La dictadura de Stroessner y los derechos humanos* (Asunción: Comite de Iglesias, 1990). Simón was among the very few and certainly one of the most prolific authors to write on Paraguay's international relations and, quite extensively, on U.S.-Paraguayan relations in the 1980s and into the next decade. Some of his works include "Aislamiento político internacional y desconcertación: El Paraguay de Stroessner de espaldas a America Latina," *Revista Paraguaya de So-*

ciología 25, no. 73 (1989): 185–234; "Del aislamiento a la reinserción internacional: El Paraguay de la inmediata transición post-stronista, *Perspectiva Internacional Paraguaya* 1, no. 1–2 (1989): 163–200; and, coauthored with José Félix Estigarribia, *La sociedad internacional y el estado autoritario del Paraguay* (Asunción: Aravera, 1987). Simón contributes much to understanding the means or levers by which Washington pressured and isolated the Strossner regime and later helped Asunción reinsert itself into the international system once democratic rule was instituted in 1989. In 1989 Simón inaugurated and edited a new journal titled *Perspectiva Internacional Paraguaya* that featured a number of important articles on Paraguayan foreign policy and international relations, including U.S.-Paraguayan relations, such as Antonio Salum Flecha, "Nueva proyección de la política internacional," *Perspectiva Internacional Paraguaya* 1, no. 1–2 (1989): 157–63; Fernando Labra, "Paraguay: Un nuevo perfil internacional," *Perspectiva Internacional Paraguaya* 2, no. 4 (1990): 7–33; and Fernando Masi, "Hasta cuando la diplomacia presidencialista?" *Perspectiva Internacional Paraguaya* 3, no. 5 (1991): 7–20.

The external factor in the collapse of the Stronato was addressed in a series of academic pieces by Simón, Mora, and Fernando Masi. Some of this work is cited above, but other studies by these and other authors include Fernando Masi, *Stroessner: La extinción de un modelo político en Paraguay* (Asunción: Intercontinental Editora, 1989); Virginia Bouvier, *Decline of a Dictator: Paraguay at a Crossroads* (Washington, D.C.: Washington Office on Latin America, 1989); and Marcial Riquelme, *Stronismo, golpe militar, y apertura tutelada* (Asunción: RP Ediciones, 1992). An interesting collection of essays by the regime's principal ideologue and spokesman—Ezequiel González Alsina—published as a book reflects the sense of betrayal and resentment felt because of U.S. pressures in the late 1980s: *Paraguay ante el mundo: Verdad, democracia y derechos humanos* (Asunción: Colección Biblioteca Republicana, 1989).

During the first two democratic governments of Andrés Rodríguez and Juan Carlos Wasmosy more research appeared on Paraguayan foreign policy and democratization that focused on the role of the United States in safeguarding Paraguay's fragile democratic system. Some of these important works include Fernando Masi, "Foreign Policy," in *The*

Transition to Democracy in Paraguay, ed. Peter Lambert and Andrew Nickson (New York: St. Martin's, 1997): 174–84; Thomas Bruneau, *The Political Situation in Paraguay Two Years after the Coup* (Monterey, Calif.: Naval Postgraduate School, 1991); José Luís Simón, *La política exterior paraguaya en 1991: Modernización insuficiente, carencia de una visión global y condicionamiento de un estado prebendario en crisis* (Asunción: unpublished mimeo, 1992); Frank O. Mora, "Paraguayan Democratization from Abroad: External Determinants of Regime Survival and Democratic Deepening," *South Eastern Latin Americanist* 19, no. 3 (Winter 2001): 23–40; Arturo Valenzuela, "Paraguay: The Coup That Didn't Happen," *Journal of Democracy* 8, no. 1 (January 1997): 41–53; Arturo Valenzuela, *The Collective Defense of Democracy: Lessons from the Paraguayan Crisis of 1996* (New York: Report of the Carnegie Commission on Preventing Deadly Conflict, 1999). Each of these studies focused on a particular crisis facing democracy and how external actors, particularly the United States, responded to ensure that it was not toppled. In the end, despite some important contributions to the research on U.S.-Paraguayan relations, particularly since the 1980s, there is still much that historians and political scientists have yet to uncover about this intensifying but insufficiently studied relationship in the Western Hemisphere.

Index

ABC Color (newspaper), 208, 211
Abdo Benítez, Mario, 224
ABPC powers (Argentina, Brazil, Peru, Chile), 74–76
Abrams, Elliott, 215–17, 226, 228
Acevedo, Elpidio, 225–26, 228
Acevedo, Euclides, 257
Acheson, Dean, 119–20
Acuerdo Nacional Party, 200, 230
Adams, Nathan, 191
adoption, of Paraguayan babies, 249
Ageton, Arthur A., 134–35, 137, 142
agriculture: and Asunción-Brazil highway, 97–98; in the Chaco, 69; crops, 52, 58, 67; foreign investment in, 179–80; of German colonists, 93; and Peace Corps, 182–86
aid, from U.S.: and Alliance for Progress, 161–71; for anticommunism, 161–64; under G. H. W. Bush, 236–42; under Carter, 199–204; under Clinton, 245–46; to combat corruption, 264; to combat Nazism, 115–16; decline of, 213–14; for drug eradication, 239–40, 246; for education, 153; under Eisenhower, 121–24, 133–45; for health care, 62–64, 264; and human rights concerns, 197–98; under L. B. Johnson, 173–78; military, 96–101, 123–24, 133–45, 152–59, 200–201; and Morínigo regime, 121–24; and nongovernmental organizations, 214; under Reagan, 205–10, 213–18; in A. Rodríguez regime, 236–37, 239–40; under F. D. Roosevelt, 103–7; treaties of, 97–101, 121, 190; under Truman, 121–22, 129; World War II era, 96–101. *See also* economic development; industrial/infrastructure development
Alfonsín, Raúl, 209
Algodones, S.A., 93–94
Allen, Philip, 17
Alliance for Progress, 161–64, 183
Allis-Chalmers, 206
Almon, Collins D., 119
Alonzo, Mariano Roque, 5
Alto Paraná, 179–80
American Farms, 180
Amigas Norteamericanas del Paraguay, Las, 156
Amigos de las Américas, 219
Amnesty International, 202, 214
Amorim, Celso, 265
Anderson, Jack, 191
anticommunism: and alliance with Brazil, 174–75; civil war and seeds of, 118–21, 123; decline of, 205, 214–15; and end of cold war, 231; and Kirkpatrick, 207; and Reagan, 206; in A. Stroessner era, 125–29, 132, 143–45, 169–71; and U.S. aid, 135, 142–43, 161–64
Aranda, Bernardo, 101
Arbenz, Jacobo, 125
arbitration, 23, 40–41, 49, 71–73, 82–87
Argaña, Luis María: in Morínigo cabinet, 102; as presidential candidate, 244; resignation of, 114; at Rio conference, 104–6; in A. Rodríguez cabinet, 234–35; as vice presidential candidate, 255–57

Argentina: as arms supplier, 120; assists Paraguayan exiles, 149; and Chaco War, 69–70, 74–75, 82–87; investment of, in Paraguay, 53, 58, 67, 111, 122–23; and political factionalism, 123; and A. Stroessner, 128, 153; territorial claims of, 39–40; and Wasmosy, 251
Ariel (Rodo), 109
Arnold, Samuel G., 17
Arthur Young consultants, 180
Asboth, Alexander, 26
Asociación Nacional Republicana (ANR). *See* Colorado Party
Asunción-Brazil highway, 97–98, 168
Asunción Compañía de Luz y Traccíon, 58
Asunción Port Concession Corporation, 93, 111
autocratic rule. *See* Stronato
Axis powers, 92, 95–97, 99, 102–3, 105–7, 114–16
Ayala, Eligio, 48, 50
Ayala, Eusebio, 73, 75, 79–80, 86–87

Babbitt, Bruce, 236
Bacon, John F., 42–43
Báez, Cecilio, 48, 60
Bamberger, Louis, 18
Bank of America, 179
Bank of Boston, 179
Baptist missionaries, 61
Beach, Marianne, 184
Beaulac, Willard L., 112, 115–21
Belloti, Tony, 183
Benites, Gregorio, 36
Benítez Vera, Victoriano, 101, 112–14, 116
Berle, Adolf, 161–62
Black Jack gang, 56
Blaine, James G., 43
Bliss, Porter, 28, 30
Bliss-Masterman affair, 31, 33–36
Boccia Paz, Alfredo, 264
Boggino, Juan, 109
Bolivia: and Chaco region, 4, 66–69, 72, 81–87; landlocked, 67; Long's campaign against, 79–81; oil resources in, 77–79, 84; and Pinilla-Soler Protocol, 68; presidential election in, 265; protests U.S. arbitration, 41; recognizes Paraguay, 6
Bolivian Oil Company International, 178
Bourne, Richard, 126
Bowlin, James Butler, 18, 20–23
Braden, Spruille, 83–91, 119–20
Brazil: at Chaco Peace Conference, 82–87; democratization of, 209; on European presence, 7–8; and Farquhar Syndicate, 51–53; investments of, in Paraguay, 179–81, 205; pro-U.S. military regime of, 174–75; and A. Stroessner, 128, 131–32; on territorial claims, 40; and Uruguayan civil war, 23; and U.S. understanding, 49–50; and Wasmosy, 251–52; and *Water Witch* controversy, 14–17
Brazilian Railway Company, 51
Britain, and Latin America, 53, 55
Brítez, Francisco, 195
Brown and Root Company, 206
Buchanan James, 7, 10, 17–22
Buenos Aires, blockade of, 6
Burress, Withers A., 128
Busch, Germán, 88–89
Bush, George H. W., 236, 239–40
Bush, George W., 262
Bush Leblond, Dorothy, 237

Caceres Almada, José, 232
Campo Grande, 101–2, 112–13
Cantilo, José María, 89
Cardozo, Efraím, 90
Cargill, 180
Carter, Jimmy, 197–205

Castelo Branco, Humberto, 175
Castiglioni, Luis, 264
Castro, Fidel, 149, 161
Castro, Sara Lara, 210
Catholic Church, 102, 194–95
Catholic University, 220
cattle industry, 53–58, 67, 123
CBS News, 212
CCPA (Paraguayan-American Cultural Center), 108, 219, 225; *Land of Lace and Legend*, 156
Chaco, the: airfield in, 264; and Argentinean claim, 40; Bolivian claims to, 4, 66–69, 81–87; cattle industry in, 52–57; Farquhar Syndicate in, 55; oil resources in, 77–79, 84, 154; as Paraguayan, 40–41; and Pinilla-Soler Protocol, 68; Villa Hayes, 40–41
Chaco Peace Conference, 82–92
Chaco War, 68–79
Chaney, Samuel, 16
Chase Manhattan Bank, 81, 154, 179
Chaves, Federico, 118, 121, 123, 125, 128–29
Chávez, Hugo, 265
Chávez, Juan Ramón, 233–34
Cheney, Dick, 264
Chesapeake Mining, 180
Chile, 5, 82–87, 211
Christian Church Leagues (LAC), 192, 194
Christianity, 262
Christopher, Warren, 200
Ciudad del Este, and terrorism, 260–61
Cívicos (Liberal faction), 52
Clinton, Bill, 245
Coca-Cola Company, 178
cold war. *See* anticommunism
Colegio Internacional, Asunción, 61
Colman, Patricio, 188–90
Colorado Party, 47–48, 50, 53, 232, 256; anti-U.S. propaganda of, 203; and democratization, 117–21; deterioration of, 224, 231; and drug trafficking, 188; factionalism and economic volatility of, 122–24, 130, 140–41; MOPOCO faction of, 150, 209; and Oviedo, 244, 250, 255; *Patria* newspaper of, 164, 217, 226–27; and Peace Corps, 183; and A. Stroessner, 127–28, 130–33, 135, 138, 143–48, 150; and Taylor, 217–18; and Wasmosy, 250
Columna Mariscal López, 160
Commemorative Meeting of American Presidents (1956), 144
Commission of Investigation and Conciliation, 70
Commission of Neutrals, 71, 73–75
communism. *See* anticommunism
Concepción region, and livestock industry, 55–56
Conference of American States (Lima), 100
constitutional crises: 1996, 248–53; 1999, 254–58
Constitution of 1967, 171, 177
Consultation of Foreign Ministers, 99–100, 104–6
Continental Grain, 180
Coronel, Pastor, 188, 191, 196
corruption, 169, 211; aid to combat, 264; and infant adoption, 249; and livestock theft, 56–57; political, 52–53, 260; repression of, 235, 262
Counter-Terrorism Fellowship, 261
Coverdale, Paul, 237
CPT (Paraguayan Workers Confederation), 148–49
Cramer, Rafael, 252
Cuba, 149, 151
Cubas, Cecilia, 264
Cubas, Raúl, 256

Cubas Barbosa, Roberto, 176
cultural exchanges: and Alliance for Progress, 162–63; under G. H. W. Bush, 240, 264; under G. W. Bush, 264; in difficult times, 218–21, 249; under Eisenhower, 152–59; under L. B. Johnson, 172–73; under J. F. Kennedy, 162–63, 172–73; KPP programs, 219–20; and Peace Corps, 181–86; in A. Rodríguez regime, 240; under F. D. Roosevelt, 108–10; university programs for, 220–21

Da Costa, Juan Carlos, 192
Davidow, Jeffrey, 252–53
Davis, Arthur, 207–10
Davis, Charles H., 31, 35
DEA (Drug Enforcement Agency), 223–24
De Chiara, Enzo, 227–28
Decoud, José Segundo, 42–47
democracy: and Alliance for Progress, 162–64; and bilateral relations, 242–48, 255, 260, 263; and civil war, 118–21; and cold war, 165–66; and constitutional crises, 245, 248–58; deterioration of, 250, 254–55; under Duarte, 262; Glassman's support of, 242–48; and postwar violence, 117; under pressure, 213–18; and Reagan, 207; and A. Rodríguez, 234–35, 238; in South America, 145–48, 208–9, 211; and U.S. aid, 115–18, 121–24, 198–205
Diario de Noticias, El (newspaper), 217
dictatorships, 95, 101–3, 113–15, 145–47
Dion, J. Mark, 225
diplomacy: under Buchanan, 17–23; deficiency of, under Washburn and McMahon, 29–33; under Pierce, 17; on tennis court, 237
Dirección Nacional de Narcóticos (DINAR), 191, 233
direct foreign investments (DFI), 153
Disciples of Christ missionaries, 61
disease. *See* health care
Docking, Robert, 185
Dominican Republic, 176
Douglass, Robert, 136
Drug Enforcement Agency (DEA), 223–24
drug trade, 186–92, 211; and counternarcotic cooperation, 233; and DEA enforcement, 223–24; Paraguay decertified because of (1995), 249; under A. Rodríguez, 235; Taylor's campaign against, 215–16, 225; and UN Single Convention on Narcotics (1961), 190; and U.S. aid, 239–40, 246
Duarte Frutos, Nicanor, 262

Eaton, Dorothy, 155
Eaton, Robert, 57, 155
economic development: and agriculture, 52, 67; and airport, 113, 117, 153; and Alliance for Progress, 161–64, 183; and Buchanan administration, 18; and G. H. W. Bush administration, 236–37; and cultural links, 152–59; under Duarte, 262; and Kennedy and Johnson administrations, 167–78; and land sales, 12–13, 53, 67; and monetary reform, 110; under A. Rodríguez, 236–37; and F. D. Roosevelt administration, 103–9; as stagnant, 240–42; and World War I neutrality, 53, 58–60. *See also* aid, from U.S.; foreign investment; industrial/infrastructure development; trade
Ediger, Elmer, 184
education: cultural exchange, 108–10, 156–59; in Guaraní language, 183; integrated preschool for disabled children, 220; and Peace Corps, 182–86; repression of, in Paraguay, 149–50; university exchange programs, 220; U.S. aid for,

153; by U.S. missionaries, 61–62; U.S. scholarship, 156–57. *See also* cultural exchanges
Eisenhower, Dwight D., 132–33, 144–46
elections, 117, 244–48
El Supremo (José Gaspar de Francia), 1–3, 5
Enciso Velloso, Guillermo, 109, 123
Escobar, Mario, 246
Escuela Alegría, 220
Estigarribia, José Félix, 75, 89–90, 97–98, 100–101, 257
Eugenio Jacquet, José, 224
Evarts, William M., 41
exiles, 149–51, 158, 171
Export-Import Bank (U.S.), 96–98, 104–6, 111–12, 136, 139
exports. *See under* trade

Falcón, José, 42
Farquhar, Percival, 51–56
Farrell, Edelmiro, 114
fascism, 92, 95–96, 102–3
Febrerista Party, 93, 95, 101, 117–18, 146, 170; Vanguardia Febrerista, 150
Ferreira, Benigno, 47
Filártiga, Joelito, 197
Fillmore administration, 22
Finch, William R., 45–46, 48
First National City Bank, 154, 179
Fish, Hamilton, 37, 42
Fitzpatrick, Richard, 17
Ford administration, 191–92, 194
foreign investment: and Argentina, 53, 58, 67; and Farquhar Syndicate, 51–56; by Germany and Italy, 92, 95; and Law No. 246 (1955), 153; and Mercosur, 241; and private capital, 51, 111, 122–23, 153–54, 178–81; and sale of ships, 12
foreign policy (Paraguay): as aligned with U.S., 132–33, 264–65; and the Chaco, 66, 92; and Colorado-Liberal struggle, 47; Corrientes alliance, 8; and counterterrorism, 260–62; and early Pan-Americanism, 44; and human rights, 193–98, 208–10; and L. B. Johnson administration, 173–78; Long's attack on, 80; postwar, 64; and Ricord affair, 189–92; under A. Rodríguez, 236–40; under A. Stroessner, 129, 132–33; under Wasmosy administration, 249; and World War I, 53, 58–60; and World War II, 96–101
foreign policy (U.S.): "big stick" nonintervention, 141; under Buchanan, 10; under Carter, 197–98, 214; and Chaco War, 66; Food for Peace program, 167; Good Neighbor policy, 66, 92, 120; in Guatemala, 125; and hemispheric/national security, 91, 100–101, 121–24, 129–33, 141; and human rights, 193–98; as interventionist, 49–50; 1914 T. Roosevelt expedition, 61; on Paraguayan independence, 38; under Pierce, 16–17; as pragmatic, 165–67, 193, 198; under Reagan, 206–10, 213–18; and reestablishment of diplomatic relations, 234–37; and A. Rodríguez regime, 237–40; and A. Stroessner, 121–24, 129–33, 213–18; Truman Doctrine, 120, 129
Fourteenth of May Movement, 150–51
Francia, José Gaspar de (El Supremo), 1–3, 5
Franco, Rafael, 95
Franco, Ricardo, 151
Freire Esteves, Gómez, 95
Freire Esteves, Luis, 95
French Connection (Ricord), 188
Frente de Guerra, 95–96, 101–3, 114, 117
Frost, Wesley, 105–7
Fuertes Caminos project, 247

FULNA (United National Liberation Front), 150, 160
Fuster, Marcos, 95

Galvin, John, 222
Gang of Four, 232
Gaviria, César, 252–53
Gelbard, Robert, 218
Generalized System of Preferences (GSP), 223, 237, 239–40
Germany, 92–96, 102–3, 113–15, 205
Gibson, Hugh, 83, 85
Gil, Andrés, 5
Gilbert, Henry, 6
Gillette, Michael L., 81
Glassman, Jon D., 240, 242–48
Godon, Sylvanus, 34–35
Godoy Jiménez, Adán, 224
Golden Foursome, 232
Gondra, Manuel, 48, 59–60, 64
Gondra Collection, 108
Gondra Doctrine, 64
González, Juan Natalicio, 118, 121
González Alsina, Ezequiel, 132, 164, 186, 232
González Macchi, Luis Angel, 258, 260
Good Neighbor policy, 66, 92
Goodwin, Richard, 161
Gordon, Lincoln, 161
Goulart, João, 174
Grace, Joaquín, 195
Grant, Ulysses S., 37
Grant administration, 33
Great Britain, assistance to Paraguay, 153
Griscom, Richard, 182–83
Gross, Nelson, 190
Grow, Michael, 94
Guaraní aquifer, 264–65
Guaraní language training, 183, 219
Guatemala, 125
Guevara, Che, 151
Guggiari, Herman, 220
Guggiari, José P., 60
Gulf and Western, 180

Hamas, in Asunción, 261
Hancock Oil Company, 154
Harrison administration, 44
Harty, Maura, 255–58
Harza consultants, 180
Havana Conference (1928), 65
Hayes, Rutherford B., 40
health care: clinics, 220; and hookworm eradication, 62–64; immunization program, 219; Medretes assistance for, 264; and Peace Corps, 182–83, 185; Rockefeller assistance for, 62–64
Hill, Frank D., 38
Hizballah, in Asunción, 261
Hoover administration, 66, 80
Hopkins, Edward A., 7–13, 21–23, 39, 41–42
Howard, Findley "Ministro Cowboy," 105
Howard, Robert, 236–37
Hull, Cordell, 76, 83, 90, 98
Humaitá fortress, 19–20, 27
human rights: American Convention on, 235; American Declaration of Rights and Duties of Man, 201; under Carter, 197–98, 214; under Clinton, 247; under Reagan, 207, 215–16; and A. Stroessner, 234–35; as U.S. foreign policy, 193–98, 208–10, 237
Human Rights Commission of Paraguay, 210
Human Rights Watch, 214

Ibañez, Carlos, 244
IMET (International Military and Training), 175, 177
IMF (International Monetary Fund), 152–53
imports. *See under* trade

industrial/infrastructure development: and cattle industry, 53–58, 67, 123; in the Chaco, 67; and coin minting, 6; and Farquhar Syndicate, 52–53; financial and technical assistance for, 96–101, 112, 123–24, 133–45, 152–59; and mining, 180; and modern machinery, 12; and petroleum exploration, 77–79, 84, 88, 111, 123; and private capitalization, 153–54; and streetcar company, 58; and tanning, 111, 123; and telecommunications, 112; of water supply system, 136
Industrial Paraguaya company, 52–53
Institute of Inter-American Affairs, 97, 107
intellectual property rights, 241, 259, 263
Inter-American Defense Board, 136–37
Inter-American Human Rights Commission, 201
Inter-American Peace Force (IAPF), 176
International Conference of American States, 70, 100
International Military Education and Training (IMET), 175, 177
International Monetary Fund (IMF), 152–53
International Police Academy, 169
International Products Corporation (IPC), 53, 56, 58, 93, 111, 154
International Telephone and Telegraph (ITT), 112
IPC. *See* International Products Corporation
Irala, Antolín, 60
Iribar, José, 151
Islamic terrorists, in triborder area, 261
Israeli Embassy, 261
Itaipu hydroelectric project, 179, 204–5
Italian fascism, 92
Itapirú fort, 16
ITT (International Telephone and Telegraph), 112

Jeffers, William N., 16
jewel box affair, 27–29, 42–43
Johnson, Cave, 21–23
Johnson, Lyndon B., 32, 173–78
Johnson Doctrine, 176
Joint Combined Exercise Training (JCET), 264
Joint U.S.-Paraguayan Commission for Economic Development, 123

Kansas-Paraguay Partners (KPP), 184–86, 219
Kansas State University, 220–21
Karim Yassine, Salah Abdul, 261
Kennedy, Edward, 201, 217–18
Kennedy, John F., 160–69, 171–73
Kennedy, Robert F., 163
Kennedy Doctrine, 163–64
Khrushchev, Nikita, 161
Kirkpatrick, Jeanne, 207
Kissinger, Henry, 193–94
Koons, Charles, 154

Laíno, Domingo, 201, 228
Landau, George, 198–99
Land of Lace and Legend (CCPA), 156
Lane, Lyle Franklin, 205–7
Las Amigas Norteamericanas del Paraguay, 156
Latin America: and Alliance for Progress, 161–64; and Good Neighbor policy, 66; and human rights violation, 193–99; imports/exports of, 58, 122–24; missionaries to, 61–62; and neutrality policy, 80, 120; Nixon's tour of, 140–41; and Peace Corps, 181–86; Pope John on, 194; and Reagan, 206–10; tourism and trade in, 61–62, 66, 122–24; U.S. cowboys in, 56–57
Latin American Studies Association (LASA), 236
Latin Connection, 188

League of Nations, 64, 75–77, 80–81
Leblond, Dorothy Bush, 237
Levi Ruffinelli, Carlos, 170
Levi Ruffinelli, Fernando, 170
Lewis, Paul, 117; *Paraguay under Stroessner,* 221
Liberal Party: and Colorado Party, 47–48; and Estigarribia, 98; factionalism in, 52; and Monroe Doctrine, 48–49; Nazi threats to, 96; overthrow of, 87; and Radicales, 52, 59; and Renovacionistas, 170; and A. Stroessner, 146, 170, 177
Liga Nacional Independiente, 95
Ligas Agrarias Cristianas (LAC), 192, 194
Lincoln administration, 23
Lockhart, Theodore, 239
Long, Huey "Kingfish," 79–81
López, Carlos Antonio: and border opening, 5; and Hopkins, 11–17, 21; Nueva Bordeos colony of, 41; and Paraguayan War, 25, 27–28; treaties signed by, 17, 20–21; and U.S., 8, 18, 22; and Washburn, 23, 27; and *Water Witch* controversy, 14–17
López, Emiliano Victor, 37
Los Angeles Times, 211
Lugar, Richard, 237
Luque, Paraguay, 27
Lynch, Eliza, 32

Machuca, Vicente, 101
Mallownay, Richard, 36
Manifest Destiny, 7, 14
Manlove, James, 28–29
Mann, Thomas C., 173
Mann Doctrine, 174, 176
Marcy, William L., 13, 17
Mariscal Estigarribia Airfield, 264
Marshal, George, 121
Martin, Edward M., 166
Martínez, Germán, 191
Masterman, George F., 30
McCullough, Gerald, 248
McMahon, Martin T., 30–36, 38
media: censorship of, 102–3, 117; on drug trafficking, 191, 215, 217; magazines, 191; newspapers, 109, 117, 147–48, 208, 211, 225–26, 248; on overthrow of A. Stroessner, 234; propaganda, 162–63; against protesters, 195; radio, 214, 223; repression of, 203, 208–9, 211; on A. Stroessner, 210–13; television, 212, 219; on U.S. Embassy, 254–55; on U.S.-Paraguayan relations, 265. *See also specific media outlets*
Medical Readiness Training Exercise (Medretes), 264
Méndez Fleitas, Epifanio, 123, 130, 135, 137
Mennonite Church, 69
Mennonite Partners of the Americas program, 184
Mercosur (Southern Core Common Market), 139, 263, 265
Methodist Episcopal missionaries, 61
Methodist missionaries, 61
Meza Brítez, Silvio, 226
military, 75; and Alliance for Progress, 163; and bilateral ties, 238–39; and Chaco region, 69, 265; in Chaco War, 68–79; disarray and discontent of, 232; and Frente de Guerra coup, 101–3; and lend-lease equipment, 104, 107; penetrated by A. Stroessner, 130–33; support of, for Wasmosy, 252; training of, 169, 175, 177, 264; U.S. aid to, 136–37, 168, 169, 175, 207 (*see also* aid, from U.S.); and Vichy mission in Paraguay, 102, 107
Millennium Challenge Corporations (MCC), 263
Miranda, Anibal, 126, 136

missionaries, to Latin America, 61–62
Mission Impossible (TV show), 219
Mitré, Bartolomé, 25
Monroe Doctrine, 7, 48–49, 69
Montanaro, Sabino, 186, 189, 195, 203, 217, 224
Mooney, Daniel F., 51, 59–60
MOPOCO (Popular Colorado Movement), 150, 209
Morales, Evo, 265
Morínigo, Higinio, 101–7, 111, 113–18, 127–28, 136–37
Morris meatpacking, 58
Morrison, Bruce, 236
Movimiento Renovacionista, 170
Mujeres para la Democracia, 214, 222
Musgrave, George West (aka Bob Stewart), 56–57

narcotics. *See* drug trade
Natalicio González, Juan, 118, 121
National Accord Party, 200, 230
National Antidrug Secretariat (SENAD), 240, 246
National Association of Partners of the Americas, 184
National Directorate of Narcotics (DINAR), 191, 233
National Endowment for Democracy (NED), 214, 236
National Human Rights Congress, 202
nationalism, 68–69, 74, 84–85, 132
National Potable Water Authority (SANOS), 175
National Socialist Party. *See* Nazi Party
National University of Paraguay, 109, 220
Nazi Party (National Socialist Party), 92, 94–96, 99, 105–6, 113–15
New Republic, 211
newspapers. *See under* media *and specific newspapers*
New York and Paraguay Company, 54–56
New York Herald Tribune, 37
New York Times, 211–12
Nicaragua, U.S. intervention in, 65
Niemeyer, Oscar, 172
Nixon, Richard, 140–41, 193
Nixon administration, 146, 186–92
Nogues, Alberto, 203
North American Strategic Command, 136
Nueva Bordeos colony, 41

O'Brien, Edward, 50
Odría, Manuel, 145
Office of the Coordinator of Inter-American Affairs (OCIAA), 96–97, 108
oil resources, and Chaco Peace Treaty, 77–79, 84, 88
Organización Primero de Marzo/Organización Político-Militar (OPM), 192, 196
Organization of American States (OAS): and Caribbean communism, 176; and Cuba, 170; on human rights, 194, 201–2, 214; strategic alignment of, 132, 170; and Wasmosy, 251–52
Overseas Protection Insurance Corporation (OPIC), 239
Oviedo, Lino, 242, 244, 250–53, 255–56

Page, Thomas Jefferson, 14, 16, 22
Paíva, Félix, 89, 97
Pampliega, Amancio, 117
Panama, recognized by Paraguay, 238
Panama Canal Zone, 129, 169, 175
Pan-American Airways, 112–13
Pan-American Union, 43–44, 49, 59–60, 64–65, 76
Paraguay: Asunción, evacuated by López, 27–28; as buffer state, 49–50; and the Chaco, 66–67, 82–87; civil war in, 118–21; and coin minting, 6; collapse of, 221–30; Constitution of 1967, 171, 177,

Paraguay (*continued*)
245, 248–58; corporatist constitution of, 101; Corrientes alliance with, 8; development of nation of, 1–4; and drug traffic (*see* drug trade); and Farquhar Syndicate, 51–53; as focus of Peace Corps, 182; and human rights, 193–205; impeachment of R. Cubas in, 257; as ineffectual in foreign affairs, 18; intelligence buildup in, 137–38, 264; as isolationist, 2–3; and Mengele case, 211; and Pan-American Congress, 44; political-psychological dependence of, on U.S., 254; and postwar coalition, 17; as pro-Axis, 102–3; recognition of, as nation, 11; regime change in, as impossible goal, 166–67; and Ricord affair, 186–92; sociocultural changes in, 155–56, 172–73, 193–98, 250, 254; strategic value of, to U.S., 158; A. Stroessner coup against Chaves in, 125–29; tax revenue of, from Chaco products, 67; as Uncle Sam's stepchild, 50–51; U.S. community in, 156–59; and Villa Occidental, 39; water supply system of, 136. *See also* aid, from U.S.; economic development; industrial/infrastructure development
—neutrality of: in Spanish-American War, 44; in World War I, 59–60
—treaties of: in 1853, 11–13, 15–16, 18; in 1859, 20–21
Paraguay (Warren), 156
Paraguayan-American Cultural Center (CCPA), 108, 219, 225; *Land of Lace and Legend*, 156
Paraguayan Communist Party (PCP), 150, 192
Paraguayan Sanitary Commission, 63
Paraguayan University Federation (FUP), 149
Paraguayan War, 23–26, 38
Paraguayan Workers Confederation (CPT), 148–49
Paraguay Central Railway Company, 51–53
Paraguay-Corrientes alliance, 10
Paraguay Land and Cattle Company, 55
Paraguay River navigation treaty, 11–12
Paraguay under Stroessner (Lewis), 221
Paredes, Ramón, 101
Partners of the Americas, 184
Partridge, James R., 42
Patria (newspaper), 164, 217, 226–27
Peabody, Fred, 229
Peace Corps, 181–86, 219, 240, 264
Pecten Mining, 180
Peña-Irala, Americo, 197
Pepsico, 178
Pérez Jiménez, Marcos, 145
Perón, Juan D., 114, 119–20, 123, 128, 135, 145
Pierce, Franklin, 16–17
Pierson, Warren Lee, 97
Pinilla-Soler Protocol, 68
Ploeser, William, 134, 139–40
Point IV program, 121–22
political corruption, 52–53
political prisoners, 199–200
political protest, 149–50, 160, 187, 194–98
Pope John XXIII, 194
Popular Colorado Movement (MOPOCO), 150
poverty, 182
Price Waterhouse, 180
Prieto, Jorge, 250, 252
Program Committee for Military Defense Assistance, 136–37
propaganda: and Alliance for Progress, 162–63; *En Guardia* magazine, 109–10; informational films as, 108–9; Nazi, 93–95, 102–3, 114; and A. Rodríguez PR campaign, 235; and A. Stroessner–

Stevenson meeting, 165; of stronistas, 232; U.S., 96–97, 108–10
Protestants, 61–62
Pure Oil Company, 154

Quayle, Dan, 238

Rachid Lichi, Bader, 257
Radicales (Liberal faction), 52, 59
Radical Liberal Party, 171
Radio Ñandutí, 208, 214
railroads, 51–52, 88
Ramírez Boettner, Luis, 143
Ramón Chávez, Juan, 217
Reagan, Ronald, 205–10, 213–18
Recalde, Elena, 248
Record, James, 252
Redman, Charles, 234
Reducción de Melodía, 41
Renovacionista movement, 170
Republican National Committee, 227–28
Rickard, George Lewis (Tex), 54–56, 61
Ricord, August (André), 188–92
Ricord affair, 186–92, 204
Ring of Sacrifice group, 95–96
Rio-Branco, Baron (José Maria da Silva Paranhos Jr.), 49–50
Rio Conference, 104–5
Río de la Plata: and Farquhar Syndicate, 51–53; political conditions in, 6–8, 11; viewed as export market, 14
Rockefeller, Nelson, 185, 187
Rockefeller Foundation, 62–64
Rodo, José Enrique, 109
Rodríguez, Andrés, 188–89, 191, 231–34
Rodríguez, Manuel, 51–52
Rodríguez Alcala, Hugo, 221
Rojas Pinilla, Gustavo, 145
Rólon, Raimundo, 128
Roosevelt, Franklin D.: and Estigarribia, 97–98; and "Good Neighbor" policy, 66, 92; Long's attack on foreign policy of, 80; meets Morínigo, 107, 111, 113–14; purchases Paraguayan alignment, 103–7
Roosevelt, Theodore, 49, 61
Rosa Rodríguez, Ramón, 248
Rosas, Juan Manuel de, 5–6, 9, 11
Rosenberg, Tina, 211
Rostow, Walt, 166
Rout, Leslie, 74
Rubin, Humberto, 208
Rubottom, Roy, 138, 143
Ruffin, John N., 45–48
Rumsfeld, Donald, 265

Saavedra Lamas, Carlos, 76, 84, 86, 88
Saldívar, Carlos, 226
Samaniego, Marcial, 240
SANOS (National Potable Water Authority), 175
San Salvador, 55
Sapena Pastor, Raúl, 132, 138, 143, 147–48, 164, 186, 189
Sarmiento, Domingo, 36
Schaerer, Mario, 192
Schlesinger, Arthur, Jr., 164
scholarship, 156–57, 221, 240, 263
secret police, 95–96
Seifert, Angel Roberto, 244
Selecciones (magazine), 191
SENAD (National Antidrug Secretariat), 240, 246
Service, Elman, 156–57
Service, Helen S., 157
Service, Robert, 248–54, 261
Servicio Técnico Interamericano de Cooperación Agricola (STICA), 107, 122
Seventh-Day Adventists, 61
Seward, William H., 25–26, 33
Shaw, George, 124
Sherman, Jim, 183

Shriver, Sargent, 181–82
Shubrick, William B., 18–19, 23
Signal Oil of California, 154
60 Minutes (TV show), 212
slave purchases, 12
Smith, Federico, 96
Smith, Larry, 226
Smith, Rick, 183
Snow, William P., 167, 173–74
social justice, 161–64, 183
soft power: under G. H. W. Bush, 243; and constitutional crisis of 1999, 254–59; under Reagan, 205–10, 213–14, 218–19
Solano López, Francisco, 23–26
Somoza Debayle, Anastasio, 205
Soper, Fred L., 63
Sosnik, Douglas, 236
Southern Core Common Market (Mercosur), 139, 263
Spain, and *Temerario* gunboat incident, 43–45
Spanish-American War, 44–46
Special Olympics, 220
Stagni, Pablo, 101, 112, 114
Standard Oil of New Jersey, 77–81, 111
Standard Oil of Ohio, 154
Stansifer, Charles, 220
Steichen, E. F., 184
Stevens, John L., 42
Stevens, Robert T., 128
Stevenson, Adlai, 164–66
Stewart, Bob (aka George West Musgrave), 56
STICA (Servicio Técnico Interamericano de Cooperación Agricola), 122
Stimpson, Harry F., 134, 141
Stimson, Henry, 70, 83
Storm, Gustavo, 152
Stroessner, Gustavo, 229, 231
Stroessner Matiauda, Alfredo: American press condemnation of, 147–48, 211–13; characteristics of, 126–28; coup of, against Chaves, 125; final purge of, 148–52; human rights violations by, 201–3; illness and decline of, 229–30; and L. B. Johnson administration, 172–78; and J. F. Kennedy administration, 160–69; manipulation of Alliance for Progress by, 164–67; meeting of, with Carter, 199; meeting of, with Walters, 227; and Nixon administration, 186; overthrow of, 233–34; and political liberalization, 170–71; reaction of, to Galvin's appeals, 222; and Reagan administration, 205–10, 213; repression of citizens by, 149–50, 160, 192, 194–96, 208–9; resists U.S. pressure, 213–18; and Ricord affair, 186–92; as unconditional U.S. ally, 178; and U.S. ambassadors and aid, 133–45; and U.S. military, 128–29, 169; U.S. outrage at regime of, 209–10; as victim of cold war decline, 205; welcomes Kansas governor Docking, 185–86; worsening relations of, with U.S., 210–13
Stronato: collapse of, 231–34; and Colorado Party, 224; condemned by Carter, 198; decline of, 229–30; and foreign policy, 129–33; roots of, 121–24; so-called reforms of, 169–70
Stuart, Granville, 54
student protesters, 149–50
Suderman, David, 220
Swift meatpacking, 58
Szulc, Tad, 145

Talavera, Ramón, 146–47
Talbott, Strobe, 253
Tarde, La (newspaper), 217
Taxi Aéreo Guaraní, 189
Taylor, Clyde, 216–18, 221–28
Temerario gunboat incident, 45–46

terrorism, in triborder area, 260–61
Tewksbury, Howard, 122
3+1 Group on Triborder Area Security, 262
Threshold Country Program (TCP), 263
Thurman, Maxwell, 237
Tiempistas, 102, 104, 114
Tobatí (E. Service and H. S. Service), 156–57
tourism, in Paraguay, 172, 240, 247
Towell, Timothy, 228–30, 235, 237–38
trade: and Asunción-Brazil highways, 97–98, 168; bilateral, 111, 122–24, 178–81; Brazil-Paraguay, 180–81; decline of, in A. Stroessner regime, 204, 213–14; and democratization, 242–48, 255, 260–61; under Duarte, 263–64; and economic sanctions against Paraguay, 223–24; of finished goods, 57–58; and GSP restoration, 239; international, 49–50, 57–58; Paraguayan, with like-minded regimes, 225; restoration of, in A. Rodríguez regime, 237, 240–42; under A. Rodríguez, 237–39, 247; in twenty-first century, 263. *See also* economic development
—exports: decline of, after 1980, 204; hampered by WWII, 96–97; of hides and quebracho, 58; of illicit drugs, 187–92; Latin American, 58, 122–24; and oil agreements, 88; in twenty-first century, 263; to U.S., 154
—imports, 111, 154; decline of, after 1980, 204; Latin American, 58, 122–24; of modern machinery, 12, 58; in twenty-first century, 263
training: in antiterrorism, 262; in DEA enforcement, 223–24; in Guaraní language, 183, 219; IMET, 175, 177; JCET, 264; Medretes, 264
Trans-Andean railway, 51
Trans-World Airlines, 112
treaties/pacts: Advancement of Peace treaty (1914), 49; air services agreement, 112; Arbitration treaty (1909), 49; Braden-Ayala protocol, 86–87; Busch-Braden agreement, 88–89; Chaco dispute settlements, 70–72; Chaco peace protocol/treaty, 82–83, 85–87, 90–91; Economic Union (Argentina-Paraguay), 124; educational agreement (1945), 110; extradition treaties, on drug trafficking, 190–91; Foreign Assistance Act (1971), 190; Gondra Doctrine, 64; Inter-American Reciprocal Assistance (Rio Treaty), 121; lend-lease military equipment, 104, 107; Machaín-Irigoyen Treaty of Limits, 40; Memorandum of Understanding (intellectual property), 263; Military Aviation Mission, 107; Pact of San José (American Convention on Human Rights), 235; Pinilla-Solor Protocol, 68; Rose Garden Agreement, 239; Triple Alliance treaty (1865), 40
—U.S.-Paraguay treaties, 107, 134; of 1853, 11–14, 16, 18; of 1859, 20–21; for financial or technical assistance, 97–101; and *Water Witch* controversy, 15–16
Trujillo, Rafael, 166
Truman administration, 121–22
Truman Doctrine, 120, 129

Uberti, Rolando, 95
Ultima Hora (newspaper), 225
Unión Nacional Paraguaya (UNP), 146
Union Oil Company of California, 111
United Christian Missionary Society, 61
United Fruit Company, 80
United National Liberation Front (FULNA), 150
United Nations, 132
United Nations Single Convention on Narcotics (1961), 190

United Nations Universal Declaration of Human Rights, 193

United Nuclear Mining, 180

United States: accused of duplicity, 248–49; and antifascism, 94–101; and antiterrorism training, 262; and cattle industry, 53–57; and Chaco War/Peace Conference, 72–77, 82–87; change in policy of, toward Paraguay, 213–18; Chilean confrontation with (1891–92), 44; CIA, 151–52; collapse of Paraguayan relations with, 221–30; cultural and academic exchange of, with Paraguay, 108–10; and demise of Stronato, 232; and democratization program, 115–18; and denazification, 115–18; economic predominance of, 58; economic sanctions of, against Paraguay, 223–24; economic ties of, to Paraguay, 97, 110–13, 122–24; and elections in Paraguay, 244–45; human rights confrontation of, with Paraguay, 198–205; human rights policy of, 193–98; influence of, on Paraguayan politics, 135–37, 258; initial Paraguayan relations with, 6–7, 11–12, 20–23; land purchases of citizens of, in Paraguay, 12, 53; ministerial relations of, with Paraguay, 38–39; and Paraguayan alignment with F. D. Roosevelt, 103–7; respect for, in Paraguay, 218, 253–58; and Ricord affair, 186–92; role of, in Paraguayan constitutional crises, 248–58; slave purchases by citizens of, 12; support of, for A. Stroessner, 131–33; and support of Wasmosy against Oviedo, 250–53; and territorial arbitration, 40–41; and War of Triple Alliance, 24–26, 38–39. *See also* aid, from U.S.

United States and Paraguay Navigation Company, 12–13, 17–23

United States Agency for International Development (USAID), 168, 263

United States Congress: authorizes use of military/diplomatic means, 18; House Committee on Foreign Affairs, and Bliss-Masterman affair, 33–36; on human rights, 193–94, 196–97; and Selden Resolution (1965), 176–77; suspends military aid, 200–201; on Vinocur article, 212

United States Navy: and Bliss-Masterman affair, 31, 33–36; fleet to Paraguay, 17–21

United States State Department: Bureau of Intelligence and Research (BIR), 151; CIA, 151–52; and commercial expansion in Río de la Plata, 14; and counterterrorism, 260–62; Division of Cultural Relations, 96; and military mission in Paraguay, 137; Office of the Coordinator of Inter-American Affairs (OCIAA), 96; and Wasmosy, 247

United States War Department, 96

University of Kansas, Center for Latin American Studies, 220

University of Texas, Austin, Gondra Collection, 108

Urquiza, Justo José de, 11, 19–20

Uruguay: assistance of, for Paraguayan exiles, 151; and Chaco Peace Conference, 82–87; civil war of, 23; democratization of, 209; recognizes Paraguay, 5; and A. Stroessner, 128

USS *Wasp*, 31, 34

USS *Water Witch*, 14–17

Valdovinos, Arnaldo, 150

Valenzuela, Arturo, 253

Valois, Valerie, 220

Vanguardia Febrerista, 150

Van Natta, Thomas F., 95

Vargas, Getulio, 145
Vargas Peña, Benjamín, 150
Vásquez, Carlos, 220
Vaughn, Jack, 182
Venezuela, 44, 149–50
Villa Hayes, 40–41
Villa Morra Tramway Company, 52
Villa Occidental, 39–41
Villaroel, Gualberto, 114
Villasboa, Adolfo Hirohito, 95
Villasboa, Mutshuito, 95
Vinocur, John, 212
Voz del Coloradismo radio, 223

Wallace, Mike, 212
Wallace, Neil, 136–37
Walters, Vernon, 226–27
Walz, Larry, 220
War of the Pacific (1879–83), 67
War of the Triple Alliance, 23–26, 38
Warren, Harris Gaylord, 156
Washburn, Charles Ames, 23–24, 26–30, 34–36
Washington Post (newspaper), 248
Wasmosy, Juan Carlos, 244–45, 249–53, 255
Water Witch controversy, 14–17
Watson, Alexander, 247–48
Webb, J. Watson, 26–27, 31
Welles, Sumner, 83, 90, 98, 105
Westinghouse Company, 206
Wheeler, Post, 72–73
White, Francis, 72–75, 77
White, Robert, 199, 203, 236
Wiens, Frank, 184
Williams, William, 38
Williams Brothers Company, 154
Wilson, Woodrow, 59–60, 64–65
Wise, Henry, 7–8
Woerner, Fred, 228, 231, 233
Women for Democracy, 214, 222
World Anti-Communist League (WACL), 103
World Bank, 124, 139
World Court, 80–81
World War I, 53, 55–56, 59–61
World War II, 96–101

Yacyretá hydroelectric project, 206
Ylitalo, J. Raymond, 189
Ynsfrán, Edgar L., 137–38, 233–34
Ynsfrán, Pablo Max, 81, 98, 157–58
Yopo, Mladen, 213
Yost, Lyle, 184–85

Zuibizaretta, Gerónimo, 89